5ß

RETIREMENT EDENS

Outside the Sunbelt

The Fires of Autumn:
Sexual Activity in the Middle and Later Years

The Illustrated Encyclopedia of Better Health (coauthor)

The Wealth Management Handbook (coauthor)

The Complete Retirement Planning Book

Sunbelt Retirement:
*The Complete State-by-State Guide to Retiring
in the South and West of the United States*

RETIREMENT

EDENS

Outside the Sunbelt

PETER A. DICKINSON

E. P. DUTTON | New York

Published in the United States by Elsevier-Dutton Publishing Co., Inc.,
2 Park Avenue, New York, N.Y. 10016

Library of Congress Cataloging in Publication Data
Dickinson, Peter A
    Retirement Edens outside the Sunbelt.
    Bibliography: p. 294
    Includes index.
    1. Retirement, Places of—United States.
I. Title.
HQ1063.D49   1981   646.7′9   80-22629

ISBN: 0-525-93173-2 (cloth)
      0-525-93174-0 (paper)

Published simultaneously in Canada by
Clarke, Irwin & Company Limited, Toronto and Vancouver

10 9 8 7 6 5 4 3 2 1

First Edition

CONTENTS

VIII: THE BORDER STATES—RETIREMENT
WITH FORESIGHT   *259*

ACKNOWLEDGMENTS

I could not have written this book without the help of many people. My thanks to those scores of retirees, gerontologists, directors of state units on aging, doctors, tax assessors, developers and chamber of commerce directors who gave me directions and supplied information. And my special thanks to those people who gave me detailed accounts of their Retirement Edens: B. Choyce Sheehan, Amherst, Massachusetts; H. "Pat" Brigham, Southbridge, Massachusetts; Norman D. Ford, Boulder, Colorado; Kay Hillyard, Carmel, California; Louise Driggs, Berkeley, California; William P. Dumont, Sonoma, California; Charles Weikel, Mendocino, California; Kathy Bernhardt, South Lake Tahoe, California; Ruth A. Castelli, Martha's Vineyard, Massachusetts.

INTRODUCTION

A *Retirement Eden* is a place you would love to visit and like to live in. It is a haven where you will be happier, healthier and wealthier than you are now. And it is a place where you can make as well as save money.

Sound good? Wait. Some retirees think paradise lies in Anchorage, Alaska; others in Key West, Florida. Some envision the Bar Harbor area of Maine, others the San Diego area of California. Some dream of the San Juan and Gulf Coast islands off the coast of Washington state, others of the "Golden Isles" off the coast of Georgia.

Can they all be right? Of course. And so are you with a choice somewhere in between. One lesson I learned after writing *Sunbelt Retirement* (E.P. Dutton, 1978; revised and updated 1980) is that one reader's heaven is another's hell. Some like palm trees, others pine trees; some mountains, others valleys. And for every fact there is a fantasy.

Wherever your compass points, it will point to a place in this book. During the past 3 years I've bounded the map from Alaska to Texas and from Maine to the Hawaiian Islands. I've explored hundreds of Retirement Edens to suit every personal need and practical want.

How did I select these havens? I chose them from:

■ Readers like yourself—people who moved to the "garden spot of God's country" and are proud of it. I interviewed them to learn their pros and cons of living in a new place.

- The choices of experts—I received nominations from government retirement specialists, directors of all state units on aging and leading gerontologists. I then investigated and evaluated their selections.
- Personal observations—I spent months traveling several thousand miles visiting the most likely Retirement Edens. I give my firsthand impressions of these places, both the good and the bad.

I used the 6 yardsticks below to help you evaluate these places. I've seasoned facts with personal experiences of residents and the practical advice of geriatricians, retirement leaders, builders, chamber-of-commerce directors, tax assessors, climatologists—anyone who could help you find your haven.

What did I look for? Places that would rate high in these categories:

Climate — days when the temperature is 66° F. and the humidity 55 percent. This climate allows the body chemistry to function without strain; the more days like this, the better you feel.

Cost of living — where retired couples can live for around $10,000 annually and pay around 8 percent or less in state and local taxes.

Housing — a variety of 2-bedroom units from $40,000.

Medical facilities — semiprivate hospital rooms for less than $163 daily (the national average) and at least 1 doctor per 750 residents.

Recreation and culture — a place where someone interested in books, music or art would feel comfortable.

Special services for seniors — transportation programs and other services and facilities for older people.

You're not likely to find places that are perfect in all respects, and these standards don't have to be fully met. To help you find the best places in the United States, I've organized them first by *regions* (New England, Mid-Atlantic, Midwest, Rocky Mountain, Far West, Border states), then by *states* within the regions. Under each state you'll find several *towns* offering various retirement advantages. And at the end of each state section I have rated the major towns and areas from excellent to fair. You're bound to find several towns in each section that could become your Retirement Eden.

Your horizons are limited only by your vision. If you seek some place where the living is easier and the costs lower than where you live now, you'll find it. A move gets you out of a rut; you get more out of life if you respond to a challenge like moving. Challenges create opportunities. Think about it: if you move to a place because you like it and it likes you, you should find more people of similar backgrounds and interests—perhaps people from your area who have moved there for the same reasons you did.

Most of us didn't choose our present location. We moved here because of a job; if the job goes or gets stale, why stay?

Since 1970, a million more people have moved to rural areas than have moved out. In a recent Gallup poll, two-thirds of those questioned said they would move out of the city if they could. When *McCall's* magazine asked its readers, "If you could live in any place, where would you choose?" 32 percent said small towns, 27 percent suburbs, 25 percent rural areas and 14 percent cities. Among those age 50 and older, almost 60 percent wanted to live in a small town or a rural area, with twice as many preferring small towns. Why did they want to move? Most said they want to "make ends meet" or "get in touch with more important values."

If you think you'll miss family and friends you leave behind, listen to these answers from retirees who moved to Florida from northern areas:

- When the quantity of visits decreased, the quality improved.
- The new home in Florida acted as a magnet to draw family and friends down for holidays.
- With low long-distance telephone rates and reduced air fares, it was quick, easy and inexpensive to get in touch.
- Because there's more social activity and entertaining in a Retirement Eden, they had more friends than "back home."

WHERE DO RETIREES LIVE NOW?

Nearly half (45 percent) of retirees live in seven states: California and New York (each with more than 2 million), Florida, Illinois, Ohio, Pennsylvania and Texas (each with more than 1 million). Retirees make up more than 12 percent of the population in Florida (17.6 percent), Arkansas (13.4 percent), Iowa (13.1 percent), Missouri and South Dakota (13.0 percent), Nebraska and Rhode Island (12.9 percent), Kansas (12.6 percent), Oklahoma and Pennsylvania (12.4 percent), Maine (12.2 percent), Massachusetts (12.1 percent), and North Dakota and West Virginia (12.0 percent).

Since 1970 there have been increases of more than 30 percent in the number of retirees who live in Alaska, Arizona, Florida, Hawaii, Nevada and New Mexico. The growth seems concentrated in the South and West, with increases at 22.1 percent in Southern states and 20.5 percent in Western states.

More retirees left New York than any other state. A study by a group headed by University of Kansas sociologist Cynthia B. Flynn showed that of migrants over age 60 from other states, 23.5 percent moved to Florida, 9.5 percent to California and 4.3 percent to Arizona.

TABLE I: MOST AND LEAST CROWDED CITIES IN THE U.S.

MOST CROWDED		LEAST CROWDED	
Met. Area	Pop. per Sq. Mile	Met. Area	Pop. per Sq. Mile
JERSEY CITY, NJ	12,288	RENO, NV	23
NEW YORK, NY	6,908	LAREDO, TX	25
PATERSON–CLIFTON–		GREELEY, CO	27
PASSAIC, NJ	2,356	GRAND FORKS, ND	29
NASSAU–SUFFOLK, NY	2,181	GREAT FALLS, MT	32
ANAHEIM–SANTA ANA–		RICHLAND–	
GARDEN GROVE, CA	2,173	KENNEWICK, WA	35
NEWARK, NJ	1,983	DULUTH–SUPERIOR,	
NEW BRUNSWICK–PERTH		MN–WI	35
AMBOY–SAYREVILLE, NJ	1,900	YAKIMA, WA	36
CHICAGO, IL	1,886	BILLINGS, MT	37
LOS ANGELES–LONG		LAS VEGAS, NV	42
BEACH, CA	1,717	BAKERSFIELD, CA	43
TRENTON, NJ	1,396	RIVERSIDE–SAN BER-	
PHILADELPHIA, PA	1,353	NADINO–ONTARIO, CA	45
CLEVELAND, OH	1,295	FORT COLLINS, CO	45
BRIDGEPORT–STAMFORD–		FARGO–MOORHEAD, ND–MN	45
NORWALK–DANBURY, CT	1,277	TUCSON, AZ	48
SAN FRANCISCO–		ABILENE, TX	48
OAKLAND, CA	1,266	SAN ANGELO, TX	50
NEW HAVEN–WATERBURY–		PUEBLO, CO	52
MERIDEN, CT	1,259	EUGENE–SPRINGFIELD, OR	52
BOSTON,–LOWELL–BROCKTON–		TEXARKANA, TX	52
LAWRENCE, MA	1,257		
HONOLULU, HI	1,184		
DETROIT, MI	1,130		
WASHINGTON, DC	1,074		
LONG BRANCH–ASBURY			
PARK, NJ	1,034		

Source: U.S. Dept. of Commerce

WHICH AREAS ARE GROWING THE FASTEST?

According to the National Planning Association, these areas are growing the fastest (in order):

Southwest   Mountain States
Far West   New England

Great Lakes	Mid-Atlantic
Southeast	Plains States

Between now and 1985, the Bureau of Economic Analysis says these states will grow the fastest:

Alaska	Florida
Arizona	Hawaii
Colorado	Nevada
Delaware	New Hampshire

These metropolitan areas are expected to grow the most (in order):

Houston, TX	Washington, DC
Anaheim–Santa	Riverside–San Bernadino–
Ana–Garden	Ontario, CA
Grove, CA	Nassau–Suffolk, NY
Tampa–St. Petersburg, FL	Sacramento, CA
Phoenix, AZ	Portland, OR
Ft. Lauderdale–	San Antonio, TX
Hollywood, FL	Salt Lake City–Ogden, UT
San Diego, CA	Baltimore, MD
Denver–Boulder, CO	Minneapolis–St. Paul, MN
Atlanta, GA	New Orleans, LA
Miami, FL	Boston, MA
Dallas–Fort Worth, TX	Columbus, OH
San Jose, CA	San Francisco–Oakland, CA

At present, 3 out of 10 Americans live in small towns and cities with populations under 50,000; 2 live in midsized cities (50,000 to 500,000); 1.4 live in big cities (more than 500,000) and 3.6 live in unincorporated communities and rural areas.

More people are leaving cities for rural areas, where living costs run 10 to 20 percent lower than in metropolitan areas (see Table V). However, conditions such as the cost and shortage of energy for heating and cooling could alter the above patterns. An energy shortage could hasten migration toward the Ozarks, northern California, Arizona and New Mexico, where air conditioning isn't usually required and winters are fairly mild.

THE "BEST" AND "WORST" RETIREMENT STATES

What states will offer the best retirement living during the next ten years? Chase Econometrics, a forecasting company, recently projected where the *cost of living* (inflation, taxes, housing, employment) would remain favorable for retirees during the next decade. Here are the "best" retirement states for the following reasons:

Utah — low energy costs; moderate cost of living; healthy job growth.

Louisiana — inexpensive way of living; extremely low property taxes.

South Carolina — low living costs and taxes.

Nevada — abundance of new housing and jobs; no state or inheritance taxes.

Texas — service jobs plentiful; housing costs moderate outside big cities.

New Mexico — job supply growing; energy costs low; cheap housing abundant.

Alabama — cheapest and warmest of "best" states.

Arizona — good, inexpensive housing; warm climate; fine medical care.

Florida — warm climate; excellent medical services; no income tax.

Georgia — mild climate; very low living costs even in Atlanta.

The Chase group felt that *Massachusetts* was the "worst" retirement state because it has the highest cost for retirement living, utility bills that average almost $2,000 a year, high taxes, dividends and interest taxed at double the rate for earned income, high unemployment and a part-time job market dominated by college students. The Chase people felt that all of New England, New York and New Jersey fell at the bottom of the list for the same reasons.

However, there are serpents in the "best" Edens, including poor medical care, rising taxes and weather extremes. And the Chase group acknowledged that the "worst" states offered "great medical and cultural institutions."

Some 25 million of us have retired in the United States—in some surprising places. Each of us has our own idea of what makes a Retirement Eden. The answers are as personal as your dreams and as practical as your pocketbook. Fortunately, there are so many good places to retire in this country, you are almost certain to find the right one for you.

RETIREMENT EDENS

Outside the Sunbelt

I.

WHAT MAKES

A RETIREMENT EDEN?

1. THE CLIMATE HAS A LOT TO DO WITH IT

A good climate is easy on the pocketbook and health. It should have:

no sharp changes in temperature
lots of sunshine
gentle breezes
minimum dampness and pollution

mild seasons
no heavy snowfalls or bitter cold
minimal threats of hurricanes, tornadoes, floods

Around the ideal of 66° F. and 55 percent humidity, you would like these variations:

winter — an average of 66°F to 72°F. with a relative humidity of 35 to 40 percent.
summer — an average of 72°F to 78°F. with a relative humidity of 55 to 65 percent.

The *temperature humidity index* (a measurement of summertime discomfort resulting from the combined effects of temperature and humidity) should be under 72. Above that you begin to feel uncomfortable.

Why these ideal temperatures and humidities? Because the older we get, the more difficulty we have in adjusting to drastic changes in climate.

1

Drastic changes or extreme variations aggravate certain illnesses. For instance, too much *heat and humidity* damage older hearts and blood vessels. The expanding of blood vessels to help the body eliminate heat induces changes in blood composition, body chemistry and oxygen supply to the brain. This adversely affects both mind and body.

As the outside temperature nears 98.6° F. (body temperature), watch out! It's impossible for heat to dissipate through the circulatory system because the temperature of the capillaries is the same as the surrounding air. You can't sweat to cool the body because the perspiration can't evaporate. And when the temperature is above 90° F. and the humidity is over 75 percent, the heart struggles to pump blood through the dilated blood vessels. This causes a severe strain to older bodies: temperature and humidity levels that cause heat cramps in a 17 year old may bring on heat exhaustion in a 40 year old and heat stroke in someone over 60.

Dr. George E. Burch of Tulane University finds that more heart-attack victims were admitted to hospitals and died in August than in any other month. Even dry heat can be fatal; several studies show that increased deaths occur on the day following the high temperature of a dry heat wave. That's the day it takes to overwork and wear out an aging or tired circulatory system.

Older bodies can't tolerate *extreme cold* either. When it is cold, our muscles don't generate as much heat as they did when we were younger, although we may not feel the cold as much. Unfortunately, this makes us more prone to accidental chilling, which may be fatal. Some older people die in a room with a temperature that a younger person could tolerate.

Cold weather costs more. In addition to the money you'd spend for clothing and heating, you eat an average of *15 calories more per day* for every one degree drop in temperature. Thus, your food bill in winter is a lot higher than in summer.

Extreme heat and cold affects our reaction to medication. Aspirin, for instance, dilates the blood vessels and quickens loss of body heat. Alcohol does the same thing. We should go easy on both aspirin and alcohol in winter.

Sudden changes in the weather aggravate asthma, hay fever, bronchitis, skin cancer, influenza, ulcers and the common cold. Many people suffer "barometric pains" when it is about to rain. When the barometer suddenly drops, body cells lose water to equalize the atmospheric pressure. Inflamed cells (usually because of arthritis) can't depressurize fast enough and start to hurt. Other tissues swell, reducing blood flow. This places a slight pressure on the brain, prompting some people to behave peculiarly. The pain and pressure usually ease when it starts to rain.

A research team from the University of Pennsylvania found high barometric pressure to be a factor in depression, while low pressure was a factor in excessive drinking. The team reported fewer homicides on days with more sunshine.

They also correlated air pollution with increased drug use and violent crimes. Unfortunately, pollution increases with altitude, because the thinner air can't absorb hydrocarbons. Higher altitudes are also bad for people with heart problems, since the heart must pump faster to supply oxygen to the brain.

Air conditioning isn't much help. One study found that people in air-conditioned offices had more headaches and felt worse than people in non–air-conditioned quarters. And the situation grows worse toward the end of the summer, because air conditioning interferes with acclimation to heat.

Which cities have the worst air pollution? A recent study by the Environmental Protection Agency showed that only 1 American urban area with a population over 200,000—Honolulu—had air within acceptable levels for all pollutants. However, another 20 made the grade in all but 1 pollutant—petrochemical oxidants from combustion engines. These were:

Aurora–Elgin, IL	New Orleans, LA
Austin, TX	Newport News–Hampton, VA
Baton Rouge, LA	Norfolk–Portsmouth, VA
Columbus, GA	Orlando, FL
Fort Wayne, IN	Richmond, VA
Grand Rapids, MI	Rockford, IL
Jacksonville, FL	Shreveport, LA
Lawrence–Haverhill, MA-NH	Tampa, FL
Little Rock–North Little Rock,	West Palm Beach, FL
AR	Wilmington, DE
Miami, FL	

What about water pollution? The EPA tested water in several urban localities and found the water supplies in these areas to have the lowest level of cancer-causing agents (those of the trihalomethane group):

Baton Rouge, LA	Provo, UT
Boston, MA	Pueblo, CO
Fresno, CA	Rockford, IL
Greenville, MS	Spokane, WA
Jacksonville, FL	Tacoma, WA
Madison, WI	Whiting, IN

What's the Forecast for Tomorrow?

Leading climatologists forecast that we're in for a "little ice age." Dr. Hurd C. Willet, who has correctly predicted major weather trends over the past 20 years by observing sunspots and storms, says the weather will continue to be erratic, tending toward colder conditions until the end of the 1990s. He observes: "In the course of the next 15 years I would expect some of the coldest weather we've had for many years."

HOW TO CONVERT FAHRENHEIT INTO CELSIUS

As most of us are used to discussing temperature in terms of the *Fahrenheit* scale, I've used this scale as the primary one throughout this book. However, the *Celsius* scale is part of the international system of measurement, and will become the official scale in the U.S. Already, most weather reports are given in Celsius as well as Fahrenheit. To convert, note the basis of each: the key numbers are the *freezing* and *boiling* points of water. In Fahrenheit, this range is from 32° to 212°; in Celsius, it's from 0° to 100°. Thus, each Celsius degree is almost twice as large as a Fahrenheit degree. To convert from a Fahrenheit temperature to Celsius, subtract 32 and then multiply by 5/9 or 0.56. Thus, 50°F. becomes 10°C. $(50-32=18$ and $18 \times 0.56=10)$. To convert from Celsius to Fahrenheit, multiply by 9/5 or 1.8 and add 32. For example, 55°C = 131°F. $(55 \times 1.8=99$ and $99+32=131)$. Here are some other examples:

Temperature	Celsius	Fahrenheit
Water freezes	0	32
Water boils	100	212
Body temperature	37	98.6
Warm winter day	10	50
Mild day	20	68
Hot day	30	86
Heat wave	40	104

You can get educational materials concerning the metric system by writing to the Metric Information Office, National Bureau of Standards, Washington, D.C. 20234.

Drs. Leona M. Libby and Louis J. Pandolfi agree, with the following variation: they forecast continued cool weather all over the earth through the mid 1980s, with a global warming trend then setting in for the rest of the century, followed by a severe cold snap that might last throughout the first half of the twenty-first century. How much colder might it get? "Easily 1 or 2 degrees annually," they say, adding, "It was less than a

TABLE II: CLIMATIC DATA FOR LEADING AMERICAN CITIES

State & City	Average Temp., °F. Winter	Average Temp., °F. Summer	Sunny Days	Humidity, %	Precipitation Rain (in.)	Precipitation Snow	Average Wind (mph)	Elevation (ft.)
ALABAMA (Montgomery)	55.1	76.0	233	71.8	47.1	0	1.5	183
ALASKA (Juneau)	25.8	49.1	100	77.2	53.7	150.2	8.2	114
ARIZONA (Phoenix)	60.5	96.4	289	33.5	10.87	0	7.3	1117
ARKANSAS (Little Rock)	41.3	82.1	212	69.3	43.08	4.0	6.0	257
CALIFORNIA (Los Angeles)	60.6	72.5	293	63.3	6.54	0	7.8	270
CALIFORNIA (San Francisco)	52.7	59.6	211	76.0	20.79	trace	9.3	52
COLORADO (Denver)	36.3	63.5	210	55.0	16.87	83.2	8.7	5280
CONNECTICUT (Hartford)	33.7	64.0	165	71.0	64.55	58.2	8.5	169
DELAWARE (Wilmington)	41.1	76.1	181	69.5	48.13	9.5	9.1	74
FLORIDA (Tampa)	66.5	79.8	233	75.25	42.18	0	8.7	19
FLORIDA (Miami)	72.1	79.7	252	76.25	63.11	0	8.3	7
FLORIDA (Orlando)	67.9	80.7	231	72.0	51.35	0	8.5	108
GEORGIA (Atlanta)	50.2	71.5	206	70.8	50.61	trace	9.2	1010
HAWAII (Honolulu)	72.9	79.6	244	68.8	26.90	0	13.2	7
IDAHO (Boise)	34.5	62.3	216	57.5	11.43	21.4	9.1	2838
ILLINOIS (Springfield)	35.3	67.8	176	74.3	32.03	26.2	11.2	588
INDIANA (Indianapolis)	36.4	66.9	159	72.3	40.27	18.1	9.7	792
IOWA (Des Moines)	29.1	62.3	176	73.5	36.02	36.7	10.4	938
KANSAS (Topeka)	37.7	68.4	180	69.8	31.21	26.1	9.9	877
KENTUCKY (Louisville)	42.4	69.5	177	69.0	49.38	10.4	9.0	477
LOUISIANA (New Orleans)	59.7	77.5	234	78.8	63.98	0	8.5	4
MAINE (Portland)	28.6	58.1	178	74.8	48.62	123.7	9.6	43
MARYLAND (Baltimore)	41.8	67.7	186	69.0	52.33	13.0	8.8	148
MASSACHUSETTS (Boston)	36.5	64.3	175	68.3	53.11	40.7	11.4	15

TABLE II: CLIMATIC DATA FOR LEADING AMERICAN CITIES

State & City	Average Temp., °F.		Sunny Days	Humidity, %	Precipitation		Average Wind (mph)	Elevation (ft.)
	Winter	Summer			Rain (in.)	Snow		
MICHIGAN (Detroit)	25.6	63.8	188	66.5	29.96	30.6	10.6	619
MINNESOTA (Duluth)	15.2	53.9	165	74.0	39.61	110.2	9.8	1428
MISSISSIPPI (Jackson)	55.0	77.4	226	76.0	50.03	trace	7.4	310
MISSOURI (Kansas City)	38.7	70.6	194	66.8	27.75	15.9	10.3	1014
MONTANA (Helena)	27.1	55.1	169	57.0	8.22	40.0	8.3	3828
NEBRASKA (Omaha)	32.6	66.3	185	71.8	35.56	27.1	9.8	977
NEVADA (Reno)	37.0	60.8	245	48.3	5.52	trace	8.4	4404
NEVADA (Las Vegas)	52.4	80.1	297	28.8	4.85	0.4	9.5	2162
NEW HAMPSHIRE (Concord)	27.7	58.8	167	77.0	42.07	100.3	7.2	342
NEW JERSEY (Trenton)	40.2	66.8	193	70.6	47.13	17.2	6.4	56
NEW MEXICO (Albuquerque)	44.0	69.4	271	42.3	10.11	6.4	9.7	5311
NEW YORK (New York)	39.9	67.8	232	67.8	67.03	22.9	8.8	132
NORTH CAROLINA (Raleigh)	47.8	69.1	201	70.5	51.74	4.0	8.6	434
NORTH DAKOTA (Bismarck)	19.9	58.8	171	67.0	15.16	45.6	9.6	1647
OHIO (Columbus)	36.4	63.4	151	69.8	45.60	27.1	9.7	812
OKLAHOMA (Oklahoma City)	45.2	74.0	226	65.5	27.63	14.6	12.8	1285
OREGON (Portland)	44.4	63.6	156	61.0	38.82	6.5	8.1	21
PENNSYLVANIA (Harrisburg)	38.8	66.8	191	68.0	59.27	33.4	7.5	338
RHODE ISLAND (Providence)	35.8	63.4	179	71.0	65.06	30.4	10.5	51
SOUTH CAROLINA (Charleston)	56.2	74.7	226	75.5	42.86	0	9.2	40
SOUTH DAKOTA (Rapid City)	28.5	59.6	202	64.3	17.19	23.1	11.1	3162
TENNESSEE (Nashville)	47.4	71.8	198	71.8	54.41	2.5	9.1	590
TEXAS (Austin)	57.9	79.0	221	67.5	26.07	trace	9.0	597

UTAH (Salt Lake City)	37.5	67.2	211	51.3	15.74	76.8	9.5	4220
VERMONT (Burlington)	25.5	59.2	151	73.0	38.10	121.6	8.0	332
VIRGINIA (Richmond)	45.9	66.8	188	73.5	59.34	14.3	7.4	164
WASHINGTON (Seattle)	42.9	69.4	151	72.5	48.36	22.2	8.6	400
WEST VIRGINIA (Charleston)	42.9	66.1	128	71.3	51.15	26.5	6.1	939
WISCONSIN (Madison)	25.2	60.8	163	75.5	30.96	50.2	10.0	858
WYOMING (Cheyenne)	31.8	57.6	204	53.3	12.04	48.6	13.5	6126

Source: U.S. Dept. of Commerce National Oceanic and Atmospheric Administration. Based on standard thirty-year period.

half-degree drop in the annual temperature that led to the little ice age during the 1770s."

2. THE HIGH AND THE LOW COSTS OF LIVING

No matter what your income, if you live in the right state you can cut your state and local taxes by 50 percent and more. For instance, if you make $50,000 to $100,000, you pay more than $10,000 in state and local taxes in New York but only $1,433 in Wyoming. And if you make between $10,000 and $15,000, you pay more than $1,600 in Massachusetts but only $557 in Louisiana (see Table III).

Your state's tax burden depends upon what tax bracket you're in. If you earn a lot, you're better off in one of the Southern or Western states which tax incomes less and tax sales and use more. High-bracket taxpayers suffer less in Illinois, Indiana and Pennsylvania, which tax rich and poor with the same percentages.

Table III on pp. 9–11 shows taxes according to adjusted gross income, and how your state ranks in tax burden (the higher the number, the lower the burden; the District of Columbia is included, so 51 is the highest number and therefore the lowest tax burden).

How Big Are Property Taxes?

Although property taxes have increased about 50 percent in the last 5 years, you're probably paying at or below the rate you paid then. Inflation is pushing up taxes.

You pay an average of 1.8 percent of market value ($900) on a $50,000 house in 90 major cities. Cities with more than 100,000 people levy lower taxes than cities of 50,000 to 100,000—1.6 percent compared with 1.9 percent.

You'll find taxes steepest (average 4 percent of market value) in Northeastern states and lowest (average 1 percent of market value) in Southern states. For instance, in Mobile, Alabama you pay about $200 on a $50,000 house; in Trenton, New Jersey $2,445. Other cities with high taxes include Jersey City, Boston and Worcester, Massachusetts.

In the Midwest you pay the highest taxes (3 percent of market value) in Detroit. Other Midwestern cities tend toward the median of 1.8 percent. Western cities average in between, with hardly any over 2.5 percent of market value and nearly all under 1.5 percent.

The table on p. 12 shows how property taxes on a $50,000 house compare in major cities.

TABLE III: AVERAGE STATE AND LOCAL TAXES FOR VARIOUS INCOME BRACKETS

Adjusted Gross Income

	$10,000 –15,000	$15,000 –20,000	$20,000 –25,000	$25,000 –35,000	$35,000 –50,000	$50,000 –100,000
ALABAMA	$817 (39)	$1,094 (38)	$1,342 (38)	$1,760 (38)	$2,543 (36)	$3,381 (41)
ALASKA	1,069 (21)	1,403 (18)	1,693 (27)	2,162 (24)	3,083 (22)	4,685 (22)
ARIZONA	950 (28)	1,309 (26)	1,589 (30)	1,929 (35)	2,574 (33)	4,214 (30)
ARKANSAS	782 (44)	991 (42)	1,326 (39)	1,731 (41)	2,556 (35)	4,393 (28)
CALIFORNIA	1,232 (13)	1,657 (9)	2,090 (7)	2,700 (6)	4,045 (5)	7,432 (4)
COLORADO	1,111 (16)	1,533 (15)	1,938 (13)	2,435 (14)	3,352 (17)	4,726 (20)
CONNECTICUT*	1,321 (8)	1,586 (13)	1,699 (24)	2,042 (27)	3,408 (15)	4,993 (17)
DELAWARE†	974 (25)	1,263 (29)	1,777 (16)	2,404 (15)	3,208 (19)	6,778 (6)
DISTRICT OF COLUMBIA	1,085 (19)	1,519 (16)	1,751 (19)	2,654 (8)	3,733 (9)	6,023 (10)
FLORIDA*	715 (45)	785 (49)	991 (47)	1,305 (46)	1,565 (47)	2,502 (45)
GEORGIA	804 (41)	1,187 (33)	1,488 (34)	2,137 (26)	3,065 (24)	4,692 (21)
HAWAII	1,192 (14)	1,607 (12)	2,022 (11)	2,539 (13)	3,193 (20)	5,835 (12)
IDAHO	972 (26)	1,314 (25)	1,736 (20)	2,217 (22)	2,969 (27)	4,533 (25)
ILLINOIS	1,137 (15)	1,370 (21)	1,719 (22)	2,033 (29)	2,677 (31)	3,891 (36)
INDIANA	900 (33)	1,124 (36)	1,350 (37)	1,562 (43)	2,121 (43)	3,068 (43)
IOWA	961 (27)	1,371 (20)	1,695 (25)	2,247 (19)	2,827 (29)	4,645 (23)
KANSAS	911 (32)	1,292 (28)	1,564 (31)	2,038 (28)	2,972 (26)	3,961 (35)
KENTUCKY	1,034 (22)	1,396 (19)	1,769 (17)	2,286 (17)	3,145 (21)	4,287 (29)
LOUISIANA	557 (51)	755 (51)	913 (51)	1,102 (50)	1,612 (46)	2,234 (48)
MAINE	1,096 (18)	1,257 (30)	1,723 (21)	2,150 (25)	3,468 (13)	4,816 (19)
MARYLAND	1,468 (3)	1,839 (4)	2,212 (5)	3,040 (4)	4,014 (6)	6,072 (9)
MASSACHUSETTS	1,636 (1)	2,124 (2)	2,549 (2)	3,096 (2)	4,399 (2)	7,047 (5)
MICHIGAN	1,366 (7)	1,720 (8)	2,075 (9)	2,660 (7)	3,724 (10)	5,152 (15)
MINNESOTA	1,317 (10)	1,830 (5)	2,397 (3)	3,059 (3)	4,284 (3)	7,708 (3)

TABLE III: AVERAGE STATE AND LOCAL TAXES FOR VARIOUS INCOME BRACKETS

| | Adjusted Gross Income | | | | | |
	$10,000 –15,000	$15,000 –20,000	$20,000 –25,000	$25,000 –35,000	$35,000 –50,000	$50,000 –100,000
MISSISSIPPI	835 (37)	1,079 (39)	1,308 (41)	1,770 (37)	2,704 (30)	3,540 (39)
MISSOURI	947 (29)	1,256 (31)	1,557 (32)	1,935 (34)	2,481 (37)	3,771 (38)
MONTANA†	1,000 (24)	1,236 (32)	1,665 (29)	2,218 (21)	3,273 (18)	4,987 (18)
NEBRASKA	922 (31)	1,358 (22)	1,769 (18)	1,989 (31)	2,650 (32)	4,400 (26)
NEVADA*	843 (36)	854 (46)	1,016 (46)	1,250 (47)	1,622 (45)	2,419 (46)
NEW HAMPSHIRE*†	1,320 (9)	1,351 (23)	1,679 (28)	2,017 (30)	2,173 (41)	3,434 (40)
NEW JERSEY	1,400 (6)	1,771 (6)	2,055 (10)	2,582 (12)	3,606 (11)	5,464 (14)
NEW MEXICO	788 (43)	1,057 (40)	1,297 (42)	1,745 (40)	2,221 (40)	4,396 (27)
NEW YORK	1,574 (2)	2,161 (1)	2,742 (1)	3,656 (1)	5,321 (1)	10,135 (1)
NORTH CAROLINA	938 (30)	1,305 (27)	1,694 (26)	2,235 (20)	3,017 (25)	5,536 (13)
NORTH DAKOTA	792 (42)	952 (44)	1,388 (36)	1,947 (33)	2,260 (39)	3,813 (37)
OHIO	829 (38)	1,111 (37)	1,402 (35)	1,775 (36)	2,558 (34)	3,971 (34)
OKLAHOMA	692 (47)	888 (45)	1,181 (43)	1,753 (39)	2,271 (38)	3,996 (33)
OREGON†	1,099 (17)	1,631 (10)	2,085 (8)	2,647 (9)	3,744 (8)	6,357 (8)
PENNSYLVANIA	1,252 (11)	1,570 (14)	1,847 (14)	2,328 (16)	3,073 (23)	4,210 (31)
RHODE ISLAND	1,450 (5)	1,731 (7)	2,121 (6)	2,620 (11)	3,487 (12)	5,924 (11)
SOUTH CAROLINA	813 (40)	1,176 (34)	1,511 (33)	1,987 (32)	3,373 (16)	5,064 (16)
SOUTH DAKOTA*	865 (35)	1,055 (41)	1,152 (44)	1,667 (42)	1,463 (49)	2,353 (47)
TENNESSEE*	682 (49)	827 (48)	970 (48)	1,188 (49)	1,502 (48)	1,972 (49)
TEXAS*	646 (50)	839 (47)	916 (50)	1,213 (48)	1,414 (50)	1,944 (50)
UTAH	1,023 (23)	1,472 (17)	1,716 (23)	2,216 (23)	2,942 (28)	4,198 (32)
VERMONT	1,235 (12)	1,629 (11)	2,022 (12)	2,643 (10)	3,852 (7)	6,665 (7)

VIRGINIA	1,079 (20)	1,322 (24)	1,835 (15)	2,285 (18)	3,442 (14)	4,616 (24)
WASHINGTON*	866 (34)	1,137 (35)	1,325 (40)	1,507 (44)	2,128 (42)	2,562 (44)
WEST VIRGINIA	702 (46)	980 (43)	1,045 (45)	1,442 (45)	2,071 (44)	3,323 (42)
WISCONSIN	1,461 (4)	1,976 (3)	2,373 (4)	3,026 (5)	4,175 (4)	7,829 (2)
WYOMING*	691 (48)	764 (50)	969 (49)	1,065 (51)	1,090 (51)	1,433 (51)
U.S. AVERAGE	$1,131	$1,503	$1,869	$2,409	$3,368	$5,384

*States with no personal income tax. (New Jersey's income tax was imposed July 1, 1976; Connecticut taxes capital gains and dividends; New Hampshire and Tennessee tax income from interest and dividends.)
†States with no sales tax.

Source: Internal Revenue Service

City	Tax	City	Tax
ALBANY, NY	$1,730	LINCOLN, NB	$835
ALBUQUERQUE, NM	665	LITTLE ROCK, AR	520
ANCHORAGE, AK	635	LOS ANGELES, CA	1,135
ATLANTA, GA	765	MADISON, WI	1,205
BALTIMORE, MD	1,270	MIAMI, FL	880
BILLINGS, MT	670	MINNEAPOLIS, MN	1,020
BILOXI, MS	625	MOBILE, AL	195
BIRMINGHAM, AL	275	NASHVILLE, TN	495
BOISE, ID	760	NEW ORLEANS, LA	230
BOSTON, MA	1,905	NEW YORK CITY, NY	955
BRIDGEPORT, CT	1,400	OGDEN, UT	580
CHARLESTON, SC	460	OKLAHOMA CITY, OK	545
CHARLESTON, WV	305	OMAHA, NB	1,040
CHARLOTTE, NC	690	PHILADELPHIA, PA	1,055
CHICAGO, IL	830	PHOENIX, AZ	730
CINCINNATI, OH	600	PORTLAND, ME	1,280
COLORADO SPRINGS, CO	835	PORTLAND, OR	1,170
COLUMBIA, SC	575	PROVIDENCE, RI	1,550
DENVER, CO	665	RENO, NV	615
DETROIT, MI	1,735	ST. LOUIS, MO	820
HARRISBURG, PA	1,085	SALT LAKE CITY, UT	455
HONOLULU, HI	325	SAN FRANCISCO, CA	655
HOUSTON, TX	520	SEATTLE, WA	440
JACKSONVILLE, FL	505	TAMPA, FL	500
KANSAS CITY, KS	1,045	TUCSON, AZ	670
KANSAS CITY, MO	590	WASHINGTON, DC	615
LAS VEGAS, NV	655	WILMINGTON, DE	890
LEXINGTON, KY	545	WORCESTER, MA	1,670

Cigarette, Gas and Sales Tax

The District of Columbia and 45 states levy general sales and use taxes, ranging from 2 percent in Oklahoma to 7.5 percent in Connecticut.

You pay the highest cigarette taxes—21¢ a pack—in Florida, Massachusetts and Connecticut. North Carolina levies the lowest cigarette tax, 2¢ a pack.

Gasoline taxes range from a low of 5¢ in Texas to a high of 12¢ in South Dakota and Washington. See pp. 13–14 for tax rates in the 50 states and the District of Columbia. Many cities and counties impose taxes of their own in addition to these state levies. Rates are those in effect August 1, 1980.

What about utility rates? Here's the average bill for 500 kilowatt hours of electricity in major cities as of early 1980:

State	Cigarette Tax (per pack)	Gas Tax (per gallon)	Sales Tax
ALABAMA	16¢	11¢	4%
ALASKA	8¢	8¢	0
ARIZONA	13¢	8¢	4%
ARKANSAS	17.75¢	9.5¢	3%
CALIFORNIA	10¢	7¢	4.75%
COLORADO	10¢	7¢	3%
CONNECTICUT	21¢	11¢	7.5%
DELAWARE	14¢	9¢	0
DISTRICT OF COLUMBIA	13¢	10¢	5%
FLORIDA	21¢	8¢	4%
GEORGIA	12¢	7.5¢*	3%
HAWAII	40%	8.5¢	4%
IDAHO	9.1¢	9.5¢	3%
ILLINOIS	12¢	7.5¢	4%
INDIANA	10.5¢	8.5¢	4%
IOWA	13¢	10¢	3%
KANSAS	11¢	8¢	3%
KENTUCKY	3¢	†	5%
MISSOURI	9¢	7¢	3.125%
MONTANA	12¢	9¢	0
NEBRASKA	13¢	10.5¢	3%
NEVADA	10¢	6¢	3%
NEW HAMPSHIRE	12¢	11¢	0
NEW JERSEY	19¢	8¢	5%
NEW MEXICO	12¢	8¢	3.75%
NEW YORK	15¢	8¢	4%
NORTH CAROLINA	2¢	9¢	3%
NORTH DAKOTA	12¢	8¢	3%
OHIO	15¢	7¢	4%
OKLAHOMA	18¢	6.58¢	2%
OREGON	9¢	7¢	0
PENNSYLVANIA	18¢	11¢	6%
RHODE ISLAND	18¢	10¢	6%
SOUTH CAROLINA	7¢	10¢	4%
SOUTH DAKOTA	14¢	12¢	5%
TENNESSEE	13¢	7¢	4.5%
TEXAS	18.5¢	5¢	4%

	Cigarette Tax (per pack)	Gas Tax (per gallon)	Sales Tax
LOUISIANA	11¢	8¢	3%
MAINE	16¢	9¢	5%
MARYLAND	13¢	9¢	5%
MASSACHUSETTS	21¢	10¢	5%
MICHIGAN	11¢	11¢	4%
MINNESOTA	18¢	11¢	4%
MISSISSIPPI	11¢	9¢	5%

	Cigarette Tax (per pack)	Gas Tax (per gallon)	Sales Tax
UTAH	10¢	9¢	4%
VERMONT	12¢	9¢	3%
VIRGINIA	2.5¢	11¢	3%
WASHINGTON	16¢	12¢	4.5%
WEST VIRGINIA	17¢	10.5¢	3%
WISCONSIN	16¢	9¢	4%
WYOMING	8¢	8¢	3%

*Plus 3 percent of the retail price excluding the 7.5-cent tax.
†Kentucky's gas tax is 9 percent of the average wholesale price.

City	Average for 500 kwh	City	Average for 500 kwh
NEW YORK, NY	$42.85	DETROIT, MI	$28.35
PHILADELPHIA, PA	31.08	LOS ANGELES, CA	28.18
HONOLULU, HI	30.85	BALTIMORE, MD	28.08
BOSTON, MA	30.76	WASHINGTON, DC	27.97
CLEVELAND, OH	30.36	DENVER, CO	27.40
SAN DIEGO, CA	28.84	PITTSBURGH, PA	27.37

Some states provide special utility rates for seniors. In Indiana, those 60 and older get a $15 annual tax credit on utility bills. If combined income doesn't exceed $15,000, the rebate is $50.

Ohio allows low-income seniors a 25 percent credit on winter heating bills. In some states, utility companies will install insulation and other energy-saving devices and add the cost to the customer's bill. The San Diego County government has ordered that all new homes be equipped with solar-energy collectors.

What Cities Have the Highest Taxes and Cost of Living?

If you earn $50,000 or more you pay the highest taxes in New York City. At lower levels you pay more in Boston. Other high-tax cities include Milwaukee, San Francisco and Los Angeles.

You pay the lowest taxes in Jacksonville, Nashville, Seattle and New Orleans. There's a breakdown of state and local tax loads in 62 cities on pp. 16–18.

What does it cost a retired couple to live in the various cities? Table V shows the budget figures for a retired couple, based on estimated 1981 prices.

3. HEALTH IS WHERE YOU FIND IT

Generally, hospital beds and doctors tend to be where most people live. See the table at the bottom of p. 19 for how the 4 major regions compare in hospital beds per 1,000 population.

Perhaps because they are more active outdoors, people in the South and West have a poorer health record than those in the Northeastern and North Central states. According to the National Center for Health Statistics, the average Westerner has 21.5 days of restricted activity because

TABLE IV: STATE AND LOCAL TAX LOADS IN MAJOR CITIES

	$7,500 INCOME		$15,000 INCOME		$25,000 INCOME		$50,000 INCOME	
	Taxes	% Income	Taxes	% Income	Taxes	% Income	Taxes	% Income
Atlanta, GA.	$713	9.51%	$1,121	7.47%	$1,884	7.54%	$3,817	7.63%
Baltimore, MD	962	12.83	1,621	10.81	2,672	10.69	5,190	10.38
Boston, MA	1,313	17.51	2,129	14.19	3,185	12.74	5,676	11.35
Chicago, IL	802	10.69	1,260	8.40	1,804	7.22	3,074	6.15
Cincinnati, OH	653	8.71	1,097	7.31	1,768	7.07	3,503	7.01
Cleveland, OH	705	9.40	1,151	7.67	1,801	7.20	3,477	6.95
Denver, CO	718	9.57	1,078	7.19	1,836	7.34	3,555	7.11
Detroit, MI	864	11.52	1,440	9.60	2,328	9.31	4,801	9.60
Houston, TX	542	7.23	728	4.85	927	3.71	1,348	2.70
Indianapolis, IN	862	11.49	1,316	8.77	1,856	7.42	3,089	6.18
Jacksonville, FL	481	6.41	656	4.37	841	3.36	1,236	2.47
Los Angeles, CA	787	10.49	1,299	8.66	2,145	8.58	5,142	10.28
Memphis, TN	584	7.79	813	5.42	1,052	4.21	1,558	3.12
Milwaukee, WI	947	12.63	1,923	12.82	3,289	13.16	6,665	13.33
New Orleans, LA	380	5.07	666	4.44	919	3.68	1,696	3.39
New York, NY	976	13.01	1,684	11.23	3,037	12.15	7,875	15.75
Philadelphia, PA	1,108	14.77	1,851	12.34	2,766	11.06	4,932	9.86
Pittsburgh, PA	1,049	13.99	1,683	11.22	2,463	9.85	4,275	8.55
Phoenix, AZ	798	10.64	1,155	7.70	1,845	7.38	3,537	7.07
Seattle, WA	609	8.12	797	5.31	996	3.98	1,420	2.84

over 500,000

City								
St. Louis, MO	821	10.95	1,295	8.63	2,055	8.22	3,816	7.63
San Francisco, CA	596	7.95	996	6.64	1,714	6.86	4,422	8.84
Albuquerque, NM	457	6.09	828	5.52	1,420	5.68	3,419	6.84
Birmingham, AL	694	9.25	1,055	7.03	1,668	6.67	3,000	6.00
Charlotte, NC	718	9.57	1,192	7.95	2,040	8.16	4,135	8.27
Dayton, OH	681	9.08	1,134	7.56	1,805	7.22	3,820	7.64
Des Moines, IA	867	11.56	1,352	9.01	2,194	8.78	4,301	8.60
Grand Rapids, MI	618	8.24	1,116	7.44	2,054	8.22	4,173	8.35
Jersey City, NJ	1,231	16.41	1,931	12.87	2,776	11.10	4,793	9.59
Louisville, KY	863	11.51	1,418	9.45	2,298	9.19	4,250	8.50
Miami, FL	632	8.43	892	5.95	1,179	4.72	1,799	3.60
Minneapolis, MN	475	6.33	1,282	8.55	2,534	10.14	5,688	11.38
Nashville, TN	563	7.51	782	5.21	1,007	4.03	1,483	2.97
Newark, NJ	1,113	14.84	1,747	11.65	2,512	10.05	4,352	8.70
Norfolk, VA	698	9.31	1,104	7.36	1,777	7.11	3,478	6.96
Oakland, CA	813	10.84	1,334	8.89	2,195	8.78	5,225	10.45
Oklahoma City, OK	541	7.21	796	5.31	1,345	5.38	3,013	6.03
Omaha, NB	766	10.21	1,315	8.77	1,969	7.88	4,055	8.11
Portland, OR	413	5.51	1,051	7.01	2,247	8.99	4,986	9.97
Richmond, VA	788	10.51	1,257	8.38	2,004	8.02	3,870	7.74
Rochester, NY	1,119	14.92	1,852	12.35	3,119	12.48	7,187	14.37
Syracuse, NY	947	12.63	1,575	10.50	2,737	10.95	6,550	13.10
Wichita, KS	696	9.28	1,066	7.11	1,646	6.58	3,262	6.52
Berkeley, CA	827	11.03	1,356	9.04	2,226	8.90	5,277	10.55
Billings, MT	629	8.39	981	6.54	1,717	6.87	3,458	6.92

200,000–500,000

TABLE IV: STATE AND LOCAL TAX LOADS IN MAJOR CITIES

	$7,500 INCOME		$15,000 INCOME		$25,000 INCOME		$50,000 INCOME	
	Taxes	% Income	Taxes	% Income	Taxes	% Income	Taxes	% Income
Biloxi, MS	708	9.44	962	6.41	1,658	6.63	3,107	6.21
Burlington, VT	576	7.68	1,432	9.55·	2,467	9.87	5,312	10.62
Clearwater, FL	507	6.76	697	4.65	900	3.60	1,334	2.67
Columbia, SC	672	8.96	1,045	6.97	1,844	7.38	3,876	7.75
Fargo, ND	597	7.96	955	6.37	1,820	7.28	3,758	7.52
Huntington, WV	490	6.53	696	4.64	1,067	4.27	2,321	4.64
Las Vegas, NV	545	7.27	745	4.97	970	3.88	1,461	2.92
Little Rock, AR	633	8.44	986	6.57	1,640	6.56	3,556	7.11
Manchester, NH	846	11.28	1,196	7.97	1,615	6.46	2,548	5.10
Pontiac, MI	689	9.19	1,242	8.28	1,970	7.88	4,133	8.27
Providence, RI	1,121	14.95	1,780	11.87	2,558	10.23	4,870	9.74
Salt Lake City, UT	673	8.97	1,063	7.09	1,794	7.18	3,371	6.74
Savannah, GA	682	9.09	1,094	7.29	1,864	7.46	3,812	7.62
Sioux Falls, SD	780	10.40	1,110	7.40	1,472	5.89	2,257	4.51
Terre Haute, IN	872	11.63	1,038	6.92	1,460	5.84	2,429	4.86
Trenton, NJ	1,338	17.84	2,098	13.99	3,014	12.06	7,619	15.24
Wilmington, DE	757	10.09	1,322	8.81	2,454	9.82	5,672	11.34

under 200,000

TABLE V: COST OF LIVING FOR A RETIRED COUPLE

The Bureau of Labor Statistics defines a retired couple as a husband age 65 and older and his wife. They are assumed to be self-supporting, in reasonably good health and able to take care of themselves. Budgets include food, housing, transportation, clothing, personal care and medical expenses, but *not* personal income taxes. Annual budgets for estimated 1981 prices based on moderate standard of living:

NORTHEAST

Boston, MA	$11,924	New York, NY	$11,794
Buffalo, NY	11,007	Philadelphia, PA	10,495
Hartford, CT	11,296	Pittsburg, PA	9,965
Lancaster, PA	10,005	Portland, ME	10,662

NORTH CENTRAL

Cedar Rapids, IA	9,849	Green Bay, WI	9,717
Champaign-Urbana, IL	10,406	Indianapolis, IN	10,010
Chicago, IL	9,966	Kansas City, MO	9,868
Cincinnati, OH	9,574	Milwaukee, WI	10,313
Cleveland, OH	10,439	Minneapolis-St. Paul, MN	9,996
Dayton, OH	9,609	St. Louis, MO	9,836
Detroit, MI	10,011	Wichita, KS	9,640

SOUTH

Atlanta, GA	9,146	Durham, NC	9,556
Austin, TX	9,348	Houston, TX	9,702
Baltimore, MD	9,803	Nashville, TN	9,565
Baton Rouge, LA	8,861	Orlando, FL	9,353
Dallas, TX	9,359	Washington, DC	10,587

WEST

Anchorage, AK	13,977	Los Angeles, CA	10,049
Bakersfield, CA	9,401	San Diego, CA	9,809
Denver, CO	9,678	San Francisco, CA	10,871
Honolulu, HI	11,439	Seattle-Everett, WA	10,602

U.S. AVERAGE $10,022

Source: U.S. Bureau of Labor Statistics

Region	General medical, surgical	Nursing homes, etc.	Total
Northeast	4.9	4.1	9.0
North Central	5.2	2.3	7.5
South	5.0	2.4	7.4
West	4.8	1.5	6.2

of illness or injury and the average Southerner 18.7 days. Westerners also
had the highest level of bed disability—8.1 days a year—followed by
Southerners, with a 7.6 day average.

Surprisingly, the longest-lived persons in the United States live in the
coldest states in the country—Nebraska, North and South Dakota, Minnesota, Iowa. Perhaps if they've survived the extremes of heat and cold
for a long time, they can survive most anything.

The same holds true for people who live in high altitudes. While some
people with bad hearts or respiratory problems might find it difficult if not
impossible to retire in the mountains of New Mexico, which lie above 7,000
feet, once you've learned to adjust to high altitudes, you might improve
your chances of survival. A team of doctors from Harvard, Case Western
Reserve and New Mexico universities found that the death rate from
coronary heart disease was 28 percent lower among men who lived above
7,000 feet than those who lived at 3,000 to 4,000 feet. The doctors theo-
rized that men get more exercise when they work in a thin mountain
atmosphere; once they became acclimatized, they became less prone to
high blood pressure. In fact, New Mexico has the lowest death rate from
heart attacks of any continental state.

What About Health Care If You Move?

If you must find a new doctor, telephone your county medical society
and ask if its listing includes internists who specialize in geriatrics (the
medical science of aging). Another way to find a good doctor is to call a
nearby medical school or accredited hospital (preferably one affiliated
with a university medical school) and ask for a list of internists or general
practitioners who are on staff as attending physicians. Generally, the best
doctors are affiliated with accredited hospitals and medical schools in a
teaching, consulting or other staff capacity.

An alternative is to seek out a group medical practice in which spe-
cialists pool their talents and expensive equipment and offer a group
rate. You might also investigate Health Maintenance Organizations
(HMOs), which emphasize preventive medicine. If you can't locate an
HMO near you, write HMO Program, 12420 Parklawn Drive, Rockville,
MD 20852.

If you're covered by Medicare, find a doctor who accepts Medicare
assignments; he will limit his charges to the "reasonable" rates set by
Medicare for services in his area. If he doesn't accept Medicare assignments, Medicare will pay you only 80 percent of what it considers "reasonable" and you must pay any excess that the doctor chooses to bill you for.
Most HMOs have arrangements with Medicare to receive payment for

covered services. You can get Medicare treatment throughout the United States and its possessions.

Below is a table of average rates for semiprivate hospital rooms, along with the number of doctors per 100,000 residents. Ideally, there should be 133 physicians per 100,000 population (or 1 doctor per 750 residents). Anything below 133 is considered substandard:

TABLE VI: HOSPITAL COSTS AND MEDICAL COVERAGE*

State	Average Rate for Semiprivate Hospital Room	Physicians per 100,000 Population
Alabama	$120	111
Alaska	222	116
Arizona	130	183
Arkansas	100	109
California	199	219
Colorado	145	198
Connecticut	174	224
Delaware	136	155
District of Columbia	189	592
Florida	136	175
Georgia	124	136
Hawaii	133	174
Idaho	132	105
Illinois	187	172
Indiana	130	117
Iowa	123	115
Kansas	124	144
Kentucky	106	128
Louisiana	112	141
Maine	157	136
Maryland	147	271
Massachusetts	190	245
Michigan	195	145
Minnesota	129	177
Mississippi	84	102
Missouri	126	155
Montana	132	126
Nebraska	123	138
Nevada	148	128
New Hampshire	148	159
New Jersey	177	177
New Mexico	141	146
New York	193	126
North Carolina	106	139

TABLE VI: HOSPITAL COSTS AND MEDICAL COVERAGE*

State	Average Rate for Semiprivate Hospital Room	Physicians per 100,000 Population
North Dakota	120	118
Ohio	177	150
Oklahoma	121	128
Oregon	159	173
Pennsylvania	159	173
Rhode Island	171	195
South Carolina	99	123
South Dakota	109	98
Tennessee	108	147
Texas	114	146
Utah	145	163
Vermont	141	203
Virginia	126	162
Washington	154	178
West Virginia	130	131
Wisconsin	132	141
Wyoming	120	113
U.S. AVERAGE	163	174

*Rates prevailing in 1981. Source: Health Insurance Association of America and National Center for Health Statistics

II.

ARE THERE SERPENTS

IN EDEN?

If there were an ideal place, everyone would want to live there—and it would no longer be an ideal place. Fortunately, perhaps, there are pitfalls in any paradise that keep some people away.

Let's look at the good and bad points of the regions of the United States. The table below shows how they compare in the various qualities of living (S = South; W = West; NC = North Central; NE = Northeast).

As you can see, no one region has it all good or bad. Although many people move from the city to the country and from the Snowbelt to the Sunbelt, you'll find a reverse trend, also, and for good reason. Listen to

lowest cost of living	fastest economic growth	fastest popul. growth	lowest income taxes	mildest climate	most health facil.	lowest crime rate
S	W	W	NC	W	NE	S
NC	S	S	S	S	NC	NC
W	NE	NE	W	NE	S	NE
NE	NC	NC	NE	NC	W	W
highest cost of living	slowest economic growth	slowest popul. growth	highest income taxes	harshest climate	least health facil.	highest crime rate

these comments from people who have moved back from the rural South to the urban East:

- "The heat was so intense and the bugs would drive you out of your mind."
- "We found the life quite dull. People there seemed to have nothing to do except sit all day and talk or stare into space."
- "I couldn't stand the barren desert. I'm used to green grass and blue ocean."

As do the regions, each type of community has its advantages and disadvantages. See pp. 25 and 26 for some of them.

I'm sure you could add some goods and bads to the above lists. The main point: every place has its advantages and disadvantages. The hope is that some place offers more pros than cons for you.

To help you select a place that appeals to you, here is a check list to help you decide. Add up the score of various places; the one with the most points may be your Retirement Eden.

TABLE VII: CHECK POINTS FOR PICKING RETIREMENT EDEN
(Rate each item from 0–5 in each column. Multiply A, B and C by importance.)

Item or Factor	Importance to You	Place A	Place B	Place C
1. Climate, geography scenery	_____	_____	_____	_____
2. Health and medical facilities	_____	_____	_____	_____
3. Cost of living, housing	_____	_____	_____	_____
4. Family, friends and associates	_____	_____	_____	_____
5. Religious and social facilities	_____	_____	_____	_____
6. Recreation and sports facilities	_____	_____	_____	_____
7. Cultural and historical advantages	_____	_____	_____	_____
8. Accessibility to important things	_____	_____	_____	_____
9. Employment opportunities	_____	_____	_____	_____
10. Type and size of town	_____	_____	_____	_____

TOTALS: Add columns

THE GOOD AND BAD ABOUT THE COUNTRY

Good	Bad
Generally more friendly—if you feel you belong	Shortage of good service facilities
More social clubs—especially in towns with retirees	Poor television and radio reception
Helpful neighbors provide security	Limited transportation
More respect for seniors	Limited cultural attractions—libraries, theaters, adult education, museums, etc.
Lower food costs—if local products available	Sometimes no door-to-door mail delivery
Lower housing costs	Fewer sales and less merchandise
Lower taxes	Fewer municipal services
Greater freedom in landscaping, zoning and altering housing to personal preferences	Less opportunity for passive activities (spectator sports, reading, watching drama, etc.)
Outdoor living close at hand	More bugs and other insects
Fresher air	
Less noise	
More "breathing" space	

THE GOOD AND BAD ABOUT THE CITY

Good	Bad
Greater variety of cultural events—movies, theater, music, education	More noise and air pollution
Better mass transit and intercity transportation	Higher sales and other taxes
Better hospitals and medical care	Higher rents and housing costs
More municipal services	More crime
Greater variety of restaurants	High garage and parking costs
More easily available repair and service facilities	Higher auto and other insurance
More discount stores and greater variety of sales in regular stores	Higher clothing costs because of more "dress up" occasions
More newspapers, radio, television programs	More costly for "night on town"
Lower real estate taxes if taxes absorbed by business and industry	
More job opportunities	

THE GOOD AND BAD ABOUT A RETIREMENT COMMUNITY

Good	Bad
People your own age—peer support	Age segregation
Organized activities and recreational facilities	Isolation—often far from city
	Lack of transportation to city
Easy housing maintenance	Sameness in housing
Usually good in-community transportation	Sometimes escalating maintenance and recreation costs
Good housing value	Less civic pride and responsibility
Stress on active living	Lack of privacy
Attractive surroundings	Less intellectual stimulation
	Not suitable as you grow older and more passive
	Widow may be out of place in couple-oriented community
	Keeping up with "Retiree Jones"
	Restrictions on landscaping and altering housing
	Good hospitals often not close

THE GOOD AND BAD ABOUT A COLLEGE COMMUNITY

Good	Bad
Can rent out room to students (if zoning okays)	Higher real estate taxes because of lower base
Free or low-cost adult education	Higher housing costs
Many university activities open to seniors	Fewer public recreation facilities (golf courses, etc.)
Higher intellectual level	Higher cost of living because of better taste, standards
Top-quality hospitals and medical care often associated with university	Some congestion in student areas
Rapport with sympathetic students to "keep young"	Student noise and rowdiness
Job opportunities associated with university	Parking problems
Attractive surroundings	Research firms located near university may cause congestion and higher taxes
Outdoor sports and recreation for participants and spectators	
Good libraries, art, museums	

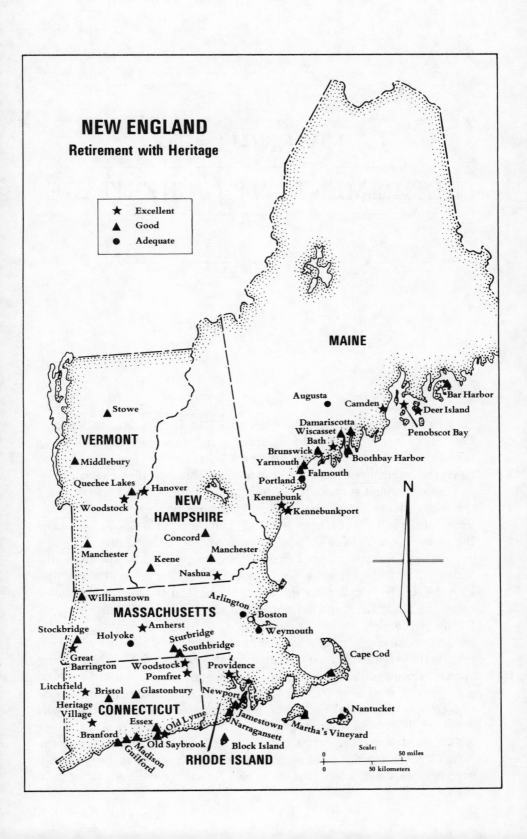

NEW ENGLAND
Retirement with Heritage

★ Excellent
▲ Good
● Adequate

MAINE

VERMONT

Stowe ▲

Middlebury ▲

Quechee Lakes ★   Hanover ★

Woodstock ★

NEW HAMPSHIRE

Augusta ●   Camden ★   Bar Harbor ★
                                  ★ Deer Island
Damariscotta ▲   Penobscot Bay
Wiscasset ★
Bath ★
Brunswick ★   Boothbay Harbor
Yarmouth ▲
Portland ▲   Falmouth ▲

Kennebunk ▲
★ Kennebunkport

Concord ▲

Keene ▲   Manchester ▲

Manchester ▲   Nashua ★

N

Williamstown ▲   Arlington

MASSACHUSETTS   Boston ○

Stockbridge   Amherst ★   Weymouth ●

Holyoke ●   Sturbridge ▲
                    Southbridge ▲

Great
Barrington ▲   Woodstock ★   Cape Cod ▲
                 Pomfret ★   Providence ▲

Litchfield ★   Bristol ▲   Glastonbury ▲   Newport ★

Heritage
Village ★   CONNECTICUT   Nantucket ●

Essex ★   Old Lyme ★   Jamestown ★   Martha's Vineyard ▲
Branford ▲   Narragansett ★
          Old Saybrook ★   Block Island ●
     Madison ▲
     Guilford ▲   RHODE ISLAND

Scale:
0 _____ 50 miles
0 _____ 50 kilometers

III.

NEW ENGLAND—

RETIREMENT WITH A HERITAGE

New England is a nice place to "come home" to. It is the land of heritage: Colonial charm, Currier and Ives scenes, Christmas-card settings. Even towns with grimy brick business districts boast tidy residential areas with neat green-shuttered houses and gleaming white-steepled churches.

New England is flaming fall foliage in Vermont, breakers pounding the rocky Maine coast, green village commons in New Hampshire, the graceful Berkshires of Massachusetts, clam chowder in Rhode Island and the Connecticut Yankee holding court in a wood-beamed tavern.

But if the land wears Pilgrim garb, its people are apt to be the taciturn Scots who settled in Vermont and New Hampshire, the clannish French-Canadians in Maine, the volatile Irish and Italians in Massachusetts, the stolid Germans in Connecticut and the colorful Portuguese in Rhode Island.

It takes a hardy people to survive the weather. The same whimsical climate that creates flaming autumns dictates frozen winters; blossoming spring heralds suffocating summer. And while the beaches of Cape Cod and Rhode Island offer blessed summer relief, the mountains and woods of New Hampshire and Vermont offer winter solace mainly to those who crave icy sports and roaring fireplaces. The annual average temperature is 44°F., with winters averaging 20°F. in northern New England and summers 67°F. An average of 36 inches of rain falls throughout the year until it freezes to snow, averaging 78 inches. Relative humidity averages 73 percent, bearable if the weather is mild. While fog blankets the coast during many nights and early mornings, it dissipates as you move inland. Clear days average 100 annually, cloudy days 130. The sun shines about 50 percent of the daylight time.

The population hugs the coast and disperses inland. Western Connecticut and Massachusetts, as well as large portions of Vermont, New Hampshire and Maine, are sparsely populated; you can often find a well-kept farm or Colonial house for sale.

But bring money. Charm costs, and taxes soar to pay the price. In Vermont, Connecticut, Rhode Island, Maine and Massachusetts, income, sales and property taxes are among the highest in the nation. They don't call Massachusetts "Taxachusetts" for nothing; Vermont taxes are 50 percent higher than in neighboring New Hampshire, but the services aren't necessarily better. Connecticut, which has no income tax, taxes dividends and capital gains at 7 percent and has among the highest cigarette, gasoline and sales taxes anywhere. The Boston area has the highest cost of *retirement* living in the continental United States, with Hartford, Connecticut close behind. New Hampshire has the lowest taxes (no state or sales tax) and only a 5 percent tax on interest and dividends.

Maybe it takes a special kind of person to retire in New England. Those who take pride in dry stone fences . . . who get misty-eyed when you mention Harvard, Yale, Dartmouth, Wellesley, Radcliffe, Smith, Mt. Holyoke and Amherst . . . who feel that harsh winters, torrid summers and stratospheric taxes are just something else to "put up with" . . . and especially those who feel that New England is a "nice place to come home to."

1. MASSACHUSETTS—THE "WORST" OFFERS SOME OF THE BEST

For the "worst" retirement state, Massachusetts offers some of the best retirement areas—Pioneer Valley, the Berkshires, Cape Cod, Nantucket, Martha's Vineyard, to name just a few. And for a small state (forty-fifth in size), it offers big contrasts: eastern lowlands, western uplands; frigid winters, torrid summers; liberal politics, conservative religion.

Some 16.5 percent of the state's 5.81 million population is age 60 and over, living mostly in Berkshire, Franklin, Worcester, Essex, Middlesex, Norfolk, Bristol, Barnstable and Dukes counties. Here are some of the advantages and disadvantages of retirement in the Bay State:

Climate and Environment

Massachusetts has cold winters and warm summers, with the colder and drier climate in the western region. It has a jagged, indented coast from Rhode Island around Cape Cod; flat land yields to stony upland pastures near the central region and gentle hilly country in the west; except in the west the land is rocky, sandy and not fertile. In the capital, Boston, the average winter temperature is 36.5°F.; in summer, 64.3°F. There are 175 sunny days, with an annual average humidity of 68.3 percent. The Bay State averages 53.11 inches of rain annually and 40.7 inches of snow.

A Leader in Health Care

Massachusetts has 189 hospitals with a total of 45,456 beds. There are 528 nursing homes with 38,942 beds and 341 personal-care homes with 11,998 beds. It has 245 doctors per 100,000 residents, among the highest ratio in the nation. However, the average cost for a semiprivate hospital room runs $190 daily, compared to the national average of $163 daily.

Innovations in Housing

Massachusetts has been an innovator in both housing laws and architecture. The Bay State was the leader in calling for inclusionary rather than exclusionary zoning. This means communities must allow a variety and choice of housing to meet the needs of all categories of people who might choose to live there. The state passed its "antisnob" law in 1969, requiring that communities make available a percentage of land or housing units for low- and moderate-income families. It is also the only state with a zoning appeals law.

Massachusetts, blessed with a bountiful supply of building materials, has also excelled in architectural styles, including still-standing seventeenth-century frame houses, Cape Cods and saltboxes; the glass, steel and concrete structures of Walter Gropius (longtime chairman of Harvard's architecture department); the geodesic creations of Buckminster Fuller, born in Milton.

Again, charm costs. Housing prices keep pace with the high cost of retirement living in the Bay State.

The Highest Cost of Retirement Living

Not only does the Boston area have the highest cost of retirement living in the continental United States, but state and local taxes average 17.8 percent of income—about the highest in the United States (the national average is 12 percent). Here's how the tax breaks down:

Income Tax—interest, dividends and capital gains (exclusive of interest on Massachusetts savings deposits), 10.75 percent; all other income 5.375 percent. *Personal exemptions:* single, $2,000; married filing jointly, $2,000 plus (1) an amount not exceeding $2,000 equal to the earned income (salary, wages, pensions, annuities and other earnings) of the spouse having the smaller of such income and (2) $700 if such spouse's income is $2,000 or less (but not more than $4,600 in the aggregate). Married filing separately, $1,000; persons 65 and over and each qualified dependent, $700; if household is maintained for dependent under 12, $600; blind, $2,200. There is no tax if taxable and nontaxable income does not exceed $3,000 if single, or $5,000 if married. Tax credits, if total income does not exceed $5,000, are $4 for singles, $8 for married, and $8 for each dependent.

Special Treatment of Retirement Income—income from federal and Massachusetts governmental contributory annuities, pensions, endowments or retirement fund is exempt. Income from such funds of other states is exempt on a reciprocal basis.

Property Tax—an exemption of $4,000 in assessed value or $500 in actual tax, whichever results in the greater amount of taxes being abated, is granted to persons 70 or over whose gross receipts are less than $6,000 (single) or $7,000 (married), who have lived in the state for the preceding 10 years, who have owned and occupied the residence for 5 years and whose whole estate does not exceed $40,000 ($45,000 if married) or $17,-000 ($20,000 if married) exclusive of residence owned and occupied. In computing gross receipts, amounts received under Social Security, Railroad Retirement or a public pension plan may be deducted in an amount equal to the minimum Social Security benefit then payable. *Property tax deferral:* Persons 65 or over, who have lived in the state for the preceding 10 years, who have owned and occupied the residence for 5 years and who have gross receipts of less than $20,000 (whether single or combined if married) may postpone payment of all or a portion of real estate taxes up to 50 percent of their interest in the real estate when a tax deferral and recovery agreement has been entered into with the assessors. Effective July 1, 1981, property taxes are reduced to 2.5 percent of market value from the previous average of 3.4 percent.

Sales Tax—5 percent. *Exemptions:* Food, clothing (up to $175 for any one article of clothing), prescription medicines, eyeglasses, hearing aids, prosthetic devices, utilities, heating oil.

Leadership in Culture

As the "cradle of liberty," the Bay State has led in both culture and education. The first free American public school, the Mather, was founded in Dorchester (Boston) in 1639. The state has 119 institutions of higher learning including Harvard and the Massachusetts Institute of Technology.

Cape Cod has summer theaters, sports and an artists' colony at Provincetown. Tanglewood, in the Berkshires, has the summer concerts of the Boston Symphony Orchestra. In New Bedford, the Old Dartmouth Historical Society and Whaling Museum has a large and unique collection of whaling implements, scrimshaw and logbooks as well as furniture, costumes and firearms. In Pittsfield, the Berkshire Athenaeum has memorabilia of Herman Melville, who lived there while writing *Moby Dick*. In Plymouth, Pilgrim Hall contains relics of the Mayflower Pilgrims. And Old Sturbridge Village, in Sturbridge, is a re-created early New England village of 35 authentic and functioning homes and shops.

Unique Services for Seniors

Massachusetts is home of the Elderhostel program, in which 200 colleges and universities in 30 states offer on-campus, college-level courses to older people at very low cost. Classes are held year-round and sessions generally last 1 week. For further information write Elderhostel, 100 Boylston Street, Boston, MA 02116. Massachusetts is also the birthplace of Project HIRE, a program that helps people age 55 and older find full or part-time jobs. It is implemented by the Division of Community Colleges in Bedford and supported by the Minuteman Home Care Corporation of Lexington. Functioning through local intake centers where job applicants can register and receive career counseling, Project HIRE is designed to "create a broad range of opportunities for older people to enhance their lives and increase their income." Unfortunately, the Massachusetts Department of Elder Affairs has not matched the zeal of the above organizations in helping seniors find Retirement Edens in the Bay State.

For further information write:

Massachusetts Department of Elder Affairs
110 Tremont Street
Boston, MA 02108

MAJOR RETIREMENT AREAS

The Pioneer Valley—Scenic Beauty, Cultural Charm, Historic Appeal

In seeking Retirement Edens, one of the first places I was attracted to was the Pioneer Valley in western Massachusetts. Lying midway between Vermont and New Hampshire to the north and Connecticut to the south and embracing Hampden, Hampshire and Franklin counties, this is a land of scenic beauty, historic charm and cultural appeal.

Bisected by the second longest river in the East, the Connecticut, the valley includes hills, woods, fertile meadows, streams and lakes. It is criss-crossed by the Berkshire and Mohawk trails, where Revolutionary leaders assembled and Daniel Shays staged his rebellion.

Culture abounds in 5 colleges in the area. The leader is the main campus of the University of Massachusetts in Amherst, which has tripled in size over the last 20 years and has fine museums and libraries. I also found many galleries, shops, antique stores, auction houses, country fairs and delightful parks scattered throughout the valley. And I learned about annual events that range from dog and horse shows to craft exhibits and church suppers.

You'd be as impressed as I was with *Amherst* (pop. 33,000). Nestled in the Pioneer Valley about 10 miles east of Northampton, it is surrounded by rolling farmland, orchards and woodlands, and rimmed by the Mt. Holyoke–Mt. Tom ranges and the eastern Berkshires.

Amherst combines the charm of the past with the advantages of the future. The Colonial village green and Revolutionary houses mingle with the stark concrete slabs of the U. Mass. campus. History is so current that Emily Dickinson, Robert Frost, Noah Webster and Eugene Field still make their presence felt.

Residents over age 60 (16 percent of the townspeople) form a vital, vocal core of this community through active councils on aging, senior clubs and membership in scores of other clubs, civic associations and campus boards. The town responds with services and facilities geared to our needs and wants.

Climate and Environment. Every season is picturesque, and the air quality is rated "excellent" by the Pollution Control District. There are no slums in Amherst, and both town and campus police curb major crimes (vandalism, noise complaints and traffic accidents are about the worst violations). Christmas in Amherst means lighting the gigantic Merry Maple tree on the Town Common and winter sports; spring blossoms with homecoming birds, delicate flowers and fresh greenery everywhere; summer yields farmers' markets, outdoor exhibits and rallies, long, warm days to walk woodland trails or paddle meandering streams; autumn paints the landscape in brilliant yellows, oranges, reds and browns. The January temperature averages 23.9°F.; April 47.4°F.; July 72.2°F.; October 52.1°F. Rain averages 43.81 inches, with February the driest month (3.13 inches) and December the wettest (4.16 inches). Snowfall averages 53.8 inches. Unfortunately, this precipitation doesn't always provide the needed water for the town and sometimes there is a shortage.

Medical Facilities. Considering its size, there is an abundance of doctors and medical facilities in Amherst. There are 38 doctors in town, 16 of them concentrated in the Amherst Medical Association clinic on University Drive, 4 blocks west of the Town Common; this makes referral from one specialist to another convenient. You also have the services of a full-time psychologist, 3 nurse practitioners and 2 physician's assistants. Amherst boasts a Health Maintenance Organization, emergency service and 16 dentists. Within 10 miles is a general hospital with 268 beds, a Veterans Administration hospital and 2 major hospitals in nearby Holyoke. The Amherst Nursing Home, next door to the clinic on University Drive, provides a day-care center which features meals, planned recreation, entertainment and activity. All told there are 88 nursing-home beds in the community.

Housing Availability and Cost. Housing, especially rentals, is scarce because of the competing student population. However, many rentals are available during the break at the end of the spring semester, at the beginning of summer school and again at the beginning of the fall semester. You'll find approximately 15 real estate agencies in Amherst, most of which handle rentals. Rentals for 1- or 2-bedroom apartments generally start at $250 a month and require a year's lease. A month's rent is usually required in addition to the first month's rent, and a like amount is required as a security deposit, which is returned if no damage is done. The law requires all rental apartments to be furnished with a good stove and refrigerator, and the landlord must provide trash removal and all maintenance. Tenants usually pay utility bills. Single-family 2-bedroom houses, condominiums and coops and townhouses usually start at $40,000, although the best start at $50,000. Most of the better homes are tucked away in secluded spots in the woods. Make sure that your hideaway isn't too far from a public road and transportation. Also note the length of the approach from the public road to your garage. Someone will have to shovel that in the winter, and you can count on plenty of snow. Public roads are plowed before you get up in the morning, and public buses will be running when you want them.

If you want to buy a "handyman's dream" house (for under $40,000), you might consider an older home that is a designated town landmark. The federal and state governments have monies set aside for restoration of such buildings. You can find out details by writing to the National Trust for Historic Preservation, 740 Jackson Place NW, Washington, D.C. 20006; ask for the free booklet, "National Trust Service." In Amherst there are 2 areas (census tracts 8203 and 8205) in which owners are eligible for grants from the Amherst Housing Rehabilitation Program for up to 80 percent of the cost of repairs to bring property up to town standards. Check with the Amherst Office of the Town Planner to find if your property would qualify.

The ground-floor apartments of Chestnut Court on South Pleasant Street have always been the envy of older Amherst residents, but there aren't enough units (30) to accommodate all those who would like to have them. Their convenient location at the head of the business district, and back-to-back with the Amherst Carriage Shops, places them in an enviable position. But Chestnut Court in its heyday couldn't compete with the new Ann Whalen Housing for the Elderly, located at one end of Boltwood Walk, kitty-corner to the Bangs Community Center, home of the Council on Aging. The 80 units in Ann Whalen were spoken for before the plans were off the drawing board. Another building, the Clark House, has opened with 80 units, also on the edge of Boltwood Walk.

The Amherst Council on Aging is remodeling a former fraternity house, located adjacent to the Chestnut Court housing area, into a 23-bedroom residence with central kitchen, dining and social areas. This "congregate housing" is much like the boardinghouses of old. Each resident has his or her private room, although some have to share a bath down the hall. Everyone eats family style in the dining room, and parlors are set aside for socializing, visiting, television and reading. Personal assistance and homemaker services are provided.

Cost of Living. Property taxes are based on approximately $28.20 per $1,000 of market value; the tax on a $50,000 house is $1,410. Seniors may be eligible for tax exemptions, and many stores offer seniors a 10 percent discount. The main shopping center starts on South Pleasant Street across from the Common and continues up both sides of the street. There you'll find scores of boutiques, craft stores and restaurants. Although Amherst proper is "anti–shopping malls," it is surrounded by them, some right on the town line. The malls offer free bus service to Amherst residents, so you can have all the advantages and none of the disadvantages of these huge shopping complexes. Food and other costs are generally in line with major urban areas, but Amherst residents have the option of lowering living costs by taking in students, and augmenting income with part-time or full-time jobs. Job counseling is offered through the library and the Council on Aging in the Bangs Center. The Employment Resource Center in the basement of Jones Library, on Amity Street, keeps an up-to-date list of all jobs listed with the Northampton office of the Massachusetts Department of Employment Services. This saves the job hunter a trip to investigate job possibilities. Amherst is also involved in the "Green Thumb" program, a federally funded program to find jobs for seniors, and the Highland Valley Elder Service Center employs older people as Senior Companions and for their Chores Services program. The Homemaker Services of Hampshire County hires older people for light housework or for work as home health aides. These last 3 programs limit work to 20 hours a week and pay minimum wage.

Leisure-Time Activities. Amherst residents have fingertip control on culture. They have 5 colleges in the area: Amherst College, the Amherst campus of the University of Massachusetts and Hampshire College; nearby (within 10 miles) is Smith College and Mt. Holyoke. At any time of year you can attend concerts of classical and popular music, dance recitals, theater, films, lectures, debates, forums, etc.—many of them free. Additions and last-minute schedule changes can be checked through local newspapers and radio stations or the Amherst Chamber of Commerce, (413) 253-9666. Another bonus is the resource materials available within each campus. You can borrow books from the U. Mass. library, and Amherst and Hampshire colleges permit residents to use books on campus. What you can't find at these 3 sources is probably available through the Inter-Library Loan System. Jones Library has extensive collections of Emily Dickinson, Robert Frost and most other Amherst-related writers. Amherst College's Robert Frost Library has an impressive collection of material by and about him. There are 2 local newspapers, 9 bookstores, 3 art galleries, 2 museums, 4 little theater groups, 3 FM radio stations and good television reception. You have your choice of 2 programs of continuing education run by U. Mass. and the town of Amherst. There are 13 churches and 1 synagogue in town.

Nearby Tanglewood in Lenox offers summer concerts by the Boston Symphony; America's oldest dance festival, Jacob's Pillow, stages programs at Becket, about an hour's drive away.

The sports enthusiast will find 3 golf courses in town, 3 tennis courts, 3 swimming pools and many conservation trails. Also within town limits are cross-country ski trails, bike trails and jogging trails. There is also a restricted hunting area for town residents, and several well-stocked fishing streams. Horseback riding is available throughout the area and there are many wildlife sanctuaries. Camping, boating, canoeing and hiking are all within the area. In the 72.5-acre Mill River green belt are fitness trails which guide you step-by-step through physical exercises. Signs suggest exercises for each age group, and assorted bars, steps, walls and other devices help put you through the paces.

Special Services for Seniors. The Amherst Council on Aging (COA) has established excellent rapport with the town and has worked closely with the town for mutual goals. The COA is responsible for providing daily hot lunches in the Bangs Community Center and for home-delivered hot meals. The council has instituted crafts and recreational programs, arranged for discounts from merchants and shared facilities with local schools and churches. It has a continuing agenda of bus trips scheduled for out-of-town and has an ongoing agenda of live entertainment at the Bangs Center. The COA sponsors workshops in creative writing and dancing, bridge classes, folk dances and literature-discussion groups. The COA operates 2 radio-controlled minibuses which take seniors to the doctor, shopping, visiting or to the daily hot meal at Bangs Center. This service is free to anyone over 60, retired or not, and any person of this age is automatically a member of the COA and is actively encouraged to participate in its programs. Besides COA, there is a Golden Age Club which sponsors many programs. The consensus of the over-60 set is: "We've never had it so good." Transportational facilities throughout the area are also geared to seniors. You can travel at half-fare at off-peak hours, and many bus lines offer free transportation to shopping malls and through the various campuses. Good train and plane service is nearby.

Whatever interest you have, you'll find a club or organization to meet your needs. Membership activities are big in Amherst and help newcomers assimilate. But it isn't hard to "fit into" Amherst; the town has a way of making new arrivals feel like natives. However, the town is also used to people who prefer to remain reclusive, and anyone preferring peace, quiet, solitude and isolation won't be pressured to mix.

For further information, write:

> Amherst Chamber of Commerce
> 11 Spring Street
> Amherst, MA 01002

About 20 miles south of Amherst lies *Holyoke* (pop. 48,000), which has a special attraction for seniors. Many younger families have moved out of what used to be the better sections of town, and left many single and 2-family homes vacant. The result is that good housing is available for sale below $40,000 and for rent from $200 a month. Leases are rare, and the relationship between landlord and tenant is usually one of easy camaraderie and mutual trust. Holyoke is also the home of *Geriatric Village*, a Camelot for the elderly perched on an 18-acre brow of the municipal nursing-home site overlooking the city and Pioneer Valley. It offers congregate and other housing in a campuslike setting which includes a skilled-nursing facility, out-patient clinic and adult care center. Another day-care center is located in the downtown area, and the city has two community hospitals, one municipal and a state veterans' hospital. Besides these services for seniors (more than 23 percent are 60 or over), Holyoke is home of Mt. Holyoke College and Wistariahurst, a repository of museum artifacts, fine arts, exhibits, paintings, science and natural history. Spring shad fishing in the river is a local tradition. Tom Reservation, located between Holyoke and Easthampton, has picnic facilities, fishing, ice skating, a trail museum and bird-watching observation towers with panoramic views of Pioneer Valley. Nearby is Mt. Tom Ski Area and Mountain Park, an amusement-recreation family park. The Church-in-the-Round on Northampton Street is a new concept in architectural design, and has been featured in *Life* magazine and other publications. Scotts Tower, in Community Park, offers a scenic view of the city and of the Regional Stephen Chumura Pool and Recreation Area.

Despite these attractions, I do not consider Holyoke a "pretty" town. I've wandered the streets many times and driven through the surrounding suburbs. The architectural innovations are in contrast to the grimy red brick of most of the older business buildings and districts. But the fact that the town offers such good buys on retirement housing makes it worthwhile investigating. For further information, write:

Chamber of Commerce
Holyoke, MA 01040

The Berkshires—Grace Notes and Obbligatos

I couldn't sing the praises of New England without adding the grace notes and obbligatos of the Berkshires. These highlands are bounded by the Connecticut Valley on the east, Hudson Valley on the west, Vermont on the north, and Connecticut on the south. Here is the home of the Berkshire Music Center at Lenox, Berkshire Playhouse at Stockbridge, Jacob's Pillow at Becket, Lenox Art Center at Interlaken and Williamstown Theater Festival at venerable Williams College. And here you'll find elm-shaded streets, rolling meadows and wooded hills; rich culture and deep history in an area that is 74 percent forested, less than 3 percent built up.

I found downtown *Great Barrington* (pop. 7,400) to be as stately, dignified and trim as its older citizens (who comprise more than 30 percent of the population). Shops, churches and a library line the main street, and cars even stop for pedestrians. Just off the business district I could see gracious houses on large lots. Further on were tidy clapboard houses on smaller plots.

Climate and Environment. Located in southwestern Berkshire County, Great Barrington is the subregional center, and only 30 minutes from *Pittsfield* (pop. 55,000), the county seat. Great Barrington is the quintessential New England town, with ancient trees spreading leafy shade; stone churches and white clapboard houses; historical markers studding the lush green landscape. The annual average temperature is 49.1°F. (January 24.8°F.; July 72.7°F.), with 43.77 inches of rainfall annually.

Medical Facilities. Fairview Hospital has 70 beds, and there's a clinic which provides emergency service. The Berkshire Medical Center (393 beds) in nearby Pittsfield is superior to many hospitals serving much larger communities, and meets the needs not only of Great Barrington and the rest of the county, but draws patients from New York, Connecticut and Vermont. Great Barrington also has 3 nursing homes with 310 beds, 15 physicians and surgeons and 8 dentists, which adds up to more than adequate medical facilities.

Housing Availability and Cost. Housing is generally scarce. When rentals are available, 2-bedroom houses rent from $300 a month; 2-bedroom apartments, $250–$450; townhouses, $250–$450. You can buy 2-bedroom houses from $50,000, although some "rustic retreats" start at $45,000. Building lots range from $1,000 to $6,000. No mobile homes are allowed.

Cost of Living. Property taxes run about $49 per $1,000 valuation (about 3 percent of market value), but seniors get a $350 exemption. Retail sales tax is 5 percent with clothes and food exempted, and seniors get a 10 percent discount at some stores. Food and utility costs are classed as high, but are reasonable compared to similar communities. Some part-time jobs are available, and you can get job counseling through the Southern Berkshire Employment and Counseling Services. Some residents plant gardens to grow their own vegetables.

Leisure-Time Activities. Great Barrington has 2 local newspapers, 2 libraries, 3 bookstores, 4 art galleries, a little theater, an FM radio station and good cable-television reception. It has 35 clubs, including 2 garden clubs, chess and bridge clubs. Adult-education classes are available at Monument Mountain Regional High School. The town also features parks, swimming pools, 3 golf courses and riding trails.

Special Services for Seniors. Great Barrington has a senior center and a chapter of the American Association of Retired Persons. The Office on Aging (8 Castle Street) gives referral services of all kinds. There is also a hot meal program, homemakers service, visiting nurses, meals on wheels, transportation program, income-maintenance program, a help phone for emergencies and legal-aid services. Seniors go on regularly scheduled tours and attend yearly Christmas parties and a Veterans of Foreign Wars Christmas luncheon.

For further information, write:

Southern Berkshire Chamber of Commerce
Great Barrington, MA 01230

Everything about *Williamstown* (pop. 10,000) is elegant: the rustic setting in the northern Berkshires, the smart shops, gourmet restaurants and stately homes. I, along with many others, think this is one of the loveliest towns in New England. You'd be convinced, too, just by walking around the campus of Williams College. Starting as a free school in 1791, it became a men's college in 1793 and coeducational in 1970. It retains all the romantic charm of those earlier days. The Thompson Memorial Chapel on Main Street has beautiful stained-glass windows that can stand a long look. Diagonally across the street is the octagonally shaped Lawrence Art Museum, with its Greek rotunda housing fine collections of glass, pottery, bronzes and sculpture. On South Street, just west of the center of town, is the Sterling and Francine Clark Art Institute, which boasts a memorable collection of Renoirs along with antique silver, furniture and china. Many college events are open to the general public, which makes Williamstown an attractive place to retire (some 20 percent of the population is age 55 and older). Williamstown is a "4 season" community, having the same climate and environment as Great Barrington. Williamstown residents share the medical facilities of North Adams Regional Hospital (188 beds) about 5 miles away, and the town itself has 18 physicians and surgeons and 9 dentists—more than enough for medical needs. Like Amherst, Williamstown has a shortage of rentals, especially during the college season, but some charming homes are available, ranging from $45,000 (average price in the $60,000s). The town also has a 60-unit housing project for seniors and a senior center on Church Street. Property taxes run a bit higher than in Great Barrington (about 4 percent of market value) but, like many college towns, Williamstown offers good low-cost eating and shopping facilities for the modest-incomed student body and faculty. Besides the Williamstown Theater Festival and the many college activities, there are 2 18-hole pro golf courses, tennis courts (at the college) and many tree-shaded streets and paths that have earned Williamstown the right to be called a walkable town. Green Mountain Park (Vermont) and Jiminy Peak and Brodie Mountain ski areas are just a short drive away. An active Council on Aging provides the older citizens with luncheons and programs at the Friendship Center, including movies, instruction in arts and crafts, bus trips, free tax service, senior discounts and health programs. Many a Williams grad has it in the back of his mind to retire here some day, but it doesn't take an alumnus to realize that this could be an ideal retirement spot.

For further information, write:

Williamstown Board of Trade
Williamstown, MA 01267

Between Williamstown and Great Barrington lies *Stockbridge* (pop. 2,300), which certainly rivals both towns in charm if not in size. You can't help but become captivated with the Red Lion Inn (established in 1773), which dominates the main street (Highway 7). This elegant summer-resort inn caters to discriminating vacationers as well as gourmets; it and the Colonial Merwin House and Old Corner House have drawn sightseers as well as artists. Playwright Robert E. Sherwood summered here for many years, and it has been the home of playwright William Gibson, writer Norman Mailer, and painter Norman Rockwell. Famous actors trod the boards at the Berkshire Playhouse and at Chestwood, a 150-acre estate, you can visit the studio of Daniel Chester French, sculptor of the Lincoln statue in the Lincoln Memorial and Concord's Minuteman. Stockbridge is certainly worth a visit as a tourist or potential resident.

Central Massachusetts—Where the Past Still Lives

In the heartland of Massachusetts, you'll find a major educational, industrial and retail center offering all retirement advantages. You'll also find the past very much alive in Old Sturbridge Village (see below), adding historic charm to gracious living.

The main retirement center is *Southbridge* (pop. 17,000), with nearly 20 percent of the population classified as retired. Southbridge is bordered by Sturbridge on the west, Charlton on the north and northeast, Dudley on the east and Connecticut on the south. It is 65 miles southwest of Boston, 21 miles from Worcester, 45 miles from Springfield and 160 miles from New York City.

Climate and Environment. Although Southbridge is a major manufacturing center, noise and air pollution are minimal. The terrain is hilly, with elevations ranging from 400 to 800 feet above sea level. Average temperature in January, 24°F.; in April, 47.5°F.; July, 69.8°F.; October, 55°F. Humidity averages 70 percent and there are 200 days of sunshine.

Rain averages 49.16 inches; snowfall 12 to 18 inches. The driest month is July, the wettest April.

Medical Facilities. Southbridge has 1 hospital with 126 beds, 1 nursing home with 210 beds, 3 clinics, 24-hour emergency service, 44 doctors, 20 dentists, 15 specialists and a mental-health clinic. Including the other health-care facilities in the area, medical care is more than adequate.

Housing Availability and Cost. Housing is generally scarce, although there are 2 senior-citizen housing projects (over 300 units) in the town. When single-family houses are available, they sell from $40,000 and rent from $300 to $400 a month. Some rental townhouses are available from $200 to $300 monthly. Building lots cost from $4,000 to $10,000 and building costs average $25 a square foot. Some vacation homes are available at $150 per week.

Cost of Living. Taxes run 3.6 percent of market value ($1,464 on a $40,000 house). Retail sales tax is 5 percent, although many senior discounts (10 percent) are available at local stores. Food costs are average for the area, but energy costs are rated high. Some jobs are available in retail stores and service industries, and some job counseling is also available.

Leisure-Time Activities. There are 2 local newspapers, a library with 40,000 volumes, 3 bookstores, 1 art gallery, a community theater, FM radio and cable television with good reception. There are 6 clubs, including 2 garden clubs; adult-education classes at the high school and various junior colleges in the area; 2 parks, 2 golf courses, 3 tennis courts and both private and public trails for biking, hiking and horseback riding, and a racquetball club.

Special Services for Seniors. The Southbridge Council on the Aging, 60 Charlton Street, (617) 764-7070, offers many services, as does the Sturbridge-Fiskdale Council on Aging, (617) 347-9412. You'll also find chapters of the American Association of Retired Persons, an elder bus program, community day centers (both social and therapeutic) and home-care services. There are also a crisis-intervention program, legal-aid service, rehabilitation programs and various senior discounts to recreational and cultural activities.

For further information, write:

Tri-Community Area Chamber of Commerce
111 Main Street
Southbridge, MA 01550

About half way along the Massachusetts Turnpike (Interstate 90), 65 miles west of Boston, you can turn off this modern speedway and drop back 150 years in time to Old Sturbridge Village, a living museum in the town of *Sturbridge* (pop. 5,000).

The Village is a restoration of a typical New England village of the period 1790–1830. Here, on several hundred acres of lush meadows along the banks of the Quinebaug River, a private nonprofit foundation has restored over 40 historic homes and buildings to re-create life as it existed before the industrial revolution. While the Village attracts tourists, the town of Sturbridge is attracting more and more retirees. This area—20 miles from Worcester, 45 miles from Hartford, 150 miles from New York City—has some of the finest medical facilities in the country, including a recently built hospital 4 miles away in Southbridge. There are also excellent metropolitan hospitals in Worcester. Besides excellent restaurants in the area (the Publick House in Sturbridge has made almost every "best" list of New England restaurants for years), you'll find good golf courses, excellent hunting, fishing, boating, ice skating and skiing. Perhaps the best recommendation for retiring in the Sturbridge-Southbridge-Worcester area is that while many natives like a trip to Florida or the Caribbean at the end of a long winter, they want to get back for the next town meeting!

For further information, write:

Chamber of Commerce
Sturbridge, MA 01566

Two Boston suburbs are worth considering for retirement living: *Arlington* (pop. 52,000) and *Weymouth* (pop. 59,000). Arlington is a substantial residential community of professional, semiprofessional and skilled workers, many of whom own their own homes. Although new homes are scarce, good older homes in several fine sections sell from $50,000. There is an ample apartment selection from $300 a month. Taxes are high—7 percent of market value—but the services are good, including an outstanding public library with 2 branches which offer a fine record library, art gallery, music appreciation and other cultural programs. Arlington also boasts an outstanding Philharmonic Society with its own large orchestra and choral groups, an unusually fine dramatic society and most service and social clubs, including a Golden Age Club. This northwest suburb is only 6 miles from downtown Boston and has easy access to suburban medical facilities. By contrast, Weymouth is a south shore residential community about 12 miles south of the city. It is more middle class, covers a wide area and has several sections, each with its own distinct characteristics. You'll find an unusually good selection of older homes from $40,000, with newer homes selling from $50,000. Taxes are lower than in Arlington: 5 percent of market value. Weymouth features many outdoor recreational areas, including 1 public beach at a lake and 1 at the seashore. It also has 3 marinas and 2 yacht clubs. It has its own 239-bed hospital which serves other south shore towns, and 36 physicians, 20 dentists and 10 osteopaths, providing good medical care.

For further information, write:

Chambers of Commerce
Arlington, MA 02174
Weymouth, MA 02188

Cape Cod—For Those Who Love the Sea

If you like the sea you'll love the Cape. The Cape is a 70-mile long peninsula, bent like an arm with its fist upraised. Buzzards Bay and the Cape Cod Canal are at the shoulder; Chatham and Nauset beach are at the elbow; Provincetown is the fist. It's a sandy spit with miles of varied beaches, 300-year-old villages with green-shuttered white clapboard houses and gray-shingled Cape Cod cottages, pine woods, grassy marshes, rolling dunes, cranberry and bayberry bogs.

Its 15 townships comprise an entire county, Barnstable. Each village offers a type of life and atmosphere of its own. Generally, the towns on the north shore (Cape Cod Bay) retain their Colonial charm, are quiet and dignified and offer the best retirement living. Villages along the shores of Vineyard and Nantucket sounds are livelier and more commercial (and noisier and more congested).

Although the year-round population of some 146,000 nearly triples during the summer season (July and August), retirement has overtaken tourism as Cape Cod's primary industry. Currently, about 50,000 people age 62 or older (33 percent of the stable population) live on the Cape, and their Social Security, pension checks, savings and investments contribute $300 million to the economy. It is not hard to understand why they chose the Cape: it's within a few hours' drive from children and grandchildren in Boston and New York, and taxes average 25 percent less than in those metropolitan areas. Add milder winters and cooler summers, pure air and water and endless recreational and cultural facilities, and you have an almost ideal Retirement Eden.

Climate and Environment. The temperature averages 70.5°F. in summer, 35°F. in winter. Rainfall averages 43 inches a year, with heaviest amounts in summer and winter. There is little snow or ice in winter, but some rain and fog. Golf addicts claim you can play all year, but you have to be a really hearty soul.

Medical Facilities. The Cape Cod Hospital, located in Hyannis, is a private community health center for general practice. Also in this village is the Hyannis Medical Center for general practice. The Barnstable County Hospital, in Pocasset, is for chronic diseases. Also in this village is the Pocasset Mental Health and Retardation Center. The Falmouth Hospital is open for general practice, and the Cape Cod Artificial Kidney Center, located in Yarmouth Port, provides facilities for kidney dialysis. Crow's Nest Medical and Dental Clinic in Buzzards Bay provides primary health and preventive care. The A.I.M. Medical Center is located on Route 6 in Wellfleet. There are other extended-care facilities located throughout the Cape, and there are some 250 doctors and dentists scattered throughout the villages, providing more than adequate health care.

Housing Availability and Cost. You'll find plenty of real estate offices to sell you housing and plenty of antique stores for furnishings. And although some housing is expensive (condominiums at the New Belmont in West Harwich start at $125,000), you'll find some unusual bargains. A recent ad in the local *Cape Cod Independent* offered a 1-bedroom efficiency cottage, furnished, for $125 a month, year round. And Nickerson Homes in Orleans recently offered to erect a shell of a home for under $10,000 (completed homes also available). Acorn Homes, North Eastham, features the "nutshell" (a modified saltbox with an exterior of weathered vertical plywood) for $45,000 to $70,000. Figure the average retirement homes sell for $55,000; lots, $6,000. You can get a list of real estate brokers and information on second or retirement homes by writing to the Cape Cod Chamber of Commerce, Hyannis, MA 02601. Be sure to specify what you are looking for.

Cost of Living. As noted, real estate taxes run 25 percent lower than in the Boston metropolitan area. Food and other essentials (household goods) might cost as much or more than they do in Boston or New York, and because of the many specialty shops catering to tourists, some luxury items may cost even more. However, after Labor Day, many stores have end of season, close-out or "going out of business" sales where you can pick up real bargains. And those who live here year round say you soon learn to shop where the locals do and where you can get the best prices. Don't count on getting a job, unless you want one associated with the "vacation business" (hotels/motels, restaurants, entertainment centers, etc.) or plan to set up your own small business. There's always room for creative people who can develop their own markets, especially along the arts-and-crafts line. Retail sales tax is 5 percent, but seniors can get discounts at many restaurants, stores and entertainment facilities and exemptions on some taxes.

Leisure-Time Activities. There are more than 25 motion-picture theaters, and summer stock productions are presented at several theaters and playhouses. Local theater groups provide entertainment in the off-season. You'll also find garden clubs, art centers, symphony and music societies, choral groups, crafts associations, women's and men's clubs, sportsmen's clubs, sports centers, libraries, senior organizations and a full array of service clubs. You can enjoy several FM radio stations and cable television is available. Of course, all outdoor activities are available, including boating, bicycling, golf, hiking, horseback riding, hunting, fishing, camping, sailing, tennis, etc. The YMCA offers a special course for seniors, "The Way to a Healthy Back." The program was developed by Dr. Hans Kraus, a world-known authority on the treatment of backache.

Special Services for Seniors. The Cape has its own area agency on aging, a home-care corporation, nutritional programs, senior aides program, retired senior volunteer program, 13 senior centers, AARP chapters, caseworker program for low-income elders, visiting nurses, meals on wheels (all 15 towns have them), a transportation program (buses, but the situation is difficult because of winding roads and isolation of some areas), an elderly law project targeted for low-income seniors, adult day-care centers in Pocasset and South Yarmouth. Persons over age 60 can ride the Barnstable-Hyannis bus for 25¢.

What are the best retirement towns? Most seniors prefer the quieter and less crowded north side of the Cape. One reason the north side (Cape Cod Bay) is less developed is because the water is colder than the south (Nantucket Sound), where most public beaches and commercial enterprises are centered. On the same summer day you can be driving serenely (with little traffic) past jelly-makers' kitchens and sprawling old inns on the north shore, while on the south shore traffic is bumper-to-bumper, crawling past motel and fast-food chains. Even the mid-Cape around Hyannis tends to become congested and noisy, because a major airport is located there. But the north shore is a land of gray-green moors, sheltered inlets, sandy beaches, and quaint towns.

Here are the preferred retirement areas:

Orleans (pop. 5,100) lies at the crook of the Cape Cod arm; 40 percent of the population is age 60 and over. It is a quiet town with many facilities for retirees, including a hospital in Hyannis with 278 beds, a nursing home with 33 beds, an emergency rescue squad and ambulance, 5 specialists and 12 dentists. Orleans also has a convalescent and retirement home (19 units) and a good selection of single-family homes selling from $70,000. There are few rental units available, but coops and condominiums sell for $34,900 to $60,000. When rentals are available they run from $300 a month for a house and from $200 for apartments. Building lots run from $20,000 to over $100,000. Taxes are only 1.25 percent of market value and

many stores offer 10 percent discount for seniors. Orleans has a council
on aging, elder services, home health-care programs, drop-in center, library, 2 bookstores, 3 art galleries, a museum, little theater, arts and
crafts clubs, chess and bridge clubs, an extensive adult-education program and a reassurance program to make sure seniors aren't ill and
unable to function for themselves.

For further information write:

Chamber of Commerce
Box 153
Orleans, MA 02653

Sandwich (pop. 9,500) is by far the prettiest of the upper Cape communities, and it still retains much of its charm as the first town to be
settled on the Cape. The steeple of the First Church of Christ, said to be
America's finest copy of a Christopher Wren spire, soars above the village
green. Nearby is the saltbox Hoxie House of 1637, believed to be the
oldest house on the Cape. More modern housing is available to retirees.
You could buy a custom-built, 3-bedroom, 2½-bath, 1-fireplace chalet with
2,100 square feet of living space set on a superbly landscaped ⅓-acre plot
for around $95,000; taxes would run about $1,000 a year. Less expensive
but elegant homes start at $75,000; attractive lots sell for $12,000 to
$30,000. Other attractions include the Sandwich Glass Museum, contain-
ing outstanding examples of pressed glass made in the area, and Heritage
Plantation, set on 75 acres of land, with woodland walks, a museum of
antiques and folk art exhibits.

For further information, write:

Chamber of Commerce
Sandwich, MA 02563

Eastham (pop. 3,415) lies at the gateway to the Cape Cod National
Seashore. Eastham is noted for fine fishing, including trout, bass, pickerel,
white and yellow perch, striped bass, flounder, tautog, fluke and bluefish,
and for its shellfish, including clams, oysters, scallops and mussels. Also
in town is the magnificent stretch of Nauset Beach, on the "back" (Atlantic) side. The town offers many other recreational facilities, including a
40,000-volume public library. The library offers a variety of activities,
including rotating art exhibits, craft programs and films. Townspeople
have access to Cape Cod Hospital, and there's a good variety of housing
available from $45,000. Many who own second homes here belong to the
Eastham Non-Resident Taxpayers Association, which holds summer

meetings and represents taxpayers the rest of the year. The property tax rate is a modest $14.50 per $1,000. Many cottages are available for rental both off- and on-season.

For further information, write:

Eastham Chamber of Commerce
Eastham, MA 02642

Other Cape Cod communities include *Chatham* (02633), a town of 2,000 on the southeast corner of the Cape and a fashionable shopping center; *Dennis* (02638), a town of 7,000 which heads a group of "Dennises" which includes the smaller townships of Dennis Port, East Dennis and South Dennis; *Harwich* (02645), population 6,000, which includes East Harwich, West Harwich, South Harwich and Harwich Port and which proclaims itself "a nice place to retire," although I found the area a bit more congested than some north cape towns; *Provincetown* (02657), population 3,000, at the tip of the Cape and a startling mixture of the heroic past and relaxed present; *Yarmouth* (02675), population 13,000, architecturally one of the choicest communities, with well-preserved old houses lining the main street. For further information, write to the specific chambers of commerce (use zip code in parentheses) or:

Cape Cod Chamber of Commerce
Hyannis, MA 02601.

Martha's Vineyard—The "Incredible Isle"

Martha's Vineyard (pop. 9,000 year round; 80,000 summer) has the advantage of being insulated but not isolated. The temperature is 10 degrees warmer in winter and 10 degrees cooler in summer than the mainland; it's only 45 minutes by ferry from Woods Hole, and there's daily scheduled air service from Boston, New York, New Bedford, Hyannis and Nantucket. Thus, you could get away from it all here without getting island fever.

The island has an older population, with 18 percent over age 60. Most of the retirees are ex-military people, educators, business and professional types of middle to upper-middle income. All races and religions are represented (it has a Black resort, an active Jewish community and Portuguese Catholic communities in a predominantly white Protestant population base) on this "incredible" (because of the store of vines) triangular island, 10 miles wide and 20 miles long. It's geography is as diverse as its people: protected harbors, lovely salt marshes and ponds, long stretches of sandy beaches. The flat pine-covered plains of midisland merge with hilly woodlands along the north shore and high, rolling land at the western end. The highest elevation is 308 feet, and there are 124.6 miles of tidal shoreline.

Climate and Environment. The climate is mild, with January averaging 30.3°F. and July 69.5°F; the annual average is 49.4°F. During July and August the waters around the island have a temperature range in the upper 60s and low 70s, and the water remains warm until early October. The Gulf Stream, flowing north and east, is only a few miles to seaward; this, coupled with the rather shallow waters that can warm the ocean over sandy shoals, accounts for much of the warmth in winter. And the curled arm of Cape Cod protects the area against the cooler water from the coasts of Labrador and Maine.

Medical Facilities. The Martha's Vineyard Hospital is a new 80-bed health-care center. Facilities include an emergency room which is open 24 hours, an acute-care section, intensive-care section and long-term-care section. There are 2 operating rooms, a radiology facility, a laboratory, a physical therapy department and a respiratory therapy department. The emergency room is staffed with physicians on duty 24 hours from June 15 to September 15; during the rest of the year there is full-time staffing on weekends, and from 6 P.M. to 7 A.M. Monday through Friday. Physicians are on call at all other times.

Housing Availability and Cost. While 2-bedroom homes are available from $45,000, the average *winterized* home starts at $65,000. I know one retired couple who bought a home on the shore of a big tidal pond in Vineyard Haven for $80,000. It is a kind of guest cottage on a piece of property which the owner split, reserving the larger house for himself. It has 71 by 278 feet of land, and the house itself is on a dead end, right on the water, with a private beach and a dock that can accommodate a 50-foot yacht. The pond is bordered by trees, and has a drawbridge to allow access to the open sea for boats that pass by. It is an incredibly tranquil and serene spot, a little point that juts out into the lagoon. The large living room has a cathedral ceiling; there are 2 bedrooms and a sleeping loft reached by ladder, a galley-type kitchen and a bath. There's a wood-burning fireplace, a space heater and baseboard electric heating. When not using this charming house, they can rent it for $650 a week during the season and $400 in fall. A winter rental commands a minimum of $250 a month.

Cost of Living. In Vineyard Haven, property is assessed at 100 percent of its taxable value; the taxes on the above house run $800 annually. Taxes in the rest of the island vary widely. In fiscal 1979 the tax rate per $1,000 assessed value was $23.20 in Chilmark, $24.00 in Edgartown,

$101.00 in Gay Head, $21.20 in Oak Bluffs, $32.00 in Tisbury and $54.00 in West Tisbury. And since many items must be transported from the mainland, things cost a few pennies more than on Cape Cod. The cost of utilities also runs high; perhaps as much as $250 to $300 a month in winter, $100 a month in summer.

Leisure-Time Activities. To whom it may concern: alcoholic beverages are sold only in Oak Bluffs and Edgartown; the other island towns are dry. And in order to preserve the natural beauty, there are no bathhouses or concessions at any of the public beaches. But you'll find many recreational facilities: tennis courts in Oak Bluffs, Vineyard Haven and Edgartown: horseback riding in West Tisbury, Vineyard Haven, Oak Bluffs and Edgartown; bicycle trails everywhere. You'll also find ample movie theaters, little theaters, art galleries, boutiques of all kinds, good libraries and good television reception. Much of this activity goes on during the season, which lasts from about May to after Columbus Day in October. Then summer homes close down, the population thins out and activities dwindle. And although roses may bloom into November, people start to fade about that time. Yet in winter music groups give concerts; performers come to the island; you can take courses at the regional high school and at the Nathan Mayhew Seminars. Each town also has its public library (West Tisbury is the exception) and has various clubs and artists' and writers' colonies. A number of restaurants and shops are open during the winter, so there's no shortage of supplies; and the relatively mild weather allows you to explore the woods and nature preserves and comb the beaches. Outside of these activities, there's "nothing much to do" during the winter and boredom threatens the fabric of many families. A friend of mine, a retired publisher of some means, and his wife bought a house on Martha's Vineyard with an eye to staying year round. But they had to return to their former home in Westport, Connecticut because they couldn't cope with the winter doldrums.

Special Services for Seniors. Councils on aging flourish throughout the island. Included are Elder Services of Cape Cod and the Islands, (617) 693-4394, for questions on services and community resources, Islands Council on Aging, Up-Island Council on Aging (covering West Tisbury, Chilmark and Gay Head), Tisbury Council on Aging, Oak Bluffs Council on Aging, Edgartown Council on Aging, Martha's Vineyard Senior Citizens and Vineyard Haven Senior Citizens. The services they offer include information and referral, transportation, social workers, meals on wheels, nutrition programs (daily hot meals) at various sites, a newsletter, Social Security information, health screening, companion services and reassurance services. To assure good programs, advisory councils representing participants, elder-service board members, community agencies, volunteers and staff meet regularly to coordinate activities.

Each of the villages on Martha's Vineyard has its own personality and apperance and tends to attract year-round and summer residents who have common interests and backgrounds. Here are thumbnail sketches of the major villages:

Vineyard Haven (pop. 3,000), which some locals still call "Tisbury," is a bustling little town with a rather decrepit intersection known as the "Five Corners," where traffic proceeds at the discretion of the drivers— without any visible sign of traffic lights or stop signs. Most of the island's visitors land here so the town has a bustling air that's most inviting. The many shops and spirited activity of the harbor, with ships of all sizes milling about, provide grand excitement, particularly when the beautiful schooner *Shenandoah* puts in. This is also the largest of the island's towns and home of the only Jewish house of worship on the island: the active and contributive Hebrew Center. Vineyard Haven lacks the architectural and historic interest of Edgartown, because much of the old whaling and fishing town was destroyed by the great fire of 1883. Still, it contains a seaman's and a D.A.R. historical museum and Association Hall, the largest and one of the oldest church structures on the island.

Oak Bluffs (pop. 1,800), located across the harbor from Vineyard Haven, was originally called "Cottage City," a name stemming from the days when Oak Bluffs was a center for Methodist camp meetings. These began as tent revivals, with a great conical tabernacle built in the center of the campground. But as more and more people kept coming back to the meetings, tiny Victorian gingerbread cottages were built, each brightly painted and ornately decorated. Once every summer, their owners celebrate "Illumination Night" with brilliant Japanese paper lanterns, turning the area into a stage setting for Gilbert and Sullivan's *The Mikado*. Many other homes in Oak Bluffs were built around the same time and retain the whimsical, ornate designs. In addition to being a Methodist center, Oak Bluffs is also one of the oldest Black resort communities in the United States. And as it and Edgartown are the only two "wet" towns on the island, the bars do a lively business.

West Tisbury (pop. 700) has more of the character of an inland New England village, with rolling farms where sheep and cattle graze, a white church with a tall steeple, a post office and general store, and even a mill pond. You'll find some fine old captains' houses in town and in the Lambert's Cove area, on the northwest shore.

Chilmark (pop. 520) combines country and coastline in a matchless crazy-quilt of hills and dales, pastures and stone walls. A fishing, fowling and farming community, it boasts a rolling landscape with ponds and sea, reminding visitors of Scotland. You'll see many scenic views of the ocean and two beautiful ocean beaches are open to residents. And in the fishing village of *Menemsha* to the north, you can buy fresh fish or eat it in a nearby seafood restaurant. And right next to town is Menemsha Beach, a large, pleasant public beach.

Gay Head (pop. 160), with its towering mile-long cliffs of dazzling colors, its 100-million-year-old history and its famous Gay Head Light, is an Indian town. It numbers among its population some 150 descendants of the Wampanoag Indians, who taught the early settlers how to kill whales and were steerers in the old whaling days. This is the town and these are the people who figured so prominently in Melville's *Moby Dick.* Unfortunately, the town has lost some of its historic charm as souvenir shops and concessions have given the area a Coney Island look.

Edgartown (pop. 2,300) is the oldest town on the island, and it still retains its eighteenth-century charm. The entire town is a treasure trove, with Greek revival houses beautifully preserved, cupolas and widow's walks, elegant fanlights and century-old trees. So narrow are the streets that most of them are one-way, inviting leisurely strolling and window shopping at the elegant stores, fine hotels and superb restaurants. This is where the whaling captains made their headquarters and this is where most of the fashionable people live, some in restored and well-preserved eighteenth- and nineteenth-century white Colonial homes. In the summer, Edgartown is host to many yachts and cruisers, and in the fall it is a surf-casting mecca. It has excellent beaches, many small "open all summer" boutiques, a good library and bookstores. There's a 200-acre wildlife preserve to wander through, and on *Chappaquidick* you'll find two lovely untainted areas owned by the Trustees of Reservation that are favorite spots for fishermen. Houses are more expensive here than in the other towns, but you could still find a good winterized retirement home for around $50,000. Edgartown is also the home of the *Vineyard Gazette,* a lively informative newspaper now owned by the James Restons (of *New York Times* fame). If you want to keep up on the island's developments, it would pay to subscribe. Two issues are published during summer weeks, one during winter weeks. For further details write *The Vineyard Gazette,* Box 66, Edgartown, MA 02539.

And for further details on Martha's Vineyard, write:

Martha's Vineyard Chamber of Commerce
Vineyard Haven, MA 02568

Nantucket—The "Far Away Little Gray Lady by the Sea"

Nantucket is a place you have to court. Although accessible by air, most people take the 2½-hour auto ferry from Woods Hole or Hyannis. And once you approach this 15-mile-long, 3.5-mile-wide living museum, you'll often find her shrouded in mists that hug her scrub oaks and pines and nestle around her wharves. And although there are those days when she is stunning with the blue of the sky, the russet of her moors and the crimson of her wild cranberry bogs, most of the time she is weathered in gray.

She is aloof to tourists and to summer residents alike. Yet she can be kind to her elders; the average age of the population is over 38, and 20 percent of her population of 6,500 is age 60 and over. Nantucket is an experience, not just an occasion, and if you fall deeply in love with her, you'll never forget her.

Climate and Environment. While all who know her are aware of her charms, most people describe this small island as shaped like a pork chop or a shrimp. It covers 55 square miles with 88 miles of coastline and over 60 miles of beaches. It's low-lying, with few trees and little stone. The air is pure and the moors—carpeted with heather, wild indigo, viburnum and sweet fern—are made for walking. The rest of the island is covered with shrubs, cedar bushes, scrub oak and wild trees sculptured weirdly by the winds. You'll find sassafras and tupelo, cranberries and bayberries and enchanting views everywhere, from flat meadows and clay cliffs to water ponds and marshes. Nantucket enjoys the same moderating influences of the Gulf Stream as does Martha's Vineyard, so the climate is milder than on Cape Cod. The average January temperature is 33°F. and average July temperature 67.5°F. Normal rainfall is 43.6 inches annually. The main towns are *Nantucket Town* and *Siasconset* ('Sconset), which haven't allowed the tourist trade to dominate them and remain quiet and charming. There is elegant, secluded *Shawkemo; Squam, Shimmo* and *Quaise,* where estates are tucked at the ends of long drives; *Madaket,* the fisherman's dream; *Wauwinet,* whose old-fashioned sprawling summer cottages edge the harbor; *Quidnet,* with more modern beach homes; *Polpis,* rich in birds and wildflowers. Then there are *Cisco* and *Surfside* on the ocean front, *Sankaty Head's* bluffs and two subdivisions at *Tristram's Landing* and *Tom Nevers Head.* The population is mainly WASP (White Anglo-Saxon Protestant) or of Portuguese extraction; there is only one Catholic Church and no synagogue on the island.

Medical Facilities. Nantucket Cottage Hospital has about 50 beds. There are 10 doctors, 4 dentists and 2 opthalmologists; visiting specialists, surgeons, orthodontists and other health professionals offer generally adequate medical care. More specialized care is available by a short flight to the mainland.

Housing Availability and Cost. Nantucket has rigid strictures against the building of modern homes whose style doesn't harmonize with the old. It even dictates the color of the paint which homeowners may use: white, a discreet yellow or gray. There isn't a single neon sign on the island, nor a billboard, traffic light or fast-food chain, and virtually every building must be covered with unpainted shingles. New homes tend to be reproductions of the older Georgian, Federal or Greek revival structures. This insistence on reproduction has led to almost nothing in the way of significant new architecture on the island. At Tristram's Landing, condominiums designed as mock saltboxes are plopped down in no apparent order on an open marsh. Most islanders feel that this fake Colonial style ends up looking sillier than anything modern ever could. A good-sized building lot starts at $20,000; and while some cottages are available for $75,000, most comfortable year-round places start at $125,000. However, property taxes are low: around 1 percent of market value.

Cost of Living. As most items must be brought from the mainland, costs for basics like food, clothing, furnishings and household supplies tend to run higher than on Cape Cod. Utilities are very high: the average heating cost of a 3-bedroom home with electric heat and thermostats set at 65°F. is at least $300 a month in winter and $100 a month in summer. There are no discount drugstores or major chains; an average dinner out with drinks runs $20 to $25 per person; liquor costs about $2 more per bottle than on the mainland. In fact, it seems that the key word when it comes to retirement on Nantucket is *money*—if nothing else, money to get away when you need or want to. Many islanders hold two or three jobs to make ends meet, or cater to tourists with shops or crafts.

Leisure-Time Activities. You'll find an active theater workshop, arts council and a garden club. You can take various craft courses, including needlepoint, pottery and basketry. Recreational facilities include golf, swimming, sailing, tennis and bicycling. The Atheneum Library, rebuilt after the great fire of 1846, has 45,000 volumes. The whaling museum is one of the finest in the country, and deep-sea fishing is a favorite sport. While there's much activity in the summer, many people leave or "hibernate" during the winter. People with homes in other parts of the island tend to move into town for the winter; most homes in outlying areas are shuttered and boarded up, giving a bleak, desolate look reminiscent of an abandoned Hollywood set. Fog rolls in, sometimes shrouding the island for days. Strong winds batter the island and storms from the northeast can be devastating. Older people find the town's picturesque cobblestone streets treacherous in winter, and the island's elite, many of them originally mainlanders, are said to be a closed society, difficult to break into. If you want to "go out and do something" you must head for the mainland, 3 hours away if the boats are running. Thus, it would help if you had an activity tied to the island; if you were a watercolorist, writer, bookbinder, craftsman, shopowner or businessperson who has fallen in love with Nantucket. As one innkeeper who has since left the island said, "In winter it's sad to see the lights go out and the people leave, and it's lonely, too."

Special Services for Seniors. There's an active Center of Elderly Affairs and a meals-on-wheels program. Most residents rely on their self-sufficiency, independence of spirit and hardiness. These are qualities one must have—in abundance—to retire on Nantucket. That's why it's crucial for anyone considering retirement on Nantucket to live there for a number of months—November through March if possible—to get the flavor of it. Otherwise, if the "Little Gray Lady of the Sea" has bewitched you, buy a cottage and summer there. Her wintry charms may prove too frosty for you.

For further information, write:

Nantucket Island Chamber of Commerce
Nantucket, MA 02554

SUMMARY

For the "worst" retirement state, Massachusetts offers some of the best retirement areas and some of the best educational and medical facilities. However, the high cost of living (including taxes) makes the Bay State the most expensive retirement area in the continental United States. To retire here you should have roots or some activity or business reason; otherwise there are other places that would treat you more gently. But if you do decide to retire here, you'll find plenty of places to do so. Here are my personal evaluations of the retirement areas based on (1) Climate and Environment, (2) Medical Facilities, (3) Housing Availability and Cost, (4) Cost of Living, (5) Leisure-Time Activities and (6) Special Services for Seniors:

Excellent — Amherst, Great Barrington
Good — Williamstown, Stockbridge, Southbridge, Sturbridge, Cape Cod area, Martha's Vineyard
Adequate — Holyoke, Weymouth, Arlington, Nantucket

2. VERMONT—RETIREMENT FOR RUGGED INDIVIDUALISTS

If there is a special place for rugged retirees, it is the Green Mountain State. Vermont gives much but demands more. While church-steepled towns snuggle in cozy valleys, the surrounding hills and mountains challenge hikers and skiers. Picture-postcard flaming fall freezes into frigid winter, with spring and summer little more than fleeting memories. Taxes are twice as high as in neighboring New Hampshire, but services fall far short of twice as good. And its clean air and pure water may be more vulnerable to pollution than most states.

Vermont also suffers from a split personality. While it may be the Yankees' last stand—where natives measure heritage by the depth of their roots—only about a third of Vermonters were born there. So many natives have moved out that a "Committee to Save a 'Thurd' " has been formed to lure them back. Yet even born Vermonters may be subject to the old saying, "Just because the cat had kittens in the oven doesn't make them muffins." And in many cases it's true that "Vermonters will do nothing that you tell them to; most anything that you ask them to."

In spite of some seeming drawbacks, city folks still flock here for what they can't get elsewhere: a refuge of woods and water where a man can breathe free; gentle mountains wearing a cloak of green; towns and people that fiercely defend the past and don't worry about the future. Some 15.1 percent of the state's 490,000 people are age 60 and older, most settled in the milder south; yet, like the rugged individualists they are, they are scattered where they see fit to plant their Yankee roots.

A Challenging Climate and Environment

The state is mountainous, the Green Mountains bisecting north and south. The Connecticut River is on her eastern border, 120-mile-long Lake Champlain is on her west. The average elevation is 1,000 feet, which, added to Vermont's northern latitude, makes for cold and snowy winters, but comfortably warm summers without too much heat and humidity. In Burlington, about halfway up Lake Champlain, winters average 25.5°F., summers 59.2°F.; there are 151 sunny days; 73 percent average annual humidity, 38.10 inches of rain and 121.6 inches of snow. While a sparse population (only 52.1 persons per square mile) and an emphasis on dairy farming and agriculture make for a relatively unpolluted environment, probably no other state has as much potential for pollution. This is due mainly to the fact that almost two-thirds of the homes in Vermont use wood for at least some of their heat. Unfortunately, wood is "dirty": only about 80 percent of it burns (versus almost 100 percent of gas and oil), and the soot and ash residue clouds the air like large, smoking cigarettes.

Moreover, state officials have been encouraging the use of wood by providing cut-rate prices on wood from state forests and turning to wood in some state facilities. Yet Vermont has dealt sternly with environmental problems in the past, and a new type of wood-burning furnace might be the answer to keeping Vermont's air as pure as its mountain streams.

Adequate Health Care

The Green Mountain State has generally adequate medical care, with 19 hospitals with a total of 3,306 beds; 50 nursing homes with 2,964 beds; 213 personal-care homes with 2,166 beds; and 203 doctors per 100,000 residents. The average rate for a semiprivate hospital room is $141 daily, less than the national average of $163 daily.

A Smorgasbord of Real Estate

You'll find a good variety of housing available at reasonable prices. Some recent offerings:

- Ranch retreat in the Green Mountains, 3 bedrooms, 2 baths, 7 acres, $65,000
- 270-acre estate in Lamoille Valley, $295,000
- 2 ranch-style camps on Lake Eden, 2 bedrooms each, 5,000 square foot lots, $18,000
- Wooded lots in Eden, $275 per acre
- Remodeled farm house, 3 acres, $45,000
- 2-bedroom cottage on lake with all services and 5,000 square foot lot, $21,500
- Showcase property of a classic Vermont village, all wood floors, 3 acres of land, $110,000
- Charming Victorian near Montpelier, good barn, pasture, 5 acres of hay, $69,500

Many new homes are being built with old-style "post-and-beam" construction, which is how almost all American wood houses were built during the eighteenth and early nineteenth centuries. The posts and beams are massive and heavy and must be hand cut and assembled with wooden pegs before they can be raised (traditionally, by a gathering of friends and neighbors) into place. This old-style construction and the social occasion of house-raising are enjoying renewed popularity in Vermont and New Hampshire for practical and esthetic reasons. Post-and-beam houses are sturdier than modern houses and have larger, easier-to-heat room spaces, especially for those who want to use wood stoves.

You can find out about these and other homes for sale by specifying what you're looking for and in what location and writing to Real Estate Location Service, Vermont State Chamber of Commerce, Box 37, Montpelier, VT 05602. For a list of Vermont licensed real estate brokers and salesmen, write to: Vermont Real Estate Commission, Montpelier, VT 05602. And if you're interested in businesses for sale, write Facaci Consultants, Main Street, Manchester Center, VT 05255.

High Cost of Taxes

While real estate may be reasonably priced, taxes are high. Taxes on a new home can equal 7 to 8 percent of market value, while on an existing home they can run 5 percent. However, the tax rates and assessment ratios in some towns (see below) run lower than these averages. As noted, the higher taxes (compared to New Hampshire) don't necessarily buy better services. And because of rising transportation costs, prices of basic foodstuffs and household goods are soaring in rural areas. Also, rural stores are generally too small to reap the efficiencies of buying in bulk quantities, so they can't offer discount prices. And less competition means fewer sales. You could well end up paying more for basics in rural Vermont than in urban Boston.

Here are other tax rates in Vermont:

Income Taxes—23 percent of taxpayer's federal income tax liability. Credits are given if the tax is greater than it would have been under federal law in effect on January 1, 1967. Personal and medical deductions are the same as permitted under federal law.

Special Treatment of Retirement Income—persons age 65 and older are entitled to tax credits on income up to $7,000. The *inheritance tax exemption* is 30 percent of the federal estate tax.

Sales Tax—3 percent on most items.

Property Tax Concessions—persons age 65 or over are entitled to a credit against income taxes equal to the amount by which the property taxes on his homestead (or 20 percent of the gross annual rent) exceeds a percentage of his income. Credit is amount of property tax paid in excess of 4 percent on an income up to $4,000; 6 percent on income of $16,000 and over.

Hardy Outdoor Recreation

The Green Mountain State is noted for its year-round outdoor activities, especially hiking, camping and skiing. There are more than 56 ski

areas in the state. It also has museums and art galleries, especially in its
larger cities: Bennington, Burlington, Manchester, Middlebury, Montpelier, Stowe and Woodstock. It also has its share of tourist attractions,
ranging from craft centers to a "Little Grand Canyon" and castles. You
can get a folder on various activities and events by writing to Vermont
Travel Division, 61 Elm Street, Montpelier, VT 05602 or to Vermont Attractions Association, Box 7, Shelburne, VT 05482.

Good Services for Seniors

The Vermont Office on Aging offers a toll-free statewide "Access for
the Elderly" telephone line (1-800-642-5119) open to anyone age 60 or over.
Also, five area agencies on aging offer these services: information and
referral, transportation, health, in-home, ombudsman (nursing home),
legal, nutrition, adult day care and other assistance. For further information write:

> Vermont Office on Aging
> c/o State Office Building
> Montpelier, VT 05602

MAJOR RETIREMENT AREAS

Manchester and *Manchester Center* (pop. 3,700) have been among
Vermont's best-loved summer resorts for more than 100 years. Their
wide, shady streets, surrounding mountains and restful trees make them
appealing to retirees. Besides several skiing areas, there are 3 first-rate
golf courses in the area, including the fabled Ekwanok. Other attractions
include the John Newcombe Tennis Center, clear trout streams like the
Battenkill, and hunting for bear, deer, turkey and wild fowl. All other
outdoor activities are available, as is an art center which offers a varied
program of exhibits, performances and workshops; a museum of American fly fishing; country auctions, antique shops and flea markets; summer
stock companies; craft fairs and antique shows; concerts and disco dancing. Retirement housing in the area is available from $50,000; the tax rate
is $3.65, with an assessment ratio of 48.

For further information, write:

> Chamber of Commerce
> Manchester and the Mountains
> Manchester Center, VT 05255

Middlebury (pop. 6,750) is a beautiful setting for one of the finest smaller colleges in America. And the campus of Middlebury College, the Middlebury Inn, the Congregational Church, and the Sheldon Museum all help to create the kind of collegiate community that attracts many retirees. Situated in heavy snow country, this area abounds with ski jumps, cross-country skiing, ski trails, a Snow Bowl and a winter carnival. There are also many summer activities available, including the 18-hole Middlebury College Golf Course. The Vermont State Craft Center is located at nearby Frog Hollow, and the University of Vermont maintains Morgan Horse Farm 2.5 miles northwest. Retirement housing starts at $50,000. Tax rates are $2.41 with an 81 assessment ratio. For further information, write:

Chamber of Commerce
Middlebury, VT 05753

Woodstock (pop. 3,000) has been voted one of America's prettiest towns by *National Geographic* magazine, the American Architectural Society and by the host of people who revisit the village year after year. Time seems to have stood still in Woodstock. When you first see it, it appears like a New England Brigadoon, waiting to be discovered by a Hollywood producer looking for the perfect New England town. Much of the town has been designated a historic district, and carefully preserved eighteenth-century homes and discreet shops ring the handsome village green. Any nostalgic longings will reverberate when you see the fabulous Woodstock Inn regally gracing one whole side of the green, a covered bridge dominating the other side. If you're lucky enough to be here on a Sunday, you'll hear church bells cast by Paul Revere. When I first saw Woodstock on a mellow autumn day, I hummed "It's a Great Day for Singing." The next time I saw it, covered with pristine snow, I felt "White Christmas" was more appropriate. And I'm told on a spring day that violets and geraniums are "busting out all over" in flower boxes (once used to gather syrup) along Central Avenue. No matter what time of year you visit, you'll sing its praises. And I'm sure you'll fare better than the Hollywood producers who did discover this perfect New England town, only to be told to "let us alone."

Climate and Environment. At an altitude of 700 feet above sea level, the climate is dry and healthful, with winter temperatures occasionally falling to 30°F. below zero. Summer temperatures seldom rise above 90°F., and nights are always cool. Snow falls in quantity from December to March, and skiing is often at its best then.

Medical Facilities. Woodstock boasts a splendid health facility, the

Ottauquechee Health Center, staffed by 3 internists, 2 pediatricians, 1 gynecologist, 1 podiatrist, 4 dentists and 1 periodontist. It also has an emergency room, X-ray facilities, and a laboratory. Nearby hospitals are at Lebanon, New Hampshire (18 miles), Hanover, New Hampshire (20 miles), Randolph, Vermont (25 miles) and Rutland, Vermont (32 miles). A Veterans Administration hospital is located at White River Junction (14 miles). Woodstock is also affiliated with visiting nurses associations, mental health facilities, ambulance services and other health organizations to offer complete medical care.

Housing Availability and Cost. Good 2-bedroom units are available from $50,000, although many of the more desirable properties start at $100,000. Rental 2- and 3-bedroom apartments are available from $350 a month. Land sells from $1,000 and up per acre. This is a summer and winter resort area, so if you're interested in buying or renting, it is best to do so in the spring or fall.

Cost of Living. The tax rate is $3.97 and the assessment ratio is 44. This works out to about 5 percent of market value for an older house ($2,250 on a $50,000 house) and up to 7 to 8 percent of market value of a newer home. Utilities in winter run $150 to $200 a month unless you heat with wood. In summer you certainly wouldn't need air conditioning at night and probably not during the day. Because of the tourist trade, prices in town tend to be higher than in the country, but shopping is certainly a pleasure in the well-stocked in-town stores. With original ideas and restoration savvy, merchants have revitalized the Morgan, Cabot and French blocks in the downtown area. A favorite shopping center is Gillingham's old-fashioned general store, where Robert Frost often made the trip from his summer home on Breadloaf Mountain for an afternoon of trading in the aisles and back rooms. The store seems to wander for acres and features "vittles and sundry delicacies" (including penny candy and peanut butter ground while you wait), along with household and kitchen wares, tools for workshops, barns, gardens and fields. "Your money's worth or your money back" is the guarantee established in 1886 when the store was founded, and I certainly would have paid twice what I did for the gourmet cheeses, jams, maple syrup, hams and other goodies I've stocked up on.

Leisure-Time Activities. Activities abound at the Woodstock Inn, which has been restored to its 1793 charm (with modern conveniences) by Laurence S. Rockefeller. He stocked the inn with antiques and local handicrafts, patchwork quilts on the beds, brass hinges, weathered Vermont timbers and hand-cut stone fireplaces. The panorama of activities spans the seasons: from golf to skiing, horseback rides to sleigh rides. Outside the inn you'll find historic sites, museums, craft centers, bicycling, jogging, hiking, swimming, fishing, hunting, tennis and all other outdoor activities. The Woodstock Recreation Department offers a broad range of activities, ranging from the creative and performing arts to sports and athletics. Programs for the elderly are just as important as programs for youth. A recreation newsletter is published every Friday and distributed at local stores. There's also an active historical society, drama group, craft classes and other courses at nearby Dartmouth (20 miles away). A well-stocked library circulates 40,000 volumes a year.

Special Services for Seniors. A "Senior Citizen Newsletter" is published each month. Older residents gather daily at the Woodstock Area Senior Center in the lower level of the Little Theater. The center is a resource for older persons in the community who come together to fulfill their social, physical and intellectual needs and to stimulate and expand their interests. Located in the center is the White River Council on Aging's outreach worker, an assistant and a meals coordinator. Group activities are sponsored by the Recreation Department, while the White River Council sponsors dinners at the center and home-delivered meals to shut-ins. In addition, the council provides a wide range of support services, including transportation, the Senior-Citizen Discount Card, tax assistance and a monthly visit by a lawyer from the Legal Services for the Elderly Program. The center is open to all persons 60 and over in the Woodstock, Barnard, Pomfret, Bridgewater and Reading area, and may be reached by calling (802) 457-3277.

For further information, write:

Chamber of Commerce
Woodstock, VT 05091

About halfway between Woodstock and Hanover, New Hampshire (about 10 miles from each) lies the development of *Quechee Lakes* (year-round pop. 500), where historical renovation, quality recreational facilities and good land planning are creating a unique community. This is home of the Quechee Gorge, the "Little Grand Canyon" 165-feet deep. About half of the development's 6,000 acres is being preserved as a green belt, with lakes, ponds and recreational facilities. The rest will ultimately hold about 2,000 homesites and 500 condominiums (as of 1980 more than 1,000 homesites have been sold, and some 200 homes and about 150 condominiums built). Prices start in the $60,000s and go beyond $100,000. For $1,000 yearly dues, homeowners and landowners become members of the Quechee Lakes Landowners Association, which operates all the recreational facilities. These include 2 private 18-hole golf courses, a ski area, tennis courts, beach area, clubhouse and fishing and boating areas. Wooded homesites, which include club membership, start above $12,000. At present, most residents use their homes as vacation or second homes, but the permanent retiree population is growing. The place is worth a look if you're in the area.

For further information, write:

Quechee Lakes Corporation
Box 85
Quechee, VT 05059

In Vermont's "middle mountains" (the northwestern part of the state) lies *Stowe* (year-round population about 2,990, often called the "Ski Capital of the East." It is becoming a year-round resort as well as a year-round place to live, with a growing permanent population including a number of retirees. In fact, at the Mt. Mansfield ski area, skiers over age 70 ski for free, and those age 65 to 69 are eligible for "young at heart" rates, which are the same as children's rates. Retirees also enjoy tennis, riding, theater, mountain climbing, archery, swimming, fishing and golf; browse through numerous shops, galleries and boutiques; visit the Historical Society Museum and the Bloody Brook Schoolhouse, a 1-room school. Stowe is home to the Trapp family of *Sound of Music* fame, and their ski lodge and shops are a must for visitors and residents alike. Stowe offers fine health facilities at the Stowe Clinic and Copely Hospital. And you'll find a good supply of relatively low-cost housing in the area, some starting in the $50,000s, though the best are in the $70,000s and up. Some rentals are available from $300 a month. Building lots and acreage are available from $5,000 an acre. The tax rate is $1.59 and the assessment ratio is 100, making taxes lower than in many parts of the state. Stowe offers good job opportunities in restaurants, hotels/motels, theaters and recreational areas, and in some of the light industry which is settling in 2 industrial parks in the area.

For further information, write:

Stowe Area Association
Box 1230
Stowe, VT 05672

SUMMARY

Vermont isn't for sissies; you'll like retirement here mainly if you're a rugged individualist who loves outdoor sports and indoor fireplaces. For this privilege, you'll pay higher taxes and higher prices for foodstuffs than in neighboring areas. However, you'll find a good variety of housing available at reasonable prices, plenty of indoor and outdoor recreation, and good services for seniors. Here are my ratings of the various retirement areas:

Excellent — Woodstock area
Good — Manchester and Manchester Center, Middlebury, Quechee Lakes, Stowe

3. NEW HAMPSHIRE—URBAN AND RURAL CONTRASTS

For states that share a common border and a similar size and shape, Vermont and New Hampshire are most uncommon neighbors. Vermont is content to remain rustically rural; New Hampshire prides itself on becoming urbanized and industrial. Vermont probably has the strictest development controls in the country; New Hampshire probably the most lax. Vermont is the third most heavily taxed state; New Hampshire the fourth least heavily taxed. New Hampshire's population is growing twice as fast as Vermont's and faster than any state east of the Mississippi except Florida.

Despite these differences, New Hampshire still retains much of "What America Used to Be." There's a permanence about the Granite State—from its rocky foundations to its stone bridges and churches. Traditions still smooth the edges of modern life, but you don't have to be born here to be accepted. Newcomers are welcome if "their humor doesn't bite and their voice isn't too loud." If you walk in gently, you'll find a retirement haven here.

Some 15.2 percent of the state's approximately 900,000 people are 60 and over, and many have settled (along with other newcomers) in the "golden triangle" southern section, convenient to Boston and to scenic mountain and ocean areas. It is bounded by Salem and Nashua in the south and Manchester in the north. Although it has less than 4 percent of the state's land area, it has more than 30 percent of its population. But retirees are also seeking out some of the more rural and picturesque areas like Hanover, Keene and Concord. You'll find both urban and rural attractions to suit your taste and pocketbook.

Varied Climate and Environment

The Granite State has 18 miles of seacoast followed by countless hills and mountains rising out of a central plateau. This plateau is topped by Mt. Washington (6,288 feet), the highest peak in the Northeast. You can divide the state into 4 parts: the North Country, with the spectacular

White Mountains; the Lakes Region, with Lake Winnipesaukee, the largest freshwater body east of the Great Lakes; the low, rolling seacoast bordering the Atlantic; and the Currier and Ives southwest corner, home of majestic Grand Monadnock Mountain, for which this famous region is named. Due to the nearness of high mountains and ocean, the climate is highly varied. In the capital, Concord, the average winter temperature is 27.7°F.; the average in summer, 58.8°F. There are 167 sunny days with an annual average humidity of 77 percent. Rainfall averages 42.07 inches annually, snowfall 100.3 inches. In fact, as snow usually begins in November and lasts through March, you can not only count on a white Christmas but perhaps a white Easter as well. You don't fight the snow, you learn to move with it—snow tires and maybe snowshoes. Not so easy to fight is the pollution caused by rapid industrialization, massive construction, outdated sewer systems and the fact that many smaller communities don't have garbage pickup—you must haul rubbish to town dumps that are open at odd hours.

Adequate Health Care

New Hampshire has 33 major hospitals with a total of 4,995 beds. There are 85 nursing homes with 5,751 beds and 30 personal-care homes with 627 beds. There are 159 doctors per 100,000 population; the average daily rate for a semiprivate hospital room is $148, compared to the national average of $163.

Varied Housing at Good Prices

You'll find a good supply of varied housing at prices starting from $40,000 (average retirement housing sells in the $50,000s). The most popular styles are Colonials, 2-story Garrisons (with upper front overhang), Cape Cods and Gambrels (1½ stories with or without dormers), saltboxes (2 stories with long slanting roof to rear lower floor) and ranch style. These homes vary in age from 125 years to modern, and sell from $45,000 to the low $60,000s. But be advised that except for a few cities and larger towns, New Hampshire communities rarely have (adequate) city water, gas or sewers; you may have to have a well, a septic tank and use propane gas. You can get a newspaper of current real estate available (along with pictures) by sending for a free copy of the New Hampshire edition of *Suburban Real Estate News*, 377 Main Street, Stoneham, MA 02180.

Amazingly Low Taxes

New Hampshire is the fourth least heavily taxed state. It has *no* sales or income tax (the only state to lack both); its main sources of revenue are levies on liquor, cigarettes, horse racing, business profits and real estate. Its property taxes are relatively moderate, averaging $4.50 per $100 valuation on property valued at 60 percent of market value. Thus, the tax on a $50,000 house would be only $1,350, or 2.7 percent of market value. Depending upon age and income, seniors can get a reduction on the assessed valuation on property. Any residents age 65 and older get an extra $600 exemption on the 5 percent tax on interest and dividend income. There is no inheritance tax for spouse or legal heirs. Amazingly enough, in spite of the low taxes, a recent study showed that services in New Hampshire are just about as good as those in neighboring Vermont (with the third highest tax in the nation). The state ranks fiftieth in its per capita contribution to education, and many parents send children to private schools. New Hampshire has a triple-A bond rating and balanced books, something that most states can't claim. Also, the Granite State has one of the lowest unemployment rates in the nation, thanks in part to its growing industry.

Recreational Opportunities

The Granite State is big on antique shows, fairs and seasonal events like fall foliage festivals held in Warner and at Loon Mountain in Lincoln in October. In winter the Dartmouth Winter Carnival is the big event in Hanover. Ski events and snowmobile races are held in February and March. The White Mountain National Forest contains 724,000 acres of fabulous scenery, hiking, camping sites and top winter sports areas. New Hampshire has 32 other state parks for swimming, picnicking and hiking. Throughout the Granite State you'll find extensive examples of Americana and European art of the last 3 centuries, all well housed and fascinating to visit. Perhaps the most ambitious project is at Strawberry Banke, a multimillion-dollar historic restoration of the section of Portsmouth that once was the colony's capital. The New Hampshire Historical Society at Concord is both a library and a museum. And throughout the state you'll find 29 bronze markers that identify places of historical interest. In music, the Hopkins Center at Dartmouth has a superb array of performers and orchestras throughout the summer. Other concerts take place in Meredith and Center Harbor. The Theater by the Sea in Portsmouth presents classical and modern plays staged by resident companies, and both Dartmouth and the University of New Hampshire (Durham) have year-round student theaters. You can get a free hunting-fishing license if you're a resident and are over age 68.

Varied Services for Seniors

The New England Gerontology Center is located in the University of New Hampshire, offering continuing-education courses to practitioners and information on aging to the public. It also has an extensive list of publications and periodicals. For further information, write the NEGC, 15 Garrison Avenue, Durham, NH 03824. Also, the New Hampshire Council on Aging provides a variety of services to seniors in the fields of nutrition, transportation, housing, legal information, health care and recreation. For further information write the Council on Aging, 14 Depot Street, Concord, NH 03301.

MAJOR RETIREMENT AREAS

Hanover (pop. 6,500; 3,300 college students) has drawn me back several times, mainly because of the beautiful Dartmouth College campus, the ambiance of the Hanover Inn, and the overall Ivy League quality of the town. If you feel, as I do, that you could belong to such a town, you might find retirement stimulating both physically and mentally.

Climate and Environment. The town rests in a valley set in the New Hampshire hills and mountains, across the Connecticut River from Norwich, Vermont. It is approximately at the center of the Vermont–New Hampshire border, about 64 miles from Concord and 139 miles northwest of Boston. It is part of the Upper Valley area, which also includes Lebanon, New Hampshire and Norwich and Hartford, Vermont. Winters average 28°F., summers, 60°F.

Medical Facilities. The Dartmouth-Hitchcock Medical Center is a confederation of 4 institutions: Mary Hitchcock Memorial Hospital, Hitchcock Clinic, Dartmouth Medical School and the Veterans' Administration hospital in White River Junction, Vermont. The medical center also includes the Norris Cotton Cancer Center, West Central Community Health Services, the Dartmouth-Hitchcock Arthritis Center and Hitchcock Foundation. In addition, there are visiting nurse services, mental health counseling, home-care services, long-term-care facilities including a hospice (to support the dying and their families) and a pacemaker clinic. All this assures excellent health care for residents, especially older ones.

Housing Availability and Cost. The average house within walking distance of the campus might cost $80,000, but the farther out you go, the less expensive the housing. I saw many fine retirement homes toward

Lebanon that sold in the $50,000s, and lots about a mile from town were selling for $10,000 an acre. Some rentals are available for $300 a month. Several large estates selling for $200,000 and more lend a distinctive atmosphere to the area.

Cost of Living. The tax rate in the Hanover area ranges from $24 to $27 per $1,000 assessed value. Typical taxes on a $50,000 home average $1,250 annually. Taxes are lower in Lyme, West Lebanon and Lebanon. There are excellent shops around the campus, some selling elegant clothes and furnishings catering to the country-club set. But you'll find chain stores, supermarkets and other moderately priced stores in the area.

Leisure-Time Activities. Most activities center around the campus, which lies in the heart of town. Strolling the campus is a pleasure; it is prettier and more spacious than Harvard, and the setting is quieter and cleaner. Cultural focal points are the Hopkins Center, which in addition to being the home of the Dartmouth College Department of Art, Drama and Music houses galleries, concert halls and theaters, with a wide range of exhibitions and musical, theater and dance productions; and the Baker Memorial Library, which stands at the head of the campus and is one of the chief centers of college activity. Adjacent to the Hopkins Center is the Hanover Inn, which offers gracious accommodations and food and drink in a 1780 atmosphere of Colonial decor. The inn is a delightful place to visit any time of day. Besides the campus activities, the Hanover Parks and Recreation Department offers year-round sports, concerts, theater, arts and crafts and educational programs. It also has a senior citizens' program director who can be reached by telephoning (603) 643-5315. You'll also be able to camp and swim at the Storrs Pond area, enjoy golf and tennis at Dartmouth, skating on Occom Pond and skiing at Oak Hill and College Skiway in Lyme.

Special Services for Seniors. The Hanover Senior Citizens club is located at 42 Lebanon Street in Hanover and the Upper Valley Senior Citizens at 9 Campbell Street, Lebanon (about 5 miles away). This center offers dial-a-ride, friendly visiting, good neighbor aid and meals on wheels.

For further information, write:

Hanover Chamber of Commerce
Hanover, NH 03755

Keene (pop. 23,000) lies in the southwest corner of the state. This trim, lively city retains its rustic charm, as working farms still prosper within the city limits, alongside a bustling business district, 2 colleges and more than 50 diversified manufacturing firms. The elm-shaded main street leads past an eighteenth-century tavern to a grassy common which lies at the heart of the city. Stubborn planning has preserved unspoiled the wooded hills which ring the city on 3 sides. Keene has a 173-bed hospital, a clinic, more than 30 doctors, 20 dentists and 2 orthopedic surgeons. Housing is scarce, and the best values in single-family homes are in the $45,000 to $65,000 range. Some condominiums and coops are available from $40,000 to $60,000. Taxes are $35 per $1,000, making the tax on a $50,000 home $1,750. Seniors get a 10 percent discount on medicines and entertainment. There are tennis courts and swimming pools at the Fuller Park Recreation Center, 1 private and 1 public golf course, more than 10 miles of hiking trails and a 10-acre natural lake and nature study center.

For further information, write:

Chamber of Commerce
Keene, NH 03431

Concord (pop. 35,000), the Granite State's capital, embraces 64 square miles offering both urban and rural attractions. The downtown is a busy, cosmopolitan center with no claim to the back-porch simplicity of the rural villages—*Hopkinton* (pop. 3,500), *Boscawen* (pop. 3,000), *Dunbarton* (pop. 1,100), and *Canterbury* (pop. 1,000)—surrounding it. Yet within Concord's boundaries are forests, farmland and beaches on both sides of its sandstone valley floor. And it's a city of "plain good manners," where cars stop for pedestrians and "thank you" is a spoken phrase, not just a written slogan. The mean temperature is 46°F. and precipitation occurs in about the same amount yearround; mean snowfall is 61.6 inches, rainfall 38.1 inches. Concord is a leading health center of New Hampshire, with 135 doctors, 4 osteopaths, 47 dentists and a modern 5-story hospital that operates a school of nursing and an operating-room technician program. There's also the New Hampshire Hospital for Mental Health. Older homes are available from $40,000 to over $100,000, and newer homes from $45,000. Some modern condominiums are available from $35,000. You could also live at the *Havenwood Retirement Community* in Concord Heights. Havenwood offers 1- and 2-room units in connecting wings and separate housekeeping apartments. Rates, including meals, run from $350 a month for 1 room to $550 a month for 2 rooms. It also has self-care units and an extended-care facility. In nearby *Dover* is *Jensen's Farmwood Village*, a community of manufactured homes that sell from $25,000. As the capital of New Hampshire, Concord is home for the New Hampshire Opera Company, the League of New Hampshire Craftsmen (which has craft shops throughout the state), the New Hampshire Audubon Society and the state historical society, with its renowned research room on early Americana. Excellent musical ensembles hold lunch-hour concerts at downtown Phoenix Hall, and the city also has a brass and percussion group, a community orchestra and a year-round theater group. The Walker Lecture Series, a free series of vaudeville acts, lectures, films, operettas and concerts, is also held in Concord. The city has many organizations for seniors, including senior centers, chapters of senior organizations, foster grandparent programs, housing and legal assistance programs, meals on wheels, countywide craft workshops, a retired senior volunteer program, and counseling and friendly visiting.

For further information, write:

Greater Concord Chamber of Commerce
116 North Main Street
Concord, NH 03301

Nashua (pop. 70,000), the first New Hampshire exit off the expressway from Boston, is booming in all directions—including retirement living. The population has doubled in the last 20 years and is expected to do so again by the year 2000. In fact, it is the fastest-growing town in the state. That rapid growth has tended to obscure some of its 300-year-old heritage, but it has not caused it to lose a more personal touch reminiscent of smaller towns. There's still a suggestion box outside city hall, and traffic tickets have a big SORRY printed on them. Civic plans include expansion of senior facilities and services.

Climate and Environment. The downtown area is a collage of the very new and very old—modern department stores standing alongside nineteenth-century Greek revival buildings. More than 90 diversified industries, ranging from plastics to tools to ginger ale, fill the area, but the surrounding countryside remains rural and Colonial. The city's ethnic mix contains persons of French-Canadian, Greek, Irish and Lithuanian descent, as well as those tracing their ancestry back to the Revolution. Located on the banks of the Merrimack River, the area escapes much of the bitter cold and deep snow that blankets the north. Average temperatures range from 23°F. in winter to 70°F. in summer. Rainfall averages 40.4 inches annually.

Medical Facilities. The city has 2 community hospitals and 6 nursing homes; 4 medical centers or group-practice clinics are located in nearby suburban towns. Some seniors belong to the Matthew Thornton Health Plan, which offers specialized medical care.

Housing Availability and Cost. Home building is keeping up with population growth, and many single-family homes are available for $50,-000. Housing units for seniors, accommodating 300 people, have recently been completed. Some 2-bedroom apartments are available, ranging from $200 to $400 a month.

Cost of Living. Since private business pays about one-third of the taxes in the city, Nashua's property tax is the second lowest in the state: $27 per $1,000 valuation. The tax on a $40,000 home is a little over $1,000. There is no retail sales tax, and many stores give 10 percent discounts for seniors.

Leisure-Time Activities. The Nashua region is rich with cultural activities, including summer theaters, music festivals, symphony orchestras and an arts and crafts society. Nashua's unusually large public library has more than 500,000 volumes and circulates more material (including 5,000 business volumes) than any library in the state. The Arts and Science Center provides a place for art exhibits and the performing arts. There are 2 18-hole golf courses in the area, 3 indoor tennis facilities, swimming pools and excellent skiing within a half-hour's drive. The American State Festival is held in the adjacent town of Milford, with a 600-seat playhouse on the banks of the Souhegan River.

Special Services for Seniors. Nashua has one senior center located at 221 Main Street, providing for seniors in the immediate area. There is also an adult day-care center attending to the needs of those recovering from illness. The center hosts 3 senior clubs, and there's a chapter of the American Association for Retired Persons. Transportation, once a problem for area seniors, is being solved by providing dial-a-ride door-to-door service. Public transportation is also being planned to complement the private system. Seniors have many counseling services available: Medicare counseling, information and referral services, visiting nurses, homemakers, legal assistance, human services council, community council, adult learning center and more. At the Nashua Senior Center, more than 100 meals are served each day, and a meals-on-wheels program provides food for more than 100 shut-ins. Related activities include clinics, dance and exercise classes, day and multiday trips, craft and other recreational activities.

For further information, write:

Nashua Association for the Elderly
221 Main Street
Nashua, NH 03060

Chamber of Commerce
Nashua, NH 03060

Manchester (pop. 100,000), the largest city in New Hampshire (and in the 3 northern New England states), lies midway between Nashua and

Concord. It sits astride a major highway intersection and is the northern terminus of the East Coast megalopolis. The elevation of the valley floor at the lowest point within the city is 110 feet; the highest, 570 feet. The surrounding area is largely rural, wooded and with many lakes and ponds. Thus the Manchester area maintains a balance between urban attractions and rural tranquility. Average temperatures range from 14.8°F. in January to 70°F. in July, with an annual average of 47°F. Rainfall varies from an average of 2.66 inches in February to 3.62 inches in July, with an annual monthly average of 3.28 inches. Annual snowfall averages 60.6 inches. There are 2 hospitals in the area with 498 beds. There is also a Veterans hospital in the area and an active visiting nurse program. There are 175 practicing physicians and surgeons, giving a favorable 1 doctor per 556 population ratio.

Many homes were built decades ago, but you can also find many newer developments on the northern edges of the city. A new house in this area may cost $80,000. Yet a tree-shaded Cape Cod can be purchased for $40,000, and a smaller retirement home may be purchased for as low as $35,000. Taxes are a bit higher here, with the effective property tax $32 per $1,000 valuation ($1,280 yearly on a $40,000 home). The many supermarkets in the area offer much competitive shopping and senior discounts are available. Also, the taxes provide many cultural activities and parks. Fringing elm-shaded Victory Park in the heart of the city are 3 handsome cultural emporiums: the Manchester Historical Society, the Institute of Arts and Sciences and the city library. These are the focal points for all the arts and sciences. And within the city limits you'll find indoor and outdoor swimming pools, a bathing beach, lighted horseshoe pits, baseball fields, 15 public and private gyms and 2 chair-lift ski areas. Several agencies offer comprehensive programs for seniors, and the Elderly Services Policy Committee, located at 24 Pleasant Street, plans and coordinates municipal services for seniors.

For further information, write:

> Greater Manchester Chamber of Commerce
> 57 Market Street
> Manchester, NH 03101

SUMMARY

As the fourth least heavily taxed state, New Hampshire offers low-cost retirement living with a variety of urban-rural attractions. But the rapid growth and urbanization threaten to spoil some of the magic. If you choose the right location, you can enjoy the best of the Granite State without being affected by the worst. Here are my ratings of major retirement areas:

Excellent — Hanover, Nashua area
Good — Concord, Manchester, Keene, Hopkinton, Boscawen, Dunbarton, Canterbury

4. MAINE—THE LAST RETIREMENT FRONTIER?

Maine is as rugged as its coasts, as dense as its forests, as harsh as its winters. Yet it is luring many retirees seeking a last frontier—geographically, socially and economically.

To know Maine is to understand its location and wilderness. It is situated in the extreme northeast corner of the United States, surrounded by relatively desolate regions of Quebec and New Brunswick in Canada. The more isolated sections of New Hampshire butt its western flank. Within Maine's 33,215 square miles lies almost half the land of all New England, yet 82 percent of this area is heavily forested and 10 percent is water. Most of Maine's 1.1 million people live in the southern and central areas of the state, within 30 miles (15 miles on either side) of the Maine Turnpike. The 6 southernmost counties, York, Cumberland, Sagadahoc, Androscoggin, Kennebec and Lincoln (about 12 percent of the state's total land area) have a the population density is 145 persons per square mile. This is still substantially less than the more than 600 persons per square mile living in Massachusetts and Connecticut. And 70 percent of the population still lives in communities of 10,000 persons or less.

"Downeasterners" (from the prevailing winds blowing down Maine's coast) are mostly of Yankee stock, with about 5 percent each of German, Swedish and-Norwegian; 2 percent Canadian, 1 percent Polish, English, Czech, Russian and Austrian. About 6 percent are Black, Native American and other races. Some 50 percent of the population is between 20 and 65 years of age, 16.5 percent over age 60 and 12 percent over age 65.

Timber is the principal source of wealth in the Pine Tree State, followed by agriculture (mainly potatoes), mining, manufacturing and fishing. The wilderness is the basis of a major tourist industry, offering thousands of locations for camping, fishing and hunting.

Rugged Terrain and Climate

The Appalachian Mountains extend through the state, creating rugged terrain on the western borders. The southern coast contains long sandy beaches, with a myriad of capes, peninsulas and harbors totaling

3,500 miles of magnificent shoreline. The northern coast consists mainly of rocky promontories, peninsulas and fiords, causing scolding surf. The state is divided into 3 regions—coastal, southern interior and northern interior. Climatic conditions of the coastal division, which extends for about 20 miles inland along the entire length of the Maine coast, are tempered by the Atlantic Ocean. Annual coastal temperature averages 46°F. The southern interior division extends in a longitudinal belt across the southern portion, encompassing about 30 percent of Maine's total area. Annual average temperature in this division is 44°F. The northern interior division occupies about 60 percent of the state's area and has continental climate, with wide variations in temperature. The annual average in the northmost section is 37°F. and in the south 43°F.

Peak temperature, normally occurring in July, averages 70°F. throughout the state. Summer nights are usually cool and comfortable. Winters are generally cold, but prolonged cold spells are rare. Temperature variations are greater in winter, with northern parts registering 40 to 60 days of subzero temperatures annually, while coastal stations normally report 10 to 20 subzero days.

Maine averages measurable precipitation, including snow, in 1 out of every 3 days. January is normally the snowiest month, with an average of 20 inches. Some heavy ground fogs appear in low-lying inland areas and most frequently and heavily along the coast. The sun shines an average of 50 percent of the time in Eastport, about 60 percent in Portland.

While the air and water are generally clean and clear, I must issue this personal warning: *Don't settle within smelling distance of a pulp mill.* They are a gaseous insult to a newcomer's nostrils. As pulp and paper mills are prevalent throughout the state, you must pick your site carefully—usually along the coastal areas.

Abundant Health Facilities

Maine's medical facilities are abundant, modern and relatively inexpensive. The Pine Tree State has 54 hospitals with 7,324 beds, 133 nursing homes with 6,587 beds and 174 personal-care homes with 2,453 beds. A semiprivate hospital room costs $157 daily (vs. $163 U.S. average) and there are 136 physicians per 100,000 population, a bit more than adequate. In comparison with the other New England states, Maine claims to have more hospital beds per citizen and a greater reserve bed capacity than either New England or the United States.

Vacation-Type Housing

About half of Maine's housing lies in rural, the other half in urban areas. However, "urban" in Maine usually means medium and small-sized communities with relatively generous amounts of open space nearby. About 70 percent of the population lives in communities of 10,000 persons or less and only 6 percent in communities over 50,000. In fact, Portland, Maine's largest city, has only 70,000 people and Lewiston-Auburn (the largest urban area) has only 75,000.

Much housing is vacation type, located in or near camping areas and/or the seashore. Some retirees have built homes themselves or have contracted to have them built for as little as $25,000. Many small "retirement" homes (6 to 8 rooms, generally with 2 bedrooms) are available from $35,000. And even some 12-room Colonials on large lots sell for under $50,000. Vacation-home lots are available from $5,000. But remember, most of Maine is heavily forested, and any "lot" might be at least half-wooded. In short, a good building lot might cost $10,000. You can get a better idea of what's available by sending for a free copy of "Maine Real Estate Opportunities," State of Maine Publicity Bureau, Gateway Circle, Portland, ME 04102.

Relatively Modest Taxes

Maine's taxes are among the lowest in New England. Here is the breakdown:

Income Tax—rates vary from 1 percent on the first $2,000 of income for single taxpayers ($4,000 for couples) to $1,700 plus 10 percent on income over $25,000 for singles ($3,400 plus 10 percent of income over $50,000 for couples). There is a $1,000 exemption for each federal exemption.

Special Treatment of Retirement Income—a tax credit equal to 20 percent of the federal credit for the elderly is permitted residents on their Maine returns.

Property Taxes—the average municipal tax rate is $25 per $1,000 of equalized full value. Elderly householders age 62 and over with household income not exceeding $5,000 ($6,000 if there are two or more members of the household) and unmarried widow(er)s who are 55 or over and receiving disability benefits are entitled to a tax refund equal to the amount of the homestead property tax (or 25 percent of annual rent). The maximum refund is $400. Tax on a $50,000 home runs around $1,250.

Sales Tax—the rate is 5 percent. Exempt are food for home consumption, prescription drugs and prosthetic devices, including hearing aids and eyeglasses.

All told, the cost of living in Maine is slightly above the average for the United States for a retired couple: $10,022 U.S. average, $10,662 in Maine.

Big Outdoor Recreation

Since 82 percent of the Pine Tree State is forested, camping and wilderness activities are most popular. Acadia National Park alone encompasses more than 30,000 acres on Mt. Desert Island in the Bar Harbor vicinity, and there are 25 state parks in other areas. The Maine Forest Service maintains more than 260 wilderness camping areas, and many rural homes and farms have guest facilities. Yet for all its outdoor activities, Maine is surprisingly rich in historical and cultural societies and events. The Maine Historical Society and Bangor Historical Society maintain ambitious programs, as do many local organizations. There are many art museums, including those in Ogunquit, Portland, Rockland, Orono, Waterville, Brunswick and Wiscasset. Also, art colonies and art schools are available at Skowhegan, Kennebunk, Kennebunkport and Monhegan Island. Maine is the birthplace of summer theater, and performances are presented in converted barns and old movie houses. The best theaters are located in Boothbay, Brunswick, Skowhegan, Ogunquit, Monmouth and Kennebunkport. And there are many local crafts shops located throughout the state, as well as many members of the Antique Dealers Association. Factory outlets are popular, and the hunter, camper and outdoorsperson shouldn't miss the L.L. Bean Store in Freeport.

Services for the Independent

Maine's seniors pride themselves on their independence. Yet there are good services for seniors where the greatest concentrations of older people are (generally in the most populous counties): Cumberland, York, Penobscot, Kennebec and Androscoggin. Good facilities and services are also available in counties with the highest rates of growth in the number of older people: York, Hancock and Lincoln. The counties with the highest proportions of elderly are those with either high rates of in-migration of older people (York, Hancock and Lincoln) or those with high rates of out-migration among the young, such as Piscataquis and Washington. In these places you'll find local and area agencies on aging.

The Bureau of Maine's Elderly is located in the State House in Augusta and maintains comprehensive programs in nutrition, transportation, volunteer services, legal services, housing and health. Other services are also available to older residents, including homemaker, home health and senior centers.

For further information, write:

Bureau of Maine's Elderly
Department of Human Services
State House
Augusta, ME 04333

You can also contact regional agencies on aging in Presque Isle, Bangor, Augusta, Wilton and Portland.

MAJOR RETIREMENT AREAS

Kennebunk area (Kennebunk, pop. 8,000; Kennebunkport, pop. 3,-000) is the place for those who like the tang of the sea, the tickle of the beach, the crash of the surf. For here sights and scents of land and sea blend fascinatingly. The vacationer becomes a stay-put summer resident, then a retiree (if he can afford it).

Climate and Environment. The beautiful beaches, picturesque rocky coastlines, snug harbors and acres of forest and farmland are dominated by the mighty Atlantic —usually placid but sometimes frightening. Divided by the peaceful Kennebunk River, the town of Kennebunk lies on the west bank and the villages of Kennebunkport and Arundel on the east. Within their borders are the communities of *Kennebunk, Kennebunk Beach, Kennebunkport, Cape Porpoise, Goose Rocks Beach* and *Arundel.* The Atlantic Ocean tempers the climate, resulting in lower summer and higher winter temperatures than in interior zones. Annual average temperature is 46°F. Rainfall averages 46 inches annually; snowfall 50 to 70 inches, although the area rarely has more than 20 days with 1 inch or more of snowfall.

Medical Facilities. The area has 5 physicians, 5 dentists and a scattering of specialists. The community is certified for Medicare, and emergency ambulance service is available. The nearest hospital is in Biddeford (8 miles away), with 190 beds. A Veterans hospital in Augusta (85 miles away) can be reached in 2 hours. There is 1 nursing home in the area with 33 beds. The community is also served by the Kennebunk Public Health Association, which provides free or low-cost clinics, health care in the home, skilled therapy and loans of medical equipment. With a full-time public health nurse and staff, the Home Health Agency is certified for Medicare and Medicaid patients.

Housing Availability and Cost. The area is an architectural trea-

suretrove, with houses built in many classical styles: Colonial, Federal,
Greek revival, Victorian, Cape, Georgian, Gothic, Renaissance, Italianate,
Romanesque, Queen Anne, French chateau, Colonial, Tudor and Art Nou-
veau. Some of these well-preserved eighteenth- and nineteenth-century
homes sell in the $100,000–$250,000 range. But there are more modern
homes in developments that sell from $50,000 to $150,000, and the average townhouse sells from $60,000 to $85,000. Some winterized summer
homes are available from $50,000 to $90,000, but homes built on the
waterfront generally command $150,000 and up. Year-round apartments
in older renovated buildings start at $200 a month, but summer apart-
ments rent from $300 a week. Little land or development is available at
present. No trailer parks are in the area.

Cost of Living. Prices tend to be high in stores, shops and restaurants that cater to tourists. But the locals shop at two large supermarkets
and in department stores in Biddeford-Saco and Sanford. The property tax
rate in Kennebunkport is around $20 per $1,000 at 100 percent full valuation ($1,000 on a $50,000 home) and around $15 per $1,000 in Kennebunk.

Leisure-Time Activities. The beaches are very good, with fine,
clean sand. They are free of dangerous undertow, and they are patrolled
by lifeguards to enssure safety. Golf enthusiasts can find real challenges on the well-tended fairways of 3 golf courses, and fishermen vie
for hard-fighting striped bass at the mouth of the Kennebunk or Mou-
sam rivers and along the rocky shores. Many marinas offer good facilities for yachts and other boats; racing enthusiasts can see horse races
at nearby Scarborough Downs; and many indoor and outdoor theaters
are available. Art galleries and antique stores abound, with outdoor art
classes conducted by several outstanding artists. Church bazaars and
fairs are frequent, and auctions attract bargain-hunters and collectors.
History buffs have a field day at the Kennebunkport Historical Society,
where they find displays of pictures, documents, maps, costumes, furniture and other evidences of the town's past. Area libraries have 40,000
volumes.

Special Services for Seniors. The Kennebunk area has 70 clubs,
including a 50-Plus Club. The Cumberland-York Senior Citizens Council,
Inc. provides nutritional programs, transportation, information and referral, legal services, retired senior volunteers, health and other outreach
services.

For further information, write:

> Kennebunk-Kennebunkport Chamber of Commerce
> 43 Main Street
> Kennebunk, ME 04043

Bath area (pop. 10,000), stretching from Brunswick on the west to Damariscotta on the east, contains some fine retirement areas. And although the city of Bath has been known since early days as a shipbuilding town (the Bath Iron Works is one of the leading shipyards in the nation), it contains many elegant homes and cultural centers.

Climate and Environment. The city proper is hilly, offering many intriguing views of the Kennebec River. Located near the mouth of this river, Bath has a climate moderated by both it and the ocean. The average temperature in summer is 68°F., and 21°F. in winter. Many fine old mansions, built when Bath was a great seaport, stand behind the towering elms which line its streets. On Washington Street you'll find the Bath Marine Museum, which houses more than 5,000 artifacts related to over 300 years of Maine shipbuilding. And in the city park on Washington Street, you'll see the bronze fountain "Spirit of the Sea," created and presented to the city by sculptor William Zorach. In fact, the downtown area is undergoing a transformation back to its nineteenth-century appearance, with brick sidewalks and period lighting.

Medical Facilities. The Bath Memorial Hospital contains 92 beds and has an active staff of 25 doctors. There are 2 nursing homes in the area, and 8 dentists are in practice. The Community Health and Nursing Services (CHANS) is a Medicare Certified Home Health Agency servicing the area. It offers skilled nursing and therapy service, personal and homemaking care, health screening and patient clubs.

Housing Availability and Cost. Some 10 realtors have offices in Bath, and the town has 2 "build your own" schools for those interested in homebuilding; 10 building and general contractors are available for those who need help or want outside contracting. The residential area offers a rare collection of historic architecture, with the National Register Historic District spreading for several blocks and containing numerous examples of fine homes in various architectural styles. Some of these late eighteenth- and nineteenth-century homes sell for $150,000 and up, but there are more modestly priced retirement homes from $40,000. Rental housing is limited, but when available most apartments rent from $250 per month. Single-family homes and duplexes rent from about $300 to $500 a month, with tenants paying for heat, lights, sewer and water. Two housing projects for the elderly offer a choice of city living at Washington House or a more rural setting at the Anchorage.

Cost of Living. The tax rate is $24 per $1,000 valuation. Other costs are about in line with other Maine cities, so retirees would need an income of at least $10,000 (for a couple) to retire comfortably here.

Leisure-Time Activities. Recreation facilities include outdoor tennis courts, a waterfront park, public boat launch and 2 nearby beaches. The

Performing Arts Center at Bath offers concerts including bluegrass, jazz, classical, folk, dance, theater and musical comedy. Antique and art shops abound in the area and every Saturday from May through October, the area farmers and craftsmen hold a farmers market and crafts fair on Front Street. Baked goods and local produce are also for sale here. The area has many parks and beaches, and there is a 9-hole golf club.

Special Services for Seniors. The Bath area has many social service and health agencies, including chapters of the American Cancer Society, Arthritis Foundation and American Red Cross. There's a Bath Senior Citizen Club on Summer Street and nearby senior centers and associations in Augusta and Brunswick. The Central Maine Area Agency on Aging provides a comprehensive program of services.

For further information, write:

> Bath Area Chamber of Commerce
> 45 Front Street
> Bath, ME 04530

Other retirement possibilities in the area include *Falmouth* (04105), *Yarmouth* (04096), *Boothbay* (04537), *Boothbay Harbor* (04538), *Brunswick* (04011) and *Wiscasset* (04578).

Damariscotta (pop. 1,500) is a lovely seaport town where walking the main streets is like visiting with relatives. The storekeepers are as friendly as good neighbors, as happy to talk as to do business. Main Street has 2 big grocery stores, a fine town library, 3 clothing stores, 2 gift shops, a very good bookstore, 3 hardware stores, a state liquor store, barber and beauty shops, a department store with its spin-off bargain basement, plus a passel of business offices of insurancemen, lawyers, oil dealers, doctors, dentists and real estate agents. A riverfront municipal parking lot makes shopping and visiting easy, and you can walk to the twin village of *Newcastle*, which lies on the opposite shore near the headwaters of the Damariscotta River, 12 miles from the ocean. The region consists of pine-bordered lakes, shady forests, tidal rivers, protected harbors, sandy beaches and a rock-bound coast. Both villages date back to 1629 and contain many beautiful homes and buildings of the Colonial period. But housing is expensive ($50,000 and up) and land values have tripled in the last decade. Taxes have increased by 25 to 30 percent annually, making these villages increasingly expensive. But there's a class-A hospital in the area, and you save on frills, entertainment, clothes, tips and keeping up with the Joneses. Outdoor sports—tennis, swimming, riding, canoeing, golf, fresh- and saltwater sailing and fishing, hunting— are all here. And you can enjoy bowling, first-run movies, summer theater, square and modern dancing. Some retirees have found part-time work (especially during the summer tourist season) and others have opened small businesses.

For further information, write:

> Damariscotta Region Information Bureau
> Damariscotta, ME 04543

Camden (pop. 5,000) lies further up the coast, a peaceful retirement village which offers the best of both sea and mountains. The setting, on Penobscot Bay, where the Megunticook River spills into the harbor, has been described as one of the most beautiful on the Atlantic coast. The village is one of elm-shaded streets, white houses, neat gardens, flower-decorated lampposts, church steeples and schooner-filled harbors. Nearby Camden Hills State Park offers most recreational facilities; cultural activities include the Shakespearean Amphitheater, art and antique stores, music centers, a classic movie house and a splendid library. Many culture-conscious retirees have settled here, renovating some Colonial homes. Until a few years ago you could have picked up such a house for under $50,000. Now, house prices start at $60,000 and smaller houses are scarce. Camden has a good community hospital, another close by in Rockport, and there's a Veterans Administration hospital in Togus, about an hour's drive.

For further information write:

> Chamber of Commerce
> Camden, ME 04843

Camden lies on *Penobscot Bay,* which holds more than 400 islands. By their very number they assure there won't be any crowded highways among the island traffic. This area ranks as a Retirement Eden, perhaps because there aren't too many things on which to spend money. And you won't find much in the way of formal entertainment around these islands, but you'll find a lot of healthful recreational opportunities in the coves and inland lakes and ponds—swimming, fishing, sailing. If you're a bird watcher, this is *the* place to try your observational skills because it lies squarely on the Atlantic flyway. A couple of islands of special note:

Deer Island (pop. 2,515) is joined to the mainland by a toll-free bridge over Eggemoggin Reach. There are 2 towns: *Deer Isle* (pop. 1,215) and *Stonington* (pop. 1,300). The fifth largest island off the Atlantic coast, Deer Island has 80 miles of coastal road, passing through pine-scented hills and skirting coves, rocks and an unspoiled panorama of nature at her best. Many local crafts people live here and display wares in the Barn Gallery and adjacent shop. Stonington is the kind of fishing village, with scores of picturesque fishing boats, that artists rave about.

Vinalhaven (pop. 1,135) forms a geographic unit with *North Haven* (pop. 400), a small strip of water between them. Both islands are fashionable summer resorts, and numerous deep coves and inlets make them a choice yachting and boating haven. Vinalhaven boasts good electricity, city water, a good public library, a hospital and clinic. The island is usually reached by an hour-and-a-half cruise around the other islands, but despite its remoteness, Vinalhaven is attracting more and more retirees to whom time is no longer of paramount importance. And, while winters will always be winters, here among the coastal islands you are still in a temperate zone. If you have a fund of projects to do inside the house during the winter, you'll get a bonus of enjoyment when the weather creates things to do outside in spring, summer and fall.

Further up the coast lies *Bar Harbor* (pop. 2,400), the largest town on Mt. Desert Island. This is one of the most popular "get-away-from-it-all" areas in the East. "Eden seekers" have been coming here for a hundred years, and many have come back to stay. In fact, it was *the* place until the great fire of 1947 destroyed many of the magnificent estates that lined the shores. But the fire didn't destroy the rugged beauty that still serves as a magnet for young and old, many of whom hike to the summit of 1,532-foot Cadillac Mountain to gain a bird's-eye view of the granite, forests, flowers, bays and inlets that are Maine in its most natural state.

Most of Acadia National Park, reached by bridge from the mainland, is on Mt. Desert Island, and in addition to Bar Harbor, the area contains the villages of *Southwest Harbor, Northeast Harbor, Seal Harbor, Tremont* and others. In these villages you'll find both the beauty you expect in an Eden and the modern conveniences you hope for.

For further information, write:

> Chamber of Commerce
> Deer Island, ME 04627
> Vinalhaven, ME 04863
> Bar Harbor, ME 04609

SUMMARY

Maine is a great state for retirees seeking a last frontier. But you have to be a hardy soul to cope with the harsh winters and to settle in the wilderness. That's why the best retirement areas are along the coast where the weather is more moderate. This is prime vacation country and year-round costs are higher than the national average. Also, your Retirement Eden *must* be beyond smelling range of a pulp or paper mill (most of which are inland). Here are my ratings of the major retirement areas:

Excellent — Kennebunk, Kennebunkport, Camden, Bath area, Penobscot Bay area, Deer Island
Good — Boothbay, Boothbay Harbor, Bar Harbor, Falmouth, Yarmouth, Brunswick, Wiscasset, Damariscotta
Adequate — Augusta and Portland areas

5. RHODE ISLAND—A LOT IN A LITTLE PACKAGE

For the smallest of the 50 states, "Little Rhody" packs a lot of quality in a small space. Only 48 miles long and 37 miles wide, it contains over 400 miles of coastline, which provides ideal swimming, sailing and fishing. And on a "Quality of Life" scale designed by the Midwest Research Institute, Rhode Island ranked in the top 10 of all 50 states as one of the most desirable places to live. The Ocean State scored "excellent" in individual equality, living conditions, agriculture and health and welfare; "high average" in individual status, technology, economic status; "average" in education and state and local governments.

Rhode Island was founded on religious freedom, racial tolerance and respect for individual rights. The early settlers were Puritans from Massachusetts Bay Colony, and successive waves of immigration brought French-Canadians, Portuguese, Irish and Italians. The importance of agriculture and shipping has shrunk, as has the rural population; now more than 90 percent of the population live in urban settings.

Some 17.6 percent of the state's 1 million people are age 60 or over, and 12.6 percent are age 65 and older, giving the state one of the nation's highest proportions of older citizens. There are good reasons why older people come to live here and stay.

Invigorating Climate and Environment

The more than 400 miles of shoreline give the Ocean State a rich saltwater heritage; the fact that more than 80 percent of the state still consists of wooded and farmland areas gives it a rural base. The variable climate is stimulating and invigorating. It is influenced by the Gulf Stream and Narragansett Bay and averages 72°F. in July and 35°F. in January. (50°F. year-round). But the weather can be extremely variable, marked by occasional hurricanes and tidal waves. The topography consists of the eastern lowlands of the Narragansett basin, an interior of rolling hills and small lakes and western uplands of flat and rolling hills.

The major ethnic groups are Italian, English and Irish; racial distribution is 93.6 percent white, 3.0 percent Black, the rest Hispanic and other.

High-Grade Health Care

Rhode Island has 21 hospitals with a total of 6,700 beds. A semiprivate hospital room costs $171 daily (the national average is $163). The Ocean State has 195 doctors per 100,000 people, higher than the average of 174 per 100,000. There are 80 nursing homes with 5,980 beds and 40 personal-care homes with 1,422 beds. All in all, medical facilities are above average, in both quality and cost.

Adequate, Varied Housing

The Ocean State provides a wide range of living styles with adequate housing. The price of new homes is $50,000 and up, although some smaller retirement homes are available for less. The range for 1- and 2-bedroom apartments is from $200 to $450 and up a month, and some garden-type apartments are available from $250 a month for the smallest units. Most Rhode Island real estate agents subscribe to the state-wide multiple-listing service and can provide information on areas and homes suited to your particular life style. You can also get a free copy of "Suburban Rhode Island Real Estate News" by writing to 377 Main Street, Stoneham, MA 02180. And *The Providence Journal,* the state's largest newspaper, services the entire state and provides valuable listings. You can get a copy of the real estate section by inquiring at the newspaper's office, 75 Fountain Street, Providence, RI 02902. Note that condominium living is becoming more and more popular in the state, and that year-round living in the Narragansett Bay area is increasing as more homes are being winterized. Also, there are two retirement home complexes now available in Warwick.

Above-Average Cost of Living

Local taxes in Rhode Island are lower than average for some parts of the Northeast, although they are high by other standards (the state ranks sixth in tax burden for those with taxable incomes of $25,000 or less).

Income Tax—19 percent of the taxpayer's federal income tax liability. Personal and medical deductions are the same as permitted under federal law, as is special treatment of retirement income.

Property Taxes—real estate taxes range from $18.50 to $72.56 per

$1,000 valuation, with assessment ratios ranging from 31 percent to 100 percent of market value. The average tax on a $50,000 home is $1,550. But homeowners or renters age 65 or older are eligible, within certain income limits, for a tax credit and refund. And certain cities and towns may exempt some taxes for older residents (although residency requirements vary up to 7 years).

Sales Tax—rate is 6 percent. Exemptions are for food, prescription drugs, electricity, gas, heating fuel, water and clothing.

Outstanding Leisure Activities

Ever since Colonial times, Rhode Islanders have been appreciative patrons of the fine arts: concerts and dramatic performances were offered in Providence and Newport as early as 1761. It is estimated that there are more legitimate theaters in Rhode Island than in many of the larger cultural centers in the nation. And the Rhode Island Ballet Company ranks among the nation's best, as does the Philharmonic Symphony and the Trinity Repertory Theater. The 400 miles of coastline offer the best in boating, fishing and swimming, with more than 100 beaches, 200 marinas, yacht clubs and launching sites, and more than 50 charter boats for deep-sea fishing. Freshwater fishing is readily available in the well-stocked lakes, and ice fishing is a popular winter recreation. More than 8,000 acres are set aside for state parks and forests, which offer complete camping facilities. And both Newport and Providence (see below) are rich in galleries and museums. Bristol has the largest Fourth of July parade in the nation and Newport has the America's Cup races every 3 years.

Abundant Services for Seniors

The Rhode Island Department of Elderly Affairs provides a vast array of services covering health, transportation, meal programs, nursing home ombudsman, legal services, widow support, employment counseling, telephone reassurance, information and referral, in-home services and walking clubs for physical fitness. Programs are open to seniors age 60 and over, except for the widow-to-widow program, which is open to all ages. The nutrition program (daily hot meal) is on a donation-only basis. Many cities and towns offer special programs, and there are some 40 senior centers throughout the state (about half of them in Providence). The Ocean State has an annual senior prom, preretirement fair, Governor's Centenarian May breakfast, preretirement training and planning programs.

For further information, write:

Department of Elderly Affairs
State of Rhode Island
79 Washington Street
Providence, RI 02903

MAJOR RETIREMENT AREAS

Aquidneck Island contains the towns of *Newport* (pop. 35,000),
Middletown (16,500) and *Portsmouth* (15,500).

Climate and Environment. The island juts into Rhode Island Sound,
joined to the mainland by bridges. It is 30 miles south of Providence and
74 miles south of Boston. The climate is moderated by water, with the
mean January temperature of 28.7°F., July, 71.6°F. and a mean annual
precipitation of 39.29 inches. The main attraction is Newport, "America's
First Vacationland," best known for its museum mansions. The area,
formerly a big naval center, has been losing population since the navy
fleet withdrew in 1973. However, this has allowed renovation of some of
its run-down neighborhoods.

Medical Facilities. Island-wide there are 56 physicians and surgeons
and 46 dentists. Each community provides a rescue truck. The Newport
Hospital has 217 beds and the U.S. Naval Regional Medical Center provides both in-patient and out-patient services. There are 6 nursing homes
in the area.

Housing Availability and Cost. As this is a summer resort area,
summer rentals can be prohibitive, ranging upwards from $1,000 a month.
But on a year-round basis, a good 2-bedroom apartment can be rented
from $300 a month, and homes from $400 a month. And while the average
3- or 4-bedroom house might cost $80,000 to $90,000, smaller retirement
homes and cottages sell from $40,000. A good selection of housing is
available, including many coops and condominiums as well as single-
family units. The museum mansions (former private homes of historic
value and architectural significance) were the vacation "cottages" of the
Vanderbilts, Morgans, Astors and others of that era who put their stamp
on the area. Nowhere else in America can you see such extravagance as
in this assortment of French chateaus, Rhine castles, brooding Irish for-
tresses and sixteenth-century Italian palaces. These are now showplaces
for public tour rather than living quarters—no one could afford the up-
keep.

Cost of Living. Costs are relatively high, with the following tax rates
per $1,000 of assessed valuation: Newport, $58.50 at 35 percent assessed

value; Middletown, $64.40 at 60 percent of 1967 market value; Portsmouth, $23.78 at 70 percent of 1978 assessed value. The tax on a $50,000 home runs about $1,930 annually.

Leisure-Time Activities. The island boasts 17 parks and playgrounds, 6 public sandy beaches, 2 private and 3 public golf courses, 2 yacht clubs and 10 marinas, indoor and outdoor tennis (including grass) courts, 1 racquetball and handball court, 1 tricinema, 1 twin cinema, 1 movie theater, a bird sanctuary and organized sports. Newport perhaps has more points of interest than any community of similar size in the country. Besides the mansions along Bellevue Avenue and Ocean Drive, Newport is still what it has been for 340 years—a pretty port town on a breeze-swept island. Offshore are some of the finest sailing waters along the East Coast. Onshore there is a layering of history that begins at the edge of the harbor with the Colonial section of town. Annual events include a fair at the Elms (the Berwind home), a street fair and a maritime fair. Newport is big on music, with two festivals of opera and chamber music: the Newport Jazz Festival, which had been held in the resort since 1954, moved to New York in 1971. There are scores of elegant restaurants in town (most are jammed in the summer) and many shopping centers. Many of these can be found in some of the newly refurbished sections of the old waterfront. This area also has the White Horse Tavern, the oldest tavern in the country. Next to the Newport Historical Society stands Touro Synagogue, a National Historic Site, the oldest synagogue building in America. Each town has a library.

Special Services for Seniors. The area has a legal services branch, meals-on-wheels program, medical assistance services, mental health agencies, nursing-home information, a nutrition program, two senior centers, a Social Security office and transportation services.

For further information, write:

> Newport County Chamber of Commerce
> 10 America's Cup Avenue
> Newport, RI 02840

Across the Newport Bridge is *Jamestown* (pop. 3,000), which includes all of Conanicut Island, one of the three main islands in Narragansett Bay. The entire island is a summer resort, and some of the older homes and resort hotels (like the Bay View Hotel) are being restored to their former splendor.

Narragansett (pop. 7,500) is home of the Narragansett Pier, which has been referred to as "one of the finest beaches in the world." The

Tower, designed and built by Stanford White, is a landmark of the pier, and the beaches are lined with luxurious summer residences and more modest seaside cottages, selling for $40,000 and up.

The *Block Island* (pop. 500) ferry leaves from a point near Narragansett. Only 9 miles from the mainland, the island, dubbed an "air-conditioned summer resort," is 10 to 15 degrees cooler than the mainland in summer and milder in winter. Block Island offers some of the best surf and deep-sea fishing in the area, and Old Harbor is where much fish is caught before being shipped to eastern markets.

For further information, write:

> Chamber of Commerce:
> Block Island, RI 02807
> Jamestown, RI 02835
> Narragansett, RI 02882

Providence (pop. 175,000; area, 850,000) contains about one-third of the state's population. It is a city where "the past and present merge." But the past isn't just preserved in museums; it lives on streets like Benefit Street, which has more than 100 houses considered notable by the Providence Preservation Society. Most of them are eighteenth- and early nineteenth-century houses with a scattering of early Victorians. And there are hundreds more on surrounding streets, called "A Mile of History." In the Federal Hill section of town, streetlamps from another era line Atwells Avenue.

Grandiose buildings look at ease on streets aptly named Gold, Silver, Bullion, Power, Sovereign, and Doubloon. And where else in a city with a downtown of only 25 blocks can you walk from a neighborhood with the charm of Boston's Beacon Hill past an enclosed shopping mall (The Arcade) built in 1827 in the style of a Greek temple and then on to the Biltmore Plaza Hotel, which rivals the elegance of New York's Plaza Hotel?

Climate and Environment. The modern city centers around the junction of the Woonasquatucket and Moshassuck rivers. Skyscraping hotels and office buildings look across river flatlands to the State House, considered one of the most beautiful in the nation. The view is one of spaciousness rare in most U.S. cities. The average winter temperature is 35.8°F; summer, 63.4°F. There are 179 sunny days, 65.06 inches of rain, 30.4 inches of snow, and an average 71 percent humidity annually. Besides being the state capital, Providence is an important manufacturing center for silverware, jewelry, machine tools, hardware and rubber products. It is also a major port of entry.

Medical Facilities. The majority of the state's physicians, dentists, specialists and medical facilities are located here. There are 7 major hospitals and 1 Veterans Administration hospital.

Housing Availability and Cost. Some of the houses are brick mansions in the Georgian style, like the John Brown House at Benefit and Power streets, which John Quincy Adams called "the most magnificent and elegant private mansion I have ever seen on this continent." But most are simple, symmetrical wooden clapboard houses of graceful proportions. Many of these homes, as well as commercial buildings, are undergoing renovation. The city distributes up to $100,000 in federal funds to merchants fixing up dilapidated storefronts. Property owners who want to renovate commercial buildings can get up to $150,000, and any business that wants to restore a building in the city's historic district can get a tax reduction. The city also gives 3 percent loans to fix up homes and *the elderly can get their homes painted free* by federally paid city employees. Generally 1- and 2-bedroom apartments rent from $200 to $450 a month; garden-type apartments start at $250 a month for the smallest units. The average selling price of new homes is $50,000.

Cost of Living. Taxes on a $50,000 home are $1,550 a year. Other living costs are a bit above the national average; thus it would take *more than* $10,000 annually for a couple to retire comfortably here.

Leisure-Time Activities. The educational facilities are dominated by Brown University, founded in 1764, one of the oldest colleges in the nation. Other institutions are Providence and Rhode Island colleges and the Rhode Island School of Design. Cultural facilities include the Trinity Square Repertory Company, Rhode Island Philharmonic, Rhode Island School for Design Museum and the Rhode Island Historical Society. One of America's most attractive recreational areas centers around Providence: 69 saltwater beaches, 26 freshwater beaches, 50 golf and country clubs, 4 ski areas, 29 yacht clubs, 28 parks—all within 45 minutes of the city.

Special Services for Seniors. Providence is the center of many senior facilities and services. The Providence *Bulletin* (and some other state papers) prints a weekly question-and-answer column prepared by the Department of Elderly Affairs. The department also hosts "First Sunday," a monthly half-hour radio program of particular interest to seniors, and publishes a quarterly, "Older Rhode Islander." There's a branch of Retired Senior Volunteer Program (RSVP) here as well as some 18 senior centers. And Providence has scores of senior clubs located in most neighborhoods. You can find the location of the nearest senior club by calling the Department of Elderly Affairs' Information Service at (401) 277-2880.

For further information, write:

Chamber of Commerce
10 Dorrance Street
Providence, RI 02903

SUMMARY

"Little Rhody" could be a retirement haven, especially if you find a charming retirement home in the historic areas of Newport, Providence, Jamestown or Narragansett. The state offers some of the best of both the historic past and vibrant future. Living costs are above the national average, but so is the quality of living, medical care and special services for seniors (the Department of Elderly Affairs does a comprehensive job). And Rhode Island is especially attractive to the sailor, fisherman, swimmer or surf watcher. Here are my evaluations of the major areas:

Excellent — Newport area, Providence area
Good — Jamestown, Narragansett, Block Island

6. CONNECTICUT—THE PRIDE OF THE PAST WITH THE PROMISE OF THE FUTURE

As the gateway to New England, Connecticut guards its Yankee heritage with pride. Old-timers in 1774 houses sniff at "newcomers" in 1784 houses. Some residents with deep ancestral roots feel that you're not a proper Connecticut Yankee if you haven't lived here for at least 3 generations.

But if Connecticut has one foot planted in the Colonial past, the other foot is striding the Space Age future. Part of this is due to the "Gadget State's" reputation for high-skilled technology. Jet engines, helicopters, tools and dies, marine hardware all are stamped "made in Connecticut." And as corporate offices move out of New York City and into Connecticut, waves of immigrants move with them, and the once-solid Puritan base erodes. Italians, Irish and Jews predominate in many cities. This has added élan to a once staid countryside, but the Constitution State has been able nonetheless to preserve its historic past. Tall white church steeples still preside over quiet green hills and deep blue lakes. And as more people choose to live here, more people choose it as the place to retire.

Some 15.6 percent of the state's 3.15 million people are over age 60; 10.9 percent are over age 65. Here are some reasons why they chose Connecticut.

Varied Geography and Climate

With only 5,000 square miles, Connecticut is the third smallest state in the union. Yet it offers a diversity of topography and weather: western uplands (the Berkshires), narrow central lowlands, eastern uplands drained by rivers. Winters are a bit colder than the U.S. average; summers are a bit above average in both heat and humidity. But both spring and fall make up for these extremes. In Hartford, the capital, winters average 33.7°F. and summers 64°F. Humidity averages 71 percent annually. There are 165 sunny days, 64.55 inches of rain and 58.2 inches of snow annually.

Top-Quality Medical Care

Connecticut has one of the highest ratios of physicians per resident: 224 per 100,000 population; the national average is 174 per 100,000. The cost of an average semiprivate hospital room is $174 daily (national average, $163). The state has 64 hospitals with a total of 18,791 beds. There are 222 nursing homes with 19,883 beds and 134 personal-care homes with 4,690 beds.

High-Cost but Available Housing

If you want to buy a single-family retirement residence, it will be almost impossible to find anything decent under $50,000. And if you have your heart set on an old Colonial home, be prepared to pay exorbitant prices for substandard housing. Most Connecticut towns have housing projects for the elderly, but there are residency and income requirements that exclude most newcomers. However, one of the most attractive (although expensive) retirement villages in the country is located near Southbury: *Heritage Village* (see below).

Higher Than Average Taxes

Although Connecticut doesn't have a state income tax, it has other taxes that make it rank eighth in tax burden in the $10,000 to $15,000 tax bracket and thirteenth in the $15,000 to $20,000 bracket. Here is the breakdown:

Capital Gains and Dividends Tax—there is a 7 percent tax on capital gains income. Sale of a residence by an individual over age 65 which has been owned and used as a residence during 5 of the last 8 years is exempt. Dividends are taxed on a graduated scale from 1 to 9 percent if the taxpayer's adjusted gross income is $20,000 or more. The maximum applies only if the adjusted gross income is $100,000 or more.

Property Tax—rates are fixed locally and are based on a uniform percentage of true market values. In Bridgeport, the tax on a $50,000 house is $1,400. But homeowners over age 65 who have lived in the state for the last 5 years are eligible for certain tax credits, as are renters.

Sales Tax—the rate is 7.5 percent, with exemptions for heating fuel, utilities, grocery food, restaurant meals under $1, magazine subscriptions, newspapers, meals to patients in hospitals, homes for the aged, convalescent homes, nursing homes and rest homes. The gasoline and cigarette taxes are among the highest in the nation.

Historical Past, Cultural Present

Connecticut displays its pride in the past in museums and galleries at Yale University (New Haven), Bristol, Bridgeport, Litchfield, Danbury, Middletown, New Britain, New London, Norwich, Mystic (a complete seaport museum), Waterbury, Stamford and many other towns. Historic sites dot the state as do famous libraries, old estates, gardens, and theaters (the Shakespeare Theatre at Stratford is worth a visit). The state is big on tours: river, bus, fall foliage, agricultural, nature and industrial. From June through August you can attend pop concerts in New Haven, and there are string concerts at Norfolk's Music Shed and Sunday afternoon chamber-music concerts at Falls Village. Outdoor sports are big; some of the best golf courses are located at Greenwich and New Haven. Other good 18-hole courses are located in Middlefield, Southbury, Groton, Norwich, Hamden, Norwalk, Moodus, New Milford, Southington, Stonington and Waterbury. Tennis courts are open to the public in all city parks and schools. There is boating at state parks; boat launching sites with access to saltwater are at Branford, Bridgeport, Groton, Guilford, New Haven, Old Lyme, Stonington and Waterford. Trout, bass, pickerel and shad can be caught in lakes and streams, bluefish and striped bass in salt water. Fishing boats for charter and marinas are located in Groton/New London. Although Connecticut doesn't have the high slopes of other New England states, skiing and affiliated water activities are increasingly popular. Of the state's 8 skiing areas, the largest is Mohawk Mountain at Cornwall.

Active Department on Aging

The Department on Aging offers comprehensive programs and counseling on health, nutrition, housing, finances, legal matters and leisure-time activities. Every part of the state is covered by an area agency on aging, and most communities have local councils for the elderly. Senior centers are located in most major towns and villages. The Department on Aging has good literature available for seniors interested in moving to the state. Among these materials is a directory of housing for older people.

For further information, write:

Department on Aging
90 Washington Street
Hartford, CT 06115

MAJOR RETIREMENT AREAS

Western Connecticut—The Land of Nostalgia

This area is the setting for Indian summer: harvest moons, frost on the pumpkins. It is a land of state parks and semideveloped countryside, where deer, pheasant and wild duck roam across slopes and in the thick woods. The Colonial house is embedded as a natural part of the landscape, and even the new housing pays homage to the old in style and appearance. Quaint, charming Brigadoon-type towns like *Cornwall, Kent, Sheffield, Canaan* and *Salisbury* appear like romantic mirages. Yet this is also the setting of one of the most "aristocratic" of retirement communities, *Heritage Village* (pop. 4,000), where "every day is like Saturday."

Heritage Village is located in *Southbury*, about 1 hour from New York City. Many residents are former executives and professionals from Manhattan who still sample its good theaters and restaurants on the weekly bus trip to Manhattan on Wednesday (matinee day). Some residents even commute to New York to work part-time, but most Heritage Villagers (about 70 percent) are fully retired (average 65 plus) and enjoy the good life. That doesn't come cheap in this adult community of 2,500 condominium units on 1,000 acres of countryside. The original units are all sold, but about 10 percent are usually up for resale. Prices range from $55,000 for a 1-bedroom, 1-bath unit to $125,000 for 3-bedrooms, 2-baths. Monthly charges, including grounds and maintenance, electricity (heat and general), taxes, sewer and water, range from $250 to over $400. This doesn't include membership in the Heritage Village Country Club, which offers 9- and 18-hole golf courses. Annual dues run from $450 to over $1,000.

Heritage Village offers a "total living" concept: complete exterior maintenance of home and grounds; 24-hour security; daily village mini-bus; a recreation complex; clubs and social organizations. There's plenty of activity, much of it centering around the Bazaar, a barnlike structure where amateur artists cart canvases and sculptures to an upstairs art gallery. There are shops for all crafts and hobbies and a teeming bookstore. This is the place where leaflets and posters give notice of cooking classes, language lessons, bridge games, dances, amateur theater and lectures. For entertaining, there's the Country Tavern, where you can enjoy gourmet dining in a Colonial atmosphere. I had one of the best meals ever in this elegant setting; it was crowded even on a snowy winter evening. And while many residents winter in Florida and other sunspots, there is enough activity to hold retirees year-round—including the 26.5 percent of the residents who are single (24 percent of all units are occupied by single women). There are no health facilities in Heritage Village, but good ones are available in nearby Danbury and Waterbury. Many Heritage Village residents volunteer at hospitals in nearby communities (volunteering is a major activity). More than 100 volunteer for the emergency ambulance corps: "rallying around" is a way of life in this unique community. Heritage Village even has an award-winning biweekly news magazine, *The Heritage Villager*, which is distributed free to residents (for a sample copy, send 50¢ to The Heritage Villager, Box 269, Southbury, CT 06488).

For further information, write:

> Heritage Village
> Development Group
> Southbury, CT 06488

About 20 miles north of Heritage Village lie the Litchfield Hills, regarded by many as the most beautiful section of Connecticut. The rolling hills and sparkling lakes are spectacular, and they hold historic and serene villages. Chief among them is *Litchfield* (pop. 7,500), a picturebook community of beautiful homes. The Litchfield Green, dominated by the gleaming white-steepled Congregational church, is charming enough, but you'll gape at the elegant white clapboard houses with traditional green and black shutters that line both sides of elm-shaded North and South streets. The entire area has been declared a historic site, and no exterior changes can be made. If you want to retire here, bring money; this is the place for those who love beauty and can pay for it.

For further information, write:

> Chamber of Commerce
> Litchfield, CT 06759

Southwest of Litchfield lies *Washington*, another Colonial gem of exquisite white houses, a small green, and elm-shaded houses. Nearby *Kent* and *Cornwall* have covered bridges.

East of this area, toward Hartford, lies *Bristol* (pop. 56,000), where 15 percent of the population is retired. The town has 1 hospital with 250 beds and 4 nursing homes. There are 111 doctors and 82 dentists, more than adequate for the population. Housing is plentiful, with 463 units especially designed for seniors. You should be able to get a modest 2-bedroom unit for $50,000. The area is especially strong on senior services, with a Retired Senior Volunteer Program (RSVP), a chapter of the American Association of Retired Persons (AARP), a municipal agent who counsels seniors, a hot meal program, homemaker services, visiting nurses, meals on wheels, transportation program and legal-aid service.

For further information, write:

Chamber of Commerce
Bristol, CT 06010

The Connecticut River Valley—The "Revolutionary Valley"

This valley is steeped in history. Many battles for freedom were fought here and many innovations occurred here during the industrial revolution. Today a nuclear-power plant at Haddam Neck lies not far from a state park whose major attraction is a sprawl of a thousand or more dinosaur tracks. But just as the ancient footprints have been preserved, so has the Colonial charm. And more and more retirees are finding their Retirement Eden in such places as:

Branford (pop. 23,000), a residential suburb of New Haven, whose bays, beaches, and greens attract many newcomers. The town appeals especially to those interested in crafts: some 40 craftspeople have shops at Bittersweet Farm. Some retirees have bought sites on the offshore *Thimble Islands* (there are 365 of them, 30 habitable).

Guilford (pop. 15,000) has 150 old houses of various designs on original sites, many of them on the impressive town green. The oldest stone house in the state is here, as is its longest greenhouse. The Congregational church (1829) is a perfect example of Greek revival architecture.

Madison (pop. 14,500) is a former resort that is now a town for all seasons. As soon as summer homes come on the market, they are snapped up at prices ranging upwards of $125,000 (winterized for another $15,-000). Retirees are also settling in *Kensington Acres*, a project of small Cape Cods and attached houses at the Hammanasett end of town. And there's a new, expensive inland development called *Five Fields* that has attracted many newcomers. This town is so booming that it is being called the "new Greenwich," referring to Greenwich, Connecticut, a town near the New York border that mushroomed in the past decade.

Old Saybrook (pop. 10,000) is another former resort that is building for tomorrow with pride in the heritage of the past. Some 20 percent of the people in the area are classified as elderly and they are attracted by the good municipal services, including a new medical clinic supervised by the Middlesex Memorial staff. An effective volunteer ambulance unit is on call 24 hours to provide transportation within 30 minutes of 4 major hospitals. Old Saybrook offers diversified recreational activities for all age groups and maintains facilities including a 180-acre park of natural woodlands and meadows.

Old Lyme (pop. 5,000), across the river from Old Saybrook, was the nation's first art colony. Artists were attracted by its beauty, as were the sea captains who built the mansions that line the shady streets. The sea captains have gone, but not the artists. The Lyme Art Association, a prestigious summer gallery, offers 3 major shows each season. Paintings, along with rare antique dolls, toys and furnishings, are also on display at the Florence Griswold House (1817), a handsome Greek revival mansion that housed the community's and the nation's first organized group of painters. This is a Colonial gem of a town—a well-preserved antique.

Essex (pop. 5,000) has been described as a "mint-condition eighteenth-century village." The center of town is built on a peninsula that juts out into the Connecticut River. With water everywhere, it is a major yachting center and its streets are lined with handsome clapboard houses, inns and taverns. One of the most famous is the Griswold Inn located on Main Street near the harbor. It contains a potbellied stove, antique fixtures and furnishings, a valuable collection of Currier and Ives prints and other memorabilia of its Colonial past.

Retirement homes in this area aren't cheap. The average home sells for $70,000, with many selling for over $100,000. The lowest price is $50,000. Also, it could take you three or more years before you would be "accepted" by some of the older families, although the recent influx of newcomers has broken some of the social barriers.

For further information, write:

> Chamber of Commerce
> Branford, CT 06405
> Guilford, CT 06437
> Madison, CT 06443
> Old Saybrook, CT 06475
> Old Lyme, CT 06371
> Essex, CT 06426

Farther up the Connecticut River lie the hamlets of *Deep River,* *Haddam, East Haddam* and *Middletown,* all offering retirement possibilities. And just south of Hartford (the state capital) you'll find *Glastonbury* (pop. 28,000 including *South Glastonbury*) which holds promise as a Retirement Eden. Spacious wooded lots are the rule, not the exception, and a great many expand into acreage. Beautiful, restored Colonial homes line Glastonbury's main thoroughfare and reflect the town's early American heritage. Prices aren't cheap (many homes sell for over $100,000) and the tax rate is 49.4 mils with an assessment ratio of 70 percent. But there are many doctors in Glastonbury and hospitals in Hartford and Manchester. So the area can offer comfortable as well as elegant retirement living. While some might dub Glastonbury a WASP area, the town has a scattering of minorities who join with the old families at the town meetings to air local problems. This is a good place to be retired, but not "out of things."

For further information, write:

Chamber of Commerce
Glastonbury, CT 06033

About 50 miles northeast of Hartford lie the hamlets of *Pomfret* and *Woodstock* (pop. 1,000). This area of rolling hills and valleys is one of the most pastoral sections of Connecticut. In fact, airline pilots who fly commercial routes up and down the East Coast say this northeastern part of Connecticut is the only real break in the megalopolis that stretches from Boston to Washington. Many state parks and forests are in this section, and it is dotted with small pastoral estates that grow their own food. Flowers, shrubs and trees are not merely grown but cultivated by people who love the land and country arts as well as country living. Housing and other living costs are more reasonable than in other parts of the state. This area attracts teachers and professional people who seek quiet, sunlit days to indulge in hobbies, walk familiar paths, smoke a pipe in peace outside the country store or gather for carols on a white Christmas Eve. If it sounds poetic, that's what Woodstock and Pomfret do to people of discernment—and they're only about 3 hours from Manhattan and 1½ hours from Boston.

For further information, write:

Chamber of Commerce
Woodstock, CT 06281
Pomfret, CT 06258

SUMMARY

Connecticut is a good retirement state for those seeking Yankee roots. The Colonial past is lovingly preserved here in many historic villages. But charm costs, and if you want to live like a Connecticut Yankee it helps if you have a lot of money. The contrasts between the cities and the countryside are great: the more rural your setting, the more it costs. Here are my evaluations of the major retirement areas:

Excellent — Heritage Village, Litchfield, Old Lyme, Pomfret, Woodstock
Good — Bristol, Branford, Guilford, Madison, Old Saybrook, Essex, Glastonbury, South Glastonbury

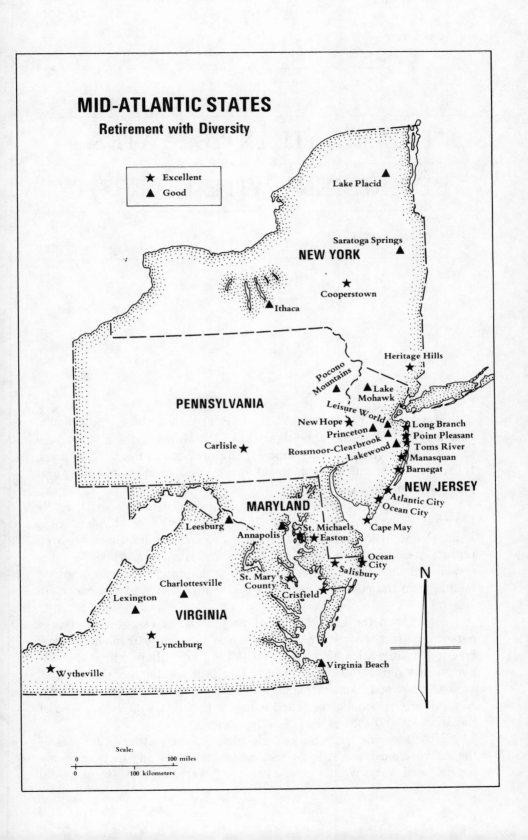

MID-ATLANTIC STATES

Retirement with Diversity

★ Excellent
▲ Good

Lake Placid

Saratoga Springs

NEW YORK

Cooperstown

Ithaca

Heritage Hills

Pocono
Mountains

Lake
Mohawk

PENNSYLVANIA

Leisure World

New Hope

Princeton

Rossmoor-Clearbrook

Lakewood

Long Branch
Point Pleasant
Toms River
Manasquan
Barnegat

Carlisle

NEW JERSEY

Atlantic City
Ocean City

MARYLAND

Leesburg

Annapolis

St. Michaels
Easton

Cape May

Ocean
City
Salisbury

St. Mary's
County

Crisfield

Charlottesville

Lexington

VIRGINIA

Lynchburg

Wytheville

Virginia Beach

N

Scale:

0   100 miles

0   100 kilometers

IV.

THE MIDATLANTIC STATES—

RETIREMENT WITH DIVERSITY

The Mid-Atlantic region takes tidbits from its neighbors: the Colonial charm of New England, the folksiness of the Midwest, the relaxed pace of the South. The area has some of the best museums, art galleries, theaters, restaurants, entertainment, recreation . . . and some of the worst poverty, crime and grime.

Parts of New York state wear a Pilgrim's hat. The South really begins in Virginia. And the accents flatten the further west you move in Pennsylvania. Italians, Jews, Germans, Poles, Irish and Slavs are well represented in many cities, as are Blacks and Hispanics, while the countryside remains mostly Anglo-Saxon. Each ethnic and racial group resists melting into the pot; each remains an identifiable part of the American stew.

Along with the individuality of people and places goes a distinct personality to the weather. Temperatures can range from just below freezing to torrid. Humidity can soar in the river valleys and in the low-lying areas along the coasts. But spring is a spectacular parade with azaleas, dogwood, camelias, apple and cherry blossoms leading the way. And fall brings a mellowness and mildness that rivals the homeyness of the Midwest and the color of New England.

You'll also find a diversity of topography. The magnificent vistas of the Appalachians and Adirondacks are matched by the inviting sandy beaches and warm waters off the coasts of Maryland and Virginia. And winter sports in the Alleghenies vie with the Christmas festivals in Williamsburg, Virginia and Bethlehem, Pennsylvania.

Take the best and leave the worst; you'll find good places to retire in this region. It is home to about one-third of the nation, and their Retirement Eden could lie just around the corner.

1. NEW YORK—HEAVEN AND HELL

If New York State were vertical, upstate could be heaven and downstate (New York City) hell. New York City has the best—but definitely the worst—of urban living. Upstate is pastoral, bucolic—perhaps the "pastures of heaven."

I recall my first visit to New York City. Although I was born and reared in Detroit and lived 17 years in the San Francisco Bay area, I was frightened by New York City's concrete jungle of narrow, congested streets. But I was awed when I traveled upstate. I was used to spectacular scenery in California, but this was better! I soon learned you don't have to travel to New Hampshire or Vermont for flaming fall foliage—it is just as brilliant in New York State.

I've since become convinced that if you live outside the metropolitan sprawl and go into New York City only when you want to—to have a gourmet meal or see a first-run show—you can have the best of both heaven and hell.

A lot of folks feel this way. New York state ranks second only to California in the number of seniors (over 2 million). Some 16.3 percent of the state's 18 million residents are 60 years of age and over; 11.6 percent over 65. Almost half these seniors live in New York City, but the upstate counties of Columbia, Sullivan, Essex, Greene, Montgomery, Albany, Broome, Cattaraugus, Cayuga and Hamilton all have over 14 percent elderly population.

Contrasting Geography and Climate

Although it is the largest of the Northeastern states and stretches 412 miles east to west and 312 miles north to south, the Empire State is only thirteenth in size. It is second in population.

The state slopes from 1-mile high Mount Marcy in the Adirondacks to the sea-level beaches of Long Island. The climate ranges from 200 inches of annual snowfall at Boonville in the north to 105°F. heat waves along the southern shore.

The northeast Adirondack uplands contain the highest and most rugged mountains. The St. Lawrence–Champlain lowlands extend from Lake

Ontario northeast along the Canadian border. The Hudson-Mohawk lowlands follow the flow of rivers east and west, and the Atlantic coastal plains lie in the southeast.

Along the eastern edge of the Catskills lies the Hudson River Valley. Well below the capital, Albany, the river cuts through the hills, forming the romantic Highlands region, where Rip Van Winkle and the last of the Mohicans roamed.

New York is the only state with shores on both the Atlantic Ocean and the Great Lakes. Water also dominates the interior, with more than 4,000 lakes and ponds and 800 miles of barge canals. Almost one-third the state is forested. Between the Hudson, Mohawk and St. Lawrence rivers and the forests lie some of the state's best retirement areas.

As to climate, here are averages for different parts of the state:

	Winter	Spring	Summer	Fall
Albany (central)	29°F.	34°F.	66°F.	61°F.
Buffalo (northwest)	25°F.	44°F.	68°F.	51°F.

Statewide, rainfall averages 67 inches; snowfall, 30 inches; humidity, 68 percent.

Contrasts in Medical Care

New York offers some of the best and worst, some of the most and least expensive, health care. The reason for these ambiguities: the best and most expensive health care is in New York City. The least expensive and worst (in number of physicians per 100,000 population) are in the upstate, rural areas. The state has 368 hospitals with a total of 134,425 beds. There are 547 nursing homes with 77,758 beds and 480 personal-care homes with 26,765 beds. The average rate for a semiprivate hospital room is $193 daily (national average, $163 daily). Again, this figure is skewed by New York City hospitals, which can cost upward of $300 a day for a semiprivate room.

The High and Low Cost of Housing

The farther you are away from the bedroom communities of New York City and the state's other large cities, the lower your cost of housing. It is possible to find good retirement homes in desirable rural areas for $50,000 and apartments for $300 a month. New York is big on specially designed apartment units for the elderly, with special facilities such as hand rails, alarm systems and doors wide enough to be used by people in wheelchairs. Many of these are located on the fringes of metropolitan areas: Westchester County, just across the New York City line, has a majority of such units.

Vacillating Taxes

At one point New York (especially New York City) was one of the highest taxed areas in the United States. However, recent tax cuts that become fully effective in 1981 mean that the tax burden will ease in all income brackets. For those with an adjusted gross income of $10,000, the burden will drop the most to twenty-fourth highest ($130 on $10,000 taxable income); in the $15,000 range, the state will rank fifteenth, ($295.20 on $15,000 taxable income); and in the $25,000 range, the burden will drop to seventh highest ($1,048.50 on $25,000 taxable income). In property tax, the burden is higher in smaller communities. In Albany you pay $1,730 taxes annually on a $50,000 home, but in New York City (where most people live in apartments) the tax would be $955 annually.

Also, New York has a circuit breaker real property tax credit or rebate—a maximum of $200 credit or rebate to homeowners or renters with a gross annual income of $12,000 or less (this will be raised in future years). Also, for homeowners with incomes from $3,000 to $8,000 annually (may be raised), localities can offer senior citizens a real property tax exemption up to 50 percent of the assessed value. And the state is reducing the percentage of sales tax charged on home heating oil, with some localities offering tax concessions to seniors. Here is a further tax breakdown:

Sales Tax—the state rate is 4 percent, but many counties and localities add additional levies up to 7 percent. In New York City and Yonkers the rate is 8 percent, but in many retirement areas the effective rate is only 5 to 6 percent. Exempt are most foods, drugs, eyeglasses, hearing aids, prosthetic devices, medical equipment and supplies.

Because of the heavy sales tax and high cost of medical care (and food and other essentials) the cost of living in *New York City* can run 10 to 15 percent above the national average. But in upstate New York, particularly in rural areas, the costs could well be below the national average. Nevertheless, you would need an annual income (for a couple) of at least $10,000 annually to retire in the Empire State.

Vast Indoor and Outdoor Recreation Programs

Most of the best indoor recreational and cultural facilities are located in New York City. The Metropolitan Museum of Modern Art, Whitney, Frick, Guggenheim, and numerous other art museums are here; on- and off-Broadway theater productions, Lincoln Center for the Performing Arts. Upstate has most of the outdoor recreational regions, with vast park systems in the Allegheny, Finger Lakes, Genessee, Niagara, Saratoga, and Thousand Lakes areas.

The Recreation Program for the Elderly, a matching state-aid program for municipalities, is unique. Because of it, hundreds of thousands of older New Yorkers can participate in special activities (arts and crafts; dramatic, literary, musical excursions; hobbies; indoor and outdoor games and sports; social) provided by localities.

Complete Services for Seniors

The New York State Office for the Aging provides funding and programs on the state and local levels in such areas as finance, health, housing, transportation, leisure activities, legal services and nutrition. These programs are among the most advanced in the nation, and the information published by this office and local offices on aging, is among the most comprehensive in the field. The office even has a hot line (1-800-342-9871) for seniors to call for help with a problem and/or for information about programs and services in their areas.

For further information, write:

New York State Office for the Aging
Empire State Plaza
Albany, NY 12223
or
2 World Trade Center
New York, NY 10047

MAJOR RETIREMENT AREAS

Heritage Hills (pop. 2,000) lies outside *Somers* (pop. 13,000) in northern Westchester County (about 50 miles north of New York City). Heritage Hills is a sister development of *Heritage Village* (see section on Connecticut), but is younger both in terms of development and age of residents. By 1980, about 1,000 units had been built at Heritage Hills; when completed in 6 or 7 years, it will contain 3,000 units on 1,000 acres of prime land. The average age of Heritage Hills residents is 54 years of age (compared with 65 at Heritage Village), and while the first settlers grow older, newcomers to the community will be in their late 40s and 50s. Most residents still work full time, commuting to New York City, an hour's drive or train ride.

Heritage Hills attracts upper-income professionals and white-collar workers, most of whom formerly lived in central Westchester County; 25 percent formerly lived in New York City. An increasing number of new residents are from northern Westchester.

These people generally have incomes averaging $40,000. They need a good income to live in Heritage Hills, because units range from $75,000 to $140,000. Monthly costs, including association and society fees, sewer and water, electricity (including heat), and taxes, run $350 to $600 a month. Add the burden of a mortgage and monthly carrying costs could easily be $600 to $800 a month.

What do residents get for their money? A 9-hole and an 18-hole golf course, and a main activities center which includes a private health club especially designed and equipped with a gym, whirlpool bath and saunas. It is located next to a large heated swimming pool, 2 tennis courts and 2 paddle-tennis courts. In addition, satellite recreational facilities, each with swimming pool and tennis or paddle courts, are located throughout Heritage Hills.

Recently, Heritage residents passed a $580,000 bond issue to build a library. And many residents participate in the full range of activities and clubs, recreational and cultural, available in Somers.

You can keep up with developments by sending for a sample copy of the slick newsmagazine, "The Heritage Reporter." Write Heritage Reporter, Heritage Development Group, Heritage Village, Southbury, CT 06488.

For further information, write:

Heritage Hills of Westchester
Somers, NY 10589

Saratoga Springs (pop. 28,000) is for those who like to recapture a sense of the past while enjoying the comforts of the present. Located 200 miles north of New York City, this was a fashionable health spa in the nineteenth century. The fashionable crowds may have disappeared except in August, but the beautiful scenery is still there, and a dozen operating springs and geysers remain in the town. Many smart retirees take advantage of the opulence that attracted their ancestors while avoiding the crowds that flock here in July and August for horse racing and other activities.

There is certainly a lot to see and do year-round. The state mineral baths and health clubs are open at convenient hours; there is harness racing from April to November and thoroughbred racing in late July and August. The Saratoga Performing Arts Center, summer home of the New

York City Ballet and the Philadelphia Orchestra, has an amphitheater
seating over 5,000 persons with lawn space for 100,000 more, and Skidmore College holds its own music festival.

Saratoga Lake offers excellent swimming, boating and fishing. There
are indoor and outdoor pools around the city, and there are several golf
courses in the area. Besides the activities at Skidmore College, cultural
events take place at Yaddo, an estate at the edge of town which is a
working haven for artists and writers.

Those with arthritis and/or cardiovascular ailments will be most interested in the spa. The baths have all the accouterments of the Gay 90s,
from the rose-colored tones of the lobby to cushioned wicker chairs and
elegant fountains. A 90-minute bath and massage in a private room costs
$15.

Wherever you go in Saratoga Springs you'll see mementos of the
opulent past. Congress Park on Broadway features the casino and two
historical museums. New shops and boutiques are opening in restored
brick buildings dating from the 1890s, and the smaller streets that branch
off Broadway are lined with Victorian homes of every style, from Italian
villa to French mansard, chateau and baroque. Many were in rundown
condition only a few years ago, but are now restored to their former
grandeur. These mansions are worth hundreds of thousands of dollars
today but it is possible to buy more modest housing in the area, starting
from $40,000. Some rentals on a year-round basis are available from $200
a month. Saratoga Springs also has 3 retirement apartment buildings and
a nursing home.

For further information, write:

Chamber of Commerce
Saratoga Springs, NY 12866

Lake Placid (pop. 3,000), the site of the 1980 winter Olympics, lies
about 100 miles north of Saratoga Springs, 150 miles north of Albany, and
60 miles south of Montreal, Canada. The town is surrounded by the highest peaks in the Adirondacks (including the highest, 5,344-foot Mount
Marcy), and itself surrounds Lake Placid and Mirror Lake. The mean
temperature is about 10° cooler than in New York City, but it can range
from 20°F. in winter to 80°F. and higher in summer. Average annual
precipitation totals 40-inches of rain and 140 inches of snow.

Medical facilities are extensive, with 11 practicing physicians and 3
dentists in the area. Hospital facilities include Placid Memorial, Uihlein
Mercy Center (for extended geriatric care) and W. Alton Jones Cell Science Center (tissue research).

Housing and rentals are short in season (which usually means summer, although the town is a year-round resort). But some retirement homes are available from $50,000 and some rentals from $200 to $400 monthly on a year-round lease. The town contains a low-income housing complex that has units available for seniors.

The sales tax in town is 7 percent, and the combined property tax rate is $107.46 per $1,000 of assessed value outside the village. There is also a town-county tax within the village limits of $92.02 and within the Lake Placid School District of $122.32.

There's something going on year-round, with ice shows and games in winter and boat trips in summer. Many indoor cultural events are offered at the Center for Music, Drama, and Art and at the Lake Placid School of Art. You'll find two museums in the area: the Lake Placid Historical Society and the John Brown Farm, where the noted abolitionist is buried. You have an unusually large number of clubs to join, ranging from the bobsled and skating clubs to organizations for rocks and minerals, bridge, barbershop singing, square dancing, community theater, gardening. All service clubs have chapters, as do most of the religious groups, including a synagogue sisterhood and United Methodist Women. And there are organizations of special interest to seniors: a senior center and a meals-on-wheels program.

For further information, write:

Lake Placid Chamber of Commerce
Lake Placid, NY 12946

Cooperstown (pop. 2,500), a pleasant little town, is known as the "Village of Museums." It has a lot more to offer than the National Baseball Hall of Fame and a lot more activities than summer sports. Set in the midst of "Leatherstocking country," 70 miles west of Albany, it combines Victorian charm with modern facilities. Main Street retains a nineteenth-century appearance in its red brick public buildings and the cast-iron lampposts that have hanging planters of petunias. Some historic homes are also on Main; at the corner of River Street is a 1790 2-story white clapboard that sits back from the sidewalk behind a low hedge. A block from Main are more elaborate homes facing Lake Otsego. Some, like Edgewater, built in 1809 of brick with a bow front and 4 side chimneys, are private mansions half-hidden behind protective hedging. Others, like the 1816 Basset House around the corner on Fair Street, mingle with white Colonial-style houses with black shutters. Most of these homes are on maple- and elm-shaded streets and are surrounded by white picket fences.

Some of these homes are available from $70,000, but you can find more modest accommodations from $50,000. Some year-round rentals are available for $400 to $500 a month. Taxes are relatively low, and Cooperstown has one of the best hospitals in upstate New York.

Once you're settled, you can live for a lot less than in most urban areas. Many retirees raise their own vegetables or buy local produce in the Farmers Market in Middlefield, 5 miles away. And there are many activities: adult-education classes, hunting and golf, swimming, hiking and social clubs like the Glimmerglass Circle or the Mohican Club.

In addition to the Baseball Hall of Fame, there is a Farmers' Museum and the resurrected Village Crossroads (a living history museum of the early New York frontier), Fenimore House (a distinguished museum) and the Doubleday Batting Range, equipped with automatic pitching machines. Nearby is the Mt. Otsego Ski Area and Glimmerglass State Park, offering major outdoor activities.

For further information, write:

Chamber of Commerce
Cooperstown, NY 13326

Ithaca (pop. 28,500) is my ideal college town. It was my first introduction to the Ivy League (Cornell University), and its red brick campus, lush trees and vines, cascading waterfalls, deep gorges and lakes are picture-postcard stamped on my mind. Located on Cayuga, the largest of the 11 Finger Lakes, it offers all the amenities of a college town: low-cost eating and living and cultural activities associated with the university. On campus are the Herbert F. Johnson Museum of Art (permanent and loan exhibitions) and the Franklin Hall Art Gallery (student work and other exhibits); little theater groups; musical activities. Off campus is the DeWitt Historical Society and Museum, a state park and marvelous swimming, boating, and fishing facilities on Lake Cayuga. The great depth of this lake (420 feet) ensures that it stays cool until late in July and is warm through October.

Ithaca is a shopping and browsing paradise. The DeWitt Building, on the corner of Seneca and Cayuga streets, houses an impressive array of shops, including the Bookery, a wood-beamed secondhand bookstore. In fact, Ithaca probably has one of the highest per capita ratios of bookstores in the country—17 in all, including the oldest, the Corner Bookstore, on South Cayuga Street. At Handwork, on State Street, you'll find a cooperative store offering patchwork, weaving, wood, pottery and other craft items. Both crafts and hobbies are big in this town, with annual craft fares and hobby shows. This is also a great area for local produce (especially apples), and every Saturday and Wednesday local growers sell organically fertilized zucchini, tomatoes, corn, fresh honey and many varieties of apples not available in most cities.

Thanks to the student population and modestly salaried faculty, many good small retirement homes are available for under $50,000, and year-round rentals are available if you can snap one up before the college season begins. And if you can settle in like the students and faculty, you'll find that you can enjoy an Ivy League existence on a sandlot income.

For further information, write:

Chamber of Commerce
Ithaca, NY 14850

For those who want to retire nearer New York City but not be sucked in by the urban sprawl, there are the *Hamptons* and *Montauk* on Long Island, and towns in Putnam County like *Brewster, Pawling* and *Wingdale.*

SUMMARY

Retirement in New York State can be heaven or hell. Just skip New York City (except for an occasional visit on your own terms) and you'll avoid the one and enjoy the other. And if you do retire upstate, you'll have the best of both the Victorian and modern worlds. Here are my ratings of the major retirement areas:

Excellent — Heritage Hills, Cooperstown
Good   — Saratoga Springs, Lake Placid, Ithaca

2. NEW JERSEY—SEASHORE AND COUNTRYSIDE

New Jersey has some of the problems but most of the privileges of neighboring New York. If you avoid the ugly cities but seek the lovely countryside and seashore, you'll know why this is called the "Garden State."

And although New Jersey has more people per square mile than any other state in the union, most of them are jammed into the cities of Newark, Trenton (the capital), Jersey City, Orange, Elizabeth, Passaic and Atlantic City, leaving the countryside relatively unspoiled.

Another aspect often overlooked: except for the 48 miles along its northern border with New York State, New Jersey is washed on all sides by water, giving it a varied seacoast that makes it prime vacation land.

New Jersey also has a varied population with major ethnic groups—
Italians, Germans and Poles lead the list. There are the white-collar com-
muters of Bergen and Passaic counties; the dairy farmers of the northern
lake country; the dockside workers of Port Newark and the shipbuilders
of Camden: the students and faculty at Princeton and Rutgers; the Blacks
that make up half of Newark; the retirees that live by the shore.

Some 15.8 percent of the 7.5 million population is age 60 and over and
11 percent is over age 65. Greatest numbers of seniors live in Essex,
Bergen and Hudson counties although the greatest percentages live in the
seacoast counties of Cape May, Ocean and Atlantic.

From Highlands to Lowlands

Like New York, New Jersey slopes from the highlands of the northwest to the lowlands of the southeast. It has Appalachian highlands, a
piedmont plateau and a coastal plain in the southeast that covers three-
fifths of the state.

The climate is relatively moderate, with marked differences between
the northwest and southeast. At Trenton, in the center of the state,
winters average 40.2°F., summers 66.8°F. There are 193 sunny days, 47.13
inches of rain and 17.2 inches of snow, with 70.6 percent humidity annually.

Above Average Health Care and Costs

New Jersey has 177 doctors per 100,000 population, a bit above the
average of 174 per 100,000. There are 139 hospitals with a total of 44,157
beds. A semiprivate hospital room costs $177 daily (national average,
$163). And the state has 290 nursing homes with 28,396 beds and 177
personal-care homes with 5,580 beds. New Jersey hospitals bill by the
illness, not the stay, which reduces cost.

Plenty of Good Retirement Housing

You'll find a good selection of retirement housing in the countryside
and seashore areas. Much of this is in adult communities in Middlesex
County (Clearbrook and Rossmoor Leisure World), Monmouth County
(Shadow Lake Village, Cheshire Square and Covered Bridge) and Ocean
County (Leisure Village and Leisure Knoll, Holiday City, Silver Ridge
Park, Crestwood Village). You'll pay an average of $70,000 for a 2- to
3-bedroom home.

Above Average Tax Burden

The personal income tax is at the rate of 2 percent on the first $20,000 of taxable income and 2.5 percent on taxable income in excess of $20,000. This places New Jersey sixth highest in tax burden in the $10,000–$20,000 income bracket and tenth in the $20,000–$25,000 bracket. Persons over age 65 and those who are blind get an additional $1,000 exemption.

Amounts received under Social Security or Railroad Retirement are totally excluded, as is a person's contribution to a private or public pension fund. Some exemptions are granted persons 62 or over on pension income up to $7,500 for a single person ($10,000 for a couple). Here are other tax breakdowns:

Property Tax Concessions—residents age 65 or over whose annual income does not exceed $5,000 (exclusive of Social Security) are allowed a tax deduction of $160. Rebates on taxes are also allowed according to place of residence, with the average rebate being $240. Renters are eligible for a credit of $65 against state income taxes, and those age 65 or older get an additional credit of $35.

Sales Tax—the rate is 5 percent, with food, clothing and prescription drugs exempt. Some localities add an additional tax.

Historic and Cultural Attractions

As some 4 major battles and 90 minor engagements were fought in New Jersey during the Revolutionary War, the state has more than its share of historic sites. It also has 4 unique historic villages or communities, including *Ringwood* on State Highway 511 near the New York border; *Batsto Village* in the southern area; *Allaire Village* near the Monmouth battlefield and *Liberty Village* near Flemington. Each parklike site offers a full day of sightseeing and recreation. You can also visit the Thomas A. Edison laboratory in West Orange, where the famous inventor worked for 44 years. Other museums include the New Jersey State Museum Cultural Center in Trenton, which has a collection of Jerseyana: glass, ceramics, dioramas of the Lenni Lenape Indians (early settlers), industrial models, carriages, home and farm tools, historic and modern art. There are famous libraries at both Princeton and Rutgers. Musical events take place in Ocean City, Sea Isle City, Asbury Park and Newark. As to sports, New Jersey offers skiing in Sussex and other higher-elevation counties, thanks to snow-making equipment. For spectator sports, there is nothing like the Meadowlands Sports Complex (near East Rutherford), which features year-round nighttime trotting and thoroughbred racing, professional soccer and football. There is also thoroughbred racing and trotting at Atlantic City, harness racing at Freehold, thorough-bred racing near Asbury Park and auto racing at the Trenton International Speedway.

Selective Services for Seniors

The New Jersey Division on Aging works with community and area agencies on aging to provide programs and services in each of the major areas: nutrition, health, housing, finance, legal matters and leisure time. The division publishes a helpful list of retirement housing in the state and has an ombudsman program for institutionalized elderly.

For further information, write:

New Jersey Division on Aging
CN800
Trenton, NJ 08625

MAJOR RETIREMENT AREAS

The Jersey Shore—Retirement with Sun and Fun

The fabulous Jersey shore contains more than 100 miles of beaches, resorts, marinas, fishing piers, bird sanctuaries, bay areas and even gambling casinos. The area starts at Sandy Hook, a 1,600-acre peninsula whose gorgeous beaches are open to the public, and ends at Cape May, the southernmost tip of the state, which was America's first, and at one time foremost, seaside resort.

In between are a string of oceanfront resorts, each with its special characteristics and appeal. Each seems to have attracted its own "crowd" from sections of New Jersey or New York or from religious groups. Some resorts operate like exclusive clubs and have special regulations. But these barriers are coming down, and even if you don't flock with your birds, you'll find a place where you can feel at home.

These areas have attracted many seniors; the numbers tell the story. Of the major counties forming the Jersey coast, Atlantic County has 21.8 percent over age 60, Cape May 27.4 percent, Middlesex 11.2 percent, Monmouth 15.1 percent and Ocean 25.4 percent.

Using Ocean County as a focal point for this area, here are some facts about retirement along the Jersey shore.

Climate and Environment. Sun, sand and surf mark this area. Much of this outdoor playland is on a long, narrow strip of barrier beach, with sheltered bay bathing and water sports only a short walk from the broad white beaches on the ocean side. Towns like *Point Pleasant Beach*, *Seaside Heights* and *Beach Haven* combine beach and boardwalk with amusement rides and arcades. During the summer there are special events, ranging from fishing tournaments, yacht races and powerboat races to art festivals and band concerts. Spring and fall offer Easter parades and boat shows. But during the winter most residents hibernate or fly south. In January the temperature averages 25°F.; in April, 65°F.: July, 75° F.; October, 40° F. There are about 5 inches of snow a year, and noise and air pollution are "moderate."

Medical Facilities. You'll find major hospitals in Toms River, Lakewood, Manahawkin and Point Pleasant. The latter hospital gives free health and medical information from its tape library, (609) 899-2400. For shut-ins there are an active visiting nurse program operating out of Toms River and Manahawkin, and meals-on-wheels programs centered in Toms River, Lakewood, Manahawkin and Atlantic City. Nursing homes are located in Bayville, Point Pleasant, Toms River and Lakewood.

Housing Availability and Cost. Some of the major retirement communities (with population figures) are: Crestwood Village (4,500), Leisure Village (2,500), Holiday City (2,300), U.S. at Greenbriar (1,500), Leisure Village East (1,500) and Cedar Glen Lakes (1,100). Mobile-home parks are also plentiful, with major ones located in Barnegat, Lakehurst, Toms River, Jackson, Laurelton, Beach Haven, Manahawkin, Whiting, Mantoloking and Lakewood. And there are senior housing developments in Lakewood, Manchester Township, Toms River, Manahawkin, Brick Town, Tuckerton and Berkeley Township. Generally, 2- and 3-bedroom homes sell from $60,000. You can rent small homes, condominium and coop apartments and townhouses from $350 a month. Building lots sell from $8,000.

Cost of Living. Living costs aren't necessarily low, but seniors enjoy many discounts. Property taxes run 2 to 4 percent of market value. Many stores offer discounts to seniors, and anyone 62 or older can get a half-fare bus pass. For those 65 or older, the toll on 4 bridges owned by the Delaware River Port Authority is only 30¢, or you can buy a book of 20 tickets for $6. Seniors also enjoy a hot-meal program (where they can pay what they like) at Toms River, Lakewood, Jackson, Point Pleasant, Tuckerton, Brant Beach and Barnegat.

Leisure-Time Activities. The shore areas have many county, state and national parks and forests (including Gateway National Park at Sandy Hook). Fishing is great here on ocean, bay and river. Catches include bluefish, striped bass, flounder, perch, weakfish, fluke, mackerel, cod, whiting, ling and trout. You can go after the plentiful Jersey blue claw crabs or clams. Waterfowl hunting is also a major sport. And, of course, boating is a favored activity from dozens of fine marinas. There are several golf courses and tennis courts in the area as well as racquetball and handball courts. Add summer concerts, the Garden State Art Center at Holmdel (concerts, theatrical productions, lectures), Ocean County College (which offers seniors courses at no cost) and major libraries at Toms River, Beachwood, Brick Town, Point Pleasant and Tuckerton. There are 200 clubs serving all major interests.

Special Services for Seniors. There are scores of senior centers and clubs, located in most areas. Ocean County has a senior coordinating council and several county-wide organizations, including a chapter of the American Association of Retired Persons (AARP), a Golden Key Club and organizations serving retirees belonging to the Bell System, retired federal employees, retired policemen and firemen, educators and Western Electric employees. Major services are provided by area and local councils on aging, which have senior outreach programs. These programs are designed to seek out seniors and identify their needs. All outreach programs have vans and provide limited transportation. In addition, outreach projects provide telephone reassurance, friendly visitors and information and referral. Outreach programs are located in Berkeley and Brick Townships, Lakewood/Jackson, Manchester Township, Shore Area and Southern Ocean County. Also, the Ocean County Handicapped Elderly Transportation program provides transportation for kidney dialysis, cobalt and chemotherapy patients. Dover Township has a multipurpose senior center providing outreach, transportation, health services, counseling, information and referral. The Church of St. Martha, Point Pleasant, provides similar services plus a daily round of activities open to all seniors.

Jersey Shore Communities

Long Branch (pop. 35,000) was the nation's leading playground in the 1870s and 1880s, when it played host to President Grant and rich New Yorkers, including Diamond Jim Brady, who built elaborate summer homes here. Some of these homes still survive as a faint reminder of bygone days, but more modern structures have taken over, including an 800-foot fishing pier, longest on the East Coast, which is open 24 hours. Long Branch boasts 3 miles of sandy beaches and 5 city-run beach areas supervised by lifeguards. At *Oceanport*, near Long Branch, is the Monmouth Park Jockey Club, the nation's oldest center for breeding and racing horses.

Asbury Park (pop. 18,000) has been a popular shore resort since its founding in 1817. Not only does the Atlantic Ocean lap its beaches, but 3 lakes are part of the town. Asbury Park claims to be the center of one of the best saltwater fishing grounds in the world. Just south of Asbury Park is *Ocean Grove* (pop. 7,000) which is notable because, until April 1980, this Methodist community had local "blue laws" banning Sunday driving and sunbathing. In an attempt to circumvent the court ruling striking down such laws, several residents began a campaign to have the community incorporated as a borough so it could enforce its own laws.

Lakewood (pop. 40,000) is an active resort town offering both indoor and outdoor activities. About 20 percent of the residents are retired, and the area offers excellent medical care: a major hospital with 265 beds, 8 nursing homes, 3 personal-care homes, 10 doctors, 20 dentists and 36 specialists. Many people live in modest retirement homes selling for $60,-000, or rent 2- and 3-bedroom units from $350 a month. Adult-education classes at the community school are popular. There are 3 parks, 3 tennis courts, a golf course and biking and hiking facilities. Lakewood has 2 major retirement developments, *Leisure Village* and *Leisure Village East.* Both offer residents arts and crafts clubs, lakes stocked for fishing, a golf course, swimming pools, and year-round sponsored trips. *Leisure Village West* is located in nearby *Lakehurst.* The township also has 2 country clubs (1 private) and 2 parks, the major one being 323-acre Ocean County Park. Most senior activities are centered in nearby *Toms River.* Also nearby is 10-mile long *Island Beach,* one of Jersey's loveliest stretches of seashore dunes, and *Long Beach Island,* a 19-mile-long sandbar which is ideal for sailing, boating, fishing, shelling and swimming.

Atlantic City (pop. 50,500), home of bathing beauties, the Boardwalk and now legalized gambling, is the best known of Jersey's beach resorts and has been dubbed "Playground of the World" and "Las Vegas with a Seashore." Besides honeymooners, conventioneers and gamblers, Atlantic City attracts many retirees, who bask in its equitable year-round climate. The city is built on Absecon Island and is shielded by the curve of the coast from battering northeast winds. The nearby Gulf Stream warms the waters and keeps the weather relatively mild year-round. The residents enjoy strolling or rolling (in the famous chairs) along the Boardwalk, a 60-foot-wide partly wooden structure that runs 5 miles along the length of the beach. To protect the beaches from erosion, 5 huge piers jut out into the ocean; the piers, too, offer food and entertainment. With the introduction of gambling, Atlantic City is undergoing renovation— whether for better or worse, it is too soon to tell. But it is worth a look as a possible Retirement Eden.

Ocean City (pop. 15,000) would be a fine place if you were a churchgoing Methodist, preferably from Philadelphia, and had lots of money. The town was founded in 1879 to appeal to such people, and some of that aura remains. You won't find any bars or liquor stores here, but you will find 8 miles of lovely beaches, 2.5 miles of boardwalk and excellent swimming, boating, fishing, tennis and golf. A very good hospital, Shore Memorial, is close by, as is the Atlantic City Community College, which offers many adult-education classes appealing to retirees. And the many churches have "standing room only" at Sunday morning and evening services.

Cape May (pop. 5,000), one of the nation's first resorts, has been restoring many of its famous old homes and hotels to create a Victorian city. This resort is situated at the southernmost tip of the state (the same latitude as Washington, D.C.) and enjoys a southern climate moderated by sea breezes. Its 4 miles of beautiful beaches and 1¼-mile paved promenade offer vacationers and residents varied entertainment. Fishing is a big sport here, and at Fisherman's Wharf you can watch the activity while eating in a seafood restaurant. Transportation is good here, with a local airport and ferry service across the estuary to Delaware.

For further information, write: Chamber of Commerce

Asbury Park, NJ 07712   Manahawkin, NJ 08050
Atlantic City, NJ 08401   Ocean City, NJ 08226
Barnegat, NJ 08005   Ocean Grove, NJ 07756
Brick Town, NJ 08723   Point Pleasant, NJ 08742
Cape May, NJ 08204   Toms River, NJ 08753
Lakewood, NJ 08701   Tuckerton, NJ 08087
Long Branch, NJ 07740

Central New Jersey

Rossmoor and *Clearbrook* are adult communities located near *Jamesburg* (pop. 6,000), about 45 miles from New York City and 12 miles from Princeton and New Brunswick. Many residents commute daily by bus to New York City, so the average age is younger than in many retirement communities (many residents are in their late 40s and 50s). These are completely self-contained communities, offering full recreational services, clubhouses, swimming pools, tennis courts, libraries, golf, shuffleboard, security protection and 24-hour emergency medical service. Housing starts in the $60,000s in Clearbrook, with monthly maintenance fees of $100 a month and real estate taxes of $120 a month. At Rossmoor, housing is available in a wider range of prices starting around $40,000 and going up to $125,000. Monthly maintenance fees run over $100 and taxes average $130 a month. These places appeal to younger retirees (including widows) or the semiretired who are seeking "active retirement living" in a country-club atmosphere.

For further information, write:

Rossmoor and Clearbrook
128 Sussex Way
Jamesburg, NJ 08831

Princeton (pop. 14,000), considered one of the prettiest of university sites, offers all the advantages of retirement in a college town: moderate cost of living and housing in a pleasant environment. Most of the activities center around the university campus, which includes the Firestone Library, Woodrow Wilson School of Public and International Affairs, University Art Museum, Nassau Hall (where Congress met when Princeton was the national capital), the Putnam Sculptures and McCarter Theater. Many retirees take an active part in campus activities and attend classes. Besides stimulating intellectual events, Princeton offers many outdoor activities, including golf, riding, tennis, swimming and hiking. The town has many eighteenth-century buildings and homes, most of which have been lovingly preserved. The entire setting is soothing to the body as well as stimulating to the mind.

For further information, write:

Chamber of Commerce
Princeton, NJ 08540

Northern New Jersey

Lake Mohawk is located near *Sparta* (pop. 28,000), about 40 miles northwest of New York City. This area has been dubbed "Pilotsville, N.J." because of the large concentration of pilots who live here. These highly paid, sophisticated and intelligent people have upgraded this community as well as increased the value of its properties. Many pilots have bought the former luxury summer homes of wealthy New Yorkers and have renovated them so that their selling price is around $100,000 (the average home in Sparta costs $80,000). The aviators have also developed sailing, tennis, skiing and other outdoor recreational facilities and many other community activities. Some pilots have even retired here to become local merchants and real estate agents. You don't have to be a pilot to live here, but it would be wise to be one if you want to feel at home.

For further information, write:

Chamber of Commerce
Sparta, NJ 07871

SUMMARY

The Garden State offers good retirement living if you concentrate on the seashore and countryside and ignore the cities. Living costs aren't necessarily low, although a retired couple could live moderately on around $10,000 annually (exclusive of taxes). And for those who would like an occasional trip into New York City while enjoying the advantages of country living, New Jersey might be the Retirement Eden. Here are my ratings of the major areas:

Excellent — New Jersey shore
Good   — Rossmoor, Clearbrook, Lake Mohawk (if you're a pilot), Princeton, Leisure World

3. PENNSYLVANIA—RICHNESS IN RESOURCES

Perhaps no other Eastern state offers such a rich variety of topography, communities, religions, people and resources. Starting with gently rolling farmland in the east, the land swells westward in 3 mountain ranges, leaving mountain and valley, river and stream, farm and mine in its wake.

At the eastern edge lies the historic city of Philadelphia. Toward the western edge towers the steel-forged town of Pittsburgh. In between are factory and mill towns; communities so rural they don't use electricity; coal mines and oil wells deep in the bowels of the earth; smoke stacks towering toward heaven and belching the brimstone fire of hell.

The people are just as diverse. While the major ethnic groups are the Italians, Poles, Germans and English of many eastern states, no other state has the Pennsylvania Dutch (actually a mixture of German and Swiss) who settled the countryside mainly to escape religious persecution in the old country. Many of the "Plain People"—Amish, Mennonites and Dunkards—live as they did centuries ago. They shun electricity, gadgets, automobiles and fancy clothes, preferring to dress in simple black and drive a horse and buggy. Many are farmers and, ironically, they often outproduce their mechanized neighbors: they are able to work when the fields are too soggy for tractors.

Residents of the Keystone State have a tradition of religous tolerance stemming from the Friends (Quakers), who originally settled here. This tolerance prevails today in literally hundreds of sects that practice their faith here and the numerous ethnic groups and races (although only 9 percent of the state is Black or Hispanic).

Some 16.9 percent of the approximately 12 million residents are over age 60; 11.8 percent over age 65.

Varied Topography and Climate

Although Pennsylvania is only thirty-third in size, it is the third most populous state. It is a horizontal state, 169 miles from north to south and 307 miles from east to west. Both eastern and western borders are relatively flat, with gently rolling farmland in the east, the Great Lakes and Great Plains in the west. Mountain ranges cut diagonally across the state: the Poconos in the northeast, the Appalachians and Alleghenies in the center portions. The climate is basically continental, with prevailing winds from the west that make for extremes of cold and heat, with heavy snows in the mountains and northern part of the state. At Harrisburg (the capital), winters average 38.8°F., summers 66.8°F. There are 191 sunny days, 59.27 inches of rain and 34 inches of snow annually. Annual humidity averages 68 percent.

Adequate, Below Average Health Care Costs

The number of physicians per 100,000 residents, 173, is more than adequate, and a semiprivate hospital room costs an average $159 daily, vs. the U.S. average of $163. The state has 313 hospitals with a total of 86,474 beds. There are 573 nursing homes with 55,289 beds and 103 personal-care homes with 6,602 beds.

Good Rural Housing Available

You can find good buys in small farms and in recreation-type housing, ranging in price from $25,000 for a 2-bedroom cabin to $200,000 for magnificent country estates. In between are many small farms and old country homes in the $50,000 to $70,000 range. In short, housing here is cheaper than in neighboring New Jersey and New York, with a greater variety available.

Moderate Cost of Living

Living costs and taxes are lower than in most eastern states, and they are generally lower in the western part of the state. Where the average retired couple needs $10,022 to retire moderately in the United States, they would need $10,495 annually in Philadelphia, $10,005 in Lancaster and $9,965 in Pittsburgh. Pennsylvania ranks eleventh in tax burden in the $10,000 range, fourteenth in the $15,000 to $20,000 range and sixteenth in the $25,000 taxable bracket.

Property Taxes—average 2 percent of market value (a little over

$1,000 annually on a $50,000 home). Persons 65 and older and widows and widowers 50 and over are entitled to rebates if their incomes are below $9,000 annually. Rebates are on a sliding scale, with a maximum of $400 annually. There's also an "intangibles property tax," which some counties impose at the rate of 4 mils per dollar on mortgages, shares of stock and public loans.

Sales Tax—the rate is 6 percent, with exemptions for medicines and medical supplies, utilities for residential use and household supplies. Food is exempt except when consumed at a restaurant.

A Keystone of Culture

Pennsylvania has always been a leader of culture, especially in music (world-class symphony orchestras in Philadelphia and Pittsburgh), more than 140 institutions of higher learning, celebrated art galleries and museums. Probably the most famous outdoor museum is at Gettysburg, scene of the famous Civil War battle and Lincoln's Gettysburg address. The town of Bethlehem boasts the first museum in the United States and was the center of the first serious music heard in the colonies. The state is resplendent in historic sites from the Revolutionary War (Valley Forge) as well as the Civil War. A unique feature of Pennsylvania is the many farms and ranches that take in guests. City folks can spend several days working, eating and visiting with the farmer and his family, and learn an entirely different culture, especially if the farm is Amish, Mennonite or one of the other "Plain People."

Many Services for Seniors

The Pennsylvania Department of Aging brings to the state's older citizens (through 49 area agencies on aging) services including information and referral, neighborhood senior centers, homemaker service, meals on wheels, domicilary and foster care, protective services and senior community service employment programs.

For further information, write:

> Office for the Aging
> Health and Welfare Building
> Rm. 540, P.O. Box 2675
> Harrisburg, PA 17120

MAJOR RETIREMENT AREAS

The Bounty of Bucks County

New Hope (pop. 1,500), just across the Delaware River from Lambertville, New Jersey, is the gateway to historic Bucks County and the keystone of lovely retirement country. Its rolling hills, wooded valleys, stone houses and colorful barns have long drawn landscape painters like Daniel Garber, William Lathrop, Edward Redfield, and John Folinsbee. With the artists came the writers and actors. The Bucks County Playhouse is one of the nation's oldest and most famous summer theaters. It opened on July 1, 1939 with Edward Everett Horton playing *Springtime for Henry*, and has been in business ever since.

Today, New Hope remains much of what it was and what it wants to be—a lovely village of fine art galleries, bookshops, antique shops, restaurants and outdoor cafés on the banks of the river and canal. The natural setting and quiet charms have attracted many retirees to this area.

Climate and Environment. The temperature in January averages 30°F., April 60°F., July 80°F., October 65°F. The driest month is August, the wettest April and May, with an average of 55 inches of rain (and some snow) falling annually. And although the area is only 20 miles from Trenton and 40 miles from Philadelphia, there is no noise or air pollution.

Medical Facilities. The town has 4 doctors, 3 dentists and 2 specialists. There are 2 hospitals within 12 miles and 2 clinics within 2 miles. And, of course, the vast medical resources of Philadelphia and Trenton are within 40 miles.

Availability and Cost of Housing. There is much actual and proposed building on the outskirts of town. Single-family homes average $90,000 and townhouses $65,000. Building lots start at $15,000. Some 1- and 2-bedroom homes and apartments are available for rent from $400 a month.

Cost of Living. Property taxes are 2 percent of market value (sometimes less). The retail sales tax is 5 percent. Food costs are medium-high, energy costs about average; other costs are in line with those in Trenton or Philadelphia.

Leisure-Time Activities. This area is alive with cultural activities, including theater, art, music, books, you name it. There are several clubs in New Hope covering gardening, crafts and hobbies, most sports and other interests. Adult-education classes are also popular, as are biking, hiking and horseback riding.

Special Services for Seniors. New Hope offers a hot-meal program for seniors, meals on wheels, visiting nurses, a transportation program, mobile units for the elderly and a legal aid program.

For further information, write:

New Hope Borough Council
P.O. Box 141
New Hope, PA 18938

I found the area around New Hope equally fascinating. Washington's famous crossing point on the Delaware is only 10 miles from town. About 4 miles south is the village of *Lahaska,* where there are about 50 shops in pleasant, landscaped grounds at Peddler's Village. At nearby *Doylestown* is the chateaulike structure belonging to Dr. Henry C. Mercer, who was curator of American and prehistoric archeology at the University of Pennsylvania. About 30 miles north is the "Christmas country" of Pennsylvania, with towns named *Bethlehem, Nazareth, Zionsville* and *Emmaus.* Bethlehem has year-round displays, climaxing at Christmas time. Pine Creek Gorge is the site of Pennsylvania's 50-mile-long Grand Canyon. This area also contains several nonprofit life-care communities, including *Cathedral Village* (Philadelphia), *Dunwoody Village* (Newtown Square), *Foulkeways* (Gwynedd), *Gloria Dei Village* (Holland), *Pennswood Village* (Newtown), *Rydal Park* (Rydal) and *Springfield* (Wyndmoor). The area has two total-life-care communities sponsored by the Religious Society of Friends (Quakers). These are *Kendal* and *Crosslands* located at Longwood in historic Chester County. Costs are shared by all members of the community based on apartment size and number of occupants.

For further information, write:

Kendal-Crosslands
Box 100
Kennett Square, PA 19348

The Pocono Mountains Playground

Some retirees have opted for the Pocono ("stream between the mountains") Mountains in northeastern Pennsylvania, about 70 miles from Philadelphia. Long a resort and honeymoon country, this 2,400-square-mile area extends north from the Delaware Water Gap into Pike, Carbon, Monroe and Wayne counties.

The Poconos offer something for everybody. Outdoor enthusiasts can have a field (and stream) day in more than 200 sites and lakes in the area, including 52-mile-long Lake Wallenpaupack. Nature lovers can wander through dense forests and view such sights as Bushkill Falls, billed as the "Niagara of the Poconos." There are plenty of hiking and riding trails, which are especially colorful during the fall and spring. There are many resorts and cabins to stay in year-round.

A note of caution: there have been a number of land sales and vacation home developments that have been promoted and sold in some questionable ways. If you do buy retirement acreage or a home here, be especially careful—have the deal checked by a lawyer familiar with local real estate laws.

For further information, write:

> Pocono Mountains Vacation Bureau
> Box K
> 1004 Main Street
> Stroudsburg, PA 18360

The Charm of Carlisle

Carlisle (pop. 20,000) was the scene of many historic events, and retains its eighteenth-century charm in its Colonial homes and lovely gardens. Beautiful Georgian doorways and village squares mark the area, and the town is the home of Dickinson College, named after John Dickinson, one of three Carlisle men who signed the Declaration of Independence. Carlisle is strategically located 18 miles west of Harrisburg, 184 miles east of Pittsburgh, 109 miles west of Philadelphia and 85 miles north of Baltimore. Its country-near-city locale has attracted retirees from all over who seek the advantages of the area.

Among these are the 254-bed Carlisle Hospital; homes that sell from $45,000 to $65,000, with rentals from $250 a month; property taxes that are generally under $1,000 for the average home; living costs that are lower than most neighboring urban areas; some job opportunities in service industries and in light manufacturing (shoes, carpets, rubber, crystals, electronics, clothing, manganese steel, paper products, glass); recreation that includes hunting and fishing, state park facilities, 2 summer theaters, tennis courts, 1 9-hole and 4 18-hole golf courses and 5 libraries, including the Dickinson College Library and Dickinson School of Law Library. In fact, many seniors attend classes at the college and some have part-time jobs there. Harrisburg Area Community College is also located in the area, offering other educational opportunities. The many churches and clubs in the area provide sociability for many older people. Other facilities include a Salvation Army Senior Action Center, a Golden Age

Club, a hot meal program for seniors, homemakers services, a transportation program, health clinics, counseling through a local office on aging, mobile units for the elderly and rehabilitation programs.

For further information, write:

Greater Carlisle Area Chamber of Commerce
P.O. Box 572
Carlisle, PA 17013

SUMMARY

Pennsylvania can offer a range of resources for the retiree at a generally lower price than New York or New Jersey. Medical facilities, housing and recreation programs in major retirement areas are especially good in the Keystone State. Here are my ratings of the major areas:

Excellent — New Hope, Carlisle
Good   — Pocono Mountains area

4. MARYLAND—WHERE THE NORTH MEETS THE SOUTH

As a border state, Maryland combines characteristics of both North and South: soft-spoken good manners and gracious rural living combined with modern urban hustle and bustle.

The Free State also contains a sampling of sandy beaches, gently rolling hills and blue-ridged mountains. Probably Maryland's most distinguishing feature is 195-mile-long Chesapeake Bay, which is intersected by 48 rivers and 102 branches. This creates 3,190 miles of tidal shoreline, providing every kind of aquatic sport. Chesapeake, meaning "great shellfish," is accurately named, for the bay yields crabs, clams and oysters that are a gourmet's delight.

Sportsmen find room to roam. You can bet on horse races at Pimlico, hunt deer in the mountains and geese on the Eastern Shore and visit historic sites of the Revolutionary and Civil wars.

There is also room for religious tolerance and racial harmony. Some 78.6 percent of the population is white, 20.1 percent is Black or Hispanic. Major ethnic groups include Germans, Italians, Russians, English and Poles.

Some 12.7 percent of the state's approximately 4.2 million people are over 60, and 8.7 percent over 65. While this makes Maryland somewhat sparse in older people, it doesn't mean that there aren't attractive places to retire.

East to West Topography, Climate

On the Eastern Shore and Maryland mainland are coastal plains. These rise to piedmont plateaus in the center of the state and soar to the Blue Ridge Mountains in the west. The climate also runs east to west, being humid subtropical in the east and continental in the west. Statewide, winter averages 35°F.; spring, 54°F.; summer, 74°F.; fall, 56°F. On the Eastern Shore, these temperatures might be 3 to 4 degrees warmer; in the mountains they could be 7 to 8 degrees cooler. There are an average of 186 sunny days per year, with 52.33 inches of rain and 13 inches of snow. Annual humidity averages 69 percent at Baltimore, higher on the Eastern Shore and lower in the mountains.

Top-Quality Health Care at Low Cost

Maryland has 271 doctors per 100,000 residents, vs. the national average of 174 per 100,000; a semiprivate hospital room costs $147 daily vs. the national average of $163. There are 85 hospitals with a total of 25,210 beds, 157 nursing homes with 16,825 beds and 34 personal-care homes with 2,329 beds.

Good, Low-Cost Rural Housing

The further you get from Washington, D.C. and Baltimore, the lower the cost of housing. In some of the more desirable rural areas you can get a good 2- to 3-bedroom house for $50,000; 2- to 3-bedroom apartments rent from $400 a month. Some residential developments have been built along the coast and Eastern Shore, where you can get good building lots for around $10,000.

Relatively High Taxes

The tax burden in Maryland is relatively high, with the burden ranked third in the $10,000 to $15,000 range, fourth in the $15,000 to $20,000 range and fifth in the $20,000 to $25,000 range. Here is the breakdown:

Income Tax— the state rate ranges from 2 percent on the first $1,000 to 5 percent on over $3,000 of taxable income. The 23 counties and Baltimore city levy local income taxes as percentages of state income tax at rates from 20 percent to 50 percent of the dollar amount of state income tax. Single persons and dependents get an $800 tax exemption, married people $1,600. Persons over 65 get an additional $800 exemption. There is some exclusion for pension income, but it is reduced by the amount of Social Security and/or Railroad Retirement benefits.

Property Taxes—homeowners, regardless of age, whose income doesn't exceed $200,000 may receive a tax credit against real property taxes. And renters age 60 or older may receive an additional tax credit against "assumed" property taxes in their monthly rent. Full taxes on a $50,000 house in Baltimore run $1,270 annually.

Sales Tax—the rate is 5 percent, with foods, medical supplies and medicines exempt.

Outdoor, Indoor Recreation

Maryland has 35 parks and recreational areas. They provide a variety of topography, scenery and recreational experiences for all age groups and for activities from strenuous to mild. Museums include those of the army (at Aberdeen) and navy (Annapolis). Other museums feature Colonial houses, rural activities, marine life, fine arts and wildfowl. Most of the historic sites are located in central Maryland, within an hour of Baltimore. And Washington's new metro system has service to suburban Maryland, bringing the nation's capital within easy reach.

Active Area, Local Agencies on Aging

In the major retirement areas and cities, area and local agencies on aging provide most of the basic services, including employment opportunities, hot meal programs, transportation, health clinics, legal services, housing and financial assistance. The state office on aging funds many of these programs and works with local leaders.

For further information, write:

> Office on Aging
> State Office Building.
> 301 West Preston Street
> Baltimore, MD 21201

MAJOR RETIREMENT AREAS

The major retirement areas surround Chesapeake Bay. These are divided into *Western Shore* and *Eastern Shore* communities. The Western Shore was the first part of Chesapeake Bay to be settled by Europeans, and its length is dotted with churches and other building dating from the 1600s. It is uncrowded and accessible, only 50 miles from both Washington and Baltimore. Two counties embrace the Western Shore.

Calvert (pronounced "culvert") County is the state's smallest, only 35 miles long and averaging 9 miles in width between the bay and the Patuxent River. St. Mary's County (where the state's first European settlers came ashore in 1634) provides 15 miles more of bay shoreline. And both counties feature cliffs, miles of good beaches, and crisp, salty air.

The Eastern Shore is better known, although the stakes are higher. It costs money to retire here, and it would help if you were a WASP (the telephone book lists mainly English names). Society is divided into three parts: the top stratum includes the DuPont estates, featuring acres of rolling lands and horses, which operate like a fiefdom. The second layer includes industrialists like Arthur Houghton (chairman of Steuben Glass) who cluster along the Wye River and dedicate themselves to philanthropic efforts to improve the neighborhood. And the third echelon includes writers (James Michener), TV personalities (Walter Cronkite) and politicians (Barry Goldwater) who vacation or summer here. Most of these arrived after the Bay Bridge was built which linked this remote area to the "mainland." But, even today, much of the Chesapeake Bay area remains unspoiled, with Colonial villages the rule rather than exception.

In general, land on the Chesapeake commands top dollar, with two acres of undeveloped waterfront going for as high as $60,000. Land values are 20 to 25 percent lower in Dorchester County which has marshland (and mosquitoes). Yet there is something for almost anyone who seeks Colonial charm so remote yet so near major metropolitan areas.

St. Mary's County for Unspoiled Retirement

St. Marys County, a long narrow peninsula jutting into Chesapeake Bay, is only an hour's drive from Washington, D.C. But this birthplace of Maryland still looks much as it did 300 years ago. At *St. Marys City* (pop. 500), the place in the riverbank where the first settlers came ashore is still covered with wild growth and marked only by a small stone bench. The Old State House is intact in its original form. And in nearby *Leonardtown* (pop. 2,000), there is a village green, clean air, lots of clear water and mild climate.

Large plantations still raise cash crops of corn, soy beans and tobacco. But these large farms and estates are gradually being split up into small parcels and sold to retired ex-servicemen and government employees who want to be within easy range of the capital.

There's much to be said for retirement in this area. The St. Marys-Leonardtown area has 38 physicians, 28 dentists and an excellent 95-bed hospital and 48-bed nursing home—more than adequate for the population. Housing is plentiful at a wide range of prices. A 2-bedroom retirement home may sell from $40,000 to over $100,000. Lower-cost housing is available in the 129-unit Cedar Lane Apartments, a project of the St. Marys Home for the Elderly in Leonardtown. Thanks to the naval air station at Lexington Park, ample apartment units are available, renting from $100 per bedroom. Taxes are low, only $2.15 per $100 assessed value. Building costs range from $35 to $40 a square foot.

Costs are generally lower here than elsewhere because most of the area merchants offer lower prices for seniors on such items as air conditioners, automobile parts, beauty shops, electrical appliances, energy (gas and oil), food and drugs, restaurant meals and theaters. And because there are many Amish farmers in the area, seniors can buy farm-fresh fruits and vegetables at lower prices, too.

For recreation and cultural activities, there are several theater groups in the area, many craft shops, clubs and antique shops. The library is located in a lovely old mansion, and there are many bookstores and newsstands. A wide range of adult-education classes is offered. There are almost 50 clubs in the area, including many which cater to older people. In fact, the St. Marys County Commission on Aging is unusually active, with programs in crisis intervention, friendly visiting, information and referral, in-home health care, legal and financial counseling, an outreach program, radio station, informative newsletter, shopping assistance, telephone reassurance, transportation, senior centers and many other activities.

For further information, write:

> St. Marys County Chamber of Commerce
> 5 East Park Avenue
> Leonardtown, MD 20650

Annapolis for Colonial Pride and Charm

Annapolis (pop. 35,000) is not only the capital of Maryland and home of the United States Naval Academy, but it is also one of the most attractive towns in America. It is reputed to have more Georgian homes and buildings than London; so much so that a square mile of these red brick and white-trim buildings has been made into a historic district.

Yet Annapolis is a living, vibrant city offering the most modern conveniences and services. Included are excellent hospitals (both public and private); reasonably priced homes (2- to 3-bedroom units sell from $60,000) considering the area; an adult country-club community where single-family patio and ranch houses sell from $70,000 to $90,000 (Heritage Harbour); a year-round recreational program including yachting, sailing, swimming, fishing, crabbing, tennis, golf and other sports. Annapolis even has a sailing school where beginners can learn the ropes in 2 days (Annapolis Sailing School, P.O. Box 3334, Annapolis, MD 21403).

Annapolis is particularly appealing to the northerner, since spring arrives earlier, autumn lingers longer and winter is a bit softer than the northern states.

For further information, write:

Chamber of Commerce
171 Conduit Street
Annapolis, MD 21401

The Eastern Shore for Retirement Living at High Cost or Low

The tidewater country of Maryland is probably one of the most unspoiled sections of our nation. The shore was settled mainly by farmers, with land grants stretching back to Colonial times. Now, 300 years later, the area is still mainly farmland, with the original landscape of forests, marshes and long, sandy beaches intact.

But the Eastern Shore is more than just a few scattered plantations. It is a neat harmony of river and stream and fine homes with grounds that go down to the water's edge.

This area has attracted both rich retirees (who buy $100,000 homes and $350,000 farms) and poor retirees (who buy $35,000 cottages) who want to be within an hour and a half of Washington (and just across the bridge from Annapolis). Here are the main areas in which they settle:

St. Michaels (pop. 1,500), a shipbuilding community which today houses the Chesapeake Bay Maritime Museum, where old sailing vessels are on display. The town also boasts a nineteenth-century lighthouse and the Log House, an example of pioneer building. You can take a boat tour around the river and get a fine view of some of the estates in the area.

Easton (pop. 8,500) is the seat of Talbot County. In a county with a population of only 26,900, it is estimated there are some 200 millionaires, including the DuPonts, Houghtons and Chryslers, who have built homes here. It is a picture-postcard pretty town with charming old brick houses, antique shops of art-gallery quality, the Academy of Arts, the Third Haven Quaker Meeting House (dating from 1682) and the big and popular Tidewater Inn, which offers hunters a 4:30 A.M. breakfast in season. The area is rich in game, as each fall the waterfowl fly south from Canadian nesting grounds and stop on the Eastern Shore. Some 550,000 geese and 200,000 ducks winter in this area, and it is estimated that hunters kill almost 300,000 birds a year. One drawback: erosion is a constant threat, and one landowner recently spent $65,000 trying to save 100 yards of shoreline.

Salisbury (pop. 16,000) is the Eastern Shore's only big town. It has a modern shopping center, a community center, state college, big country club and industrial park. Salisbury is a duck-hunting and deep-sea-fishing mecca and is also the heart of Maryland's vast broiler (chicken) industry. The annual National Indoor Amateur Tennis Championship is held here.

Crisfield (pop. 3,300) is the jumping off place for *Tangier* and *Smith Islands.* The inhabitants of these islands speak a near-Elizabethan form of English that is hard for outsiders to understand. Both islands are flat, sandy and surrounded by marshland. Houses are built on pilings, and Smith Island has tiny frame houses with small gardens, a raised pier for one of its streets and some old automobiles. There is no government, and no elected officials, jails or police on the islands, which helps to explain some of their charm.

Ocean City (pop. 2,000) is Maryland's only Atlantic Ocean resort. In summer 10 million tourists come here, where condominiums and carnival rides sprawl along 10 miles of beaches. At the south end of the development area are several fine hotels—including the Atlantic, which opened for business in 1875—and there is a shop-lined boardwalk which was built in 1902 and covers 3 miles. Many homes, farms and estates are for sale, ranging from $75,000 for a 2-bedroom ranch home near the beach to $90,000 for an estate on 5 acres of land. Some poultry farms are available near the beach, selling for $85,000 for 12 acres of land. You can buy 1 acre of prime development land for about $30,000.

For further information, write:

> Chamber of Commerce
> St. Michaels, MD 21663
> Easton, MD 21601
> Salisbury, MD 21801
> Crisfield, MD 21817
> Ocean City, MD 21842

This tidewater country continues down into Virginia. Even without a road map and a "Welcome to Virginia" sign you'll know when you've crossed the border. In Virginia the towns, creeks and rivers have retained their original Indian names—Nassawadox, Pungoteague, Onancock, Accomac and Assawoman—while Maryland uses the English names for its counties: Worcester, Somerset, Dorchester, Queen Annes and Kent.

SUMMARY

Maryland offers good retirement country within easy reach of Washington, D.C. This is especially attractive to ex-servicemen and government retirees who want to maintain ties with the capital. The retirement areas (especially those in St. Mary's County and the Eastern Shore) offer a rural contrast to bustling Baltimore. But while most costs are relatively low, taxes can be high, especially for those in upper-income brackets. Here are my ratings of the major areas:

Excellent — St. Marys County (St. Marys City and Leonardtown), the Eastern Shore (St. Michaels, Easton, Salisbury, Crisfield, Ocean City)

Good — Annapolis

5. VIRGINIA—WHERE THE SOUTH BEGINS

Virginia has a courtliness of manner and a graciousness of speech that stems from its geographical location (the first Southern state) and its 4 centuries of history. Here were fought major engagements of the Revolutionary and Civil wars, and here is the birthplace of 8 presidents. Memorials to these famous men are everywhere in the Old Dominion, to remind the visitor and newly arrived retiree of this state's rich heritage. There's something here for everyone:

In the highlands and mountains you can hike the famed Appalachian Trail, canoe on the Shenandoah, sail on the many lakes and ski in the Blue Ridge Mountains.

In the piedmont you can hunt, farm or just enjoy the rolling scenery.

In the tidewater country you can sail, fresh- and saltwater fish, swim and surf. And golf is a year-round activity, with more than 400 courses.

Virginia is home to many groups. The state is approximately 80.5 percent white and 18.7 percent Black and Hispanic. Major ethnic groups are English, German and Italian. Virginia's population is growing 40 percent faster than the national average.

Of the state's estimated 5.3 million residents, 12.8 percent are age 60 or over; 8.8 percent 65 and older.

Equable Topography and Climate

Like many of its neighbors, Virginia has a mountain and valley region in the west, including the Blue Ridge Mountains; rolling piedmont plateau in the central area, which is the main agricultural and manufacturing area;

and a tidewater or coastal plain that is flat, arable land cut by rivers and bays into a magnificent system of natural harbors. The climate is generally mild, with an early spring bringing a dazzling display of dogwood, azaleas, and rhododendrons; a long and sunny autumn that assures a rich harvest of fall foliage, especially along the Blue Ridge Parkway and Skyline Drive; a moderate summer and mild winter. Statewide, the temperature averages 40°F. in winter, 58°F. in spring, 76°F. in summer and 75°F. in autumn. In Richmond, the capital, annual statistics show an average of 188 sunny days, 59.34 inches of rain, 14.3 inches of snow and humidity of 73.5 percent.

Low-Cost Health Care

Virginia has 135 hospitals with a total of 32,138 beds. Some 90 percent of these hospitals are accredited by the Joint Commission on Accreditation—one of the highest averages of accredited hospitals in the 50 states. A semiprivate hospital room averages only $126 daily, vs. the national average of $163. There are 169 nursing homes with a total of 16,747 beds and 172 personal-care homes with 8,688 beds. These are augmented by 15 adult day-care centers around the state, and by a nursing-home bed registry that assures the best utilization of beds and facilities. Virginia averages only 162 doctors per 100,000 residents, which is a bit below the national average of 174, but more than adequate for the state's needs.

Good, Low-Cost Housing

As in Maryland, the further you get from the metropolitan area around Washington, D.C., the lower the cost of housing. In some of the best retirement areas, you can buy a good 2- or 3-bedroom home for $50,000 and rent one from $350 a month. If you want to settle in a planned community like Reston, you can buy good housing for around $40,000. Also, many areas in Virginia are providing specially designed public housing for the elderly. Major projects are being built or developed in Bristol, Charlottesville, Hampton, Hopewell, Norfolk, Petersburg, Richmond, Roanoke, and Wytheville.

Relatively Low Taxes

Virginia ranks twentieth in tax burden in the $10,000 to $15,000 tax bracket, twenty-fourth in $15,000 to $20,000 and fifteenth in $20,000 to $25,000.

Income Tax—the rate ranges from 2 percent on the first $3,000 taxable income to 5.75 percent over $12,000. A $600 exemption is allowed for each federal exemption and an additional $400 is granted to persons 65 or over. Some credits are allowed for retirement income.

Property Taxes—there is no state levy, so each locality sets its own rates, and all property, including intangibles, is assessed at fair market value. Most localities give exemptions for persons age 65 or over, depending upon income and assets. Taxes average about 1 percent of market value.

Sales Tax—the state rate is 3 percent, but all cities and counties levy an additional 1 percent, making a total of 4 percent. This applies to all retail sales except motor vehicles, which are subject to a 2 percent sales tax.

High Quality Indoor and Outdoor Activities

The main cultural centers are Jamestown, Williamsburg and Richmond, successive capitals of the Old Dominion. The Virginia Museum of Fine Arts in Richmond and the Barter Theatre at Abingdon are state supported. The arts, sciences and humanities are emphasized in all sectors of the commonwealth. Virginia also has 15 state-controlled and 28 privately controlled institutions of higher learning, including William and Mary, the University of Virginia, Virginia Polytech and the Virginia Military Institute. Persons 65 or older can attend classes free of charge if space is available. As to outdoor recreation, Virginia offers it all—fishing, boating, swimming, golf, tennis, hunting and all other sports. The state's well-distributed park system includes 20 state parks, 6 historical parks and 6 natural areas. In short, the Old Dominion is tops in both indoor and outdoor activities.

Vast Services for Seniors

The Virginia Office on Aging is unusually active in many areas, including income, health, nutrition, recreation, information and "prime time" programs including the Retired Senior Volunteer Program and the Foster Grandparent Program. Top priority goes to those projects designed to make it possible for older persons to remain independent and active—homemaker services, home health aides, chores services, visiting nurses, senior companions, innovative housing programs. The director of the office, appointed by the governor, heads a staff of 20. A main emphasis is to work with the 26 area agencies on aging, which conduct programs at the local level.

For further information, write:

> Virginia Office on Aging
> 830 East Main Street, Suite 950
> Richmond, VA 23219

MAJOR RETIREMENT AREAS

Tidewater Virginia—History Today and Yesterday

Like Maryland, Virginia has a tidewater area that combines charming
Colonial history with modern living. This area, 120 miles of coastal plain,
includes the towns of *Jamestown,* where the first white settlers landed;
Williamsburg, where patriots plotted the course of history; *Yorktown,*
where a decisive war was won and a nation born. It also includes the less
attractive towns of *Newport News* and *Norfolk,* primarily shipbuilding
and seafaring towns, which may be rundown but which offer depressed
property values.

Probably the most popular town in the area is *Virginia Beach* (pop.
270,000), which attracts large summer crowds. It offers 3 miles of concrete boardwalk, 12 miles of beaches, all water sports, an amusement
park, an active social life and famous seafood, notably the Lynnhaven
oyster.

Located 90 miles southeast of Richmond and 200 miles south of
Washington, D.C., Virginia Beach offers a steady climate averaging 59.3°F.
annually; January averages 40.5°F.; July 78.3°F. Annual rainfall averages
44.68 inches, snowfall 7.2 inches. Medical facilities include 222 doctors,
123 dentists and 2 hospitals with 513 beds. This is more than adequate to
serve the needs of the population.

A wide variety of housing and accommodations is available in all price
ranges, especially if you're looking at the area with the idea of renting
year-round or buying.

For further information, write:

> Chamber of Commerce
> 4512 Virginia Beach Boulevard.
> Virginia Beach, VA 23462

The Piedmont Province—The Rolling Hills of Virginia

This area covers about half the state and consists of gently rolling
hills. Virginia's leading tobacco farms and apple orchards are located
here. It is also an area of light industry.

Lynchburg (pop. 67,000) is the prime retirement area. It is located about 70 miles south of Charlottesville, 110 miles west of Richmond, and 180 miles southwest of Washington, D.C.

Climate and Environment. There are four distinct seasons, with temperatures averaging 32°F. in winter and 74°F. in summer. Average rainfall is 45 inches per year, average snowfall 5 inches. The humidity averages 65 percent.

Medical Facilities. There are 2 general hospitals and 1 long-term hospital with a total of 630 beds. There are also a clinic for emergency treatment and a home health service providing visiting nurses who make house calls. Lynchburg has 8 nursing homes and many health agencies to assure more than adequate health care.

Housing Availability and Cost. Two- and three-bedroom retirement houses are available from $50,000. Rentals are plentiful and start at $300 for 2- and 3-bedroom units. Some building lots are available, averaging $10,000 for a 20,000-square-foot lot. There are 5 mobile-home parks in the area, with monthly rentals starting at $100. And many 5- and 6-acre farms are available, some selling for as low as $10,000.

Cost of Living. The personal property tax rate is $1.24 per $100 of assessed value. The state income tax is usually reduced to zero if a person is 65 or over and earns less than $12,000. There is also tax relief for people who have owned property in Lynchburg for 5 years or more and earn less than $10,000 a year with less than $35,000 in net assets (excluding home and auto).

Leisure-Time Activities. Lynchburg's recreation division has organized 6 centers for seniors. Besides offering courses on art, dancing and health, the centers sponsor group trips to historic areas of the South. There are 13 city parks, 6 golf courses, 8 community centers and a major lake for fishing. Nearby are 8 educational centers that offer adult-education courses. And throughout the year the Fine Art Center sponsors music, dance, theater performances and art exhibits. Other attractions include a symphony orchestra, a theater league, historic society and a Quaker Meeting House.

For further information, write:

> Lynchburg Chamber of Commerce
> Box 2027
> Lynchburg, VA 24501

The Pioneering Highlands

Mountains, lakes, handicrafts and a frontier spirit characterize this section of southwestern Virginia. The focal point is Wythe County, a land area of 460 square miles lying in a broad picturesque valley bounded by the Blue Ridge and Allegheny mountains. *Wytheville,* the county seat, is approximately 80 miles southwest of Roanoke. The mountains along the northern border and those in the southwest and central sections have altitudes varying from 2,800 to 4,000 feet; the valley sections of Wythe County have altitudes from 2,000 to 2,500 feet.

Recent estimates put the population of Wythe County at 25,000 with 8,000 in the town of *Wytheville* and 1,100 in the town of *Rural Retreat.* About 15 to 20 percent of the population of this area is retired.

Climate and Environment. Average annual temperature is 53°F., with summer averaging 72°F. and winter 36°F. Rainfall averages 36.66 inches annually, with an average snowfall of 19.3 inches. The humidity averages 70 percent; in summer it reaches 80 percent in the morning then drops to 50 percent in the afternoon, thanks to the elevation of 2,350 feet.

Medical Facilities. There are 2 hospitals with 150 beds, 2 nursing homes with 190 beds and 1 personal-care home with 25 beds. Also, there are 2 clinics, emergency service, 15 doctors, 8 dentists and 8 specialists —more than enough to provide good medical care.

Housing Availability and Cost. Larger homes, selling from $50,000 are plentiful, but smaller ones are scarce. Townhouses and smaller homes rent from $250 to $400 a month, and mobile homes are available from $15,000 to over $40,000. Building lots sell for $5,000 to $20,000 and building costs are $35 to $42 a square foot. Some nonprofit housing is available.

Cost of Living. Property taxes run about 1 percent of market value. Seniors are eligible for some property tax exemptions, depending upon income. Some senior discounts are also available at supermarkets, and other stores feature discounts and sales on occasion. Farm produce in season is a bargain. Seniors find part-time jobs in stores and with services, as senior service aids and through the Green Thumb program, which aids rural beautification.

Leisure-Time Activities. For a small town, Wytheville has good cultural and recreational facilities, including a biweekly newspaper, 2 libraries with more than 50,000 volumes, 2 bookstores, a historical museum, a little theater, good television and radio reception, some 60 clubs, craft and hobby classes, adult-education classes, 3 swimming pools, a golf course, 5 tennis courts and nearby recreation areas and parks. Mt. Rogers National Recreation Area, the Appalachian Trail and Jefferson National Forest offer camping, fishing and other activities.

Special Services for Seniors. The area has 3 senior citizen clubs (which include concerned citizens) and 2 other clubs for seniors, a local office on aging which offers counseling service, a hot meal program, homemakers services, visiting nurses, transportation program, special health clinics, emergency service, weatherization program (where homes are insulated to save fuel costs), legal-aid program, rehabilitation program, fuel program and free classes at Wytheville Community College.

For further information, write:

Wytheville-Wythe-Bland Chamber of Commerce
P.O. Box 563
Wytheville, VA 24382

SUMMARY

As the first Southern state, Virginia offers gracious retirement living at low cost. It also offers excellent health care, recreational facilities (both indoor and outdoor), exceptional services for seniors and low-cost housing in the rural areas. Here are my ratings of the major retirement areas:

Excellent — Wytheville-Wythe-Bland area; Lynchburg area
Good   — Virginia Beach area

Other Virginia retirement towns worth considering: *Charlottesville* (22906), *Leesburg* (22075), *Lexington* (24450).

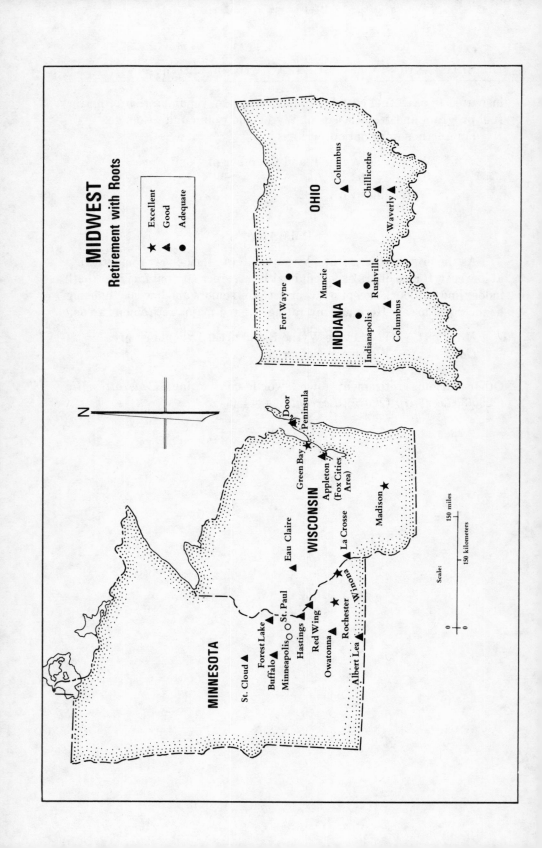

V.

THE MIDWEST—RETIREMENT
WITH ROOTS

To paraphrase an old saw: I took myself out of the Midwest, but I couldn't take the Midwest out of me. I was born in Detroit, and although I left when I was 23 (and have lived since then on the West and East coasts), I'm drawn back to America's heartland.

Maybe it is an urge to dig for my roots. But every time I'm in Detroit, Chicago or Minneapolis, the accents sound sweeter, the sights seem familiar and the natives friendlier. And I now revere Chicago as "the Paris of the Midwest."

Strangers wouldn't understand. They see this 700-mile stretch of prairieland as the "Mild West," perhaps because of the flatness of the land and the blandness of the people. I've joined tourists on top of the John Hancock Building in Chicago, looking west at sunset. All you can see is a vast flatness silhouetted only by the setting sun. Someone usually remarks that "the only hill out there must be the Rocky Mountains" (more than 1,000 miles away). But this ignores that fact that no two fields or farmhouses are the same; that parts of Minnesota lie north of Bangor, Maine and that Illinois dips farther south than Richmond, Virginia. And the longitude can be as varied as the latitude, with much of this generous expanse of land washed by water: the Great Lakes, the Ohio, Mississippi, Missouri and Red rivers.

There is also a paradox in the people. Some outsiders think Midwesterners are as friendly as puppies banging their tails against garbage cans.

This attitude may spring in part from insular self-defense. It may also stem from the camaraderie of those who live in a region with extremes of weather (anyone who shares torrid summers and frigid winters forges a common bond). And while the puppy may act friendly, he can snap at "outsiders" if rubbed the wrong way.

This isolation is fading as Midwesterners move out and the rest of the country pours in. The fact remains that the Midwest—in spite of metropolises like Chicago, Minneapolis, Detroit and Cleveland—is a land of small towns and rural people. And when the farmer retires he's as likely to opt for Buffalo, Minnesota; Spring Lake, Michigan or Appleton, Wisconsin as he is for Sun City, Arizona; Harrison, Arkansas; Fairhope, Alaska or St. Petersburg, Florida.

1. OHIO—THE TYPICAL STATE FOR RETIREMENT?

Statisticians like to think that the Buckeye State is an index of the nation. While it is true that Ohio is somewhat a microcosm of the United States—a farmland dotted with industrial centers—this ignores the macrocosms. Four-fifths of America's major industries are found in Ohio's cities, manufacturing a bewildering array of tires, rubber products, matches and glass. Ohio leads the nation in the production of variety items, from Chinese food to Liederkranz cheese, from Bibles to playing cards, from coffins to cash registers.

Yet of the 50 percent of the state's acreage not given over to farming, much is devoted to state and national forests and 62 state parks. Boats dot Lake Erie and rambling farmhouses dominate the quiet rural landscape. And the Ohio River, in spite of its heavy volume of industrial and commercial traffic, remains one of the cleanest rivers in the nation and a top recreational area for the southern part of the state.

"Beautiful Ohio" is not only a song, it is a statement. There is much beauty in the rugged sandstone caves and cliffs of the Hocking Hills, the serenity of the Lake Erie Islands, the fall colors of the Mohican State Forest and the peach blossoms at Catawba. Some 14.6 percent of Buckeye residents are over 60 and 10.3 percent over 65. The largest settlements of older people (more than 17 percent over age 60) are in Logan, Van Wert, Wyandot, Franklin, Highland, Belmont, Brown, Jackson, Scioto, Monroe, Morgan, Noble, Coshocton and Harrison counties, most in the central and southern parts of the state.

Square and Flat Topography

Ohio is square at least in size, 225 miles wide and 215 miles deep, and is bordered mainly by Lake Erie on the north and the Ohio River on the south. The state is essentially a gently rolling plain, with the Allegheny plateau in the east, Lake Erie plains in the north and central plains in the west and south. The temperate but variable weather makes up for any monotony in the landscape: it is subject to many extremes and plentiful precipitation. Statewide, winter averages 32°F., spring 53°F., summer 74°F, and fall 56°F.

Higher Cost—Lower Quality Health Care

While adequate, the cost and quality of medical care is not the best. A semiprivate hospital room costs $177 daily (vs. the national average of $163 daily) and there are 150 physicians per 100,000 residents (vs. the national average of 174 per 100,000). Ohio has 241 hospitals with a total of 64,158 beds and 825 nursing homes with 58,211 beds. There are also 128 personal-care homes with 6,692 beds.

Moderate Cost Homes and Land

Moderate 2- to 3-bedroom retirement homes in outlying areas start at $45,000 and rural land is available for a little over $1,000 an acre. Many small farms are also available (with house) from $1,000 an acre. You could retire in a rural area and farm to whatever scale suits you.

Low Cost of Living

Ohio's cost of retirement living is lower than the national average. While it costs a little over $10,000 annually for a couple to retire moderately in most parts of the United States, a couple could retire in the Dayton area for $9,609 annually and in the Cincinnati area for $9,574. However, the Cleveland area is higher than average—$10,439 annually. Taxes are also lower than average: the tax on a $50,000 house in Cincinnati is around $600 annually.

Other taxes are also moderate. Here's a breakdown:

Income Tax —the range is from 0.5 percent on taxable income up to $5,000, $900 plus 3.5 percent of the excess on taxable income over $40,000. Exemptions are $650 single or dependent, $1,300 for married. Taxpayers 65 or older get a $25 credit against tax, as well as an energy discount.

Property Taxes —if one of the spouses is age 65 or older, a homestead exemption is granted that reduces (depending upon income) assessment by 25 to 75 percent.

Intangibles Tax —income-producing intangibles are taxed at the rate of 5 percent.

Sales Tax —5 percent, with most counties levying an additional 0.5 to 1 percent. Food and prescription drugs are exempt.

Leader in Education

With more than 90 institutions of higher learning. Ohio has a number of important firsts in education: the first university (Ohio University) in the original Northwest Territory, first coeducational college (Oberlin) and one of the first to have coed dorms during the 1960s. Of historical interest: one of the leading universities, Western Reserve, took its name from a 500,000-acre tract claimed by Connecticut and given to New England settlers who had been burned out during the Revolution. These settlers brought their New England traditions with them, and that is why many Ohio towns bear a resemblance to those of New England. Ohio remains rich in historic sites, and contains extensive remains of the ancient race of "mound builder" Native Americans. The state has many museums and galleries: the National Pro Football Hall of Fame in Canton, the Air Force Museum in Dayton, the Toledo Museum of Art, the Jonathan Hale Homestead and Western Reserve Pioneer Village near Akron.

Progressive Office on Aging

The Ohio Commission on Aging has been among the most progressive in the nation, and its annual Governor's Conference draws thousands of participants. It helps fund and establish many programs, including crime prevention, discount services, training and education, nursing ombudsman, public information, transportation, financial assistance, information and referral, legal assistance, employment, multipurpose senior centers and 2 golden-age villages (in Columbus and Toledo).

For further information, write:

Ohio Commission on Aging
50 West Broad Street
Columbus, OH 43215

MAJOR RETIREMENT AREAS

Columbus Area—"The Largest Small Town in America"

I've visited this state capital area several times, and each time I'm more impressed. It is an area that is too big to be small and too small to be big. And while it retains a hometown atmosphere, it is growing, while other Ohio cities—Cleveland, Akron, Youngstown, Toledo, Dayton and Cincinnati—have been shrinking.

It is easy to see why. The town was created and laid out to be the state capital, and the streets are wide and tree-lined, with parks, Ohio State University and a handsome Greek revival state capitol building. The downtown area is clean and modern and the suburbs neat and tidy. Its people are civic minded, sports minded and cultured, thriving on hard work, low pay and plenty of church-going. And although the population has been growing, less than 3 percent of its citizens are foreign born. The city has been rated excellent for its overall quality of life by *Time* magazine. As one retiree puts it: "This is an oasis in the middle of the desert. If it wasn't for the good life here, I'd retire to Florida."

Climate and Environment. Located at the crossroads of Ohio's heartland, this city of 600,000 extends economic, educational and cultural horizons to a 5-county area containing 1.1 million people. The city is situated on the banks of the Scioto River. In January the temperature averages 28°F., in July 74°F.; its annual average is 51.5°F. Annual average rainfall is 37.01 inches and snowfall 28.5 inches, with 179 days of sunshine. For most of the year the humidity averages 50 to 60 percent during the day, and is higher at night and early morning. For a town its size, Columbus is remarkably free of air pollution, perhaps because its major "industries" are government and education.

Medical Facilities. There are 11 general hospitals with 4,509 beds providing the Columbus area with outstanding health care. Every hospital is fully accredited, and an accredited hospital emergency room is within 15 minutes of every Franklin County resident. The Ohio State University Hospital, with over 1,000 beds, has received international acclaim as a leader in medical research. A pioneer in emergency cardiac care, its Heartmobile, a specially staffed coronary-care unit, can respond within 15 minutes to emergency cardiac calls anywhere in the city. Quality cancer treatment and research has established Ohio State as a major cancer treatment center. There are 1,805 doctors and 708 dentists in the area, more than adequate for the area's needs.

Housing Availability and Cost. Columbus offers a wide choice of residential living and retirement housing ranging from the low $40,000s to over $100,000. Just a short walk from downtown is *German Village*, a unique and continuing restoration of homes built in the 1800s. Most of these are being sold for $100,000. A few minutes ride from downtown are communities like *Bexley*, where big, beautiful older homes on spacious lawns sell for under $100,000. *Upper Arlington*, 20 miles from the city center, features exquisite new homes on rolling terrain for $70,000 to $80,000. And there is wooded land, with trails and winding streams, for sale. If you prefer apartment living, you'll find plenty of townhouse units with private yards and recreational facilities renting for under $400 a month. Some of the other desirable residential areas are *Canal Winchester, Dublin, Gahanna, Grandview Heights, Grove City, Hilliard, Reynoldsburg, Westerville, Whitehall* and *Worthington*.

Cost of Living. Taxes vary according to school district, and the rate ranges from $42 to $55 of assessed value, or about $15 per $1,000 of actual value ($750 on a $50,000 house). On an Inter-City Cost of Living Indicator where 100 represents the national average, Columbus rates:

All Items—102.1	Transportation—99.9
Groceries—100.7	Health Care—98.3
Housing—99.9	Misc. Goods and Services—102
Utilities—114.5	

Leisure-Time Activities. The area boasts 8 major colleges and universities. The focal point is Ohio State University, with more than 200 undergraduate and 120 graduate programs and a campus enrollment of 51,000 (including many seniors who monitor classes here or take them for credit). The Columbus Recreation and Parks Department maintains more than 10,000 acres of parklands and waterways and has an elaborate program offering everything from paddleboats to tennis matches. The Columbus Zoo (northwest of the city) houses a total of 3,500 specimens of 623 species. The arts are a vital part of the life-style, and a glance through the area's arts directory reveals an organization for every artistic interest. The outstanding Columbus Gallery of Fine Arts houses works by Picasso, Cézanne, Monet and Rubens. The Columbus Symphony Orchestra provides metropolitan Columbus with quality musical events throughout the year. Also, there are numerous community theaters, dance groups and other performing arts. Unique to the area is Qube—Warner cable television, which provides for 2-way communication between listener and station. Listeners can vote on programs or questions by pushing buttons attached to their sets, select programs and communicate with stations and sponsors. Most of the Qube sets are located in *Upper Arlington*. Outdoor sports include an auto race track, 2 horse race tracks, 11 skating rinks,

9 swimming pools, 29 golf courses, 25 tennis courts and 39 recreational centers. There are also 29 libraries in the area.

Special Services for Seniors. Franklin County offers many programs and services for seniors, including consumer protection, credit counseling, crime prevention, day care, discounts and courtesy services, emergency services, employment opportunities, food and nutrition services, health clinics, homemaker and nursing services, home visits and companionship, housing referrals, information and referral services, legal services, library services, mental-health services, nursing-home care, senior centers and recreational centers, telephone reassurance, transportation, utility discounts, volunteer opportunities and voter information.

For further information, write:

> Columbus Area Chamber of Commerce
> P.O. Box No. 1527
> Columbus, OH 43216

Chillicothe (pop. 23,000), lying about 45 miles south of Columbus, is a bit warmer, averaging 33.4° F. in winter and 75.8° F. in summer. The area has 1 hospital with 230 beds and 4 nursing homes with 284 beds. There are 16 general practice doctors, 28 dentists and 36 specialists, offering good medical care. There is a fair supply of housing, ranging from $60,000 for 2- to 3-bedroom units. Some special senior citizen housing is available at *Hopeton Village*, where housing is available at about 25 percent of income. Some building lots are for sale from $5,000, and building costs are about $45 per square foot. The taxes on a $60,000 home are $250, and some senior discounts are available on food and other costs. Many retirees grow their own food or shop at farmers' markets. There are about 75 clubs in the area, an art league, vocational school, 2 swimming pools, 3 golf courses and excellent television and radio reception. At the YMCA the senior club meets once each month, and there is a local office on aging which supervises a hot meal program, homemaker services, visiting nurses, meals on wheels, transportation program, special health clinics, emergency service, legal-aid service and rehabilition programs. Most churches also have programs and activities for seniors.

For further information, write:

> Chamber of Commerce
> Chillicothe, OH 45601

Waverly (pop. 5,200), where 13 percent of the population is retired, lies 16 miles south of Chillicothe. Weather is even warmer here, averaging 34.6° F. in winter and 76.2° F. in summer. There is 1 hospital with 65 beds,

2 nursing homes with 134 beds and 4 personal-care homes with 80 beds. There is 1 clinic, emergency medical service, 11 doctors, 4 dentists, 4 specialists and 2 surgeons, offering better-than-average medical care. One of the chief housing attractions is *Bristol Village,* a community of 400 homes, dedicated to retirement living. The community is open to church members who are 55 years of age or older, although there is an "underage fee" for those under 65. A basic home costs $75 a month or a lifetime lease for $7,500. Other homes cost from $13,000 to over $40,000. Residents have access to an activities center providing craft and hobby projects, literary activities, card games and other entertainment. A physician in residence maintains office hours in the village and will make house calls. There are some mobile-home parks in the area, where housing runs from $6,000. Building lots are available from $2,500, with building costs around $40 a square foot; 1- to 2-bedroom homes rent from about $200 a month and some nonprofit retirement housing is available for $100 a month. The tax on a $40,000 home is $600. Some senior discounts are available, and frequent sales make this a low-cost living area. There is good television and radio reception, a library, 5 tennis courts, a golf course and several walking trails. The town has 1 senior center and features a hot-meal program, homemaker services, visiting nurses, meals on wheels, transportation program, special health clinics, legal-aid service and other senior programs.

For further information, write:

Chamber of Commerce
Waverly, OH 45690

Other possible retirement areas include *Zoar* (44679) and *Marietta* (45750).

SUMMARY

Although Ohio may be thought of as a typical state, it offers enough diversity to make retirement living interesting as well as comfortable. Overall cost of living is lower than in most states, especially in regard to property taxes and housing costs. And you can have a choice of urban or rural living in such areas as Columbus or in towns like Waverly and Chillicothe. Here are my ratings of the main retirement areas:

Good—Columbus area, Chillicothe, Waverly

2. INDIANA—WHERE SENTIMENTAL VALUES STILL PREVAIL

When you dream of Indiana, you might conjure nostalgic images of moonlight on the Wabash, the smell of new-mown hay, kids skinny-dipping in the old swimming hole and a laconic Hoosier chawin' on a weed.

Most of these images are real. Indiana remains an agricultural state with sentimental values. There are pioneer villages north of the Ohio River where time seems to have stood still. Central Indiana is one of the richest agricultural regions in the United States. Three-quarters of the state is devoted to farming, and there are more hogs than people. In the northeastern section are forests with hundreds of secluded lakes; on Lake Michigan's south shore are miles of sand dunes and beaches.

"What's good for grandpa is good enough for me" is the motto of many Hoosiers. The small-town values of work, family, church and country hold true. And when Hoosiers take steps into the industrial future, they make sure the rural past isn't left behind.

There's no Indiana city even half the size of Indianapolis (pop. 710,-000), the state capital. There are more than 2,000 towns under 10,000 population. Some 14.5 percent of the state's 5.5 million population is over 60, 10.4 percent over 65. The largest concentrations (higher than 20 percent) of those over 60 are in Clay, Sullivan, Vermillion, Switzerland, Greene, Knox and Pike counties.

Gentle Landscape and Climate

Indiana's landscape ranges from the sand dunes on its northern border with Lake Michigan to the gently rolling prairies of the center of the state to the deep valleys and hill country of the south. The temperate climate offers 4 distinct seasons, with cool but not severe winters and warm but not torrid summers. Statewide, winter averages 28°F., spring 63°F., summer 75°F. and fall 55°F. The northern regions are about 3 degrees cooler in all seasons; southern regions about 3 degrees warmer. In Indianapolis (at the center of the state) the annual averages are 159 sunny days with 40.27 inches of rain, 18.1 inches of snow and 72.3 percent humidity.

Lower Cost and Quality in Medical Care

While a semiprivate hospital room in Indiana averages $130 daily (vs. the national average of $163), there are only 117 physicians per 100,000 residents, which is below the adequate level of 133 per 100,000. There are 135 hospitals with a total of 33,816 beds, 411 nursing homes with 32,515 beds and 95 personal-care homes with 5,096 beds.

Older Homes at Reasonable Prices

There are many older homes available throughout Indiana at prices starting at $40,000. In-town condominiums sell from $25,000, and in subdivisions, newer homes sell from $50,000. Some smaller farms are available for $5,000 an acre and some vacation homes from $25,000.

Relatively Low Taxes

In tax burden, Indiana ranks in the mid-30s of the 50 states in medium-income tax burden and in the low 40s in higher brackets. Here is how the tax breaks down:

Income Tax —there is a flat 2 percent on adjusted gross income, with a $500 exemption for each person over 65.

Property Taxes —all property is assessed at one-third of true cash value. Personal household property is exempt. Persons 65 or older may be allowed an income-tax credit not to exceed $500 for a percentage of property taxes paid. Renters may consider 20 percent of annual gross rent as property taxes. Homeowners 65 or older are entitled to a $1,000 deduction in assessed value when their and their spouse's total income does not exceed $10,000. There is a general intangibles tax of 5¢ per $20 of face value, but persons with household incomes of less than $10,000 do not pay it.

Sales Tax —4 percent, with prescription drugs and food for home consumption exempt.

Seasonal Cultural Events

May 1 is the opening day of the mammoth 500 Festival, which culminates in the world-famous Indianapolis 500, held every Memorial Day. The world's top racing drivers go for glory and gold before sold-out grandstands. Indianapolis has other attractions, including its Museum of Art (featuring nineteenth-century works) and the Connie Prairie Pioneer Settlement and Museum. Other fine museums are located in Bloomington, Fort Wayne and South Bend. There is golf throughout the state, and boating is particularly popular in the northern lakes district. Fishing is good in the south-central area. Winter sports include major college football and basketball matches at Notre Dame, Purdue and Indiana University. And many people like to follow the Lincoln Heritage Trail through parts of Indiana—places made famous by the Great Emancipator.

Active Commission on Aging

The Indiana Commission on the Aging acts as the principal advocate of older people in the state. It gathers and disseminates information about programs, services, facilities and opportunities for the aging. It publishes a bimonthly newsletter and sponsors conferences for older people and those working in the field. The commission also works with and helps fund programs and projects for older people in all the major areas: nutrition, health, financial assistance, housing, legal services, leisure-time activities (including senior centers), transportation, volunteer programs and employment opportunities.

For further information, write:

> Commission on the Aging and Aged
> Room 201
> 215 North Senate Avenue
> Indianapolis, IN 46202

RETIREMENT AREAS

Columbus (pop. 40,000), located in the heart of the prairie land, has many modern buildings designed by such noted architects as Eero Saarinen, John Warnecke, Harry Weese and I. M. Pei. These have attracted national attention, with more than 40 public and business buildings considered "outstanding" examples of modern architecture. Launched as a project in the 1930s, the buildings have lent urban sophistication to this otherwise rural region.

Climate and Environment. Located 45 miles south of Indianapolis, this prairie town lies at an elevation of 656 feet. January can get pretty cold, averaging a bit over 20°F. Spring averages 62°F., summer 75.6°F., fall 58.8°F. Average annual rainfall is 41.7 inches, average annual snowfall 15.5 inches. The relative humidity averages 80 percent in January, 67 percent in April, 69 percent in August and 76 percent in October. Annual number of sunny days is 198.

Medical Facilities. Good medical care is provided by Bartholomew County Hospital (which serves a 12-county area). It contains 275 beds, 128 staff doctors and 116 participating doctors. There are 26 dentists in the community. Good mental-health facilities are also available at Quinco, a 5-county mental health consulting and treatment facility with a staff of 102. Also, 3 psychiatrists are in practice in the community.

Housing Availability and Cost. The Columbus area contains an unusually wide variety of housing in all price ranges. This includes older homes (30 to 75 years old) in several areas where restoration and neighborhood improvements are under way. Some downtown apartments are available in single-family homes and rent from $300 a month. More than 20 subdivisions have been created in the last 25 years and are located on the fringes of the city. Here, newer homes sell from $50,000. Within 15 minutes of Columbus are 13 towns with populations ranging from 250 to 5,000, where retirement housing is available from $40,000. You also have a choice of lakeside living, as the area has a large number of lakes within 10 miles of the city; 12 of the lakes have been developed as subdivisions and couple scenic beauty and water sports with good access to the city. Housing here can run as low as $30,000 for a vacation home. There are hundreds of farms within 20 miles of Columbus with a brisk market in small farms (5 to 10 acres) which sell from $2,000 per acre. Some building lots (average size 11,000 square feet) are available for $12,000. Building costs average $35 a square foot.

Cost of Living. Property taxes average a little over 1 percent of market value. State and county taxes combined total 3.3 percent of income. Food, clothing, utilities and other costs are on a par with other areas of similar size, but local produce and raising your own food can reduce costs considerably.

Leisure-Time Activities. The Bartholomew County Library, located in downtown Columbus, is one of its outstanding architectural treasures. This library is the regional reference center for 10 counties in southeast Indiana and has a circulation of over 300,000 books annually. There's the Columbus Symphony Orchestra and other music groups, the Columbus Dance Workshop, Bartholomew County Historical Museum, the Columbus Art League, 2 little theater groups and a downtown multiuse community center. Of Indiana's 16 state parks, 5 are within 45 miles of Columbus, including 2 of the largest recreational areas in the state. Other area attractions include Nashville and Brown County (16 miles away), which is a year-round arts and crafts colony.

Special Services for Seniors. Columbus boasts a modern senior center which includes a kitchen, lounge, meeting, game and craft room. Activity programs include tours, travel, bowling, dancing, arts and crafts, card games, entertainment and outings. The center provides a semimonthly preventive health-care screening program (free of charge), homemaker aids for the homebound, meals on wheels, part-time paid employment placement service, friendly visiting program and noon hot-meal program.

For further information, write:

Columbus Area Chamber of Commerce
500 Franklin Street
Columbus, IN 47201

Muncie (pop. 82,000) became nationally famous in the 1930s as the subject of sociological studies of a "typical" small city. The results were published in *Middletown* and *Middletown in Transition*. Some 40 years later a team of sociologists, on doing a repeat of the study, found that the traditional American values, such as the work ethic and family togetherness, are very much alive in Muncie. This newest report revealed that "In Muncie, it is reasonable to say that the world in which you'll raise your children will be very much like the one in which you were raised." In other words, computer technology, atom bombs, missions into space and supersonic air travel have not deeply touched the way Muncie residents live, although its residents are far more tolerant of different ways of living and thinking today than their grandparents were. Although life-styles may have changed, the town is still the antidivorce town that the original study uncovered. There is still only 1 divorce for every 2.5 marriages. And the town remains the mostly white, predominantly Protestant community it was. But although the city's religious alignment has changed very little, the Black population today matches the national average, about 11 percent. So if you're looking for a typical small city, with typical housing, medical facilities, leisure-time activities, cost of living and special services for seniors, consider Muncie. It even has a Golden Age Retirement Mobile Home Park.

For further information, write:

> Chamber of Commerce
> Muncie, IN 47305

Other Indiana towns worth considering for retirement are *Fort Wayne* (pop. 185,000; 46802) and *Indianapolis's North Side* (pop. 710,000; 46225) which has a number of excellent retirement homes, nursing homes and recreation areas. Smaller towns include *French Lick* (pop. 2,200; 47432), which is a famous health and resort center; *Rushville* (pop. 7,000; 46173), which was the national headquarters for Wendell Wilkie in 1940; *Batesville* (pop. 4,000; 47006), which features the 1852 Sherman House Inn, which mixes antiques with modern furniture, rustic beamed ceilings with continental menus. Moderate-sized towns include *Bloomington* (pop. 50,000; 47401) and *Terre Haute* (pop. 61,000; 47808), which has become an important industrial, financial, agricultural, educational, and cultural center. *Vincennes* (pop. 20,000; 47591), a historic city on the banks of the Wabash, is the oldest town in Indiana.

SUMMARY

Indiana can provide a sentimental setting for retirement at a below average cost. And while the options for retirement aren't as widespread as in some other states, there are comfortable possibilities. Here is how I would rate the major areas:

Good   — Columbus area, Muncie
Adequate — Ft. Wayne, Indianapolis's North Side, Rushville

3. WISCONSIN—A NATURAL SETTING FOR RETIREMENT

If you like cheese, beer and sausage, you'll love Wisconsin. Most of the well-padded natives look as if they were weaned on such bucolic fare. And the buxom Guernseys and Holsteins grazing in grassy fields symbolize the lushness of this pastoral paradise.

Wisconsin's cities—especially La Crosse, Green Bay, Madison and Appleton—provide good food, drink, entertainment, and solid Midwestern values in a wholesome environment. You can have the best of city elegance with rural relaxation in the Badger State.

You'll especially like Wisconsin if you are of German, Swiss, Polish or Scandinavian descent—the ethnic groups that have put their stamp on the good way of life here. But anyone could retire comfortably here; the slow and easy pace and the naturalness of the surroundings make everyone feel welcome. Some 15.9 percent of the state's 4.7 million residents are over 60 and 11.5 percent over 65. Counties in which more than 20 percent of the residents are over 60 include Richland, Sauk, Green Lake, Marquette, Waupaca, Waushara, Door, Marinette, Shawano, Buffalo, Jackson, Trempealeau, Vernon, Barron, Clark, Pepin, Polk, Adams, Florence, Forest, Juneau, Langlade, Oneida, Vilas, Ashland, Bayfield, Burnett, Iron, Price, Sawyer and Washburn.

A Tempered Land and Climate

Both the land and climate are tempered by the Great Lakes—Michigan on the east and Superior on the north. The glaciers that formed these lakes also made ridges and other fascinating sculptures in this otherwise rolling plain. The long, cold winters and short, warm summers are moderated by these great bodies of water.

The state is divided into 3 sections: the Superior uplands, with lakes, swamps, and ridges sloping to the coastal lowlands around Lake Superior; the Great Lakes plains in the central and southeastern parts, dotted with lakes and swamps; and the western uplands in the south and west, where some of the most picturesque, hilly regions (including the Wisconsin Dells) intrigue visitors and residents. Spring is usually wet and cold; midsummer very warm; fall pleasant; winter cold. Statewide temperatures average 19°F. in winter, 43° F. in spring, 68°F. in summer and 46°F. in fall. Humidity is usually relatively low, but precipitation—especially snow—can vary considerably. In the northern parts, snowfall can average 75 to 100 inches and even double that near the upper Michigan border. But in the southern part, snowfall averages 35 inches annually. In Madison, in the center of the state, temperatures are a bit milder in winter and cooler in summer, with an average of 50 inches of snow and 30.96 inches of rain annually.

Low-Cost, Adequate Medical Care

The cost of a semiprivate hospital room per day in Wisconsin is only $132, vs. the national average of $163. However, Wisconsin has only 141 physicians per 100,000 residents, below the national average of 174, but still above the minimum acceptable standard of 133. There are 171 hospitals with 28,630 beds, 453 nursing homes with 47,262 beds and 95 personal-care homes with 5,315 beds.

Good, Low-Cost Land and Housing

Most residents live in cozy houses that begin at $40,000. Many live on dairy farms, where land sells for $1,000 an acre. Vacation homes are also available, many selling for $30,000, and good building lots are available for under $1,000 an acre.

Taxes Are Tough

Unfortunately, the good life can cost—especially when it comes to taxes. Wisconsin is one of the highest-taxed states in the union, ranking third and fourth highest in most taxable income brackets. Property taxes are also high; a $50,000 house in Madison is taxed at 2 percent or more of market value—about $1,200. Here is a breakdown of taxes:

Income Tax —the range is from 3.4 percent on incomes of $3,000 or less to $3,330 plus 10 percent on taxable income over $40,000. Personal exemptions are $20, with an additional $5 for those 65 or older.

Property Taxes —real estate is locally assessed at full market value. If income is under $14,000, persons 18 and over can receive a tax credit for up to 80 percent of taxes accrued and/or rent constituting property taxes (25 percent of rent paid).

Sales Tax —the rate is 4 percent, with food for home consumption, meals sold by retirement homes, prescription drugs and prosthetic devices (including hearing aids and eyeglasses) exempt; so is home heating fuel.

Big Indoor, Outdoor Events

From January through March, there is hardly a Wisconsin city that doesn't stage some sort of snowmobile race. And with 1.5 million choice acres of national forests, the Badger State offers the best in outdoor living and recreation. Most of Wisconsin's rural areas also offer farm and ranch vacations, from rustic to modern. The top museum is in Madison, which is headquarters for the State Historical Society. Other museums are located in Green Bay (a football and railroad museum) and Eau Claire, among others. Wisconsin lives with history, and its plentiful offerings range from a towering statue of a Winnebago chief to the preserved first home of the world's greatest circus (at Baraboo). Just about any time of year, Madison offers a variety of musical treats, and the tiny Swiss city of New Glarus in southern Wisconsin is known for its Heidi Festival and its *Volkfests*. Major cities across the state have stage organizations; one of the best is the Madison Theater Guild, which presents half-a-dozen Broadway plays during fall and winter. During the summer, water sports are popular. With almost 9,000 lakes and 1,700 rivers, Wisconsin offer excellent fishing, yachting, canoeing and other water sports. The state also boasts 200 golf courses, including the popular Bay Ridge in Sister Bay and Peninsula State Park in Ephraim.

Active Bureau on Aging

The Bureau on Aging funds and administers many programs of interest to older people, including a multipurpose senior center program, nutritional services (hot-meal sites), community service employment, model projects (a nursing-home ombudsman program and legal-services program), senior center grant program, displaced homemakers project and foster grandparent program. The state of Wisconsin also maintains a number of hot lines where residents can get help on legal, insurance and other matters.

For further information, write:

> Bureau on Aging
> Division of Community Services
> 1 West Wilson Street
> Madison, WI 53702

MAJOR RETIREMENT AREAS

Door County—New England of the Midwest

This 75-mile long peninsula juts out from Green Bay, sticking a thumb at upper Michigan. It is a naturally air-conditioned summer retreat, and the 40 miles from Sturgeon Bay to Gills Rock are dotted with charming summer cottages. This 491-square-mile area has been called Wisconsin's answer to Cape Cod, mainly for its picturesque villages, islands, coves and landscapes. Probably fewer than 25,000 people live here, and the only town of any size is *Sturgeon Bay* (pop. 8,000). Of the county's 4 incorporated villages, only *Sister Bay* has a population approaching 500. One of the unique villages is *Ephraim* (pop. 250), which was founded by Moravian colonists. The town annually celebrate a Fyr-Bal Fest patterned after the traditional Scandinavian welcome to summer. You'll also find many Scandinavian gift shops and restaurants in the area. Ephraim is near Peninsula State Park, with its fine golf course and outdoor recreation. Another attractive village is *Eagle Harbor.* Almost all its buildings are white, including the spires of two small churches. The rest of the peninsula has woodlands, sand beaches, sea- and landscapes and an arts center. Boating, fishing, scenic roads, observation towers, winter sports, and cherry and apple blossom time (late May) make this area a year-round vacation center. Many people from the East and West coasts have vacationed here, and many are returning to retire.

For further information, write:

> Door County Chamber of Commerce
> Box 219 Green Bay Road
> Sturgeon Bay, WI 54235

Green Bay (pop. 140,000), located just south of Door County, is the oldest settlement in Wisconsin, and it has a lot more going for it than the Green Bay Packers football team. In the Quality of Life rating, which judged communities on 5 basic components, Green Bay ranked fifth among *all* American metropolitan areas under 200,000. And area residents believe Green Bay's life-style is superior in the availability of outdoor recreation in a prime natural environment, the friendliness of the people and comfortable pace of living, the cleanliness of the city, the quality of schools and health-care institutions and the lower cost of living.

Like many visitors, I almost bypassed the city. It has a low profile (no big buildings) and unless you know of its old world charm and space age conveniences, you may miss one of the most delightful cities of the Midwest. Luckily, I stopped for lunch at Kaap's restaurant, a turn-of-the-century German restaurant featuring sauerbraten, roast pork, fresh-caught fish, home-baked breads and pastries and, of course, plenty of local cheese and beer. Only a few blocks away from this Victorian world was the Port Plaza shopping center, a new 2-level enclosed downtown mall. This tasteful ultramodern structure and the surrounding cozy old-fashioned buildings convinced me that this town offered the best of the old and new.

Climate and Environment. The climate is continental, with 4 distinct seasons. Summers are warm and humid (in the 80s) but nights are cool (50s). Winters are cold, with days averaging 23.9°F. and nights 6.9°F. Snow begins in November and continues until March, although the total precipitation doesn't go above 27 inches a year. Spring and fall are sometimes short, but there is always enough time for myriad spring blossoms and flaming fall foliage. Lake Michigan moderates the weather, so it's not too cold or too hot any time of year, averaging 43.7°F. annually. Green Bay is 582 feet above sea level, and is on relatively level terrain on either side of the Fox River.

Medical Facilities. Green Bay offers excellent health care, with 3 hospitals and over 900 beds. The largest hospital, St. Vincent, has 542 beds and is a complete cancer treatment facility. In addition to its 234-bed capacity, Berlin Memorial Hospital is the cardiac hospital, serving northeastern Wisconsin and upper Michigan. And St. Mary's Hospital is adding a new wing to raise its capacity to 184 beds and update many of its facilities. Other health facilities include a visiting nurse association and 20 nursing homes, with more than 1,200 beds. Also, the area has some 170 physicians and 84 dentists, more than adequate for the population.

Housing Availability and Cost. There is a wide variety of housing available at a wide range of costs. Apartments in the older downtown areas are available for as low as $220 a month. A 1-bedroom apartment in a more modern complex would start at $250, 2-bedroom apartments at $270 a month. For houses, the average 2- to 3-bedroom ranch house (recently built) starts at $50,000, while older ones might cost less. More deluxe homes sell for $75,000. There are 13 retirement communities and homes listed in the area, some of which also function as nursing homes.

Cost of Living. Property taxes run 2 percent of market value or $1000 on a $50,000 house. But over all, the cost of living in Green Bay is below average, with health costs about 20 percent below average, senior discounts available and other costs near the national average. On an index where 100 equals the national average, here is how Green Bay rates:

Food—96.3   Health Care—88.2
Housing—98.6   Miscellaneous Services—101.5
Utilities—86.3   All Items—97.1
Transportation—104.4

Leisure-Time Activities. There are many opportunities to enjoy music, theater and art in the area. The Green Bay Symphony presents 4 concerts a year and the city band, the oldest continuous city band in the United States, gives weekly summer concerts at a local park. Choruses, barbershop quartets and other singing groups are popular. The Community Theater presents a repertoire of classic and modern plays, and St. Norbert College, Harlequin Players and other little theater groups also put on performances. The Neville Public Museum and University of Wisconsin house traveling art exhibits. There are several art stores and commercial organizations that offer incentives and opportunities for local artists and craftspeople to exhibit and sell their works. The Brown County Library operates a network of branches throughout the area. And there are more than 300 clubs and organizations from which to choose. The Green Bay area is a strongly religious community, with 83 congregations representing 27 denominations (including Judaism). In addition to the Green Bay Packers, sports (both spectator and active) are popular, with more than 40 parks and recreational areas offering all facilities. There are 10 golf courses in the area and good hunting and fishing in Green Bay, Fox River, Lake Michigan and nearby lakes and rivers.

Special Services for Seniors. Green Bay has senior centers, senior clubs, the Lake Michigan Area Agency on Aging and other social service agencies, a hot-meal program, visiting nurses, meals on wheels, transportation service, telephone referral service for problems of all kind, legal-aid service, bus and cab services for elderly and a curative workshop.

For further information, write:

Green Bay Area Chamber of Commerce
P.O. Box 969
400 South Washington Street
Green Bay, WI 54305

The Fox Cities—Urban and Rural Diversity

Even though the Fox River cities of *Appleton* (pop. 64,000), *Neenah* (25,000), *Menasha* (18,000), *Kaukauna* (13,000) and the town of *Grand Chute* (9,000) and town of *Menasha* (13,000) form the third largest metropolitan area in Wisconsin, they offer a richness and diversity of urban and rural living that appeals to persons of all ages. When I drove through downtown Appleton, the business district was thriving and clean, the residential district sparkling. And even though paper manufacturing is one of the main industries (other light manufacturing makes up the economic base), the area doesn't suffer from industrial noise or air pollution. In fact, in the Quality of Life study, this area rated "excellent" in all components of living. The annual average temperature is 43.7°F.; January averages 18°F. and July 68.4°F. There are 4 hospitals with 680 beds, 12 clinics, 11 nursing homes, 191 doctors and 111 dentists in the area. Appleton Memorial is the newest health-care unit and, like the others, provides general patient care. It also specializes in cardiovascular studies, diagnostic ultrasound and echophono-vector capabilities. Its outstanding cardiac surgery unit is known throughout the state and it has a highly sophisticated coronary intensive-care unit. A variety of good 2- and 3-bedroom houses are available from $40,-000 and building costs average below $40 a square foot. You can also rent homes from $500 a month while apartment rents start at $300 a month. Many duplexes are also available from $400 a month. Property taxes range from 2 to 3 percent of market value and other costs are in line with the national average. For music, theater, dance, film and art lovers, there is much to see and do every night of the week. The Fox Valley Symphony Orchestra and women's and men's choruses are very active. Lawrence University offers a concert and lecture series and houses a music-drama center. Other theater groups flourish throughout the area. The Appleton Gallery of Arts sponsors several shows each year where local, state and national artists exhibit. And museums and galleries throughout the area offer shows year-round. At least one literary magazine, *Fox Cry*, published at the University of Wisconsin Center, is locally produced, and each community has extensive book and library facilities. There are 7 golf courses, 5 indoor and 10 outdoor swimming pools, numerous tennis courts, 17 bowling alleys, 9 movie houses and 85 parks. In fact, over 1,000 acres are devoted to parkland and open space throughout the Fox Cities area. Seniors are very active in the more than 100 senior and other clubs. And the usual senior services—hot meal, transportation, visiting nurses, meals on wheels, etc.—are available throughout the Fox Cities.

For further information, write:

Fox Cities Chamber of Commerce
P.O. Box 1855
Appleton, WI 54913

Madison (pop. 170,000). was once described in the *Saturday Evening Post* as a town "where Lincoln could have grown up in harmony with his surroundings; where Galileo could have spoken his mind, and where Demosthenes could have been mayor." I found it a no-nonsense capital city, with thriving business districts and trim houses. And certainly this "City of four Lakes," situated along a natural isthmus between 2 large freshwater lakes, is one of the most livable cities in the United States. In fact, the Quality of Life study ranked Madison higher than any other Midwest city its size—and second in all the country! Here are some reasons it makes a good retirement center:

Climate and Environment. From its setting on the isthmus, the city goes on to encompass 3 more lakes and miles of rolling wooded hills and fertile farmland. The downtown area is attractive and comfortable, and the suburbs are clean and pleasant, offering easy access to cultural and recreational facilities. The average mean temperature is 44.9°F., with an average of 18°F. in January and 71.1°F. in July. There are 163 sunny days on the average during the year, with an annual average of 30.96 inches of rain and 50.2 inches of snow. The humidity averages 75.5 percent.

Medical Facilities. Madison is rapidly becoming one of the foremost medical centers in the world. Its 8 hospitals, 3,860 hospital beds and 500 physicians (85 percent are specialists) are more than adequate for the population. A new $100-million Clinical Health Sciences Center has recently been completed, and Madison has 21 medical clinics and 13 nursing homes with 1,421 beds.

Housing Availability and Cost. A 2-bedroom house starts at $40,-000, but you can rent one from $300 a month (furnished) or $200 a month (unfurnished); 2-bedroom apartments rent from $200 a month furnished, $175 a month unfurnished. There are 5 major independent housing facilities for the elderly and more have been proposed.

Cost of Living. Property taxes run 2.65 percent of market value. Other costs are generally in line with the national average, although many recreational and cultural activities are available at low or no cost, thanks to the programs at the University of Wisconsin.

Leisure-Time Activities. The Madison area offers 18,000 acres of lake surface, 4,300 acres of parklands, 10 golf courses, 23 public tennis courts, 2 toboggan runs and 60 ice-skating rinks. For a small fee, you can play one of the 12 courts of the giant Nielsen Tennis Stadium, the world's largest facility of its kind. Numerous theaters in the city offer filmed and live entertainment. Madison has a symphony orchestra, civic chorus, civic opera, theater guild, civic repertory theater, philharmonic chorus, ballet company and dinner playhouse. The Madison Civic Center has been renovated to serve as a center for the arts. The Elvehjem Art Center is located on the University of Wisconsin campus, which itself offers many galleries, museums, libraries and other facilities, many open to residents and to seniors.

Special Services for Seniors. Madison has senior centers, senior clubs, a local office on aging, a hot-meal program, transportation services, volunteer and job information services, information and referral services, health clinics, meals on wheels, legal assistance and other programs geared to seniors.

For further information, write:

> Greater Madison Chamber of Commerce
> P.O. Box 71
> Madison, WI 53701

Eau Claire (pop. 52,000), billed as an area "where industry and agriculture meet," offers the best of both worlds. About 10 percent of the population is retired. While the winters are long and cold and summers short and warm, there are enough good days to make for pleasant living. Health facilities are good: 2 hospitals with 663 beds, 6 nursing homes with 616 beds, 12 clinics, 200 physicians, 44 dentists, more than 100 specialists and an acute coronary care unit. While rentals are limited, there are some special new retirement housing projects where rent is based on income. Single-family homes sell from $40,000 and condominiums cost $100,000. Building lots start at $8,000 and building costs run $35 a square foot. Some 1- to 2-bedroom apartments are available from $225 a month. Property taxes run 2 percent of market value, and other living costs are a bit below national average (on a scale where 100 is average, Eau Claire ranks 96). Some senior discounts are available, as are some job opportunities. Eau Claire has a public library with 125,000 volumes, 3 museums, good radio and television reception, 150 clubs, adult-education classes, 15 parks, 4 swimming pools, 5 golf courses, 39 tennis courts and 3 beaches. There is a main senior center (city-county) and 30 clubs especially for seniors. Counseling services are available for seniors and there is a hot-meal program, visiting nurses, meals on wheels, transportation program, special health clinics, income-maintenance program, hot-line emergency service, mobile units for elderly and some rehabilitation programs.

For further information, write:

> Greater Eau Claire Chamber of Commerce
> 307 South Farwell Street
> Eau Claire, WI 54701

La Crosse (pop. 50,000) is a tristate city at the conjunction of 3 rivers: the Mississippi, Black and La Crosse. These rivers provide excellent swimming, fishing, boating and water sports in summer, ice fishing and skating in winter. La Crosse rated an overall "A" in the Quality of Life study for several reasons. Its hospitals are excellent, with a total of 840 beds and 177 physicians in the area, more than enough for the population. Housing is good, selling from $40,000 for single-family homes, and rentals are available from $350 a month. Municipal parks are good, with a riverside park and an island park, and there are 4 golf courses. Fishing is excellent, with pike, trout, bass, crappies, perch, bluegill, catfish, bullheads, sturgeon, carp and sheepshead most commonly caught. Hunting is also good in the area, with all types of duck and geese, ruffed grouse, pheasant, quail, raccoon, woodcock, rabbit, squirrel and deer available. The University of Wisconsin has a branch here, offering many courses of interest to seniors. And there are several art galleries, bookstores, libraries, little theaters and other cultural activities. La Crosse is a favorite gathering place for conventions, workshops and seminars as well as excursions, because of its location (near Iowa and bordering Minnesota) as well as its excellent facilities.

For further information, write:

> La Crosse Area Visitors Bureau
> P.O. Box 842
> La Crosse, WI 54601

SUMMARY

Wisconsin is a good retirement state, especially for those of German, Swiss, Polish and Scandinavian descent. The quality of its cities and the wholesomeness of its rural areas offer a good choice of both urban and rural living. Housing is good and relatively inexpensive, although taxes are among the highest in the nation. But the quality of living is worth the price. And if you can stand the cold winters and the short, warm summers, you could retire quite comfortably here. Here are my ratings for the major areas:

Excellent — Green Bay and Madison areas
Good   — Door County, Fox Cities, Eau Claire, La Crosse

4. MINNESOTA—WHERE THE WEST BEGINS UP NORTH

A Minneapolis advertising man once said, "California is the flashy blonde you like to take out a couple of times. Minnesota is the gal you marry!" And she doesn't have to be a Swedish blonde. Although there are many Scandinavians in the state, they are outnumbered by the Germans. And the Iron Range of the state (its northeast corner) finds a melting pot of Swedes, Finns, Norwegians, Italians, Croatians, Slovaks and other Europeans.

Minnesota has plenty of elbow room—the state is the twelfth largest in the nation (84,068 square miles, of which 4,059 are water), yet it has just over 4 million people. Nearly half of these live in the Minneapolis–St. Paul "Twin Cities" area, leaving thousands of square miles of lakes, pine and prairies for people to work, play or retire in.

In the Quality of Life study, Minnesota finished second to California in the overall ratings, and ranked first in "individual equality." In some ways it ranks ahead of California, with cleaner cities and more wilderness in rural areas. Certainly, it offers many excellent places to retire.

It is a wonder, then, that more people haven't discovered Minnesota's Retirement Edens. As it stands, 15.5 percent of the population is over 60 and 11.4 percent over 65. Counties with more than 20 percent age 60 and over include Kittson, Norman, Clearwater, Hubbard, Aitkin, Douglas, Grant, Otter Tail, Pope, Traverse, Wilkin, Cass, Todd, Crow Wing, Renville, Big Stone, Meeker, Chippewa, Lac Qui Parle, Swift, Yellow Medicine, Mille Lacs, Pine, Cottonwood, Jackson, Lincoln, Pipestone, Redwood, Rock, Faribault, Le Sueur, Martin, Sibley, Watonwan, Fillmore and Wabasha.

A Prairieland with five Seasons

Minnesota is part of the Great Plains, and two-thirds of the state is rolling prairie, which is broken up with rocky ridges, deep lakes and dense forests. In the north are lakes, pine- and aspen-studded forests, hills, rushing streams and cascading waterfalls. In the center is a hill and lake region covering about half the state (it's here than many of Minnesota's 15,000 lakes are located). And in the south are rolling plains and deep river valleys. The climate of the northern part of the state is affected by the Great Lakes and the southern and central portions by the Great Plains. Temperatures in the southern part of the state are generally 7 degrees warmer in all seasons, with winter averaging 16°F., spring 43°F., summer 69°F. and fall 47°F. Actually there are 5 seasons—a mellow, colorful Indian summer lasts from late September to mid-November and can be one of the most beautiful seasons of any state. One note of caution: in summer, people wear sweatshirts emblazoned with a large mosquito bearing the legend: "Minnesota State Bird."

Good Health Care at Low Cost

A semiprivate hospital room in Minnesota averages only $129 daily, vs. the national average of $163 daily. And there are 177 physicians per 100,000 population, more than adequate. There are 188 hospitals with a total of 31,050 beds, 399 nursing homes with 36,461 beds and 118 personal-care homes with 6,575 beds. Minnesotans with medical bills that exceed 20 percent of income can get help from the Catastrophic Health Expense Protection Program, and a "complaint team" at the Health Department investigates nursing home problems.

Good Housing at Moderate Cost

You can find plenty of vacation and other small housing available from $40,000, and there is much vacation land available for under $1,000 an acre. Rentals may be scarce in some small cities, but in the Twin Cities area you'll find unfurnished apartments renting below $300 a month and furnished 2- and 3-bedroom apartments from $350 a month. Although some farmland sells for under $1,000 an acre, the best (used for grazing and feed) costs more than $1,000 an acre. Good building lots sell from $10,000. Homeowners with incomes up to $7,500 can get free renovation grants to $6,000; those with incomes to $16,000 pay 1 to 8 percent interest on such loans.

Lower Cost of Living

An annual retirement budget in Minneapolis–St. Paul is a bit below the national average ($9,996 vs. $10,022) and lower than in Milwaukee, Wisconsin ($10,313). Minnesota's taxes are lower than Wisconsin's in the lower brackets (under $20,000) but are higher in upper brackets. Here's a breakdown:

Income Tax—rates on taxable income start at 1.6 percent of the first $500 and go up to 17 percent over $80,000. Everyone gets a $60 tax credit, and those over 65 get an extra $60. The first $11,000 in pension income is tax free.

Property Taxes—taxes are set locally, with the average tax on a

$50,000 house in Minneapolis running around $1,000. Senior citizens must pay a set percentage of their annual income toward property taxes, ranging from 0.5 percent to 1.5 percent. The state pays the next $850, but the maximum tax relief after that is $150 ($1,000 total)

Sales Tax—4 percent, with some cities imposing an additional tax. Exempt are food, clothing, drugs, medicines, therapeutic and prosthetic devices.

Indoor-Outdoor Activities

Both winter and summer activities are celebrated by many towns; snowmobile races are popular in winter and water carnivals in summer. Most famous is the week-long Aquatennial in Minneapolis, which includes 200 sports and entertainment events. Of the museums, the most interesting may be Duluth's historical museum, with displays and relics of pioneer days. Rochester has the Mayo Foundation Museum of Hygiene and Medicine, and in Winona, the National Savings Bank Building has a large collection of trophies and weapons from South America. In music, in addition to the Minnesota Orchestra, there are the St. Paul Chamber Orchestra and Civic Opera association. The town of Moorhead is musically active year-round, as is Rochester. Mankato and Duluth also have symphony orchestras. Seniors get reduced fishing, hunting, and camping licenses and free or low-cost admission to schools, colleges, and universities.

Active Board on Aging

The Minnesota Board on Aging has won many honors, and its director, Gerald Bloedow, has held many national offices in the field of aging. Some of the Board of Aging services available include day-care centers, health maintenance, in-home services, counseling services, nutrition (hot-meal sites), senior centers, transportation, action councils, advocacy projects, social integration projects and discount buying program.

For further information, write:

> Minnesota Board on Aging
> 204 Metro Square
> Seventh and Robert Streets
> St. Paul, MN 55101

MAJOR RETIREMENT AREAS

Hiawathaland—Switzerland on the Banks of the Mississippi

Winona (pop. 24,763) is a picturesque college town on the banks of the Mississippi River in southeastern Minnesota. I remember my first visit; I had driven across the crimson and gold Hiawatha Valley, and I hoped something equally inviting lay just over the horizon. When I saw this quiet, lovely town, with its Victorian mansions surrounded by tree-covered bluffs and lakes, I knew I had discovered a Retirement Eden. Fact is, some 25 percent of the residents are retired, which testifies to its suitability.

Climate and Environment. The bluffs help protect the city against extremes of wind and weather. In January the temperature averages 24°F., in April 47.6°F., in July 84°F. and in October 51.8°F. The humidity ranges from 64 to 76 percent in winter, 57 to 89 percent in summer. Annual rainfall averages 31.33 inches, with June the wettest month; snowfall averages 47.5 inches, with February the driest month. There is no noise or air pollution. Average length of growing season is 165 days.

Medical Facilities. There is 1 hospital with 134 beds, 3 nursing homes with 350 beds, 3 clinics, 48 doctors, 26 dentists, 1 orthodontist and 20 specialists—more than enough for the population.

Housing Availability and Cost. There are 2 special retirement housing projects, one with 118 units and the other with 169 units, available on the basis of need and income. Single-family homes start under $40,000, and there is a limited supply of condominiums, coops and townhouses selling for slightly less. Building lots costs $10,000 and total building costs come to $50 per square foot. Some 1- to 2-bedroom homes are available for rent starting at $250 a month, and some small apartments start at $200 a month. There are 8 mobile-home parks in and around Winona, where you could buy a modular unit from $20,000.

Cost of Living. Property taxes range from 1.1 to 2.78 percent of market value. Other living costs are reduced by a senior discount program and by local food discount days. Also, there are factory outlets (clothing) in the area offering special bargains. Some seniors get jobs through a local older-worker program and there is an older adult center that offers day-care services.

Leisure-Time Activities. Winona's 3 colleges, including Winona State University and Vocational Technical School, offer theater, sports and entertainment events year-round, and free courses are available to people over 65. The main library has 75,000 volumes, and there are 2 bookstores, an art gallery, 5 museums, 4 little theater groups and good radio and television reception in the area. There are 220 clubs from which to choose, including craft, hobby, bridge and other activities. For outdoor recreation, you have 23 parks, 7 swimming pools, 2 golf courses, 35 tennis courts, 1 Frisbee golf course, 1 exercise trail and a bike trail around Lake Winona.

Special Services for Seniors. The main senior center has been remodeled, and there are 4 senior clubs in the area. The area also has a local office on aging offering counseling services, including a senior advocate program, social services and community worker program. There is a hot-meal site for seniors, homemaker's service, visiting nurses, meals on wheels, transportation program, special health clinics, income-maintenance program, legal-aid service, mobile units, rehabilitation programs and a senior companion/community support program.

For further information, write:

Winona Area Chamber of Commerce
Box 870
168 West Second Street
Winona, MN 55987

Rochester (pop. 60,000), 46 miles west of Winona, is synonymous with the ultimate in health care, the Mayo Clinic. But it offers much more to retirees, so much so that in the Quality of Life study, Rochester rated second among cities under 200,000. Being inland and on the plains, it is a bit cooler and drier than Winona. It draws some 250,000 persons a year who seek the medical services of 600 leading physicians, surgeons and medical scientists at the huge Mayo complex. Health care is a major industry here, with 1,475 doctors, 2,740 hospital beds, 455 nursing-home beds and 48 dentists. Much rental housing is available, with 14 hotels and 31 motels in the area offering both weekly and monthly rates. Permanent housing is available from $40,000. Overall taxes run slightly higher than Winona (although the municipal rate is lower). Rochester's leisure-time facilities include the Rochester-Olmsted Recreational Center, 2 botanical gardens, 21 football fields, 31 tennis courts, a bird sanctuary, a ski hill and 3 golf courses. Cultural activities include the Rochester Symphony Orchestra and Chorale, summer open-air concerts, civic theater, annual arts festival and art center. The library has 145,000 volumes, and adult-education classes are available. Seniors are active in the many service and other clubs in the area, and there are many special services available for seniors.

For further information, write:

Rochester Area Chamber of Commerce
212 First Avenue S.W.
Rochester, MN 55901

Owatonna (pop. 19,000) is located 45 miles west of Rochester. This "typical American city" (as chosen by the Carnegie Foundation) considers itself Minnesota's first health resort, a claim based on a Native American legend concerning the mineral spring on the northeast side of town. I was impressed with the clean, modest, pleasant homes, business district and hospital, and by the fact that the attendant at a self-service gas station offered to fill up my car in a snowstorm. The town has 100 hospital beds and 200 nursing-home beds, 17 doctors and 15 dentists. Taxes are lower here than most southern Minnesota communities. Main cultural attractions and festivals include the county fair in August, Pumpkin Festival in October; little theater and the Owatonna Arts Center, which includes displays of old costumes, a sculpture garden and changing gallery shows. There's also a railroad museum, Village of Yesteryear and historical displays. Some modest homes in this area sell for under $40,000.
For further information, write:

Owatonna Area Chamber of Commerce
Box 331
Owatonna, MN 55060

Albert Lea (pop. 22,000) lies 34 miles south of Owatonna. This is an important dairy, livestock, manufacturing and distribution center just 8 miles from the Iowa border. The city has 115 hospital beds, 50 nursing-home beds, 30 doctors and 18 dentists, more than adequate for the population. Taxes are a bit higher than in Owatonna, but the number of food-processing plants (meat, poultry, margarine) and agricultural machinery manufacturers (ice machines, milking machines) mean that good food bargains are available. Modest homes are available from $40,000. Cultural attractions include a community theater, civic music and art center and festival, a historical museum and the Freeborn County Fair. There are 33 municipal parks, an 18-hole golf course, 16 tennis courts and 3 swimming pools.
For further information, write:

Albert Lea Chamber of Commerce
P.O. Box 686
Albert Lea, MN 56007

Retirement Near the Metroland

Although Minneapolis and St. Paul are billed as the Twin Cities, they are as much alike as a Victorian lady and a brassy blonde. St. Paul, the older city, is conservative, Catholic, Irish and "the end of the East" (some liken it to a miniature Boston). On Summitt Avenue are fine old houses built by the original settlers; some of them are still single-family homes, and in some just an old lady and 5 servants reside. Minneapolis is modern and slightly brazen; Lutheran, progressive, Scandinavian and up-and-coming. In spite of their contrasts, both offer enjoyable living. Those who seek a more stately pace opt for St. Paul; those who want a more modern tempo like Minneapolis. And not too far distant from these cities, in undulating pastureland, lie some of the state's best retirement areas.

Buffalo (pop. 5,000), 35 miles northwest of the Twin Cities, is a small farming town which offers possibilities for retirement. There are 65 hospital beds and 165 nursing-home beds, 12 doctors and 10 dentists, more than enough for the population. Modest 2-bedroom homes are available for under $40,000; some rentals from $300 a month. Some low-income senior citizen housing is also available. Taxes and other costs are unusually low, thanks to Buffalo's proximity to the Twin Cities and its location in the center of farming and dairy-products country. The main cultural attractions include Buffalo Days, RCA Rodeo, the Wright County players and the Wright County Historical Society. There are 7 parks, 1 9-hole golf course, good television and radio reception from the Twin Cities and a public library with 21,000 volumes. Adult education and other classes are available in nearby St. Cloud (see below).

For further information, write:

Buffalo Chamber of Commerce
205 Central
Buffalo, MN 55313

St. Cloud (pop. 42,000) lies 30 miles northwest of Buffalo and 65 miles northwest of the Twin Cities. This town's architecture reflects the German and New England roots of its early settlers. And while it is a diversified industrial town, it avoids a commercial appearance. It has 522 hospital beds, 681 nursing-home beds, 93 doctors and 55 dentists, more than adequate for the population. Good 2-bedroom housing is available from $40,000 and some rentals are available from $350 a month. Main cultural attractions are the Benedicta Arts Center, St. John's University Community Theater, State University Art and Lecture Series, Performing Arts Center and the city's recreational areas, which include a riverside park and a sportsmen's island. Taxes run higher here than in Buffalo and

smaller communities, but the services are good and shopping diversified.
For further information, write:

> St. Cloud Area Chamber of Commerce
> P.O. Box 487
> St. Cloud, MN 56301

Forest Lake (pop. 5,000) is 25 miles north of the Twin Cities. Though
it is small in size, it shares the activities and facilities of a metropolitan
area of 1.9 million people. Forest Lake itself has 52 hospital beds and 161
nursing-home beds, 11 doctors and 19 dentists. Housing here starts at
$40,000, but becomes less expensive north of the city. Main cultural at-
tractions are the Masquers Theater summer stock company, civic concert
series, and many sports events, both college and professional. A swimming pool and ice arena have just been built. Taxes run higher here than
in St. Cloud and in smaller communities farther from the Twin Cities.
For further information, write:

> Forest Lake Chamber of Commerce
> Forest Lake, MN 55025

Other possibilities in the Twin Cities area include *Hastings* (zip code
55033), which has the famous Steamboat Inn, and *Red Wing* (55066),
where the historic St. James Hotel is being restored to its former glory.

SUMMARY

Minnesota offers lots of room and good, clean urban and rural areas
for retirement. Although taxes are high in the upper brackets, the overall
cost of living is lower than in Wisconsin and other neighboring states.
Buying a home will be easier in Minnesota, thanks to a new law which
permits a person saving for a first home to put $2,500 a year—up to a total
of $10,000—into a trust account at a bank, savings and loan or credit
union. Up to $1,500 of the annual deposit, plus all accrued interest, may
be deducted on state income-tax returns. Deposit limits are the same for
couples and individuals, and the account must be closed within 10 years.
There are penalties for excess deposits and for not using the money to buy
a first home in Minnesota. But without question there are many possibilities for retirement in the North Star State. Most are within easy driving
distance of the Twin Cities. Here are my ratings:

Excellent — Winona, Rochester
Good　　 — Owatonna, Albert Lea, Buffalo, St. Cloud, Forest Lake,
　　　　　　　　Hastings, Red Wing

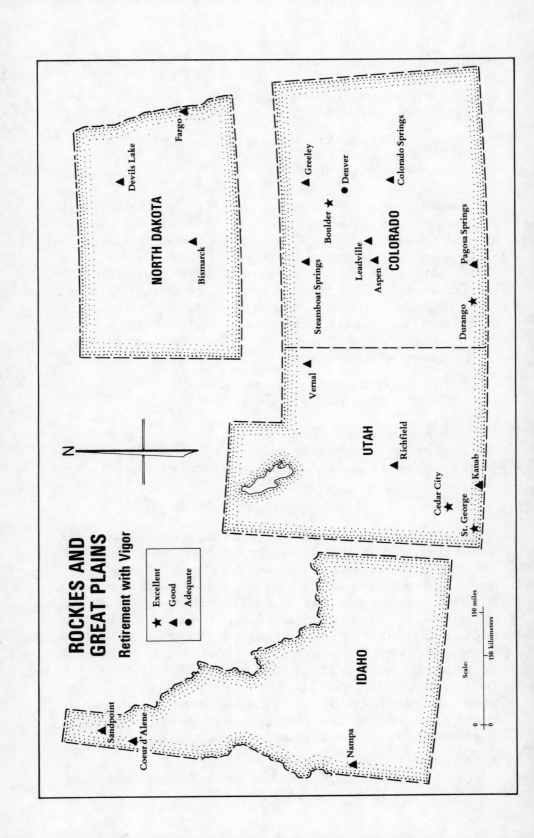

ROCKIES AND GREAT PLAINS

Retirement with Vigor

Excellent ★
Good ▲
Adequate ●

N

Scale:
0 — 150 miles
0 — 150 kilometers

IDAHO

Sandpoint ▲
Coeur d'Alene ▲
Nampa ▲

UTAH

St. George ★
Cedar City ★
Kanab ▲
Richfield ▲
Vernal ▲

NORTH DAKOTA

Devils Lake ▲
Bismarck ▲
Fargo ▲

COLORADO

Steamboat Springs ▲
Greeley ▲
Boulder ★
Denver ●
Leadville ▲
Aspen ▲
Colorado Springs ▲
Durango ★
Pagosa Springs ▲

VI.

THE ROCKIES AND GREAT PLAINS
—RETIREMENT WITH VIGOR

The Rockies are he-man mountains. They don't sweep gracefully from grassy hills as do California's Sierras; they tower massively from arid plains. They look as though they happened by accident rather than design. And they challenge the adventurous rather than lure the seeker after beauty.

The breadth of the Rockies and Great Plains is as grandoise as their height. This land stretches from the Dakotas to the Sierras, from the Canadian border to the northern border of Mexico. It ranges in altitude from 4,000 feet to over 14,000 feet.

You should be fit and outdoor-oriented to retire here. Generally, most of us can adjust comfortably to altitudes of over 5,000 feet, but from above 6,000 feet it is wise to get your doctor's approval, especially if you have heart disease or a respiratory problem.

This is warm, dry climate with humidity averaging below 40 percent and annual rainfall less than 15 inches in most places. The sun shines almost 300 days a year. Temperatures can be extreme, with summer days in the 80s and 90s., plunging to the 50s. at night. Winter temperatures can average in the 20s and 30s. during the day and dip below 0°F. at night. Thunderstorms and wind storms are not uncommon during the summer, but spring and fall are usually delightful, bringing carpets of flowers and golden fall foliage.

You can enjoy the outdoors almost any time of the year, and you can ski most of the year as well as play golf and tennis. You can couple outdoor activity with indoor adult education and cultural entertainment. And if you're a health buff, you'll find that the climate and elevation is good for asthma, arthritis, sinusitis, hay fever and respiratory disorders. In fact, the climate and elevation are similar to that of the Hunza region or the Caucasus, where many people live to exceptional ages.

1. COLORADO—FOR A RETIREMENT HIGH

Colorado can give you a retirement high both physically and culturally. It is the highest state in the nation (averaging 6,800 feet) and invites vigorous outdoor living. Its cities, filled with sophisticated refugees from both East and West coasts, offer the amenities of New York and the hospitality of San Francisco. And its scenery rivals that of Switzerland, its food that of France, its charm that of Japan.

I lived in Colorado for almost a year, and I've returned year after year. Each time I'm even more impressed with the scenic spendor and intellectual grandeur. I saw many firsts here: my first dry streambed, my first mountains and the first city I loved (Denver). And I came to share the emotions of Katherine Lee Bates, who, looking down from the Olympian heights of Pikes Peak, formed the opening lines of "America the Beautiful": "Oh beautiful for spacious skies, for amber waves of grain; for purple mountains majesties above the fruited plain."

Colorado's terrain is diverse, fascinating and spectacular, with some 53 peaks over 14,000 feet and vast plains and deep valleys grand enough to hold the universe. But some things are changing, and not all for the best.

Denver is the fourth-fastest growing metropolis in the country. This boom has clogged the freeways, polluted the air (the only major city with dirtier air is Los Angeles), crowded the airport and dried up the water. The western slope, once the proud province of mountain men and pioneer women, has been ravaged by oil, gas, and coal diggings as a result of the energy crisis. And once languid cow towns have been turned into neon and plastic fast-food cities.

Another disadvantage is the altitude. Most mountain sports take place at altitudes of 9,000 feet or higher, an elevation that would be hard even on a healthy, younger person. And a car is a necessity almost anywhere in the state, so the availability and cost of gasoline should figure into your retirement plans. Also take into account that you will need lots of heat in winter (natural gas is most commonly used) although you won't need air conditioning in summer.

Don't expect shuffleboard courts or sun cities. This is a youthful land where you are as young as you feel. Typically, a retired couple may go cross-country skiing in the morning, attend college in the afternoon and go disco dancing in the evening. You'll share a young person's environment and life-style. You might even take up bicycling for local transportation, especially if you retire in Boulder, Colorado Springs or Durango. Most other cities also have quiet, marked bicycle routes and motorists are cooperative. Local clubs offer weekend group tours for bikers of all ages.

So if you're young at heart, you can certainly find a Retirement Eden in Colorado. The best areas are the Front Range, where the cities of Boulder, Denver and Colorado Springs lie on grassy, treeless plains against the pineclad foothills of the Rockies; and the unspoiled and isolated San Juan Range in southwestern Colorado, where Durango and Pagosa Springs offer retirement havens. Some 12 percent of Colorado's 3 million population is over age 60 and 8.4 percent is over 65.

Stimulating Climate and Environment

The Continental Divide and the Rocky Mountains cut a north-south path down the center of Colorado, forming the headwaters of 6 major rivers and dividing the state into the flat eastern Great Plains and the high plateaus and deep gorges of the west. The climate is marked by sunny, pleasantly dry summers and cold winters with little rainfall (lack of water is Colorado's biggest problem). Although the climate is dry and zestful, rapid changes are common. At Front Range elevations of 5,500 feet, January temperatures range between 15° and 45°F., July 58° to 95°F., with an average relative humidity of 46 percent. Rainfall averages sixteen inches annually, snow 42 inches. Along the foothills, warm Chinook winds usually melt the average 4-inch snowfall in 2 to 4 days. Most summer days are mild, clear and sunny. Brief afternoon thundershowers cool you off and you'll need a blanket almost every night. About 20 nights a year you might appreciate a fan. July afternoons can reach 100°F., but with the low humidity, it doesn't feel as bad as some Eastern cities when the temperature is in the 80s. By mid-August the summer heat is past and cool Indian summer lasts into late fall. Wide daily ranges of temperature are common; a cloud obscuring the sun for 20 minutes can send the mercury plunging 16°F. This is just one way the climate can keep you on your toes.

Top Health Care at Low Cost

Not only is Colorado's climate healthy, the quality of health care is high and the cost is low. The clean, dry, pollen-free air breeds little hay fever or respiratory ailments. Mosquitoes are rare, termites and wood rot almost nonexistent and houseflies are easily kept outdoors. The average cost of a semiprivate hospital room is $145 a day (compared with the national average of $163) and there are 198 doctors per 100,000 residents —much more than the national average of 174 and more than adequate for the population. Colorado has 101 hospitals with 14,666 beds, 208 nursing homes with 20,525 beds and 35 personal-care homes with 2,206 beds.

Good Housing at Reasonable Costs

Most homes for sale are contemporary single, bilevel and trilevel frame structures with wood or brick veneer siding and a roof of wood or asbestos shingles. Newer houses sell from $50,000; some older, Victorian houses are available in the old mining towns and may seem like bargains. But most of these antiques are uninsulated, underwired and difficult and expensive to heat. Many of the newer homes utilize solar heating, which can also heat the water and a greenhouse. Landscaping is sometimes a problem in both old and new developments. Shade trees take years to grow. Water is scarce and green grass hard to maintain. Townhouses, apartments and condominiums are available in Colorado Springs, Boulder and at some ski resorts, but many are miles from supermarkets and other services. Before buying or leasing, make sure that the walls are thoroughly insulated and that basements are free of leaks. Most new homes come with a 10-year guarantee on materials and appliances, but some of the better homes were built in the 1950s and 1960s.

Watch out if you buy retirement land in Colorado. Suits have been lodged against some land companies. Recently the Federal Trade Commission reached a settlement with Bankers Life and Casualty of Chicago and 11 other respondents accused of using unfair and deceptive practices to market lots in southern and central parts of the state. The developments covered by the settlement were San Luis Valley Ranches, Rio Grande Ranches, Top of the World and Larwill Costilla Ranches (all in the San Luis Valley area) and Hartsel Ranch and Estate of the World in Park County.

Moderate Cost of Living

The more land your residence is on, the lower the tax rate per acre. For residential acreage only, the first acre is assessed according to its 1973 value, the next four acres at half the value of the first acre, and the rest of the acreage up to a maximum of 35 acres at one-fourth the value of the first acre. The tax is somewhat higher on a new home than on an older home of comparable size and quality. Average taxes on a new

3-bedroom, 2-bath house worth $70,000 in Colorado Springs total $900; on a 20-year-old 2-bedroom house in Boulder worth $85,000, the taxes average $600. The combined gas and electric bill for a well-insulated Boulder house averages $30 monthly in summer and $75 in winter (no air conditioning and no heat in bedrooms). In a larger home with central heating and air conditioning, figure $75 to $110 monthly. Natural gas and electricity are relatively inexpensive, and, in spite of food haulage costs, overall living costs are only about 10 percent higher than in Florida. Even in moderately expensive Denver, a couple can retire on $9,678 annually, vs. the national average of $10,022. But soaring housing prices and haulage charges have pushed up living costs along the northern Front Range and in the San Juan Mountains. And the lack of supermarkets, plus higher haulage charges, raises the cost of living in small mountain communities to as much as 20 percent more than in larger centers. Compared to food prices in Florida or California, grains and cereals often cost less, while fruits and vegetables (except apples, pears, peaches and cherries) cost more. Meats are comparable with the national average, as are most beverages, including the famous Coors beer. Most larger mountain towns have a chain supermarket supplying a wide choice of fresh produce and meat at the same prices as in larger cities. However, in any town without a chain supermarket, fresh produce is scarce and food prices about 20 percent higher.

In taxes, Colorado ranges from sixteenth in tax burden at the lowest bracket to twentieth in burden at the upper levels. Here's a breakdown:

Income Tax—rates range from 2.5 percent on taxable income under $1,134 to $544.42 plus 8 percent of excess over $11,342 taxable. Exemptions are $964 per individual plus an extra $964 for persons over age 65. There is also a food sales tax credit graduated on income.

Property Taxes—local assessments based on 30 percent of actual value. Some tax credit is available to persons 65 and older. Taxes run 1 to 2 percent of market value.

Sales Tax—3 percent, with cities and counties imposing additional taxes up to 7 percent.

Cosmopolitan Culture

Coloradans demand and enjoy the amenities of a sophisticated civilization. Denver's Stapleton Airport is an international terminus and the city is a sister city of Brest, France and Takayama, Japan. Denverites get "dressed to the teeth" for such events as the symphony at the large Denver Center for the Performing Arts, the Junior League Benefit, the Debutante Ball and the first night at Bonfils Theater of the Denver Center. This latest cultural jewel is a $13-million complex that is perhaps the most flexible and workable cluster of theaters in the country, and a perfect match between architect and artist. Denver also has a museum of natural history, the largest public library system in the Rocky Mountain region and year-round musical entertainment. Other museums, galleries and musical groups include the University of Colorado Museum and Art Gallery in Boulder, the Colorado Springs Fine Arts Center and Taylor Museum, the Colorado Ski Museum at Vail, the Matchless Mine and Tabor Opera House in Leadville, the Aspen Music Festival, the Central City Opera and summer festivals. With 7,100 miles of unposted fishing streams and 2,200 cold-water lakes and reservoirs, the state offers ample opportunity to catch Rocky Mountain trout and other fish. Hunting for pheasant, grouse, quail, duck, geese, deer, elk and other wild game is popular. And Colorado residents age 64 or older may purchase a lifetime small-game hunting and fishing license for only $2. Colorado is famous for its skiing facilities in most mountain locations, including the nation's most important centers for cross-country skiing.

Active Agency on Aging

Colorado's Division on Aging has been in the forefront of many innovations in the field, and its directors have served in many national posts. The division funds and helps administer programs in all the essential areas: nutrition (hot-meal programs), health care (both clinics and at-home services), housing and location, income maintenance, senior centers and clubs, financial counseling and assistance, employment opportunities, legal-aid services and recreation programs.

For further information, write:

> Division of Services for the Aging
> Department of Social Services
> 1575 Sherman Street
> Denver, CO 80203

MAJOR RETIREMENT AREAS

The Front Range—Retirement with Culture

Big city facilities and urban culture exist mainly in Colorado's Front Range. This urbanized area from Greely to Colorado Springs has drawn thousands of newcomers from both the East and West coasts—people seeking the culture and sophistication they left behind.

Unfortunately, their presence—and their autos and recreational vehicles—has created serious congestion and air pollution. Cold winter days create an air inversion in Denver in which a brown cloud of poisonous carbon monoxide builds up half-a-mile deep in the oygen-short atmosphere. Frequently, southerly winds blow this brown cloud as far north as Greely (60 miles from Denver) and spread the noxious brown fumes across hundreds of miles of low-lying towns and villages. At times, the brown cloud extends to the edge of Boulder (30 miles northwest of the capital), part of which, fortunately, is a few hundred feet higher than the plains and relatively pollution-free.

The *Denver* area (pop. 1.7 million) is home to more than 60 percent of the state's residents, and population projections show 2.5 million by the end of the century. The capital city offers Eastern sophistication and Western hospitality, and many advantages to retirees. Seniors get a 50 percent discount at symphony concert matinees, and they have the services of the largest medical center between Kansas City and San Francisco. Notable are the Front Range Veterans Administration hospital, the University of Colorado Medical Center, the National Jewish Hospital with a total of almost 2,000 beds and almost 1,000 doctors. Denver also has important art and natural history museums and professional baseball and football. Opera is performed each summer in the old mining town of *Central City*, about 30 miles west of Denver. Denver has several singles clubs open to all ages (20 percent of the Colorado Mountain Club singles group is over age 45). Unfortunately, the inflation rate in Denver is higher than the national average, and a good home in fashionable *East Denver* now starts at $150,000—if you can find it. But outside the metropolitan area, you can find a 3-bedroom, 2-bath, 2-car-garage trilevel home on 2 or more acres of land for $100,000. Costs are even less in unspoiled areas of attractive nearby towns like *Grand Lake, Glenwood Springs, Idaho Springs, Raymond* (near Boulder), *Georgetown* and parts of *Estes Park*. Here are other major towns in the Front Range worth investigating:

Boulder (pop. 85,000), a university town 30 miles northwest of Denver, perhaps provides the best combination of outdoor recreation and educational and cultural opportunities in the Front Range. A growth-control program limits population growth to 2.5 percent annually. As a result, a 2-bedroom, 1½-bath, 1-car-garage home on a 50 by 125 foot lot costs $85,000 to $95,000. Other costs are not as high. Bicycling is safe and approximately 10,000 residents ride bikes. An estimated 10 percent of the population is vegetarian and almost everyone is health conscious. Good hospital facilities are available at the University of Colorado Medical Center and in municipal hospitals, and there are excellent recreational and cultural facilities throughout the town. A 35-mile drive takes you to Rocky

Mountain National Park. And Boulder's own superb Mountain Parks, immediately west of the city, preserve a 7-mile long greenbelt offering scores of hikes and climbs. Education is popular in Boulder, with instruction available at all levels in everything from languages to fine arts and sciences. The parks department offers adult classes in local schools, and continuing adult-education classes are offered by the University of Colorado. One course offered recently was "Singles over Fifty—How to Have the Time of Your Life!" The University of Colorado Senior Citizens Auditing Program is a free noncredit program available to all Colorado residents 60 and over, and it permits you to enroll in any course at the university without charge. The same program is available on the university's smaller campuses at Denver and Colorado Springs. Spearheaded by the university, Boulder offers a vast array of cultural entertainment at low or nominal cost, including a summer music festival, Shakespearean festival, drama festival and a summer school with several hundred courses. Anyone over age 50, retired or not, can obtain a senior citizen's ID card entitling him or her to a 50 percent reduction at the municipal swimming pool and to a discount at most movie theaters. Many Boulder stores also grant a 10 percent discount to retirees. People 65 or older can ride free during non–rush hours on area buses, including intercity buses to Denver. A recently completed senior center offers daily recreation and nutrition counseling, plus regular tours all over the West. Anyone with a roof over his head can retire here for less than $10,000 annually (for a couple). However, plan to buy a house ($85,000), as rents are high (from $400 a month) and mobile-home living, while possible, is not the best. If you do retire here, in a single evening you could have an excellent meal at an exotic, low-cost restaurant, see a classic film, watch visiting dancers from China or India, see a Rolfing demonstration or a travelogue on Nepal and attend a concert by a prominent symphony orchestra.

For further information, write:

Chamber of Commerce
P.O. Box 73
Boulder, CO 80306

Colorado Springs (pop. 231,600) is a resort and industrial-military center lying at the foot of Pikes Peak 70 miles south of Denver. There are 3 military bases here, each with its hospital, PX and commissary, and Colorado Springs also has a large medical complex assuring excellent medical care with 1,418 hospital beds and 350 doctors. Surprisingly, housing here may cost less than in other parts of Colorado. Huge tract developments of attractive modern homes ring the city on the east, and a 3-

bedroom, 2-bath house on an 85 by 135 foot lot sells for less than $70,000. Other smaller homes in more modest neighborhoods like Pikes Peak Park cost $50,000, and you can also rent 2-bedroom townhouses from $350 a month. A contemporary trilevel house rents from $400 a month, 2-bedroom condominiums are available from $40,000 and more deluxe models sell from $70,000. The best areas of the city are the older, tree-shaded neighborhoods in the northwest section and in *Ivywild* in the southwest. The *Park Hill* neighborhood in the southeast offers good values among trees and landscaping (most eastside developments are newer). And you should make sure your housing isn't located near a military base or filled with young military families with lots of children. If you want quiet luxury, you might choose the rural *Black Forest* area north of Colorado Springs, where attractive homes on small tree-shaded lots sell from $85,000.

Golf is big in Colorado Springs, with 6 public and 5 private and military courses. At the famous Broadmoor Hotel resort, golf is played on 3 championship courses, and riding, tennis and skiing facilities are available. Colorado Springs Fine Arts Center provides year-round art exhibits, musicals and drama, and there are many concerts by military bands and choruses and the Colorado Springs Symphony.

Another city in this area worth exploring is *Longmont* (pop. 40,000), combining urban living with rural relaxation at a relatively comfortable 5,000 feet.

For further information, write:

> Chamber of Commerce
> P. O. Drawer B
> Colorado Springs, CO 80901

The Western Slope—Boom or Bust?

The broad, sparsely populated region on the western slope of the Rockies is as big as the state of Ohio. For centuries it has remained an unspoiled wilderness. But now, due to prospectors and drillers seeking coal, uranium, oil and natural gas, the population has jumped to an estimated 280,000 from 190,000 in 1970, and housing costs have more than doubled since 1975.

Industry plans to spend at least $935 million on energy projects in this area. Although this expansion is bringing wealth to the area, many natives are worried about the effects on the quality of life, and some towns are attempting to limit growth.

Crested Butte is resisting a new molybdenum mine and *Grand Junc-*

tion voters recently rejected a $20-million school bond issue. An organization, Club 20, made up of businessmen and politicians from 20 western slope counties, is helping to organize conferences between industry and government people to deal with the boom. Meanwhile, the area offers good retirement living in some of the most spectacular scenery in the West.

Leadville (pop. 5,000) is situated at 10,152 feet—"where the mountains meet the sky." It is nestled comfortably at the base of Colorado's highest and most picturesque peak, Mt. Elbert, 14,431 feet. Despite its elevation, the town has a comfortable year-round climate, with January averaging 18.7°F. and July 68.1°F. Winters aren't bitter because of low humidity, although snowfall usually begins in October and continues until April. Summer days are also comfortable because of the low humidity, and nights are always cool. Medical facilities include the 36-bed St. Vincent General Hospital and the Leadville Medical Clinic. There are 5 dentists in town and a 24-hour emergency ambulance service. Good, older housing is available in the area from $60,000 and apartments rent from $200 a month. This town was made famous by H.A.W. Tabor and Baby Doe, and Tabor Opera House and the Matchless Mine and Museum are open to the public. Service and fraternal clubs abound, and there is good fishing and hunting, golfing, scenic trips and mountain climbing. A modern, recently constructed library has a good selection of fiction and nonfiction. Leadville's economy is still tied to the production of minerals. The Climax Molybdenum Mine (the largest of its kind) is located 13 miles from the city, and the many silver mines in the area are planning to increase production if the price of silver goes up—and stays there.

For further information, write:

Chamber of Commerce
P.O. Box 861
Leadville, CO 80461

Aspen (pop. 3,000), though thought of as a "hip" town filled with young skiers, is actually a year-round resort town that caters to all ages, and its summer activities are perhaps more popular than those in the winter. In the summer, philosophers come here to discuss serious subjects and the future of the world. Graphic artists compare work and collect new ideas to take home. Photographers, weavers and potters study with the masters. Ballet dancers practice in meadows, violinists rehearse in tall pines and horn players bellow among the shaggy crags. The Aspen Music Festival attracts the best professionals and student musicians in the world. Five orchestras and numerous ensembles, ranging from rock to Bach, turn the town into a 9-week music lovers' paradise. In connection with the festival, there is the Aspen Music School just outside of town, an opera worksop, the Aspen Choral Institute, the Aspen Conference of Contemporary Music and the Aspen Jazz-Rock Ensemble. Other cultural activities abound in and around Aspen. Snowmass Resort is summer headquarters for Salt Lake City's famed Ballet West. The International Design Conference meets here annually in the late spring. The Aspen Institute for Humanistic Studies meets here in late summer, and other programs are put on during the year by the Aspen Center for Physics, Given Institute of Pathobiology, Aspen Arts Foundation, Anderson Ranch Craft Center and Colorado Mountain College. Local newspapers and town bulletin boards advertise everything from Chinese martial arts to alpine ecology. Of course, skiing is popular, and there are 4 major areas for this winter sport: Aspen Mountain, Buttermilk, Snowmass and Aspen Highlands. Other outdoor sports include golf, tennis, sailplaning and raft trips. The restaurants are outstanding and cosmopolitan, serving everything from Mexican to Cantonese to Italian food. And the refurbished, Victorian Hotel Jerome is a meeting place for locals and visitors. Many shops and restaurants are located on pedestrian malls that make for easy walking and sightseeing. With the elevation at a relatively comfortable 7,907 feet, it is an easy place to get around in and get used to. If you're considering Colorado for retirement—or if you're just sightseeing—don't overlook Aspen any time of year.

For further information, write:

Chamber of Commerce
328 East Hyman Avenue
Aspen, CO 81611

Steamboat Springs (pop. 5,000), an isolated ski resort town 165 miles northwest of Denver, might be the only small town that claims it "is a good place to visit, but would you really like to live here?" Certainly, as a picturesque resort town, it is worth a visit any time of year. I visited here in late August and found it a delightful place with a delightful climate. During the summer the temperature ranges from a low of 40°F. (at night) to over 80°F. during the day. But the low humidity prevents any discomfort. Fall temperatures range from 25°F. to 62°F., spring from 24°F. to 54°F. and winter from below 0°F. to 30°F. during the day. In fact, totals for December and January are 483 degrees below 0 and 160 inches of snow. Naturally, if you are a skier you would be in heaven. But if you're a housebound retiree, you might not appreciate the cold and snow. However, about 4 percent of the population is retired and seems to thrive in this environment. There is access to a municipal hospital with 20 beds and a nursing home with 60 beds. The town has 2 clinics, with emergency service and visiting nurses. There are 4 doctors and 6 dentists in the area, more than enough for the population's needs. There is a shortage of 2-bedroom houses, but many condominiums and townhouses are available from $70,000. Some mobile homes and modular units sell from $20,000, and there are some 2-bedroom rentals from $350 a month. The tax rate averages 1 percent of market value, but the sales tax in town is 7 percent. Clubs are popular in the area, with 40 service clubs, hobby and craft clubs, and adult-education classes available at Colorado Mountain College. For outdoor recreation (in addition to skiing) there are 2 parks, a swimming pool, 2 golf courses, 20 tennis courts and biking, hiking, and horseback riding trails (4 stables located within city limits). Steamboat Springs has a multipurpose center, an office on aging, a hot-meal program, home-maker services, visiting nurses, counseling services, meals on wheels, a limited transportation program and a free weatherization program for seniors in need of insulation to reduce utility bills.

For further information, write:

> Chamber of Commerce
> P.O. Box L
> Steamboat Springs, CO 80477

Another city in this area worth exploring is *Grand Junction* (pop. 54,000), which has the Institute for Senior Citizens sponsored by the junior college. The town is clean, neat and at an elevation of only 4,587 feet.

For further information, write:

> Chamber of Commerce
> Grand Junction, CO 81501

The San Juan Mountains—Wild and Woolly

This area of southwestern Colorado is a rugged, sparsely populated region of alpine peaks and wilderness, lakes and rivers—a perfect place for a mountain lover. And although it is more than a hundred miles west of Denver, many Denverites have bought lots here so they can retire in a smogfree environment.

Durango (pop. 13,000) is a delightful town I've visited several times, and I would certainly consider it one of my Retirement Edens. It has a well-preserved Victorian flavor and modern conveniences that make it a prime resort area. It is also a relaxed college town (Ft. Lewis) where you could monitor classes. The energy boom has created a housing shortage and high prices, so a good 2- to 3-bedroom house starts at $75,000, while small farms (1 to 2 acres) sell from $90,000. But at *Durango West*, a golf and country-club development, you can get homes and condos starting from $75,000. Coal is available locally and is often used for heating. And by raising your own vegetables and fruits you could further reduce expenses.

There's much to see and do in the town. Durango is headquarters of the San Juan National Forest and is the hub of good fishing and hunting country. There's swimming at La Plata Aquatic Center on Main Street, golf at Hillcrest Golf Club and tennis at the college and high schools. At the Southern Ute Tourist Center outside of town, you can see craft displays and demonstrations. Good skiing is available at Purgatory Ski Area north of town. And the tastefully decorated Victorian Strater Hotel offers gourmet meals and summer theater.

Durango lies in a rain pocket created by the many high peaks to the north. The result is that the entire area is greener than the Front Range. Fruit trees flourish and oak trees abound at up to 7,000 feet. The average high temperature in summer is 83°F. and the low 46°F. In the winter the average high is 45.3°F. and the average low is 14.4°F. Year-round average is 46.2°F. Just north of Durango is the fertile Animas River Valley, a popular fruit-growing area with its own mild climate. However, so many people seek homes here that prices have soared. The valley is also becoming dotted with small mobile-home parks and other commercial ventures. Yet it is still a pleasant place to live, and many of the homes have irrigation water available.

Much of the land around Durango is owned by the federal government and Native American nations. However, there are several small, quality subdivisions which cater to retirees and others. Typical is Durango West. Currently, about 100 homes have been built, and eventually this area may have a population of 5,000.

About 50 percent of the new residents in the Durango area are retirees, many from Denver or Texas (they can fly into the Durango jet airport). And Durango is considered by most Coloradans as a place where they themselves would like to retire. So this area is definitely worth a visit —either as a tourist or potential retiree.

Not far from Durango is the Victorian mining town of *Telluride*, where charming old homes are for sale at fancy prices. Just as good is the sunny village of *Dolores*, a pleasant riverside community with good gardening conditions, soil and water, reasonably priced land and modern homes within 7 miles of the supermarkets of larger *Cortez*. *Lake City* is another isolated town offering great fishing and retirement possibilities.

And don't overlook *Ouray*, a resort in a dramatic mountain setting. For further information, write:

Chamber of Commerce
Durango, CO 81301

Pagosa Springs (pop. 5,000), 62 miles east of Durango, is surrounded by the San Juan National Forest. Its main claim to fame is a remarkable mineral springs with a temperature of 153°F. which is used to heat houses and buildings. This, and the fact that the town is near Navaho State Recreation Area and Wolf Creek Ski Area, has prompted some retirement developments. Chief is *Pagosa-in-Colorado*, which is the largest golf and country-club development in the San Juan area. It's a 40-square-mile recreation complex of condos, apartments and homes clustered around an 18-hole PGA tournament golf course. It is not strictly a retirement community, as about half the 600 permanent residents live here only during the summer months. Lots sell from $10,000 to $45,000. Homes and apartments cost $40 per square foot. The average home is worth $88,000 with an annual property tax of $500. Condos sell at $80,000 for 2-bedrooms and $85,000 for 3 bedrooms. Recreation facilities also include tennis courts, horseback riding and a health spa. The main shopping area is in Pagosa Springs, 2 miles away.

As with any land development you must be careful about your rights and restrictions before buying. Have the contract checked by a local real estate lawyer.

For further information, write:

Chamber of Commerce
Pagosa Springs, CO 81147

SUMMARY

If you're a vigorous retiree who likes winter sports, you'll love Colorado. You'll also love it if you are a sophisticated refugee from either the East or West coast and settle in the Front Range cities (where it won't cost you as much). And it's a great state for anyone who's young at heart. Here are my ratings for the major areas:

Excellent — Boulder, Durango
Good — Colorado Springs, Greeley, Leadville, Steamboat
Springs, Aspen, Pagosa Springs
Adequate — Denver (excellent if it weren't for the smog)

2. UTAH—RETIREMENT IN FANTASYLAND

To me, Utah will always be the land of Oz, filled with fascinating sights and governed by that mystical force, the Mormon Church. I've visited the state dozens of times, and I can see why some people could retire here most successfully, while others might forever remain strangers.

It is a fantasyland not only in the weird sculptures of Bryce Canyon, Zion National Park and Canyonlands National Park . . . but for all those who don't understand or appreciate the influence of the Mormon Church. Fully 60 percent of the residents are Mormons (Church of Latter-Day Saints), and the church's presence is felt in the legislature (90 percent Mormon) and in businesses controlled by the church—ranging from sugar mills to finance companies, textile mills, hotels, an airline, hospitals, radio and television stations. The church also dictates morality and social behavior. Liquor is frowned upon by the church, and the only alcoholic beverage widely available throughout the state is 3.2 beer (and it is not sold on Sundays). Some restaurants serve wine or let you bring your own liquor or wine and will provide you with setups (ice and soft drinks). And, in a practice known as "liquor by the wink," customers may purchase miniature bottles of liquor in hotel lobbies and drink them in adjoining bars. Bottled liquor is also available at state-run stores and at private clubs. But a confirmed social drinker would suffer. Yet the church also encourages a respect for age and such traditional values as strong family ties and self-reliance. The tree-shaded towns are clean, law-abiding and safe at any hour, with exceptionally low rates of crime, poverty and disease.

Also, the Mormons have always had an active interest in entertainment and have produced such artists as Red Nichols, the Osmonds, Maude Adams, Laraine Day and Faye Dunaway. The church encourages sports, particularly basketball, football and boxing. And while it may seem that most Mormons are of northern European background (English, German, Danish), many converts are French, Italian, Polynesian and Japanese. And to this day the church maintains a foreign-language capability at its Salt Lake City offices that rivals that of the United Nations.

Thus, a "gentile" (non-Mormon) who accepts the fact that he would be in the minority (politically, economically, socially) and would be influenced by the moral and social strictures of the church, could retire successfully in this state. Chase Econometrics projected that Utah would become one of the best retirement states because of low energy costs, moderate cost of living, and healthy job growth. Some 11 percent of the state's 1.3 million residents are over age 60 and 7.7 percent over 65.

Spectacular Scenery and Sunny Climate

The Wasatch range of mountains cuts a spectacular seam lengthwise down the center of the state. On either side, it leaves a wrinkled, mostly arid landscape that slopes to flat deserts, relieved in the east by the powerful Green and Colorado rivers. In the southern part of the state, the mountain seam has created such wonderlands as Bryce Canyon and Zion, Canyonlands and Arches national parks. Utah's climate is generally dry, with hot summers and cold winters, except in the southwest corner, which has a semitropical climate. Statewide, winter averages 29°F., spring 48°F., summer 71°F and fall 51°F. The northern mountain regions are 6 to 9 degrees cooler in all seasons, and the southeastern regions are 2 degrees warmer. The annual average humidity is 40 percent, with 15 inches of rain annually and 2.5 inches of snow.

Good Medical Care at Reasonable Cost

A semiprivate hospital room in Utah averages $145 daily (vs. the national average of $163) and there are 163 doctors per 100,000 residents, more than enough for the population. There are 41 hospitals with a total of 5,084 beds, 86 nursing homes with 4,021 beds and 18 personal-care homes with 592 beds.

Good Housing at Reasonable Cost

Generally, a 2- to 3-bedroom retirement home costs $50,000 and apartments rent from $300 a month. You can buy a "minifarm" (less than 10 acres) for $55,000, and some recreational land sells for under $1,000 an acre.

Moderate Cost of Living

Utah ranks twenty-third in tax burden at lower levels and thirty-second at upper levels. Property taxes average 1 percent of market value.

Income Tax —ranges from 2.25 percent on $750 taxable income or less to $356 plus 7.75 percent on $7,500 and up. Personal exemptions are the same as those permitted under federal law.

Property Taxes —assessments and rates are determined locally. A circuit-breaker law allows a refund on part of the property tax paid by qualified persons 65 or over with a total household income of less than $7,000. The refund ranges from 20 to 90 percent.

Sales Tax —the state rate is 4 percent, but localities add an additional

0.75 percent. Salt Lake, Davis, and Weber counties impose an additional 0.25 percent transit tax.

Year-round Events

Utah keeps busy year-round with entertainment, cultural and sporting events and festivals. Winter attractions, given indoors, are mostly of a cultural nature. The cultural center is Salt Lake City, where events are held in the municipal auditorium, the Salt Palace, and in a new cultural center and sports arena. The Tabernacle on Temple Square is home of the world-famous Mormon Tabernacle Choir and host to the Utah Symphony. Art exhibits may be seen at the Salt Lake Art Center near the University of Utah campus, but the state's best-known art gallery is the Springfield Museum of Art. Many resort areas also hold local art shows. The Paiute Indian Museum at Cedar City and Southern Utah Museum of National History are outstanding. Most of Utah's recreational attractions are outdoors, with these outstanding national parks and monuments leading the way: Bryce, Zion, Arches, Cedar Breaks, Canyonlands, Dinosaur, National Bridges, Rainbow. There are 44 state parks in Utah; largest are Snow Canyon, Dead Horse Point and Wasatch Mountain. Tennis courts and golf courses seem to be everywhere, and there are endless possibilities for fishing, hunting, horseback riding, swimming, water-skiing and boating. Utah has 14 ski areas and many snowmobile areas. The state's finest public skating rink is in the Salt Palace.

Services for Seniors

The state's Division of Aging funds and administers programs in all the essential areas: nutrition, income maintenance, housing, legal, transportation, health care, information and referral, recreation and culture.
For further information, write:

> Division of Aging
> Department of Social Services
> 150 West North Temple
> Salt Lake City, UT 84102

MAJOR RETIREMENT AREAS

Uintah County (pop. 9,000) runs from the ridge of the Uinta Mountains on the north to the heart of the Book Cliff Mountains on the south; its eastern border is the Utah–Colorado state line. The central portion of the county lies in the Uintah basin, though *Vernal*, the major city, is within Ashley Valley. Vernal is a mile-high city whose average winter temperatures range from 5°F. to 31°F., summer from 50°F. to 90°F. The average annual precipitation is under 8 inches and the relative humidity stays low. The Vernal area has 7 practicing physicians, 5 practicing dentists and weekly services of specialists from the University of Utah Medical Center. A 48-bed hospital serves the area. Several new housing subdivisions have been built as well as a number of apartment buildings; 2-bedroom units sell from $50,000 and apartments rent from $350 a month. Costs of goods and services are generally in line with larger cities, with the exception of heavier items such as refrigerators, which cost more because of freight rates. Utilities are comparable, with the exception of natural gas, which is higher. Building costs are slightly higher and taxes slightly lower. The Mormon church has chapels in each ward throughout the county, but most Protestant sects and the Catholic church also have congregations. For cultural opportunities, the Utah Ballet West, Utah Symphony and Community Concert Association perform in Vernal each year. Name bands and entertainers are also sponsored on many occasions by Vernal's many civic and service clubs. The Uintah Potter's Guild and Little Gallery of Arts are local organizations offering cultural opportunities. Vernal boasts 2 museums and a Dinosaur Gardens (the town is next to Dinosaur National Park) where dinosaurs are depicted in natural habitat. Several clubs offer educational and cultural programs: Beaux Arts, Cultural Arts, Current Topics, Progressive Arts, State Poetry Society, Vernal Journalism Club and the Historical Society.

For further information, write:

> Vernal Area Chamber of Commerce
> 120 East Main Street
> Vernal, UT 84078

Richfield (pop. 5,500) is a halfway stop on a direct route from Los Angeles to Denver, and it is the natural gateway to 6 national parks, 2 national monuments and the Lake Powell and Glen Canyon national recreation areas. In winter, temperatures range from an average low of 16.1°F. to an average high of 43.2°F. In summer, the average low is 50.3°F. and the average high 90°F. The Richfield Care Center, a long-care nursing facility, has 98 beds, and the Sevier Valley Hospital has 28 beds. There are 5 practicing physicians and 7 practicing dentists. Housing starts at $50,000 for single-family units and there are some rentals available from $350 a month. Property taxes approximate 1 percent of market value, and other costs are in line with comparable cities. The city has parks, tennis courts and a beautiful 9-hole golf course just southwest of the city. One of the unique features of the city is the swimming pool, where more than 40,000 visitors annually splash. Many service clubs and Protestant and Catholic churches offer recreational and cultural programs. The town has a municipal airport and race track and area facilities at the Sevier County Fairgrounds, with the only quarter-mile straightaway track in the state of Utah.

For further information, write:

> Richfield Area Chamber of Commerce
> Sevier County Courthouse
> Richfield, UT 84701

Cedar City (pop. 13,500), a college town 20 miles north of Zion National Park, is surrounded by Utah's colorful red-rock country and the high, cool woods of Dixie National Forest. There are winds in spring, but the 4-season climate is pleasant all year. January temperatures range from 17°F. to 43°F.; in August, from 55°F. to 90°F. Rainfall averages 8 inches annually, and there is little air pollution. A contemporary 1,400-square-foot home with 3 bedrooms and full basement costs $62,500, with property taxes of $750 when new, decreasing slightly each year thereafter. Some 2- to 3-bedroom homes rent from $350 to $400 a month. Southern Utah State College offers a special Senior Citizens program: for $10 a year anyone over age 60 can audit as many classes as he likes, provided room is available. SUSC also presents a nationally known Shakespearean Festival each summer and an extensive adult-education program in the fall and winter. Cedar Breaks National Monument is nearby, as is Dixie National Forest and Brian Head Ski Resort. At the edge of town is Painted Hills Golf Course; in town is the Palmer Memorial Museum with Paiute and pioneer relics. Catholic, Presbyterian, Baptist, Church of Christ, Jehovah's Witnesses and Church of God are available in addition to the Latter-Day Saints Church.

For further information, write:

> Chamber of Commerce
> Cedar City, UT 84720

St. George (pop. 15,000) is the closest town to Zion National Park, and its lower elevation (2,800 feet) gives it a semitropical climate, with January temperatures averaging 40°F., April 60°F., July 84°F. and October 63°F. Rainfall averages only about 7.81 inches annually and humidity is generally under 30 percent. There is a hospital with 65 beds and 4 small nursing homes. The town also has 17 doctors, 18 dentists and 6 specialists, adequate for the population. Single-family homes start at $50,000, condominiums at $65,000, townhouses at $55,000. Some mobile homes are available from $10,000. Building lots cost $10,000 with building costs $38 a square foot. Some rentals are available from $250 a month and there are some time-share condominiums (you occupy it for only a few weeks during a year) in the area. Property taxes average 1.1 percent of market value and other costs are comparable with similar-sized cities. St. George has a library, 3 bookstores, an art gallery, a little theater and good television reception brought in by the county for a fee of $20 a year. There are 7 clubs in the area, 2 parks, a swimming pool, 4 golf courses, tennis courts and adult-education courses. Some 15 percent of the residents consider themselves retired and are active in 3 senior centers and clubs. There is a local office on aging, a hot-meal program, homemaker services, visiting nurses, meals on wheels, a transportation program, special health clinics, a rehabilitation program and numerous other programs provided by the county office on aging.

For further information, write:

Chamber of Commerce
St. George, UT 84770

Some people have also retired in *Monticello,* a smaller community near Zion National Park.

Kanab (pop. 3,000) is a town you've probably seen or read about: some 50 Hollywood movies have used the dunes, canyons and lakes surrounding it as their Western settings, and Zane Grey lived here when he wrote *Riders of the Purple Sage.* This is a little higher elevation (4,975 feet) than St. George, so the climate is 5 degrees cooler in all seasons. About 11 inches of rain fall during an average year, and the humidity stays around 20 percent. In a recent article in *Science Digest,* Kanab was listed eighth among the 10 healthiest cities in the United States. The town has 1 hospital with 35 beds and a nursing home with 8 beds. There are 2 doctors, 1 dentist and emergency service. Housing is generally scarce, but when available, single-family homes sell from $40,000 and mobile homes are available from $10,000. Building lots sell from $7,000 and building costs average $37 a square foot. Property taxes are a little over 1 percent of market value. Some senior discounts and local food bargains bring costs down further and some retirees have purchased motels and other tourist-related businesses. Energy costs are considered high and the lack of water has slowed growth. There is a public library, summer theater group, good television but poor radio reception, service clubs and women's clubs, adult-education classes, a park, swimming pool, golf course, 5 tennis courts and many biking, hiking and riding trails. There are 2 senior centers and church-oriented senior clubs. The county office on aging provides services including a hot-meal program, meals on wheels, transportation and rehabilitation programs.

For further information, write:

Kane County Chamber of Commerce
Kanab, UT 84741

SUMMARY

Utah could be a Retirement Eden if you were a member of the Latter-Day Saints (Mormon) Church or if you accepted and appreciated the influence of the church in political, economic and social matters. It would also help if you were a teetotaler or could survive without drinking; while liquor is available it isn't easy to get. Given those requirements, you could find some delightful small towns for comfortable retirement in spectacular surroundings. Here are my ratings of major areas:

Excellent — Cedar City, St. George
Good   — Vernal, Richfield, Kanab

3. NORTH DAKOTA—FOR A FREE-SPIRITED RETIREMENT

The spirit of Theodore Roosevelt still pervades the Flickertail State. The twenty-sixth president once said that he could not have become president except for what he learned in North Dakota. He regained his health there and earned the nickname "Rough Rider." And he relished the wide-open spaces, the clean, crisp air and the free-spirited independence of its people.

Many older people are realizing that they, too, can enhance their lives by retiring in North Dakota. They have lots of space in which to choose. The population density (about 9.4 per square mile) is among the lowest in the nation. And the land is a fascinating mixture of prairies, rich river valleys, small cities, huge ranches and vast stretches of wheat. The state borders Canada on the north and South Dakota on the south, the Red River of the North forms the eastern boundary with Minnesota and on the west the Great Plains extend into Montana. Eastern North Dakota is farmland, including the Red River Valley, which stretches from Canada to South Dakota and 35 miles westward. Midstate is a transitional zone between farming and ranching. In western North Dakota lie the Badlands

—deep V-shaped valleys, sculptured buttes and hills. Northwestern North Dakota is farming, ranching and oil country on rolling plains. In the northwest-central area lie farm- and ranchland and oil and lignite (a brown variety of soft coal) mining. The north-central region is glaciated upland and prime waterfowl hunting area. The southeastern part of the state is the most populated, and is dominated by the Lake Agassiz lake-bed plain. South-central North Dakota is rolling agricultural country and is dominated by the state capital, Bismarck. The southwestern part of the state is Roosevelt-Custer country—a dry, rugged unglaciated upland. But before you get the idea that North Dakota is arid country, you should know that it contains the largest man-made, freshwater lake in the United States, Lake Sakakawea, formed when the Garrison Dam was erected across the Missouri River. Covering 609 square miles with 1,340 miles of shoreline, it is a recreation lake and speedboats splash where dust once blew.

Inviting as this land might be, it challenges newcomers. The weather can be extreme—from 121° above to 60° below 0°F. in the same year. Yet even these weather extremes are moderated by the dry air. The people who pioneered here were and are a hardy lot: Norwegians, Poles, Russians and Germans who were determined to homestead farms and build cities. And if "striving is surviving," it is certainly evident in this state where some of the longest-lived persons in the United States live. Some 16.4 percent of the 654,000 residents are over age 60 and 11.7 percent over 65. Counties with the most residents (more than 25 percent) over 60 are Burke, Eddy, McIntosh and Wells.

Wide-Ranging Climate

The climate is continental, with a wide range of temperatures and little rainfall. In Bismarck, the capital, winters average 19.9°F. and summers 58.8°F. There are 171 sunny days with an annual average of 67 percent humidity. Rainfall averages 15.16 inches annually, snowfall 45.6. Daily fluctuations can equal 30 degrees or more, so on a summer day the temperature can get up to the 80s in the daytime but sink to the 50s at night.

Low-Cost, Quality Health Care

The state is noted for its people's longevity, probably because the residents are a hardy breed to begin with and the fittest have survived. Doctors are in short supply in rural areas. There are only 118 doctors per 100,000 residents in North Dakota, far below the recommended minimum of 133 per 100,000. The only consolation is that the average cost of a semiprivate hospital room is $120 daily, vs. the national average of $163. There are 60 hospitals with a total of 5,830 beds, 68 nursing homes with 5,248 beds and 35 personal-care homes with 1,630 beds.

Plentiful Housing at Low Cost

Housing is generally plentiful, with 2-bedroom, single-family homes available from $40,000, coops and condominiums from $35,000, 2-bedroom homes or apartments renting from $300 a month and some mobile-home parks available in Bismarck and larger cities.

Low Taxes and Tax Rates

In tax burden, North Dakota ranks forty-second in the lower brackets and thirty-seventh in the higher. Tax rates are also low.

Income Tax —rates range from 1 percent on taxable incomes of $3,000 or less to $1,220 plus 7.5 percent of excess over $30,000. Personal exemptions are $750, with persons over age 65 getting an additional $750.

Property Taxes —all real property is assessed at a percentage of full cash value, then reduced by 50 percent. Homeowners or renters 65 or older with incomes of $9,000 or less are entitled to a reduction in homestead assessment, ranging from 20 percent to 100 percent, depending upon income.

Sales Tax —rate is 3 percent. Electricity, prescription medicine, food and food products for off-premises consumption are exempt.

Historic Outdoor-Indoor Recreation

The Theodore Roosevelt National Memorial Park in western North Dakota displays the harsh, natural beauty of canyons and valleys, of buttes and cliffs and mounds shaped by centuries of wind, water and fire. The rebuilt Old West town of *Medora* is located at the entrance to the south unit of the park. Historical museums and sites abound in the state, with a major museum in Bismarck and many sites and remnants of forts associated with Lieutenant Colonel George A. Custer and Sitting Bull, throughout the state. There are art museums at Grand Forks and Medora. The International Music Camp, held each summer at the International Peace Garden, has become recognized as one of the leading summer schools of fine arts in both the United States and Canada. Throughout June and July, the camp gives Sunday afternoon concerts. The annual

Band Day in Bismarck, featuring bands from 4 states and Canada, is held in mid-May. For stage plays and revues, Fort Totten Little Theater offers summer musicals produced by the Devils Lake Community Theater. Dickinson State College also puts on revues, as does the town of Medora. Fishing is a major sport in North Dakota, with year-round fishing in Lake Sakakawea, Lake Oahe and the Missouri River. Hunting is extremely popular, especially for deer, antelope, bighorn sheep and for all kinds of wildfowl (one of the best duck areas in the country). Ski areas are located at Devils Lake, Bottineau, Rolla, Edinburg, Arville and Fort Ransom, with the Turtle Mountains area being particularly noted for winter sports. Rodeo is also big, and major events are held at the Minot State Fair and the Roughrider Festival at Dickinson. Hockey, curling, basketball, football and auto racing are also major attractions in the state.

A Full Range of Senior Programs

North Dakota's Aging Services provide a full range of localized services. Included are congregate and home-delivered meals, transportation, homemaker/home health aids, medical screening, social and recreational activities through senior centers and escort service. Local country social service boards provide counseling, alternate living planning, Medicaid and financial assistance. The state provides reduced fees for recreational activity and a state appropriation to develop local service programs based on community needs.

For further information, write:

Aging Services
State Capitol Building
Bismarck, ND 58505

MAJOR RETIREMENT AREAS

Devils Lake (pop. 7,500), located near the shore of Devils Lake, is in the heart of some of the best goose and duck hunting country in the north. Native Americans named the lake "Bad Spirit Lake" for its turbulence during storms and its bad drinking water. But the waters have since risen and sweetened and are now a center for fishing and water sports.

Climate and Environment. January temperatures range from a high of 16.5°F. to a low of −3.2°F.; April 66.8°F. to 43.4°F.; July 78.5°F. to 54.2°F.; October 34.2°F. to 16.1°F. The driest months are during the winter and the wettest during the summer. Noise and air pollution are minimal.

Medical Facilities. Devils Lake has 1 hospital with 110 beds, 2 nursing homes with 104 beds, 2 clinics, 13 doctors and 7 dentists.

Housing Availability and Cost. Retirement housing is plentiful, with 2-bedroom units selling for $40,000 and 2-bedroom homes and apartments renting from $250. Some retirement housing is also available in the Oddfellows Village outside of town and the Great Northern Hotel in town.

Cost of Living. Property taxes run 1 percent of market value, and the retail sales tax is 3 percent.

Leisure-Time Activities. There are 2 local newspapers, 2 libraries, cable television and good radio reception, many adult-education classes, 2 parks, a swimming pool, golf course, tennis courts, racquetball club and a bike path from town to the lake (approximately 4 miles).

Special Services for Seniors. Devils Lake has a senior citizens club and a Retired Service Volunteer Program, a local office on aging, meals on wheels, homemaker services, senior citizen's bus service, legal-aid service and other programs for seniors.

For further information, write:

> Devils Lake Area Chamber of Commerce
> P.O. Box 879
> Devils Lake, ND 58301

Fargo (pop. 61,500), which shares a border with Moorhead, Minnesota, is the largest city in North Dakota. It is the leading retail and wholesale center of the rich Red River Valley and one of the leading commercial centers in the Northwest. Its 5 hospitals with 1107 beds, 2 clinics, 220 physicians and surgeons, city and county health departments, 8 nursing homes and a number of nursing, medical technology and other schools combine to make Fargo-Moorhead the major health-care center between the Twin Cities and the West Coast. Fargo has another medical facility, the University of North Dakota School of Medicine Family Practice Center, located on the NDSU campus and affiliated with the Fargo hospitals. Fargo-Moorhead has 70 dentists, 3 dental laboratories and other specialists to assure top medical care. The area offers almost unlimited opportunity for leisure-time activity. There are 6 major parks, a bicycle path running the length of Fargo along the Red River, indoor and outdoor skating, 5 municipal golf courses and hunting and fishing areas. Cultural activities abound, with the Fargo-Moorhead Community Theater and three college theaters in the area. A 75-piece symphony orchestra and a civic opera association present year-round events, and numerous choirs, barbershop quartets and local dance orchestras offer entertainment. Fargo-Moorhead has a local daily and Sunday newspaper that covers both states, 5 AM and FM radio stations and 4 television networks. Good housing is available throughout the area, with 2- and 3-bedroom units available from $45,000 and for rent from $300 a month.

For further information, write:

Fargo Chamber of Commerce
P.O. Box 2443
Fargo, ND 58102

Bismarck (pop. 45,000), the state capital and county seat of Burleigh County, is located on the east bank of the Missouri River in a shallow basin 7 miles wide and 11 miles long. The area is almost entirely surrounded by low-lying hills about 300 to 600 feet high. The climate is semiarid, continental in character and invigorating. January averages 8°F., April 43°F., July 71°F. and October 47°F. Rainfall averages 16.16 inches, usually during afternoon thunderstorms. Winter precipitation is nearly all in the form of snow, with occasional blizzards. Freezing temperatures have occurred in every month of the year. There are 2 hospitals with a total of 453 beds, 3 nursing homes with 417 beds, 73 doctors, 29 dentists and 2 clinics. A 2-bedroom home sells for $50,000, with rentals from $300 a month. Recreational attractions include parks, swimming pools, tennis courts, skating rinks, theaters, bowling alleys and a civic center. There are 5 radio stations and 2 television stations, 1 public and 1 state library, 48 churches representing Protestant, Catholic and Jewish denominations. The city has 3 full-time recreational directors who plan year-round programs. Bismarck is surrounded by some of the finest fishing spots in the state, particularly on the Garrison and Oahe reservoirs on the Missouri River. The capital is an outstanding center of culture in central North Dakota with its art association, Community Concert Association, theater group, symphony orchrestra and concert choirs. Seniors belong to the many clubs in the area and enjoy discounts at many stores and services. Bismarck has state and local offices on aging which provide hot meals, transportation services, health care, financial and legal counseling, meals on wheels, volunteer programs and leisure-time activities.

For further information, write:

Bismarck Area Chamber of Commerce
412 North Sixth Street
Bismarck, ND 58501

SUMMARY

North Dakota could be a good retirement state if you are a hardy soul who likes cold, long winters and short, hot summers. For compensation you have clean, crisp, dry air and wide-open spaces. If this appeals to you, here are my ratings of retirement areas:

Good — Devils Lake, Fargo, Bismarck

4. IDAHO—RETIREMENT IN A MOUNTAINOUS WILDERNESS

Mountains so dominate Idaho that much of the state remains a wilderness. There are 52 peaks over 10,000 feet, including 14 peaks higher than 11,000 feet and 6 peaks over 12,000 feet. Hundreds of other peaks range from 7,000 feet to 10,000 feet. Not only have these mountains created a wilderness, they have blocked the building of roads, making travel within the Gem State difficult if not impossible in some places.

Yet it would be unfair to say that Idaho is just a mountainous wilderness. It is also a land of virgin rain forest, a blistering wasteland, gently sloping farmland and a fishing and hunting paradise.

Northern Idaho is a land of forested hills, mountains, lakes, rivers, streams and rolling farmlands. The central part of the state is an expansive, unspoiled game preserve. The south-central area is a region of extremes, with volcanic cones, crags and craters, rich forestland and rugged peaks. The southeastern section has gleaming cities and the southwestern section rich farmlands.

Just as diverse as the scenery are the people. Although northern Europeans (English, Germans, Swedes, Norwegians) are prodominant in the state, Idaho has more Basques than any place outside their homeland in the French and Spanish Pyrenees. More than half of the active church members in the state are Mormons. And it is the first state to be settled by fortune-seekers from the West (Oregon, Washington, Nevada and California) rather than the East.

Some 14.2 percent of Idaho's 920,000 residents are over age 60 and 9.8 percent are over 65. The 2 counties with the most people (more than 20 percent) over 60 are Washington and Oneida, both in the southern part of the state and near major population centers, *Boise* and *Pocatello*.

A Variable Climate

Altitude makes a difference in the climate, as you lose 5 degrees annually for every 1,000 feet of altitude. Location also makes a difference, because the southwestern part of the state is moderated by Pacific Ocean winds and the southeastern part by the continent. Statewide, winter averages 23°F., spring 58°F., summer 75°F. and fall 41°F. Average temperatures are warmer in the southwest, cooler in the southeast and cooler the higher the elevation. At Boise, the capital, which is at a relatively low 2,838 feet, the temperatures are considerably warmer, especially in winter, when the average annual temperature is 34.5°F. Its average rainfall is 11.43 inches, snowfall 21.4 inches and humidity 57.5 percent.

Low Cost, Quality Health Care

Like most of the Rocky Mountain and Great Plains states, Idaho suffers a shortage of doctors, especially in rural areas. Idaho has only 1,000 doctors (about 105 per 100,000 population), which is far below the minimum standard of 133 per 100,000 and the U.S. average of 174. More than 200 of the doctors are in the Boise area and nearly 400 others are in and around Twin Falls, Idaho Falls, Pocatello and Coeur d'Alene, leaving only 400 for the rest of the state. But a semiprivate hospital room in Idaho averages only $132 a day, vs. the national average of $163 a day. Idaho has 51 hospitals with a total of 3,737 beds, 54 nursing homes with 3,981 beds and 13 personal-care homes with 842 beds.

Low Cost Housing and Land

Some 2-bedroom retirement homes are for sale for $40,000 and for rent from $300 a month. Some wilderness recreation land is available for under $1,000 an acre, although good farm- and ranchland sells for over $1,000 an acre.

Moderate Tax Burden

Idaho ranks twenty-sixth in tax burden at lowest levels and twenty-fifth at upper levels. Property taxes average 1.5 percent of market value ($760 on a $50,000 house in Boise).

Income Tax—rates range from 2 percent on the first $2,000 to 7.5 percent over $10,000. Personal exemptions are the same as those under federal law, with an additional tax credit of $15 for each person age 65 or over (each resident gets a $15 tax credit).

Property Taxes—assessments are 20 percent of market value and rates are adjusted locally, averaging 1.5 percent of true market value. Persons 65 or older who have a household income of $7,500 or less and have owned and occupied their residence for 3 years are entitled to a property tax reduction which may not exceed $400.

Sales Tax—rate is 3 percent, with prescription drugs and prosthetic devices (exclusive of eyeglasses and dentures) exempt.

A Sportsman's Paradise

Idaho has some of the best fishing and hunting in the nation. The most famous fishing grounds are in the lakes regions: one, in the panhandle, includes Pend Oreille, Coeur d'Alene and Priest lakes; the other, in the southeast includes Henry and Bear lakes. In the 21 million acres of forest reserves can be found grizzly bear, brown bear, black bear, raccoon, badger, wolf, fox and coyote. Deer, elk and antelope are also numerous. Most of Idaho's museums are in the larger towns—Boise, Pocatello and Twin Falls. These towns also have the major art galleries. Idaho has more than 100 mineral springs, with a variety of facilities and accommodations. Most popular are those at *Lava Hot Springs, Soda Springs, American Falls* and *Hot Creek.* Winter and summer sports are popular in *Sun Valley* (see below) and there are many guest ranches throughout the state.

Active Agency on Aging

The Idaho Office on Aging funds and helps plan programs in all major areas, including nutrition, health care, housing, finances and leisure-time activities. In addition, the state office operates an advocacy assistance program including nursing home care and legal assistance.

For further information, write:

Idaho Office on Aging
Statehouse
Boise, ID 83720

MAJOR RETIREMENT AREAS

Nampa (pop. 29,500) is located 19 miles west of the state capital, Boise. It lies in the Treasure Valley, a glacial-rich area where thousands of cherry, peach, apple, pear and plum trees outdo themselves each year to produce pick-your-own fruit.

Climate and Environment. The city's location in the "comfort zone" results in consistently pleasant temperatures: mild winters and characteristically cool summer evenings; 4 seasons without harsh cold or extreme heat. The temperature in January averages 29.1°F., in April 49.8°F., in July 73°F and in October 51.2°F. for an annual mean temperature of 50.6°F. Humidity ranges from 74 to 83 percent in winter to 54 to 23 percent in summer.

Medical Facilities. Mercy Medical Center is a 162-bed acute-care hospital with more than 85 physicians on the staff, representing such medical specialties as orthopedics, urology, neurology, internal medicine, cardiology, psychiatry, dermatology and otolaryngology. There is a physician-staffed 24-hour emergency medicine department and ambulance service based at the hospital. A rehabilitation center has a 30-bed nursing service. Clinics are held regularly on blood pressure, diabetes, stroke, arthritis and cardiovascular screening. A home health department offers quality medical care to patients confined to their homes following discharge. Nampa also has a 22-physician clinic. The Yellow Pages list 4 chiropractors, 20 dentists, 2 orthodontists, 7 optometrists, 2 opthalmologists and 56 physicians and surgeons. All this assures good medical care.

Housing Availability and Cost. Sale price of existing houses ranges from $25,000 to over $85,000. Some suburban residential areas have homes ranging from $45,000 to over $90,000; 1- and 2-bedroom apartments and duplexes rent from $250 to $400 a month; 2- and 3-bedroom houses from $200 to over $450. The area also has numerous mobile-home courts.

Cost of Living. Property taxes average a bit over 2 percent of market value. But the sales tax is only 3 percent and local produce and farmers' markets bring down prices. Also, fishing and hunting and growing-your-own cut down on costs.

Leisure-Time Activities. The 200 acres of parks contain all facilities, including tennis courts and arts, crafts and hobby classes. There are 3 theaters, 2 bowling alleys and a community center. Fishing at Lowell Lake is superb, and in winter the mountains provide great skiing, although there is usually little snow below the 5,000-foot level in the residential or business areas (most of which lie below 3,000 feet). Its 3 colleges offer a wide variety of educational and cultural opportunities. There are 60 churches representing 25 denominations, a library, a local newspaper published 6 days a week, 3 radio stations and 1 television station. Radio and television reception are good, and there are more than 200 clubs in the area.

Special Services for Seniors. Nampa offers a variety of senior clubs, and there is a senior center at the community center. The local office on aging is in Caldwell and provides various counseling services. A hot-meal program, meals on wheels, homemaker and visiting nurse service are available, as are emergency service and legal-aid service.

For further information, write:

Nampa Chamber of Commerce
P.O. Drawer A
Nampa, ID 83651

Sun Valley (pop. 300) may not be a "Retirement Eden," but this world-famous resort might be one reason you would want to retire in Idaho. It is a sun-drenched, bowl-shaped valley 100 miles east of Boise, sheltered by surrounding ranges. The temperature is moderate both winter and summer, and it offers a year-round program of activities. You can enjoy bowling, swimming, ice-skating, movies and dancing. In winter there are 17 ski lifts to slopes for every type of skier, skating and sleigh rides. In summer, favorite sports are fishing, boating, kayaking, tennis, golf, skeet and trap shooting, lawn games, swimming, riding, pack trips and hayrides. The Sun Valley Center for the Arts and Humanities offers many cultural activities. And Sun Valley is a village unto itself, with its own hospital. A mile below Sun Valley is *Ketchum* (pop. 2,000), which was the last home of Ernest Hemingway. The area includes boutiques stocked with fashionable wear, excellent cafés and thriving saloons. Rows of condominiums and ski chalets fill Sun Valley proper, and the park between the lodge and inn has been replaced with a shopping mall complete with shops, restaurants, art galleries, bars and discos, service stores and a post office. A mile from Sun Valley Village lies *Elkhorn Village*, a sister condominium complex with 2,000 units.

For further information, write:

Chamber of Commerce
Sun Valley, ID 83353

The *Coeur d'Alene* (pop. 2,000) and *Sandpoint* (pop. 5,000) area is becoming a popular retirement spot. It is a lush vacation area in the Idaho panhandle, with dozen of lakes and streams. Irrigation has opened vast sections of the countryside to agricultural development, and dairying and lumbering are major industries. The temperature is moderate (elevation 2,150 feet), with four distinct seasons. Summer mean temperature is 59.8°F. and winter 38°F. Highest recorded, 109°F.; lowest −29°F. Average precipitation: 26.13 inches; snowfall 48.8 inches. There are 37 physicians in the area, 181 hospital beds, 1 nursing and 3 convalescent homes and 1 retirement home—adequate for the population. Single-family homes can cost over $100,000 but there are several low-cost retirement and resort complexes in the area, including the *Camlu Retirement Hotels,* which offer fully equipped apartments with food service, laundromat, maid service, security, craft rooms for sewing and weaving, billiards, square dancing, bingo, movies and various programs. Minimum age is 55, and fees run from $400 to $600 a month. Also in the area is *Johnson's Sandy Beach Resort,* a recreation-vehicle park with a nursing home, golf course, shopping center and marina in the area. Fees are $300 a month. Another is the *Post Falls Trailer Park,* a mobile-home park with police, fire, refuse collection, water, sewer, gas, electricity and paved streets. Fees average less than $100 a month.

For further information, write:

> Chamber of Commerce
> Coeur d'Alene, ID 83814

SUMMARY

Although Idaho is a mountainous wilderness, the best retirement spots are in relatively populated areas, offering adequate medical care. And you have access to some of the finest hunting and fishing in the nation, along with the facilities of world-famous Sun Valley. Here are my ratings of retirement areas:

Good — Nampa, Coeur d'Alene, Sandpoint

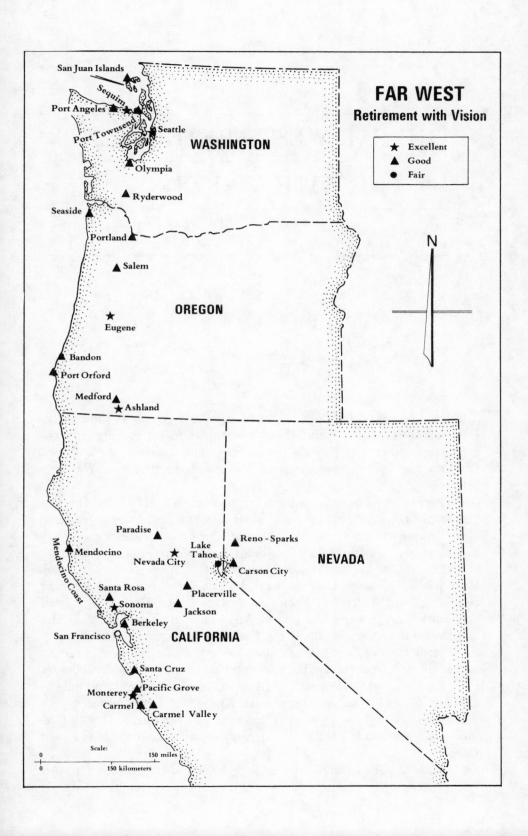

VII.

THE FAR WEST—RETIREMENT

WITH VISION

The Far West is as limitless as your horizons. Not only is the country Cinemascope in size, it's *Star Wars* in imagination—stretching from the moonscape deserts of Nevada to the towering redwoods of California, from the roguish rivers of Oregon to the stately mountains of Washington.

There is something to suit every pocketbook and taste. There is climate for the sun-worshipper and skier, housing for hostesses and hermits, living costs for princes and paupers, leisure activities for scholars and playboys, senior services for the hyperactive and the bedridden.

Once you've been to this Disneyland, you'll never forget it. If you leave you'll always want to come back. I first saw this country as a soldier returning from the Pacific. When I crossed the Golden Gate Bridge, I felt as though I had crossed the Rubicon. And when I stood on Telegraph Hill and looked over towards Berkeley, I started dreaming of returning.

It took me 5 years with many stops along the way. But when I ferried across the bay from Oakland to San Francisco, I knew I had come home. I lived in the area for 17 years and I've explored every practical mile of the Far West. I'm as enchanted with Nevada as I'm infatuated with northern California; as awed by Washington as I'm intrigued with Oregon. And I know that I will return here some day to seek my Retirement Eden.

This is the end of the continent and the end of the journey for most people. Those who find their dream settle down to live it. Those whose dreams don't come true often stop trying. But most people are limited only by their vision, and if you don't find what you're looking for, you probably haven't looked hard enough.

1. NORTHERN CALIFORNIA,WESTERN NEVADA—RETIREMENT IN THE IVY LEAGUE

Northern California is the New England of the West. In contrast to Southern California it has a rugged rather than sensual beauty, a cool rather than warm climate, sophisticated culture rather than fractured charm and rooted heritage rather than footloose life-style.

They wrote "I Left My Heart in San Francisco" for me. For although I was born and reared in Detroit and didn't leave until I was 23, I feel that I grew up in "Baghdad by the Bay" and shed my Midwestern shell there. My first meal at Fisherman's Wharf was steak and potatoes; now it's shrimp louie and sourdough bread. I thought that wine was for sissies and foreigners; now I practically brush my teeth with it. I thought that Van Camp's spaghetti was the way it was supposed to taste; now I demand my tagliarini fresh that morning. And I've long traded the sogginess of Wonder Bread for the crustiness of Parisian sourdough.

My love embraces all of San Francisco Bay and the rest of northern California and western Nevada. I have lived all over the Bay area and I've traveled all over the rest of the state. I've seen more of the Sierras than a hungry prospector, more redwood trees than most loggers and more Mendocino coast fog has washed over me than most people now living there.

My love stems from the head as well as the heart, from knowledge as well as passion, from need as well as want. Someone once said that California is a state of mind in which you hope to fulfill your image. If you have your mind set on it, you will find what you're looking for in the Golden State. Some 14.2 percent of the state's 22.5 million people are over age 60, and 10 percent over 65. While the majority live in the southern part of the state, here's what they—and you—can find in northern California and western Nevada.

Climate to Match the Mountains

The northern part of California is mountains and redwoods. The coastal sections are rugged rather than pretty. Across the coastal foothills lie fertile valleys that undulate toward the grassy foothills of the Sierras. These mountains contain magnificent valleys and stately peaks that provide barriers and sentinels for the blister-deserts that lie on the other side. The state can be said to have 2 distinct seasons: mild, wet winters and dry, hot summers. But the climate matches the mountains and valleys. California embraces 21 climatic regions, with the Los Angeles area containing 14 and the San Francisco Bay area 8. Generally, the coastal areas are cool and foggy most of the year (especially in the summer) while the further inland you get, the more extreme and 4-seasonal the climate. For instance, winter in San Francisco averages 50°F., spring 56°F.; summer 59°F. and fall 61°F. But there are challenging variations. Mark Twain once said that the "coldest winter I ever spent was one summer in San Francisco." And the tourists from Iowa, shivering in their cotton dresses, testify to the fact that July and August in San Francisco can equal November and December in most other places. But it is equally possible to leave 60°F. San Francisco, drive across the Bay or Golden Gate bridges, and be baking in 95°F. heat. The central valley regions around Sacramento and Modesto do tend to get hot in summer and cold in winter. Probably the most equable areas lie in the Sierra foothills, where the altitude (figure a 5 degree drop in temperature for every 1,000 feet) determines the limits of the 4-seasonal climate. Rainfall is also influenced by the altitude, with 60 to 100 inches falling in some northern sections while coastal areas average only 20 inches. The humidity stays fairly high (around 75 percent) but unless it's hot, you don't feel uncomfortable (and humidity usually drops in summer).

The Best of Medical Care

In keeping with the overall high quality of life, the quality of medical care is tops (as is the cost). California has 219 physicians per 100,000 population, far above the national average of 174. But, as in many places in the west, these doctors are concentrated in major cities while some rural areas may be short on medical help. And a semiprivate hospital room averages $199 daily, vs. the national average of $163. There are 613 hospitals with a total of 114,836 beds, 1,279 nursing homes with 104,346 beds and 2,221 personal-care homes with 33,976 beds. This adds up to top-quality (and cost) care in the major population centers.

Plenty of Housing at High Cost

Plenty of good housing is available, but it is probably overpriced. The average small house in California costs over $100,000. Condominiums and coops start at $60,000 and even mobile homes in this area start at $25,000. Where rentals are available, they generally start at $400 a month. And even in retirement communities, it is hard to find housing that sells for under $80,000 or rents for under $500 a month. So if you move here from some other state, plan to pay more and get less for housing than you did in almost any other part of the country.

Higher Cost of Living

While the average American retired couple spends $10,022 for basics in 1981, the same couple needs $10,871 in the San Francisco Bay area. This is less than Boston, Buffalo, Hartford and New York, but more than Denver, San Diego and Los Angeles. Costs tend to be lower in outlying areas, especially for housing, but the cost of some essentials—like food —may be even higher. As far as taxes are concerned, property taxes are limited to 1 percent of the market value of the home; the income tax burden ranges from thirteenth in lower brackets to fourth heaviest in higher brackets.

Income Tax—ranges from 1 percent of first $2,240 of taxable income to 11 percent on taxable income exceeding $17,430. For married couples, income in each tax bracket is doubled. Each person gets a $100 exemption. Personal exemptions are $27 single; $54 head of household and surviving spouse.

Property Taxes—limited to 1 percent of market value as of 1975, with increases limited to 2 percent a year until the property is sold, at which time it is reassessed. Seniors are eligible for a refund on property taxes, ranging from 4 to 96 percent, depending upon income. And seniors with incomes under $25,000 can delay part or all their taxes in return for a lien on the property when the house is sold or the owners die.

Sales Tax—the combined state-local rate is 6 percent, with an additional 0.5 percent added for transit taxes in Alameda, Contra Costa, San Francisco, Santa Clara and Santa Cruz counties. Food for home consumption and prescription medicines are exempt.

Where Culture Is King

Symphonies, art galleries, museums, theaters, adult education—you name it and it is here. Major cultural centers are in San Francisco, Berkeley, Fresno, Monterey, Palo Alto, Sacramento and San José. Historic sites abound, with Columbia, one of the best preserved of the Gold Rush towns, only 4 miles from Sonora in the Sierra foothills. Other landmarks are Donner Memorial State Park, 2 miles west of Truckee; San Juan Bautista State Historical Monument between Gilroy and Salinas and Sutter's Fort in Sacramento. Music ranges from Bach to rock, with the Monterey Jazz

Festival in mid-September and summer chamber music festivals in Saratoga. The San Francisco Symphony is world-renowned, and the Opera House cultural complex in San Francisco rivals Lincoln Center in New York. The gambling casinos of the Lake Tahoe region (on the Nevada side) offer varied entertainment. Outdoor sports are as big as the whole outdoors. And the fact that you can live, work and play outdoors most of the year means that you can fish, hunt, swim (not necessarily in the cold, dangerous ocean), ski, boat, golf and play tennis almost all year-round.

Top Services for Seniors

Again, in keeping with the high quality of life in the state, the California Department of Aging offers outstanding services. Most communities have Golden Age clubs, senior centers and chapters of senior organizations. They also offer hot-meal programs, meals on wheels, health care, housing information, financial assistance and leisure-time counseling. California was one of the first states to ban mandatory retirement, and it is the first state that allows people to make "living wills" prohibiting artificial means to prolong life during the terminal stage of an illness. California's Supplemental Security Income (SSI) and Medicaid (Medi-Cal) are among the highest in the nation.

For further information, write:

Department of Aging
1020 Nineteenth Street
Sacramento, CA 95814

MAJOR RETIREMENT AREAS

The Monterey Bay Area—Feast for the Eyes, Food for the Soul

I know what Sebastian Vizcaino meant when he first saw Monterey Bay in 1602: ". . . the best port that could be desired, for besides being sheltered from all winds, there is much wood and water . . . this port is surrounded by settlements of friendly natives who will give what they have, and would be pleased to see us settle in this country. . . . There are good springs of water; beautiful lakes covered with ducks and many other birds; most fertile pastures; good meadows for cattle, and fertile fields for growing crops."

Nothing much has changed. People still settle here to search their soul as much as find their fortune. And what they may not gain in money they gain in spirit. For this is one of the "pastures of heaven" and a place

I've come to often to make my peace. If you haven't visited here you've missed one of the heavens on earth; it's not only a good place to visit but a wonderful place to retire.

While the major towns in this area share similar climate, services and facilities, each has its own characteristics. Here's a thumbnail description of the most desirable places.

Monterey (pop. 40,000), the first capital of California, is a historic and cultural blend of Spain, New England, sea, mission and ranch. It is graced with a calm harbor, red-roofed white stucco houses, white sandy beaches, colorful ground cover and the unique Monterey cypress and pine, twisted into odd shapes by the wind.

In many ways this is the most complete town, blending historic charm with modern necessities. It is a small town with friendly "howdy," a museum piece that lives its history. The air is like wine and the streets are as clean-swept as the skies. Classical music blends with foghorns that sound a siren call to Cannery Row and Fisherman's Wharf. A couple of years ago *New West* magazine named Monterey "the best small city." It gave it highest ratings for air purity, lack of poverty, amenities and employment opportunities. It also rated it good or better in affluence, crime, health, growth rate, weather and education. Even if you didn't want to retire here, Monterey would be worth a visit for its 3-mile-long "Path of History," an orange-red line painted down the center of the streets, leading to every old house of distinction. Each stop is marked with a plaque explaining the history and architecture. Included are the Old Customs House (which houses a museum), California's First Theater, Colton Hall (site of the state's first constitutional convention) and the home of Robert Louis Stevenson. Most buildings are open to the public and some have been turned into tasteful restaurants. Be sure to visit and sample the wares on Fisherman's Wharf; it's a lot less commercialized than San Francisco's.

Carmel-by-the-Sea (pop. 5,000) looks like something out of Snow White and the Seven Dwarfs. The cottages appear to have bloomed like flowers in a pristine forest—so much so that it is difficult to find any particular house or even road, since they go around the trees. In fact, there are more trees (10,555) than people in the village, and they have the right of way. It is illegal to trim or cut down a tree without consent. The town was originally settled by wealthy recluses, artists and writers who wanted to be in the loveliest spot on earth. Unfortunately word leaked out, and up to 40,000 people a day come here to window-shop (most can't afford to live here). The town is a delightful mix of galleries, restaurants (200), shops (150), and boutiques (you lose count). Each one is "whimsical" in design, wares, and/or name. There's the "Come Fly a Kite" and "Every-

day is Christmas" shops and the "Sticky Wicket" tearoom. The "Watering
Hole" is a favorite bar. The zoning in town is just as whimsical. Strict
limitations on signs, extensive use of malls and capricious landscaping
preserve some of the natural charm. The houses within the village don't
have numbers or mail boxes. If you want to find a house you have to count
trees. And if you want to get your mail, you gather at the post office
around 11 A.M. Of course, this turns getting the mail into a social occasion,
with chats and gossip. Coffee and donuts are even served by a local
savings-and-loan. Villagers also check the town bulletin board to see
what's lost or found, for sale or rent, plus notifications of upcoming
meetings and births and deaths. Architecture ranges from California
Spanish to redwood modern to forest troll. But before you get the idea
that the place is too "cute" for living, realize that its natural and historical
assets are superb. Set on a curving beach at the foot of rolling hills, it is
one of the loveliest spots on earth. The crystal white beach is almost too
beautiful to walk on. And the historic Mission San Carlos Borromeo del
Rio Carmelo (just call it Carmel Mission) is one of the best restored of all
California's lovely missions. It is a historic marvel and a fitting place for
a tribute to God.

Carmel Valley (pop. 4,000) is home to some modern subdivisions of
no particular charm. Some shopping centers, notably the Barnyard (a
complex of rustic barns housing bookshops, arts and crafts shops, artisan
demonstrations, theaters, restaurants, entertainment), also lie out toward
the valley. This is flatter, drier, less interesting land, especially at its
mouth. But as the valley winds between the golden hills, you travel back
in time and see what the early settlers, poets, painters, writers and photographers saw. Several retirement developments and other housing has
sprung up here, most of it condominium type.

Pacific Grove (pop. 17,000) has attracted two groups of transients:
monarch butterflies, who come by the thousands each winter to settle in
the trees, and the Methodist faithful, who come here by the thousands to
pray. The town was founded in 1875 as a Methodist summer retreat, and
the flock kept retreating and returning until many of them started retiring here. The town still has a Victorian flavor, which is jealously guarded.
As nice as this may be, some of the buildings and houses look as though
they could do with some modern facelifts, and the town is moving to
change its image. Still, if you're a Monarch butterfly or Methodist faithful, you'll feel at home here.

Pebble Beach (pop. 1,000) is home of the Bing Crosby Golf Tournament, the fabulous 17-mile drive along the Monterey Peninsula, Cypress
Point (with the famous pine tree), the "ghost trees," the Del Monte Lodge
and the palatial homes of the rich and famous. Unless you're a millionaire,

forget about retiring here. And unless you're a movie mogul or star, you may not even be able to visit here. The film company Twentieth Century–Fox has bought up the land for a permanent film location.

While the above villages and towns are unique, they share certain common characteristics, services and facilities. Here are some of them:

Climate and Environment. "Cool" is one word to describe it; it has left more people shivering than enchanted. You can always tell the residents from the tourists: the natives are the ones wearing the tweed jackets and wool slacks, the tourists are the ones wearing shorts and goosebumps. I don't think I've ever been to this area (and I've been about 100 times) when there hasn't been some fog at least some of the time—summer more so than winter. That's fine if you're in the mood for a hot toddy and a roaring fire; but if you've come for sun and surf, you may be disappointed. The yearly averages don't sound bad: a high of 65.2°F. and an average low of 47.5°F. In Monterey it averages 63°F. in winter, 62°F. in spring, 65°F. in summer and 69°F. in fall. Inland, the temperatures are more extreme. While the winter and summer months tend to be cool and foggy, the autumn months, October through December, usually offer beautiful crisp, clear days with bright sun. The area has had its share of windstorms, which often knock out electricity. The wise natives usually have candles and firewood for such emergencies.

Medical Facilities. There are more than 200 physicians, 2 acute-care hospitals, 7 convalescent hospitals and 3 retirement communities that offer lifetime care, including hospitalization and surgery. One big plus, especially for those in the Carmel area, is the free emergency ambulance service provided by the Red Cross. One at the Carmel Fire Station covers Carmel and all the unincorporated areas up to the Mid-Valley Shopping Center. Another well-equipped ambulance looks after the needs of Carmel Valley; a third services the Big Sur area, a picturesque coastal retreat. Medical care is so good that the community hospital has been called the "country club on the hill." It is a showcase, designed by Edward Durell Stone. It ranks with the 17-mile drive, Cannery Row, Carmel's white sands and the mission as a landmark. A new diagnostic center opened recently for cancer, heart and lung diseases; it has a $550,000 EMI scanner. There are also a mental-health center, a clinical lab, the Eskaton Monterey Hospital (which is being updated) and the $15.5-million Silas B. Hayes Hospital at Fort Ord, home of the Seventh Infantry. There are 6 skilled nursing homes on the peninsula. Beverly Manor (99 beds) has the advantage of a private physical-therapy office next door, and the community hospital is around the corner. Two other nursing homes sit side by side and look out over the forest (they are Driftwood and Skyline, both 99 beds). And there are convalescent hospitals in Carmel, Monterey and

Pacific Grove. If you or your relatives have problems in a convalescent hospital, you can turn to the ombudsman program, which acts as facilitator, educator, mediator and record keeper. The area also has visiting nurses, meals on wheels and homemaker services.

Housing Availability and Cost. When houses are available, they're out of reach of most pocketbooks. The average single-family house costs $150,000, with highest prices in Pebble Beach, followed by the Carmel Valley, Carmel, Monterey, Pacific Grove, Marina and Seaside. It's hard to find any single-family house for under $100,000; it is easy to find them over $200,000. When rentals are available, they usually start at $500 a month on a long-term lease. Some retirement housing is available, including some that have life care. Included are *Canterbury Woods,* Pacific Grove, which has 160 apartments and cottages with kitchenettes. Age limits are 60 to 75 and prices start at $20,000 for a small studio with fees (for meals, maid service, maintenance, medical care) of $500 a month. *Carmel Valley Manor* is 5 miles up Carmel Valley Road. Minimum age is 65 and you must be ambulatory at time of entrance. Apartment costs start at $30,000 for a small studio, with monthly fees of $500. *Forest Hills* is in Pacific Grove. Formerly a hotel, it is now a retirement residence. Room costs start at $20,000, with a monthly fee of $500. Further up the Carmel Valley are some active retirement communities which have condominium units selling for $70,000, with monthly maintenance and recreation fees of $150. *Del Mesa Carmel* is located on a tree-covered mesa of 70 acres. The units all have kitchens and most have 2 bedrooms and baths. There are no medical facilities and minimum age is 40. *Hacienda Carmel* is located by the Carmel River. All of its 300 units (studio to 2-bedroom) are on a resale basis through local realtors. However, the association must approve the sale. Minimum age is 54 and 6 months, maximum 70. You'll find the usual clubhouse and dining-room facilities, swimming pools, putting greens, etc. In Monterey there is *Park Lane,* a pleasant apartment-hotel on the American plan. After acceptance (medical and financial statement) a new resident is required to pay only the first month's rent, a modest move-in fee and a security deposit. The monthly bill includes both luncheon and dinner (each apartment has a kitchen or kitchenette), mail service, utilities, limousine service, cable television and use of the health spa as well as activity rooms. Studios start at $700 a month, a 2-bedroom unit at $1,000 a month. Add $300 for a second person.

Cost of Living. You've got the message: it is not cheap to live here. I estimate that a couple would need an income of at least $15,000 annually to live moderately here ($9,000 if single). And you'd have to learn to avoid the stores, groceries, services, etc. that make most of their money from tourists. This presumes that you can afford to buy the type of housing that you want, realizing that it is probably going to cost you more than what you got when you sold your previous housing. So you'd have to pay more and settle for less, at least in material goods. But you would be rewarded with being able to maintain yourself in one of the most delightful places on earth.

Leisure-Time Activities. Each town has its senior centers, clubs and recreational programs. The Carmel Foundation Town House offers counseling and all kinds of activities: classes in art, French, sewing, history and current events, photography, wood carving, bridge, creative writing, bingo . . . you name it. The foundation also offers express-bus shopping trips to San Francisco and other places. Shopping is the biggest "game" around, and there are plenty of choices. Most visitors and residents start with Carmel with its delightfull inner courts, plus a big 3-story plaza with 46 shops that sell everything from beads to kites to Tinker Toys. You could drive out to the Barnyard on Highway 1 and shop in a complex of 90 shops, restaurants and businesses. Next to the Barnyard is the Carmel Rancho Shopping Center, with stores of all kinds—supermarkets, banks, dress shops, pet stores, druggists. On the other side of Rio Road is Carmel Center, another big shopping complex with professional offices. If antiques are your hobby, there are 51 such establishments on the Monterey peninsula, and some 77 art galleries. Some of these are located on Cannery Row in Monterey. But there is a lot more to do besides shopping: there is ample opportunity for volunteer work, 100 or so deliver meals on wheels; another 100 or so "sunshiners" deliver flowers and help admit and discharge hospital patients, and there are 450 active "pink ladies" (including 24 men) who also supplement the hospital staff and who have just bought a second tram to bring visitors up the hill to the hospital. Many seniors attend scores of adult-education classes. Others enter bridge and chess tournaments. Tennis is popular and golf is more so, with 15 courses, including two on military property. You can dig with the Gem and Mineral Society, count birds with the Audubon Society, hike with the Sierra Club. Local theater is alive and well: the historic First Theater and wharf theaters in Monterey, the Studio Theater and Forest Theater in Carmel. The Forest Theater is the first outdoor community theater in the United States, originating in 1910, and it produces Shakespearean and other plays. Many musical performances take place in Carmel's cultural center, which seats 733. Here is where trumpets announce the 2-week Bach Festival established in 1931. The Carmel Music Society presents outstanding artists throughout the year, and in Monterey, the annual Jazz Festival and the Monterey County Symphony highlight activities. Over in Pacific Grove, the Monterey Peninsula Concert Association presents a fine concert series. Incidentally, the Chautauqua series began in Pacific Grove and eventually ended up on the beach now known as Asilomar—"retreat by the sea."

Added to all this are the idyllic blend of trees, birds, and flowers; the rhythm of the ocean; the mysteriousness of the fog; and the people who choose to live here. They live and let live. They respect your privacy. They want to continue learning and living—and you will, too.

Special Services for Seniors. Alliance on Aging, Inc., serves all of Monterey County. Its 130 "friendly visitors" bring a smile and a bit of the outside world to 450 bedridden seniors. They also arrange shopping and sightseeing trips, visits to doctors, luncheons, recreational and religious programs. Under the National Council of Senior Citizens, the alliance works on the senior aides program in which the government furnishes part-time employment for those 55 or older. Some are paid to work on meals on wheels and other senior programs. One of the alliance's newest programs is to distribute 15,000 "vials of life" through various senior activity centers. "Vials of life" look like elongated medicine bottles into which you put a special form giving necessary information to paramedics and hospital emergency staffs. Each closed vial is taped under the top refrigerator shelf or medicine cabinet, and a decal pasted on the door. Other senior programs of the alliance include anticrime, elderly escort, neighborhood security and residential awareness and aid to victims of crime. Fishnet, a ministry of the Carmel Presbyterian Church, helps seniors with emergency problems, such as need for food, rent money, clothing, housing, employment. It also arranges the distribution of free vegetables to needy seniors.

For further information, write:

> Chamber of Commerce
> Monterey, CA 93940
> Carmel, CA 93921
> Carmel Valley, CA 93924
> Pacific Grove, CA 93950
> Pebble Beach, CA 93953

Santa Cruz (pop. 40,500), located at the north end of Monterey Bay 74 miles south of San Francisco, was one of the original "sunshine resorts." It is now a bustling arts and crafts center as well as an agricultural center. And many retirees are choosing to live here for its convenience to both the San Francisco and Monterey Bay communities. Santa Cruz has 2 general hospitals with 330 beds, 300 physicans and surgeons, 122 dentists, 28 optometrists and 57 chiropractors. The average price of a 2-bedroom home is $100,000 (lower than in Monterey or Carmel) and you can rent 1- to 2-bedroom apartments and duplexes for $350 to $500 a month, 2- to 3-bedroom houses for $400 to $600 a month. There are approximately 100 mobile-home parks in the area, including the adjacent incorporated community of *Scotts Valley*. Santa Cruz is located on the warmer side of Monterey Bay, so you can enjoy outdoor sports year-round. Facilities include 5 state beaches, 20 parks, 3 golf courses and a small-craft harbor. There are 100 churches, 14 libraries, 15 theaters and the Santa Cruz campus of the University of California, which offers educational opportunities to seniors.

For further information, write:

> Santa Cruz Area Chamber of Commerce
> P.O. Box 921
> Santa Cruz, CA 95061

Don't overlook *Aptos,* a bedroom community of Santa Cruz, which has attracted many seniors. Much of the housing is on high bluffs overlooking fine beaches. There are many delightful towns and shopping centers in the area and many activities and clubs. Many seniors take classes at nearby Cabrillo College, and the mobile-home park in the area has an activity center and recreational events.

For further information, write:

> Aptos Chamber of Commerce
> Aptos, CA 95003

San Francisco Bay Area—Mecca for Many

If I left my heart in San Francisco, I left other parts of me in the Bay area—Marin, Alameda, San Mateo and Contra Costa counties. I have lived in *Mill Valley, Berkeley, Crockett* and *Redwood City* at various times over a 20-year period and got to know these areas as well as San Francisco.

However, the city by the Golden Gate was always a mecca. Visiting the city was like living in Alice's wonderland, where all the sights and characters are probable but not very possible. Every day in San Francisco seemed like Christmas: delights and surprises that never seemed to end. Whenever I crossed either the Golden Gate or Bay bridges, it was with the anticipation of a child on his first holiday.

But much as I love San Francisco, I wouldn't want to retire there— or any other big city. I want to retire near there, in some quieter, smaller town that offers easy access to and an escape from the stimulating city. That is why I prefer some of the smaller towns in the Bay area.

I remember the first time I saw San Francisco Bay. It seemed a fantasy, a mirage, a Limoges bowl filled with petits-fours. Only by sampling did I realize that the goodies were for real. And by living in the Bay area I could get a proper perspective on San Francisco.

Of all the places I lived in the Bay area, the town I preferred most was *Berkeley* (pop. 104,000). I lived there for these reasons, which would be valid for retiring there: (1) the weather is sunnier and more seasonal than San Francisco's; (2) you have low-cost or no-cost access to the many cultural activities of the main campus of the University of California; (3) it is clean and quiet; (4) by living and eating like a student or modestly paid faculty member, you could live on less; (5) Berkeley offers its own lifestyle and the alternative (country club) life-style of Contra Costa County just over the hills; (6) Berkeley is out of the San Francisco earthquake zone—during the 1906 shake that devastated the city, many San Franciscans escaped to the East Bay (Oakland and Berkeley). While tremors are common, they aren't as bad as those in the city.

There are drawbacks, of course. If you live in the Berkeley hills, the climate can be cold and foggy. The flowers, shrubs and dampness are tough on those with hay fever or asthma. The town part of Berkeley isn't nearly as attractive as the gown (University of California). With little industry, taxes are high.

Climate and Environment. From almost any street, you can look across to the Golden Gate. The city bills itself as being one of the most racially progressive towns in the country. It was one of the first to integrate its school system, and the International House on the Berkeley campus has always been home to foreigners from all over the world. It is also "one of America's most refreshing cities," as the temperature has an average high of 64°F. Both the weather and the setting are lovely— if you can afford it. That means being able to find and pay for a quaint house in the college part of town, but not too far up in the hills (where you can freeze on a summer day). The atmosphere is greatly influenced by the main campus of the University of California, 1200 acres of white granite and red-tiled buildings, groves of oak and eucalyptus trees and a 307-foot campanile that can be seen almost anywhere in town. Most residents quickly become involved in university activities, attending concerts, films, folk festivals and theater and eating and drinking where students and faculty gather. This is also a great place for people who like to browse in bookstores; Telegraph Avenue near the campus is filled with them, and sidewalk vendors fill both sides of the street.

Medical Facilities. The facilities are excellent, but the costs are high. Unless you have access to the U.C. Medical Center, you would go to a local private hospital such as Alta Bates (Berkeley) and Peralta (Oakland), where costs run over $200 a day for a semiprivate room (vs. the national average of $163 a day). Physicians' and surgeons' fees are also high, partly because of the high malpractice insurance rates in the state. Retired military and veterans have nearby hospitals and medical facilities at Oak Knoll (Oakland) and Letterman (San Francisco). There is also a Veterans Administration hospital in Martinez, 35 miles from Berkeley. Most admissions, except for emergencies, are on a space-available basis.

Housing Availability and Cost. Housing is scarce and expensive. In recent years, high student enrollment (as many as 30,000) has created the shortages, even though new dormitories have been built and many residents have student quarters for rent (garages have often been converted into student homes or apartments). Sometimes housing is available through the university, when faculty members take sabbaticals or leaves. Unless you find student or faculty housing, you could pay $150,000 for a single-family home. However, if you look hard enough, you could be living in a more attractive house than the one you left, especially if you find something in the Berkeley hills. Most of these houses are architect-designed, including some of the brown-shingled, vault-ceiling Maybeck houses that are still standing. Many other houses look as though they have been built by or for poets, artists, writers, psychiatrists, atomic physicists and the thousands of other intellectuals who are attracted to this area. In 1965 I bought a home that would be ideal for retirement—a vault-ceiling "hutch" in the midst of a botanical garden. The "cottage" had only a little over 1,000 square-feet of living space (2 bedrooms), but French doors led to an outdoor patio garden where we could and did eat most every day. There was only one gas wall heater to heat the house, plus a fireplace. And we did freeze on cold days (fortunately rare). The garage had been made into a student apartment so we parked the car in the driveway (no real problem in a climate that even treats rare books kindly). The garden was so bountiful (something was in bloom or scent 11 months of the year) that we had to hire a gardener. It was our first home and we loved it. We paid $31,000 for it (it was overpriced then, and now it is probably $150,000) with $600 a year taxes (taxes now would be slightly more than 1 percent of market value). It could be an ideal retirement home for 1 or 2 persons, but it would be impractical for a growing family. And even though it was near transportation and a public footpath, it was up in the hills around the Claremont Hotel and would be unsuitable for anyone who couldn't climb or walk up hills.

There is some strictly retirement housing in the area. In nearby *Oakland*, close to Lake Merritt, are *St. Paul's Towers* and *Lake Park*, which cost at least $1,000 a month for 2 meals a day, limited medical care and room service. In Berkeley there's the *Berkshire*, which costs from over $500 a month (semiprivate room) to $1,000 a month (private room) for 2 meals and limited medical care. The *Shattuck Hotel*, an older hotel in downtown Berkeley, has been converted into a retirement home, where single rooms with private bath cost $500 a month and suites $800 a month (2 meals and limited medical care). The *Berkeley City Club* (formerly Berkeley Women's City Club) now has permanent retired residents who pay $350 a month for a single room. Near Alta Bates Hospital on Ashby Avenue are two convalescent hospitals (nursing homes) where rooms run $50 a day (with a deposit of over $1,000). Meals, special diets and medical care are covered, any extra care or medical services are not. The *Berkeley Hills Convalescent Hospital* also charges $50 a day.

There are plenty of outdoor activities. For golf, you have a choice of two public courses, one at Tilden Park in the Berkeley hills and the other at Lake Chabot, a little further away. There are several private clubs as well. Tennis, swimming and bowling are offered at several centers, including the gracious Claremont Hotel. Bridge players can join groups that play on any level, and other card groups are available. For music, you can attend concerts by the Oakland Symphony Orchestra at Paramount Theatre in Oakland, and during the summer there are band concerts at Lakeside Park by Lake Merritt. You also have easy access to the symphonies and concerts in San Francisco. BART trains make the run into downtown San Francisco in about 30 to 40 minutes. From there it is a short ride or walk to the Opera House and the new Performing Arts Center where concerts and opera are performed throughout the year. Some retired people serve as ushers at performances and cut down the cost of attendance. Berkeley has a new repertory theater, and both San Francisco and Oakland have outstanding ballet groups that perform the year-round. The Bay area has both on- and off-Broadway shows (many groups try out here before going to New York). The Berkeley Repertory Theater puts on excellent productions, and the American Conservatory Theater in San Francisco is also rated high. Berkeley has several museums, covering art, natural history and anthropology. The Oakland Museum is outstanding, as is the De Young Museum in San Francisco and the Palace of the Legion of Honor. Spectator sports are available at the University of California stadium in Berkeley, the Oakland Coliseum and Candlestick Park in San Francisco. And for fishing, you can go down to the Oakland, Berkeley or San Francisco piers and usually catch good eating fish almost any time of year. Horse racing is available at Golden Gate Fields in Albany (north of Berkeley) and you can take gambling trips to Lake Tahoe and Reno, Nevada from the area. Older people get reduced rates at many events and reduced fares on BART trains. Most museums also let seniors in at lower rates, and quite a number of East Bay restaurants have "early bird" meals for seniors at a discount. Many other activities in this area are available at reduced rates.

For more active retirement living, you could consider *Rossmoor Leisure World* in Walnut Creek (on the other side of the Berkeley hills). Condominium units sell for $150,000, but sometimes you can sublease a place when owners are away. Rossmoor activities are many and varied— golf, horseback riding, swimming, tennis, bridge, art classes. Bus service is available around the community and into Walnut Creek and to the BART (Bay Area Rapid Transit) and other transportation into the East Bay (Berkeley and Oakland) and San Francisco.

More affluent retirees like *Grand Lake Gardens* and *Piedmont Gardens* (both in Oakland) where studio apartments start at $15,000 with monthly rates (including meals) of $400 per person (an additional person pays half the rate).

Cost of Living. Unless you live and eat like a student or modest-salaried faculty member, living costs are high. If the average retired couple nationwide needs $10,000 for a modest scale of living, you'd have to add 10 percent if you wanted to retire here under average conditions. And as Berkeley doesn't have much of an industrial base (although more than 300 industries are located here), taxes are higher than normal. They range from 11 percent on an income of under $10,000 to 9 percent on an income of $25,000. This is even higher than San Francisco's 8 percent and 7 percent at these levels. However, it is possible that by taking advantage of some of the low- or no-cost activities at the University of California you could reduce your cost of living, especially for entertainment.

Leisure-Time Activities. Besides the university events, almost every church or religious group has a full program. If you belong to a service club or a professional organization, you will soon find a local group that would be happy to have you as an alumnus member. Then, too, there are many volunteer organizations, such as the American Heart Association and Cancer Society, that welcome active members. And almost every professional, historical and military group has a local chapter here. Especially active are chapters of the American Association of Retired Persons and the Sons in Retirement (SIRS), which have luncheon meetings and activities for their members (mainly former professional or business people). Libraries have the support of the people; Berkeley residents recently favored a referendum assuring funding for the libraries for the next ten years with 7 percent annual increases to keep up with the cost of living.

Special Services for Seniors. Berkeley and the East Bay have many senior centers. At the North Berkeley Senior Center (a new building near the university and downtown Berkeley) there is a full round of activities, including special programs for ethnic groups (Japanese, for instance). Besides card games, bingo, pool and dominoes, the center provides arts-and-crafts classes and workshops and has a special hot-meal program where seniors donate what they can (suggested donation is usually less than $1 for a full-course meal).

For more information, write:

Chamber of Commerce
1834 University Avenue
Berkeley, CA 94703

Across from Berkeley and the East Bay lies Marin County. When I first saw *Mill Valley* (pop. 20,000) it was filled with woodsy Sierra Club types who lived in chalets. Now it is filled with "laid back" sophisticates who are into Zen, hot tubs, pot and sex. *Tiburon-Belvedere* (pop. 8,000) was for intellectual sailors. Now it is for cosmopolitan yachtsmen types, and even the relatively affluent people I knew who retired there have moved to Santa Rosa, Sonoma or the Sierra foothills (see below).

Santa Rosa (pop. 80,000), located 52 miles north of the Golden Gate (San Francisco), is a ranching and farming community which has attracted many retirees who seek a simpler town within reach of San Francisco and Sacramento (100 miles to the west). So far it has remained the quiet rose garden that invited Luther Burbank to develop new and better plants in the area.

Climate and Environment. Santa Rosa is located in the northern and eastern part of the Cotati valley, part of a broad and relatively flat area that extends 20 miles east to west from the Sonoma Mountains to the coast and 40 miles south to San Pablo Bay. The climate is maritime in character, but its distance inland moderates the temperature to the low 80s on summer afternoons and high 40s at night; middle 50s to mid-30s in winter. Rainfall averages 30 inches, with snow rare.

Medical Facilities. The area has 5 hospitals with 560 beds, and a number of convalescent hospitals with 300 beds. Santa Rosa also has a clinic, 9 medical laboratories, 15 dental laboratories and a number of health organizations including visiting nurses. There are more than 300 physicians and 80 dentists in the area—more than enough for the population.

Housing Availability and Cost. Housing seems relatively plentiful, with small retirement homes selling from $100,000 and some rentals available for $500 a month. Mobile-home courts are available, with rents of $100 a month. The *Oakmont Adult Community* has single and multiunits available for $50,000 to over $150,000. The community also provides recreational and other facilities.

Cost of Living. Taxes here are half what they are in San Francisco and Berkeley, and the cost of living can be considerably lowered by taking advantage of local produce and other farm products. However, this isn't necessarily a "poor man's paradise," as the average effective buying income of households (after taxes) is over $15,000.

Leisure-Time Activities. Santa Rosa has 23 parks. It also has golf courses, swimming pools, ice- and roller-skating areas. It is within easy range of activities in San Francisco and the East Bay (Richmond–San Rafael Bridge) and the Russian River resort area. Cultural activities include art groups, little theater, a symphony orchestra, chorus, public library and branches and a junior college community services program. A card file of 600 nonprofit organizations and clubs of interest to residents and newcomers is maintained by the Santa Rosa Chamber of Commerce and is available in printed form on request. Included are lists of garden clubs, men's lodges, hobby clubs, music and dance groups, women's clubs, service clubs and senior citizen groups (see below).

Special Services for Seniors. Santa Rosa has 11 senior citizens groups, plus a senior citizen community recreation program which offers exercise classes, self-defense exercises, ballroom dancing and bus tours. The town also has a senior multipurpose center which features crafts, sewing, cards, art, bingo and dancing. Other organizations offer programs and services for retired teachers, retired federal employees and members of professional organizations. There is a grandmothers' club and a Retired Senior Volunteer Program (RSVP) as well as a Filipino Community Senior Group. The Commission on Aging meets once a month in the Community Center.

For further information, write:

> Santa Rosa Chamber of Commerce
> 637 First Street and Santa Rosa Avenue
> Santa Rosa, CA 95404

Other towns in the area to consider include *San Rafael* (pop. 50,000), only a few miles north of the Golden Gate. This community uses a former railroad depot ("The Whistlestop") as a senior center and headquarters of the Marin Senior Coordinating Council, whose services include counseling, employment, recreation, education, transportation, low-cost meals and tax assistance. Also in the area is Emeritus College, which offers a variety of classes to older people. Another place of interest: *Bolinas* (pop. 1,000), a New England–type village on the west Marin coast, which is rapidly becoming a favorite retirement and arts-crafts community (the "Carmel of the North").

For further information, write:

Chamber of Commerce
San Rafael, CA 94901
Bolinas, CA 94924

Napa and Sonoma Valleys—A Bucolic Setting for Retirement

This is wine and Valley of the Moon country . . . the settings for stories by Robert Louis Stevenson and Jack London . . . the place where many San Franciscans go to retire. Just an hour's-plus drive north from the Golden Gate, this area offers a contrasting climate and environment. Hal Cammann, writing in his weekly column in the *Sonoma Index-Tribune,* says that Sonoma, like Hawaii, has much to offer in the way of pleasant, relaxing and safe living. He adds: "Sonoma will increasingly become a haven for people who have retired and have come here to escape the rat race and wall-to-wall people of the cities. Here the climate is good, the people friendly, and there is a rural atmosphere."

Using *Sonoma Valley* (pop. 30,000) as an example of what you might find in this region, here are vital statistics:

Climate and Environment. This valley community is proud of its historic roots (the plaza in the city of Sonoma was the scene of the Bear Flag Revolt, which established the California Republic), its international population, friendliness and mild climate. Here, retirees find a favorable climate, hospital and other services, organizations offering open doors to new friendships. Temperatures are mild, rains moderate, snowflakes rare (and soon gone). Summer temperatures are in the mid-80s, seldom up to 100°F., down to the 50s at night for good sleeping weather. January is the coolest month, ranging from 40°F. to 56°F. and containing 12 of the area's 45 freezing days. Annual precipitation totals 28.08 inches, about 90 percent of it between November and April. Humidity during winter nights goes up to 90 percent but down to 60 percent during the days; summertime it is in the 40 percent range during the days and up to 70 percent at night. This makes for a pleasant overall climate.

Medical Facilities. The Sonoma Valley Hospital is a fully accredited, publicly owned district acute-care hospital with 89 beds. It offers a full range of services including medical, surgical, intensive care/coronary care unit, pediatric, obstetric, inhalation therapy as well as out-patient services such as emergency, laboratory, X-ray, nuclear medicine, inhalation and physical therapy. There are also 10 convalescent and nursing programs. A hospice program, providing emotional and physical support to terminally ill patients, is also available. The hospital has over 40 physicians on staff, most of whom are active throughout the community. All told 44 doctors, 20 dentists and 2 orthodontists serve the area. Excellent medical facilities are also available in Santa Rosa and Napa, and San Francisco is readily reached by ambulance.

Housing Availability and Cost. Housing has generally been available, but a "slow growth" policy has been in effect that should slow building to 100 to 200 units a year. This could drive up prices. Meanwhile, housing costs in the area are lower than in the San Francisco and Monterey Bay areas. Here, you can still find a few single-family homes for under $100,000, while in the other areas you would spend over $100,000. Sonoma also has many mobile-home parks where units sell from $25,000 to $50,000 with additional fees of $75 to $300 a month for services and facilities. Some retirement housing is for resale, at prices from $75,000 to $100,000. Condominiums and coops generally sell from $90,000 to $125,-000 and up, townhouses for $80,000 to $100,000. Building lots, when available, cost $60,000 and building costs are $60 per square foot. Rentals start at $400 for 1- to 2-bedroom homes, from $325 for apartments. At *Oakmont,* where leisure-living attractions include 2 golf courses, lawn bowling, dining and meeting centers and complete shopping centers, new homes are under construction for $125,000. And several years ago, a retirement city was planned at *Temelec,* the former Coblentz estate. The original plans have not been completed, but building continues there.

Cost of Living. It doesn't cost as much to live here as it does in the other areas of northern California already mentioned. However, living costs may be only 5 percent less than in the San Francisco Bay area. And to be really comfortable, a retired couple should have an annual income from $15,000 to $20,000. Some retirees have found jobs in service organizations (motels/hotels, restaurants, theaters, shops) and some make money in in-home care and help services. Others have bought small acreage on which to raise grapes or vegetables. And farmers' stands and markets offering local produce can cut expenses somewhat.

Leisure-Time Activities. Meeting new friends is made easy by 25 churches and fraternal and civic groups. Altogether, there are 130 organizations representing a wide range of interests in the area. The chamber of commerce is the central source of information on all these and the town's major attractions during the year, such as the old-fashioned Fourth of July parade, barbeque, band concert and fireworks, and the Wine Festival weeks in September. The library has moved into new quarters with easy access for seniors and many items of interest to older readers, including large-type books, records and cassettes and listening stations.

Special Services for Seniors. The Sonoma area has 7 senior activity centers, 17 senior citizen clubs, 11 chapters of the American Association of Retired Persons and 6 branches of Sons in Retirement (SIRS), a Northern California organization of retired men with 20,000 members in 80 branches from Monterey north.

For further information, write:

> Sonoma Valley Chamber of Commerce
> 453 First Street East
> Sonoma, CA 95476

Other towns of interest in this area (with zip codes to write to chambers of commerce): *Napa* (pop. 50,000; 94558), one of California's oldest cities and capital of the wine-growing county, where many retirees have settled; *St. Helena* (pop. 5,000; 94574), a gracious, quiet community in Robert Louis Stevenson country; *Calistoga* (pop. 2,500; 94515), the center of numerous natural hot-water geysers, mineral springs and mineralized mud baths; *Glen Ellen* (pop. 1,000) in the heart of Jack London country and the Valley of the Moon; *Boyes Hot Spring* (pop. 1,000; 95416), a former health spa and now center for much retirement living.

The Mother Lode Country—Prospecting for Retirement

Californians have not only lovingly preserved and restored these former mining camps, they have discovered a new form of gold: tourists and retirees who want to visit and live here for the clean air, scenery and nostalgia.

The main towns stretch along Highway 49 (appropriately named) from about *Mariposa* north to *Nevada City*. This is rolling Sierra Nevada foothill country, 2,000-feet high, which assures a moderate 4-season climate. Golden hills, modest canyons and stately groves of trees mark this area.

While there are several counties in this area and literally hundreds of towns you could consider for retirement, let's concentrate on Amador County, with *Jackson* (the county seat) as typical of many towns in the area. Incidentally, I've visited all these towns scores of times over the past 30 years, and I will certainly look around here for my Retirement Eden.

Jackson (pop. 3,000) is located at the heart of the Mother Lode country. The convergence of creeks and its central location made it a natural gathering point for the '49ers. It managed to survive after the gold rush as quartz mining quickly replaced gold panning. As in most gold-mining towns, Jackson suffered a devastating fire (1862) that destroyed most of the flimsy wooden structures. But the town rebuilt around some surviving brick structures and retains the flavor (while offering modern conveniences) of the golden days.

Climate and Environment. The topography consists of flat plains, gently rolling foothills and high rugged mountains. Elevation ranges from 200 to 9,000 feet, with most of the town at 1,250 feet. The average temperature in January is 46.1°F., 58.4°F. in April, 78.1°F. in July and 61.1°F. in October. Rainfall averages 22 inches a year, falling mostly in the winter months. Humidity is also highest in winter (averaging 87 percent at noon in January) but sinks to 33 percent at noon in July, to moderate any heat.

Medical Facilities. Amador County has 1 general hospital with a 90-bed capacity and 1 convalescent hospital with an 80-bed capacity. There are 12 physicians, 14 dentists, 4 optometrists and 3 chiropractors in the area.

Housing Availability and Cost. Sales of existing homes run from $50,000 to over $100,000. There are 3 suburban residential areas within 2 to 10 miles of *Sutter Creek, Jackson* and *Pine Grove,* offering homes priced from $60,000 to $120,000. Rents for 1- to 2-bedroom apartments and duplexes start at $250 a month; homes $300 a month. There are also 25 mobile-home parks in the area.

Cost of Living. Taxes are generally lower here than in the Bay area, and the overall cost of living could be lower if you retire here for the reason most people do: to live a simpler, quieter life. Local stores may not have the discounts and sales of big-city stores, but if your needs and wants are less, your costs are lower.

Leisure-Time Activities. Amador County has 30 churches, 6 libraries, 3 newspapers, 1 FM radio station, 2 theater groups, 3 television channels received directly (1 cable), 6 parks, 3 swimming centers, 3 tennis courts (lighted at night), 3 athletic clubs and many diversified social clubs. There are many lakes and streams for water sports, 3 ski areas and 82,253 acres of public land.

Special Services for Seniors. Besides area and local councils on aging, Amador County has Senior Services, Inc., a private, nonprofit organization designed to meet the needs of older citizens. It helps members adjust to retirement living, plan activities for the future, find housing, straighten out finances, taxes and legal problems. It also offers other supportive programs and provides social contacts and recreational activities. Its mailing address is P.O. Box 335, Jackson, CA 95642.

For further information, write:

> Amador County Chamber of Commerce
> P.O. Box 596
> Jackson, CA 95642

Other towns in this area worth exploring include *Angel's Camp* (pop. 2,000), home of the famous "jumping frog" contest; *Mokelumne Hill* (pop. 1,000) one of the most authentically preserved mining towns; *San Andreas* (pop. 1,500), hangout of famous bandits; *Mariposa* (pop. 2,500), southern "anchor" of the mines and still containing old buildings; *Sonora* (pop. 4,000), one of the largest towns in the area, seat of Tuolumne County, and next to *Columbia*, a completely preserved and restored gold-rush town; *Sutter Creek* (pop. 1,200), perhaps the best preserved town in the Mother Lode.

Nevada City (pop. 3,000), located at the northern end of the mines, remains one of the most picturesquely preserved gold-rush towns. Its residential areas are dotted with multigabled frame houses, and the downtown section contains many historic landmarks, including the elegant National Hotel, which serves gourmet meals in a Victorian setting. Many museums, antique stores and historic sites are here. I never fail to stop overnight in Nevada City (staying at the National Hotel) when I'm in the area, and I'll certainly consider this town as one of my possible Retirement Edens.

Climate and Environment. Located in more rugged, rolling foot hills than Jackson, Nevada City sits at an elevation of 2,500 feet. This gives it a more distinctive 4-season climate, with little fog, little wind, no smog and about 6 snowfalls a year. Temperature in January averages 44°F., April 56°F., July 77°F., October 62°F. Annual precipitation (rain and snow) averages 55 inches, with the rainy season lasting from November to March (I've seen it snow in April). Growing season is May 20 through October 10.

Medical Facilities. Sierra Nevada Memorial Hospital has 71 beds and is staffed with 45 physicians, with an emergency staff of 8. The Grass Valley–Nevada City directory lists 40 doctors in the area, with 22 dentists. There are also 3 nursing homes in the area (with over 200 beds), a mental health department and a social services department.

Housing Availability and Cost. Housing is generally plentiful, with prices of single-family homes ranging from $50,000 to over $85,000. Rentals for 1- to 2-bedroom apartments start at $300 a month; small homes at $400 a month. Condominiums, coops and townhouses are available from $65,000. Building lots cost from under $20,000 to over $50,000 and building costs are $50 a square foot.

Cost of Living. Effective property tax is 1 percent of market value. Food costs are a bit higher than average because of transportation costs. But local food bargains and buying food in bulk can reduce expenses. Some businesses (mainly taxi) give senior discounts, and some seniors earn extra money through daily or hourly jobs, at home or in small businesses.

Leisure-Time Activities. Pioneer Park is a favorite recreation area where there are 2 lighted tennis courts, outdoor swimming pool, picnic area and playing fields. In the immediate area are bowling alleys, golf courses, a movie theater and racquetball courts. There are 125 clubs and organizations and 48 churches in the area, all with active social programs. Nevada City has both a county library and a historical library. Radio and television reception are good, with cable available in town and in some outlying areas. There are more than 20 fishing spots and good hunting in the mountains. Within easy reach are 10 skiing areas and many hiking trails are close at hand. The area has many bookstores, an art gallery, and adult-education classes are available at or through Sierra College Extension Courses and the local high school.

Special Services for Seniors. Nevada City has a branch of the American Association of Retired Persons, Sons in Retirement, a Golden Age Club and other senior organizations. There are also a transportation program, visiting nurses and meals on wheels.

For further information, write:

> Nevada City Chamber of Commerce
> 132 Main Street
> Nevada City, CA 95059

Nevada City is just "up the hill" from *Grass Valley* (pop. 5,500), a modern town with historic buildings, and *Auburn* (pop. 7,500), a new-old town that also offers possibilities for retirement. And "up the hill" from Nevada City lies *Dutch Flat* (pop. 500), a village that has attracted some of the more adventuresome retirees. Many retirees are also settling in El Dorado County (see below), which lies just south of Nevada County.

Paradise (pop. 27,000), 50 miles northwest of Nevada City, while not strictly in the Mother Lode country, started out as a gold-mining camp. There are 2 legends as to how the town got its name: that it was named after a place called "pair-o'-dice"; or that it was so named when a passenger stepped from a stagecoach, took a deep breath of air, and exclaimed: "This is paradise."

However it was named, it is paradise to the 49 percent of the population which is retired. This is God-created country—huge chasms of breathtaking beauty, warm, rolling hills garbed in green fir and tonic air constantly scented with pine. And the town's elevation of 1,300 to 2,200 feet perch it high enough to enjoy a healthy, mild 4-season climate.

Climate and Environment. The temperature averages 51.9°F. in January and 93.6°F. in July. Humidity averages 60 percent in winter and 35 percent in summer (which moderates the heat). Annual rainfall is 49.39 inches, which falls mainly during the winter months, along with about 6 inches of snow.

Medical Facilities. There is 1 major hospital with 109 beds and 4 nursing homes. The area has 32 doctors, 15 dentists, 1 clinic and 3 medical centers to supply adequate care for the population.

Housing Availability and Cost. Housing is generally plentiful, both for special retirement residences and for regular housing. Single-family homes start at $45,000. There are few rentals in the area (either houses or apartments) but there are 29 mobile-home parks that offer a wide range of services and facilities.

Cost of Living. Taxes are relatively low, averaging less than 1 percent of market value on property. Other costs, including food and energy, tend to be higher than average. Some retirees have turned real-estate agent and others have jobs in service industries. Others grow their own fruits and vegetables. Fishermen can hook rainbow, German brown and Eastern brook trout in nearby branches of the Feather River. Salmon, steelhead, catfish, striped bass, black bass and perch await lines in the Sacramento River, 20 miles away. And the area is a haven for deer, quail and other game animals.

Leisure-Time Activities. The area has 3 local newspapers, a library with 40,000 volumes, 6 bookstores, 3 art galleries, 1 museum, 1 little theater, 3 FM radio stations, 250 clubs, hobby and craft organizations, 6 parks, 1 swimming pool, 2 golf courses and adult-education classes at Butte College.

Special Services for Seniors. There is an active recreation center for seniors, and senior clubs include the American Association of Retired Persons and a council on aging. There are a senior information and referral service, hot-meal program, homemakers, meals on wheels, visiting nurses, transportation program and emergency service and assistance.

For further information, write:

Paradise Chamber of Commerce
Paradise, CA 95969

Lake Tahoe Area and Western Nevada—High, Low Retirement

Lake Tahoe, one of the largest and most magnificent lakes in the world, lies at 6,230 feet. Most of the lake is in California (El Dorado and Placer counties), where the elevation ranges from 200 to 10,881 feet. Reno, Nevada, at 4,400 feet, is situated 25 miles to the north. Thus this area gives you a choice of elevations, states, and life-styles for retirement. Starting at the western part of the area we have:

Placerville (pop. 8,000), which used to be called Hangtown by the miners, but a better name for it now would be Boom Town. The population of El Dorado County has jumped 60 percent since 1970 and is now almost 86,000. Many of these newcomers are retirees escaping from larger cities. Land speculators are thought of in much the same villainous vein as claim-jumpers were a century ago (although the speculators fared better, hanging up a "slow-growth movement" recently, rather than the other way around).

Climate and Environment. Placerville lies at an elevation of 1,850 feet. It is still largely rural and preserves many relics of its gold-mining past. But the main streets are clogged with newcomers, and services are being stretched. The weather in January averages 40°F., April 53°F., July 74°F., October 57°F. Annual rainfall is 47 inches, including 5.5 inches of snow. During summer days the thermometer may get up to 90°F., but the nights are generally cool, and the humidity, which averages 27 percent in summer, keeps the weather from feeling uncomfortable.

Medical Facilities. El Dorado County has 2 general hospitals with 111 beds, 2 convalescent hospitals with 198 beds, 60 physicians and surgeons, 50 dentists, 12 optometrists, 14 chiropractors and 1 podiatrist.

Housing Availability and Cost. The average single-family home sells for $80,000, and the construction industry is kept busy trying to provide enough housing for newcomers. Rentals are extremely scarce, with the monthly cost of 1-bedroom homes or apartments ranging from $200 to over $600. However, there are many mobile-home parks in the area and many condominiums available in the Lake Tahoe area (see below).

Cost of Living. Living costs can be high, but they can be cut by enterprising gardeners who raise vegetables during the long growing season. Local farmers sell produce below retail prices. Retail clothing and hardware stores must remain competitive with those in Sacramento, only 40 miles away. Most stores are centrally located and convenient, but crowded during the summer months. However, shopping malls in residential areas help to ease the congestion.

Leisure-Time Activities. Placerville lacks a well-defined recreational and cultural program, although there are scores of clubs and organizations that foster a wide range of activities. El Dorado County has 45 churches, 6 libraries and 1 bookmobile, 5 newspapers, 1 radio station, 1 cable-television station and 3 cable-television systems, 60 parks, 40 playgrounds and 4 theaters. Other recreational facilities include 2 drive-in movies, 2 roller-skating rinks, 2 bowling alleys, 4 18-hole and 2 9-hole golf courses, 3 community concert associations, more than 200 lakes (including Lake Tahoe), 682 miles of rivers, 50 multiple-use recreational grounds and 5 ski resorts.

Special Services for Seniors. Placerville has a senior citizen's center that provides meeting areas, trips to the Lake Tahoe casinos, referral programs for the needy, transportation services, legal aid and nutritional programs. Its new library is equipped with special services for seniors with sight or hearing problems. The American River College Extension Program gives classes in real estate, history, crafts, recreation and other special courses of interest to older persons, while the local parks and recreation department offers arts and crafts, dancing, tennis, etc. Sly Park Dam Recreational Area is at Jenkison Lake, 5 miles from *Pollock Pines*, which is fast becoming a popular retirement area. The town itself offers shopping centers, restaurants, churches and mobile-home courts. You'll find a wide variety of scenery, from the orchards and vines of Apple Hill to the pine-studded shores of Jenkison Lake, where fishing and boating are popular.

For further information, write:

> Hangtown Chamber of Commerce
> P.O. Box 151
> Placerville, CA 95667

The *Lake Tahoe area* (pop. 50,000) led Mark Twain to say, "Three months of camp life on Lake Tahoe would restore an Egyptian mummy to his pristine vigor and give him an appetite like an alligator." Maybe, but he'd become a mummy again with his first swim. Besides being the second highest lake in the world, Lake Tahoe is probably the coldest, with the water generally freezing on the hottest summer day. No matter; the setting is beautiful, surrounded by forests of ponderosa, Jeffery and sugar pine; white fir, juniper, cedar, aspen, dogwood, cottonwood and many other trees and a splendid assortment of wildflowers.

Tahoe is split into 3 distinct living areas: the south shore, with a population in *South Lake Tahoe* of about 20,000 and around 8,000 in the outlying areas of Meyers and Christmas Valley; the north shore, with the little towns of *Meeks Bay, Tahoma, Homewood, Tahoe Pines, Carnelian Bay, Tahoe Vista* and *Kings Beach* surrounding and melting into *Tahoe City* (pop. 5,000), with the other areas totaling 3,000; and the Nevada side, including *Crystal Bay* and *Incline Village*, with a combined population of 12,000, and the residential areas of *Glenbrook, Zephyr Cove, Round Hill* and *Stateline*, with a population of 5,000. The south shore has the widest cultural and recreational facilities, the north shore the costliest houses and resorts and the Nevada side the "action" as far as gambling is concerned.

All these areas live off tourists, who create bumper-to-bumper traffic (particularly on the south shore) when flocking here for fun. Almost 80 percent of the 50,000 residents are in tourist-oriented businesses or a tourist-related trade, and the other 20 percent can't ignore this economic fact of life.

The average temperatures in the area are 20°F. in winter, 38°F. in spring, 60°F. in summer and 44°F. in fall. These temperatures don't give the whole story in winter—the temperature can get down as low as −15°F., with snow falling about 1 out of every 4 days from November through April. The average winter snowpack is 20 feet, with storms dropping 8 to 36 inches at a time. Snow removal, especially after a long, hard storm, is a matter of wait and see. Although plows work around the clock to clear roads, the main arteries and emergency facilities are the first to be cleared, the residential areas last. Front-wheel-drive or 4-wheel-drive vehicles are a must, and only tourists are caught without a set of chains in the trunk.

They say that "only fools and tourists predict weather at Tahoe," and it can be so hot in January that snow runs off the roofs in riverlets, and so cold in July that the garden freezes.

Housing is generally expensive, with a 2-bedroom chalet selling from $75,000 and monthly rental for the same from $500. Low-income housing is virtually nonexistent, with a waiting list of over 2 years for what little is available. There are some mobile-home parks in the area, but costs are high and space scarce. Costs on the north shore and Nevada side are highest, with houses selling from $100,000, lots from $30,000.

The cost of living, as in any tourist area, is high. Utilities, especially propane and electricity, are outrageous. To heat a well-insulated 2-bedroom house in winter costs $50 a month for electricity and $100 for propane. Clothing and retail costs in general are high, as the shops mainly aim at the tourist trade. Most locals shop in Carson City, Reno or Sacramento.

While general medical care is good, Tahoe Forest Hospital, located 24 miles from Tahoe City in Truckee, is the nearest medical facility. It is a small emergency hospital, transferring its most severe cases to Carson or Reno. (Both hospitals can be reached only by going over Spooner or Mount Rose summits, both treacherous at best during icy winter conditions.) An ambulance service recently opened a north shore center, but in winter some hospital trips could take up to an hour.

As noted, the south shore offers the most recreational facilities. The City Recreation Center, located in South Lake Tahoe, has an indoor swimming pool, exercise rooms and offers many classes in various subjects. It also offers discount cards to residents and senior citizens. The north shore is mainly a "rich man's playground," with the majority of the homes owned by summer and winter visitors. At Tahoe City, professional theater is performed, and arts-and-crafts classes are available. The Tahoe City library is well stocked, and Tahoe City and Kings Beach both have golf courses.

The gambling casinos are necessarily on the Nevada side (where gambling is legal). Incline Village is the largest city on the Nevada side, most other areas being strictly residential. Recreational facilities include many private tennis, swimming and boating clubs, and a lovely public golf course right on the beach. Ski areas dot the slopes. Stateline, Round Hill, Zephyr Cove and Glenbrook are rapidly growing, but small houses start at $120,000. None of these areas offers community activities. Being largely residential, they depend on Incline, Carson City and South Lake Tahoe for recreation, cultural activities and medical assistance.

So unless you are a tourist or a business person living off tourists, and unless you like your winters cold and your costs high, you might find retirement in the Lake Tahoe area a little icy.

For further information, write:

South Lake Tahoe Chamber of Commerce
P.O. Box 15090
South Lake Tahoe, CA 95702

North Lake Tahoe Chamber of Commerce
Box 884
Tahoe City, CA 95730

Reno-Sparks, Nevada (pop. 140,757) is an area I've always liked. Take away the noisy slot machines and the raucous gamblers, and Reno would be one of the quietest, nicest towns in the West. In fact, if you ignore the gambling activity, you'll find that Reno-Sparks is not only a nice place to visit, but a delightful place to retire in. It has a pleasant residential section, a University of Nevada campus, many museums and art galleries.

Climate and Environment. The average temperature in winter is 34°F., spring 47°F., summer 66°F. and fall 50°F. Reno lies at an elevation of 4,400 feet and it is sheltered by mountains which provide the area with an equable 4-season climate. Rain averages 7.2 inches annually, but snow averages 82.4 inches. However, Reno doesn't have the snow and cold problem that the Lake Tahoe area has. Winter is much gentler here, with a dry climate.

Medical Facilities. Reno-Sparks has 4 hospitals with 1,000 beds, 4 nursing homes, 4 personal-care homes with 449 beds, 2 clinics, 625 doctors and 180 dentists, which provide more than enough medical facilities for the population.

Housing Availability and Cost. Housing is described as "plentiful," with single-family homes selling for $80,000, condominiums, coops and townhouses for $75,000 and rentals at $400 a month. There are several mobile-home parks in the area with fees averaging $150 a month. Reno Camlu Apartments is a 70-unit senior citizen housing project that serves 3 meals daily.

Cost of Living. Taxes are generally lower in Nevada, which has no state income tax, and the sales tax in Reno is only 3.5 percent. Property taxes average 1.78 percent of market value. Food is exempted from sales tax, and seniors get discounts at local stores. Also, there are many part-time jobs open to seniors, especially in stores, casinos, restaurants, motels/hotels, theaters and other service industries. Job counseling is available through senior centers and state, county and city employment services.

Leisure-Time Activities. Reno-Sparks has 3 local newspapers, 5 libraries, 6 bookstores, 3 art galleries, 4 museums, 2 little theater groups, 4 FM radio stations, good television reception and cable television, 7 AM radio stations, 40 service clubs, adult-education classes at Western Nevada Community College, 48 parks, 6 swimming pools (2 indoor), 6 golf courses, scores of tennis courts and a bikeway through town.

Special Services for Seniors. There are several senior centers in the area, Golden Age clubs, a division of the office on aging which offers counseling services and helps coordinate a hot-meal program, homemaker services, visiting nurses, meals on wheels, transportation program, special health clinics, income-maintenance program, emergency service, legal aid and rehabilitation programs.

For further information, write:

Greater Reno Chamber of Commerce
P.O. Box 3499
Reno, NV 89505

Many retirees are also exploring the *Carson City* (state capital) area for retirement possibilities, along with the area around the restored mining town of *Virginia City*. The *Las Vegas* area also has its share of admirers, as does the *Lake Mead–Boulder City* area.

One attraction for retirement in Nevada is low taxes. Thanks to the tourist (gambling) industry, Nevada has some of the lowest taxes in the nation, ranking thirty-sixth in tax burden at lower levels and forty-sixth in higher brackets. The state has no income tax or inheritance and estate tax.

Property Taxes —the state average is $5 per $100 of evaluation, assessed at 35 percent of market value. This equals 1.78 percent of true market value. Widows are entitled to $1,000 homestead exemption, and seniors (62 and older) with incomes below $11,000 are allowed $500 tax relief based on a sliding scale of income.

Sales Tax —3 percent with food exempted; many cities and counties add 0.5 percent to bring the effective rate to 3.5 percent.

The Division for Aging Services is making a determined effort to improve housing, transportation, health and other services for the aging, and the state has experienced the largest percentage population increase of people 55 or older in the nation.

Most of this growth is concentrated along the western borders, generally in the Reno and Las Vegas areas. *Elko* (pop. 8,000) and *Ely* (pop. 9,000) in eastern Nevada are also possibilities.

For further information, write:

Division for Aging Services
505 East King Street
Carson City, NV 89710

The Mendocino Coast—For Retreat or Retirement

The coast north from San Francisco is a great place for escape. It is made of rocky, rugged headlands, sculptured by the surging Pacific Ocean, which has also carved cloistered beaches and private coves. Thistle-swept pastures meet forests of pine, western hemlock and yew, Monterey cypress, Douglas fir, oak and sequoias and redwoods.

I used to come here as a bachelor to ponder and search my soul. I proposed marriage in one of the area's most romantic spots, Fort Ross. And after we were married, we used to come up these coasts to get away from it all.

Many artists, second-home owners and retirees are getting away from it all up here, yet this 100-mile coast (from Point Reyes to Fort

Bragg) probably has little over 35,000 people. About 10,000 reside in the biggest city, *Fort Bragg*, which is a lumber, agricultural and fishing center. The other settlements—*Bodega, Gualala, Point Arena, Mendocino*—are mere villages, each with less than 1,000 residents.

Most picturesque is Mendocino (named after Antonio de Mendoza, the first viceroy of New Spain), with a permanent population of 1,000. Because it looks like a New England village but is a lot closer to Hollywood, Mendocino has been the site of many movies you may have seen: *The Russians Are Coming, Johnny Belinda, East of Eden, Summer of '42, Same Time Next Year*. The town, 10 miles south of Fort Bragg, is a silhouette of water towers, steep-roofed clapboard houses, and a stiff, white Presbyterian Church. The false-front stores, weedy back streets and Victorian houses stand on a rocky plateau just above the sea. The town's main concessions to modernism are an efficient street-lighting system, an art center which presents an impressive year-round program of instruction and displays, and a general store which serves the town and surrounding area with everything from furniture to building materials.

As this area is being discovered, prices are going up, housing is becoming scarcer, and traffic is becoming more congested (coastal Highway 1, a 2-lane, twisting, turning roadway, is often fog-shrouded, blocked by landslides or clogged with summer tourists).

The best time to visit is in the rainy or foggy winter months when the less adventurous stay home; mist cloaks the area in a "Hound of the Baskervilles" atmosphere and hides the latest eyesore. This place is worth a visit anytime of year, and would certainly be a place to investigate for possible retirement.

Climate and Environment. The climate is dominated by the ocean. Cool, wet winters and cool summers with frequent fog and wind are the norm. The coldest temperature on record is 30°F.; the highest, 97°F. At the same time, behind the beaches and sea cliffs, are "banana belts," where highs, lows and overcast are modified. This means that it's either warmer or colder inland than it is along the coast. In fact, if you're planning to live here or stay for any length of time, find out if you're in such a "banana belt." If so, you may need extra warmth or cooling (unlikely) or at least the protection of trees and shrubs to moderate the climate to your liking.

Medical Facilities. The Mendocino Coast Hospital in Fort Bragg, with complete facilities, is the only general acute-care hospital on the Mendocino coast. It has 54 beds, which appears adequate for present population needs. The only convalescent hospital, Sherwood Oaks, is also in Fort Bragg. It is licensed for 51 skilled-nursing-care beds and 4 for intermediate care. However, there usually is a waiting list for beds, and prospective patients are referred to convalescent facilities in either Willits

or Ukiah (see below). Costs at the Mendocino Coast Hospital aren't low:
a semiprivate room costs $200 a day (the national average is $163). The
Sherwood Oaks nursing facility charges $50 a day, which is comparable
to larger-city nursing homes. The general hospital staff numbers 31 physicians and surgeons, 1 opthalmologist and 16 dentists.

Housing Availability and Cost. The building supply hasn't caught
up with demand, and the prices seem to have outstripped many pocketbooks. Also, buying property in this area is far different from buying it
in the city. You have to ask questions about water supply, utilities, ease-
ments, rights of way, emergency services, sewage system, drainage, local
fire and police protection. Search and rescue capability is also important,
as people are forever getting stuck on odd rocks and crags at high tide
and need rescuing. Also, if you're buying a second or vacation home, you'll
find that mortgage money isn't easily available, and is subject to many
restrictions.

That aside, you'll find that 1-acre "white water view" lots at the edge
of the ocean can go for $100,000 or more, although an acre a mile inland
may cost only half that much. Ready-built 2- to 3-bedroom homes with
ocean view cost over $100,000, while those inland start at $85,000. Some
mobile homes on a lot may be available for under $40,000, but if you want
one of the "charming older homes" you could pay $200,000 or more. Some
rentals are available from $400 a month. Even if you aren't looking for
housing, you'll enjoy a stay at one of the lovely inns in the area, like
Heritage House and Little River Inn, both located at *Little River,* a few
miles south of Mendocino. In Mendocino are the 100-year old Joshua
Grindle Inn and Mendocino Village Inn. Just north of Gualala lies the Old
Milano Hotel, a former stagecoach stop, which has been restored to Victorian elegance, and St. Orres, which reflects its Russian heritage. Fort
Bragg's inns include the cozy Grey Whale Inn, the tiny Victorian Blue
Rose Inn and the Colonial Inn. You'll also find several good motels in the
area. I've stayed at most of these places; my favorite is Heritage House
in Little River, which is an expanded 1876 mansion with 50 rooms and
cottages (you must reserve long in advance).

Cost of Living. Because of transportation costs and lack of competition, food costs can run 15 to 20 percent above those in San Francisco.
Mendocino's general store, which sells meats, groceries, hardware, building materials, clothing, school supplies, furniture and appliances, has no
competition, and the prices reflect this. The only other possibility is to shop
in Fort Bragg (10 miles north), but here again you'll find a limited selection, with only 1 real supermarket. Car repairs and servicing are generally
good and reasonable, if you don't drive a fancy sports car. And the services of plumbers, electricians, carpenters and other skilled craftsmen can

run $5 to $10 less than in the San Francisco area. Utility bills are comparable to San Francisco, as the same companies (Pacific Gas and Pacific Telephone) service both areas.

Leisure-Time Activities. If you live outside the immediate Fort Bragg or Mendocino area, you may find television reception less than desirable (until or unless cable television comes to the area). If you're a doer or volunteer, you'll find many opportunities to serve on local civic committees. The Art Center in Mendocino offers programs in crafts, sketching, painting, photography, sculpture and the performing arts. And, of course, there is good hunting, fishing and sailing. But you have to live here for some months before you discover what is available. As one resident noted, "No one will bother you here. If you want to get involved you can be as busy and active as you've ever been. On the other hand, if you want solitude and let that be known, people will leave you alone."

Special Services for Seniors. While Fort Bragg offers some senior services and programs, most older people in this area are independent and don't segregate themselves as to activities or services. After all, this is a place where you go to escape, not to seek protective custody.

For further information, write:

Chamber of Commerce
Fort Bragg, CA 95437

Other nearby areas which are attracting retirees are (with zip code): *Clear Lake* (95453), a popular recreation area with fishing, hunting, swimming and other sports; *Willits* (95490), a small resort town on the Redwood Highway; and *Ukiah* (95482), the seat of Mendocino County and the guardian community for Lake Mendocino, which attracts some 1 million people annually.

SUMMARY

Most of northern California and western Nevada could be a Retirement Eden if you can afford housing costs about 20 percent higher than the national average. However, you probably won't need as much shelter, since you would enjoy outdoor living much of the time, and save on heating bills and clothing costs.

Yet, although the weather is equable year-round, it is cool rather than sunshiny warm, especially along the coasts. This weather doesn't make for sunning on beaches or splashing in surf (the ocean is usually too cold to swim in any time of year). A more 4-season climate exists further inland (Mother Lode country), with warmer summers and colder winters (some snow). But this could raise costs and curtail outdoor activity.

If you appreciate the charms, culture and sophistication of San Francisco, you'd always have a mecca to go to. And if you could afford the housing and chose the right climate for you, you would probably find retirement here better than most places on earth.

Here are my ratings for major retirement areas. I've had to qualify my recommendation of several places because of these factors: the high cost and shortage of housing in Carmel and Berkeley; the preponderance of older people in Paradise (some like more of a mix); the strained facilities and transportation congestion in the Lake Tahoe area and Mendocino coasts. With these in mind, here is how I rate the areas:

> *Excellent* — Monterey, Sonoma, Nevada City
> *Good* — Carmel, Carmel Valley, Pacific Grove, Santa Cruz, Berkeley, Santa Rosa, Jackson, Paradise, Placerville, Reno-Sparks, Mendocino coasts, Mendocino, Carson City
> *Fair* — Lake Tahoe area

2. OREGON—THE BEST-KEPT RETIREMENT SECRET?

Folks in the Beaver State say that they'd like (reluctantly) for you to visit, spend your money, then go back home and not tell anyone how nice it is in Oregon.

There's a reason for this attitude. People in Oregon seems more interested in conservation than growth, status quo than progress, the glorified past rather than the glittering future. Sure, they'd like selected nonpolluting industries to widen the tax base and keep taxes low; selected, skilled, sophisticated newcomers to replace many of the native sons and daughters who escape to sunnier climes or golden opportunities—but not today; maybe tomorrow.

While the state is making up its mind, it does offer excellent opportunities for someone determined to retire here. Just pick the right spot, don't tell anyone you're a "foreigner" (especially if you're from California) and you'll find a Retirement Eden.

You have the choice of two Oregons—the coastal area and the Willamette Valley west of the Cascade Mountains. These two sections are as different as their climate, with most of the rain (some 80 inches of it annually at Brookings) falling on the coastal side. This makes for a green, misty environment that suits ducks and trees but not arthritics and nudists. By the mountains, you'll find dry streambeds, sage and sand desert. Yet fertile green stretches of farmland can be found, and most newcomers are settling here, where two-thirds of the state's population already live. With only 12 percent of the land, 3 of the biggest cities—Portland,

Eugene and Salem—are in the Willamette Valley. Southern Oregon, around Grants Pass and Medford, are getting an inflow of California businesses seeking lower overhead. And even cities in the remote central and northern parts—Bend and Pendleton—are attracting new industry and business. This still leaves over half the state to forest, semidesert and grazing lands owned by the federal government. Other brakes on growth are water and energy problems.

The northwestern part of Oregon is a combination of coastal beaches, mountains, valleys, desert, prairies, rivers and lakes. The Columbia Gorge, located near the fertile Willamette Valley south of Portland, offers spectacular scenery with waterfalls, lofty cliffs and mountains. Southern Oregon combines fruit orchards, logging, farmland and pulsing cities. Deer, antelope, wild horses and waterfowl abound in the southeast. Northeastern Oregon is a land of logging, mining, ranching and farming.

This varied scenery and climate attracts hordes of tourists who seek an away-from-it-all outdoor playground. My wife and I used to come up here often for a change of pace, climate and to attend the Shakespearean Festival at Ashland. And we'll certainly explore Oregon as our possible Retirement Eden. At present, 16.3 percent of the state's 2.5 million residents are over age 60, and 11.6 percent over 65. Counties with more than 20 percent over age 60 include Clatsop, Tillamook, Lincoln, Curry, Josephine, Wasco, Baker and Wallowa. Most of these lie along the coast or in the fertile parts of the Willamette Valley.

Wet and Dry, Hot and Cold Climate

You can practically pick a climate to order by where you live. In Eugene, in the Willamette Valley, winter averages 47°F., spring 51°F., summer 65°F. and fall 54°F. But in Pendleton, in the northeastern corner, the temperature is 10 degrees colder in winter and 10 degrees hotter in summer. At Seaside on the northwestern coast, it is cooler in both summer and winter. Rainfall is higher (70 plus inches annually) on the coast, as is the humidity (80 percent). This decreases drastically as you move inland. Dense fog occurs about 40 days a year, mostly on the coast. The annual average of 15 inches of snow occurs mainly in the valleys. Oregon is one of the most conservation-minded states, and it has done more than most other states to clean up its environment. It has made the Willamette River safe for swimmers and salmon again; cleaned up highways and campgrounds by a ban on flip-top beverage containers and a deposit on bottles; freshened the air with pollution controls and a ban on aerosol spray cans; tidied beaches and playgrounds with a volunteer sanitation crew; discouraged cars by building bike paths. But, as a former Oregon governor said, "Oregon is not a giant national park where one can live without mundane concerns of bread, health and welfare."

Good Health Care at Reasonable Cost

Oregon has 173 doctors per 100,000 population (more than enough for its needs) and a semiprivate hospital room averages $159 daily (the national average is $163). The state has 85 hospitals with a total of 11,568 beds, 190 nursing homes with 13,994 beds and 93 personal-care homes with 3,195 beds.

Good Housing at High Cost

Although housing costs and rents are generally lower than those in California, good prime land goes for over $2,000 an acre, and some goes for over $5,000 an acre. Many homes sell for $100,000, but it is possible to find less expensive retirement housing, especially in the larger cities. Marion County (near Salem) has some 200 residences in *Woodburn, Gervais, Mt. Angel, Turner* and *Four Corners,* where rents run about 25 percent of income for eligible seniors. At Sunriver, near Klamath Falls, you can buy a house and a lot from $50,000. And at Salemtowne, an adult community outside Oregon's capital city, houses also sell for $50,000. In a special section of Woodburn, about 30 miles south of Portland, relatively modest retirement homes called senior estates cluster around their own golf course, recreation complex and shopping center. Panorama 360, also in Woodburn, lists condominiums from $40,000. The rental picture varies. The oceanfront resorts of Coos Bay and Astoria are "rent short," while Portland has plenty of rentals starting at $400 a month. Mobile homes are very popular in Oregon, with over 30 mobile-home parks around Salem and 50 in the Ashland-Medford area. Purchase price is $20,000 and monthly rents $75.

Moderate Taxes for a Moderate State

The income tax burden in Oregon ranks seventeenth at the lowest bracket (5.51 percent of income) to eighth at the highest bracket (9.97 percent of income). Oregon doesn't impose a sales tax, although other taxes are relatively high.

Income Tax —the rate ranges from 4 percent on the first $500 of taxable income to 10 percent on over $5,000 taxable. Marrieds filing jointly use a schedule with income brackets doubled; 4 percent on the first $1,000 to 10 percent over $10,000. Personal exemptions are $1,000 for each exemption allowed under federal law.

Property Taxes —all taxable property is assessed at 100 percent of true market value. Rates are set locally and average $20 per $1,000 true cash value ($1,000 on a $50,000 home). Homestead tax deferrals are available to persons age 62 or over, and property tax refunds are provided for homeowners and renters with household incomes of less than $17,500.

Some retirees supplement their incomes by working in seasonal employment in the cranberry processing field, and many literally fish or hunt for their supper. Also, Oregon has pioneered a number of ways to reduce retiree expenses, including the Senior Citizens Grocery, the first discount grocery store staffed by and for seniors, located in Portland. People over 60 buy into the corporation which runs the store by purchasing a 50¢ membership card. Only members can shop at this store, whose average markup is only 3 percent (supermarkets and large chains mark up to 25 percent). Portland residents are also saving energy through a mandatory weatherization program for private residences and businesses.

Big Outdoors, Little Indoors

The Oregon life-style is geared to outdoor activity all year round. More than one-quarter of Oregon is covered by national forest, comprising 17.5 million acres. Among the most famous national sites are Crater Lake, the Siuslaw and Siskiyou national forests, the Mt. Hood, Willamette, Deschutes, Umpqua, Rouge River and Winema recreation areas (including skiing). Culturally, Oregon's outstanding contribution is the yearly Shakespearean Festival at Ashland. The entire town of 15,000 dresses for this festival, which features a replica of the Globe Theater and the Black Swan, where experimental productions are performed. The Portland Art Museum is a cultural center and gallery where world-famous paintings appear on loan and where many excellent works are permanently on display. Several other Oregon towns also have museums, but these often are in isolated buildings in backwater towns like Andrews, Ashwood, Bourne, Bradwood, Brownmead, Chitwood, Clifton, Cornucopia, Drewsey, Elk City, Frenchglen, Friend, Golden, Granite, Hardman, Jacksonville, Klondike, Lonerock, Mayger, Richmond, Sodaville, Sparta, Sumpter and Susanville. Back-to-school opportunities for seniors are good, with some classes brought to senior centers. Portland leads the way, but other smaller cities with higher-education complexes, like Eugene, and community colleges offer adult-enrichment classes. However, for most Oregonians, leisure means jogging, hiking, mountain climbing, skiing, fishing or simply getting scenic "highs."

Active Local Senior Programs

Many cities have active, well-developed programs for seniors. Portland, besides numerous senior centers and programs, has its Loaves and Fishes hot-meal program, where sociability and recreation go with the noonday repast. Salem has an active senior center with more than 2,000 members. And even smaller communities have senior clubs and other activities geared to the needs of seniors. The state program on aging provides funds and assistance in setting up programs in all major areas: finances, housing, health, leisure, legal services.

For further information, write:

> Program on Aging
> 772 Commercial Street S.E.
> Salem, OR 97310

MAJOR RETIREMENT AREAS

The Oregon Coast—Scenic Sand and Surf

The 400-mile drive along Oregon's coast is the most scenic and dramatic I've ever seen. It's wilder than Cornwall and more picturesque than Maine—rolling sand dunes, craggy cliffs, white-water rapids, jutting headlands, deep inlets, proud meadows, magnificent forests, exotic wildflowers and leaping waterfalls—one of the scenic wonders of the world. It's too bad that the fog and rain have to spoil it; but if you live here, figure on 70 to 80 inches of rain a year (mostly during the winter) and 40 days of fog (mostly in the summer). If that doesn't bother you and if you like to fish in all kinds of weather, then this might be the perfect spot for you. Add the fact that arts and crafts are big in this area (Oregon beaches are rich in agate, jasper and driftwood) and that the opportunities are excellent for growing vegetables year-round. And while the beaches are public and crowded on summer weekends, the coast is broken up by more than 30 state parks and a score of national forests, which preserve the scenery and keep the peace. Seacoast towns provide a colorful and quaint haven for tourist and retiree. Here are some possibilities:

Seaside (pop. 5,000), located just 15 miles south of the mouth of the Columbia River in northwestern Oregon, is the state's largest and oldest seashore town. It has been a resort since 1870, and it bans cars from its wide sandy beaches. A 2-mile concrete promenade encourages strolling along the shore, free from exhaust fumes. Although rainfall averages about 77 inches annually, the year-round temperature is moderate, varying only 17 degrees from the high to the low (January 43°F.; July 60°F.).

Seaside has a modern 55-bed hospital, a convalescent hospital and a health-food store. The town has 6 doctors and 5 dentists. Condominiums sell from $40,000 and 2-bedroom homes from $60,000, although homes with an ocean view cost nearer $100,000. Some seaside lots (with services in) go for $40,000 but other lots sell from $15,000. Taxes average $19 per $1,000 actual value ($950 on a $50,000 house). For recreation, there is a swimming pool, hunting and fishing (especially salmon) facilities, 2 golf courses, beaches, theater group and art association and the North Coast Friends of Musicians concerts. Many retirees have found part-time (some full time) jobs in restaurants, hotels, shops, the fishing and canning industry and nearby facilities of Crown Zellerbach, a lumber company. Clam-digging (for personal or business use) is also popular in the area.

For further information, write:

Seaside Chamber of Commerce
P.O. Box 7
Seaside, OR 97138

Port Orford (pop. 1,100), the westernmost incorporated city in the continental United States, sits on a marine terrace overlooking the ocean. The views are magnificent, with powdery beaches, a picturesque fishing harbor and wind-blown cliffs. Although the area gets over 80 inches of rain a year, the average temperature is moderate, ranging from 48°F. in January to 59°F. in July. Port Orford has a local clinic, but the nearest hospital is 27 miles away, in either Gold Beach or Bandon. The town has only 1 doctor. This place is ideal for craftspeople, since it is dotted with beautiful myrtlewood trees which grow on the Pacific coast. You'll find many myrtlewood factories and gift shops in the area, and many local artisans who work with driftwood and beach stones. Numerous streams flow from the coastal range to the sea, and some of the finest salmon, steelhead and trout fishing occurs in nearby waters. The northwest portion is dotted with freshwater lakes bordering the ocean, and all have boat-launching ramps and are open to fishing, sailing and other water recreation. Cedar Bend Golf Course, 16 miles to the south, is a PGA-rated 9-hole course. Housing costs are moderate in the area, averaging $55,000 for 2-bedroom units and renting for $400 a month. Taxes run $18 per $1,000 market value.

For further information, write:

Chamber of Commerce
Port Orford, OR 97465

Bandon (pop. 2,500) is 26 miles north of Port Orford. This resort town attracts many tourists and retirees because of its fine beach, good harbor and industry, which includes lumbering, dairying, commercial fishing, cranberry-raising and beachcombing for agate, jasper and other semiprecious stones. Oregon myrtle (California laurel) also grows here, and many craftspeople have set up studios and shops. Rainfall is 65 inches a year and the climate is mild year-round. The small but modern hospital is fully equipped and staffed, and 2 dentists, 4 physicians and an eye doctor are in Bandon. *Coos Bay* (pop. 15,000) offers more modern facilities, including a new hospital. Housing is good and reasonably priced here. Seaside lots sell from $10,000, homes cost $50,000 and apartments rent from $300. *Pine Village,* a 30-unit development, provides 1-bedroom apartments for people on limited incomes for less than $100 a month. All told, a retired couple with home and car paid for can live comfortably on $500 to $600 a month. Utilities cost less than $70 a month, and taxes are as moderate as Port Orford's. Many retirees raise vegetables, fish and go clamming and crabbing in the many tidal pools. There's golfing in the area, and the local library offers excellent service. Craftspeople and carpenters work for fun and profit, and other part-time work is available in tourist-related businesses and, during the harvest season, on farms and in cranberry-processing plants.

For further information, write:

Chamber of Commerce
Bandon, OR 97411

Other towns along the coast that offer possibilities include (with population and zip code) *Brookings* (pop. 3,500; 97415) noted for its azaleas and Easter lily bulbs; *Newport* (pop. 6,750; 97365), a Victorian resort town; *North Bend* (pop. 9,000; 97459), one of the largest cities on the coast, with a museum, golf course, and commercial fisheries, lumbering and manufacturing industries.

The Willamette Valley—Big City Retirement with Refinement

Surprisingly, Oregon's three largest cities—Portland, Salem and Eugene—all offer retirement possibilities. All are situated toward the north end of the fertile Willamette Valley. This makes for a 4-season climate with temperatures averaging 44.4°F. in winter and 63.6°F. in summer. The best weather feature is reduced rainfall—only 38.82 inches annually— less than half that on the coast. And the average annual humidity is reduced to 61 percent, down from the 80 percent that prevails on the coast. Here is a thumbnail sketch of each of the cities.

Portland (pop. 400,000), the "City of Roses," is the only true metropolis in Oregon, and it was rated highest for large cities in the Quality of Life studies. It received highest marks for its air purity (when Mount St. Helens isn't acting up), civic concern, employment opportunities and housing. Its setting, on both banks of the Willamette River and at the head of the Willamette Valley, and the surrounding countryside—the Columbia River Gorge, Mt. Hood, waterfalls, forests, ski slopes, fishing streams, hunting and camping areas—make it one of the most livable areas in the country. It is divided into 2 sections: the homey east and the elegant west, each offering comfortable living in all price ranges. The city has excellent medical facilities with 17 major hospitals, the University of Oregon Medical School, and a Veterans Administration hospital. All told, there are 5,700 hospital beds and 34,000 health service people in the area, more than enough for the population's needs. Housing costs are moderate, with 2-bedroom retirement homes starting at $60,000 and apartments renting from $350 a month. Taxes average $20.46 per $1,000 actual value. Portland also has a *Camlu Retirement Home* in the business district, where fees average $500 a month with meals. There are also a number of mobile-home parks in the area, where rents average $100 a month and purchase prices start at $15,000. Cultural attractions include the art museum, Oregon Symphony Orchestra, Oregon Historical Society, Portland State University and the University of Portland. The parks in the area are outstanding, with Macleay Park in midcity providing more than 30 square miles of dense forest untouched by the fumes and noise of the surrounding metropolis. Along the Willamette River, old factories are being torn down to create greenbelts, and the river has been cleaned up so it is suitable for fishing and swimming.

For further information, write:

Chamber of Commerce
824 Southwest Fifth
Portland, OR 97204

Salem (pop. 100,000), the state capital, is the third largest city in Oregon. Situated midway between Portland and Eugene, it lies in the fertile valley surrounded by mountains. It is a compact city, so no home is more than a few minutes from the downtown area. Medical facilities consist of 2 major hospitals with a total of 511 beds and 202 physicians, adequate for the population. Two-bedroom retirement homes start at $50,000; monthly rents are under $400, and the town also has a *Camlu Retirement Hotel* with rents of $500 a month with meals. At *Salemtowne*, on the outskirts, lots sell for $10,000 and homes start at under

$50,000. And at *Samaritan Village* you can get an apartment and 1 meal a day for $350 a month. Many mobile-home parks are in the area, with monthly fees of $75 a month. Cultural facilities include a symphony orchestra, art association, little theater, Bush House Museum, Willamette University and a civic center. There are 44 parks within a 5-mile radius, 9 golf courses within 15 miles and 70 tennis courts in the area. The senior citizens center activities list includes 2,000 events of interest to seniors.

For further information, write:

Chamber of Commerce
Salem, OR 97308

Eugene (pop. 106,000), the second largest city in Oregon, was voted the "best midsize city" by *New West* magazine. It was rated first in economic and racial balance and air purity; second in lack of poverty, employment and education; third in lack of crime, health and civic concern. Interestingly, Eugene just edged out Boulder, Colorado, with which it has much in common: a "laid-back" city where people are more concerned with the quality of life and individual freedom than they are with growth and status. It is a city filled with people who chose it as a place to live, then fought to make a life there. It is a town without pretense or an entrenched élite. As one contented newcomer said, "A social climber would die of frustration in this town; there aren't any ladders to climb." The setting is gorgeous, with the Cascade Range rising to the east and the mountains of the coast to the west. The many parks in the area offer fishing, skiing, hiking and year-round outdoor recreation. Almost everyone is a physical-fitness buff, and the health of the people shows in the vigor of the government. Costs are lower than in San Francisco, Los Angeles and other metropolitan areas, with good homes selling from $50,000, rents from $350 a month and mobile-home parks from $70 a month. The area has 675 hospital beds and 250 physicians, which is more than adequate for the population. Among cultural activities are the Maude Kerns Art Center, featuring classes in painting, ceramics, weaving and jewelry making; the Very Little Theater, one of the oldest in America; 6 golf courses and numerous tennis courts. The city's handsome mall has numerous fountains and grassy areas that dot the downtown area and make it a focal point of the town. Senior citizens activities are concentrated here, and *The Good Samaritan Center* offers life-care housing at reasonable rates.

For further information, write:

Chamber of Commerce
P.O. Box 1107

230 East Broadway
Eugene, OR 97440

Medford (pop. 50,000) may be the economic heart of Jackson County, but *Ashland* (pop. 15,000), 10 miles south, is its intellectual soul. Both lie in the Rogue River Valley, which has a different climate than the Willamette Valley. Here, the annual average temperature is 52.5°F., with a range of 31°F. to 47°F. in winter and 53°F. to 73°F. in summer. Annual precipitation averages 19.3 inches with 6 inches of snow. Humidity averages 87 percent in January but only 44 percent in July, which moderates any heat. The two towns are as different in appearance as they are in performance: Medford is surrounded by orchards (it is famous for its pears), and trees make the city parklike. The mild winters and warm summers favor outdoor living and also encourage outdoor sports: boating and fishing on the Rogue River and in the many streams and lakes in the area, including the ones in the Rogue River National Forest. Ashland, especially during festival times, looks like a picture postcard of Elizabethan England, for it is the home of the Shakespearean Festival, held in Lithia Park. This 100-acre fairyland wood is adjacent to the city plaza and contains replicas of London's Globe Theatre, where outdoor plays are held. Minstrels stroll playing ancient instruments; fair maidens in flowing gowns flit like fireflies. A plaza adjoining the park has two fountains of lithia water piped in from mineral springs. Each year the festival and setting draw more and more people, who revel in the drama and the setting. Ashland is also home of Southern Oregon State College, which adds to the intellectual quality of the community. The area has 371 hospital beds and 123 physicians, more than enough for its needs. Housing is reasonable, with 2-bedroom retirement homes starting for under $50,000. However, homes with a view of the Rogue River or the Siskiyou Mountains might cost $90,000. Good 2-bedroom apartments rent from $350 a month, and there are several mobile-home parks in the area where rents average $60 a month. This is beautiful outdoor country offering excellent swimming, boating, fishing, skiing and water sports. Add the intellectual atmosphere of Ashland and you have food for the soul as well as activity for the body. There is a senior center offering many activities. And this area is only a day's drive to the San Francisco Bay area (or to Portland) if you want a change of pace.

For further information, write:

Greater Medford Chamber of Commerce
304 South Central
Medford, OR 97501

SUMMARY

While retirement in Oregon might not be very exciting, it can be very pleasant. You would be living in one of the finest parts of the country, with moderate climate. The best scenery is along the coast, which is often rainy in winter and foggy in summer. Yet the outdoors are so inviting that most people are either surfing at the beaches, hiking in the woods, riding down the rivers or climbing the mountains. If you like the outdoors or just admire scenery, you'll love Oregon. Here are my ratings of major retirement areas:

Excellent — Eugene, Ashland
Good — Seaside, Port Orford, Bandon, Portland, Salem, Medford

3. WASHINGTON—AN EVERGREEN EDEN

A prominent national magazine once called Washington "America's Scenic Storeroom." The article went on to say that whatever was left over from making the other states was stacked in the northwest corner. This includes bits of sandy beaches, craggy cliffs, dense forests and majestic mountains. It also includes bits of weather no other state wanted: one or another part of Washington has recorded temperatures as low as −36°F. to as high as 118°F.! Some areas record little or no precipitation; others 200 inches. Some areas never get snow; others get almost 100 feet.

All this is packed into the smallest of the continental Western states: Washington is 360 miles wide and 240 miles deep. Expect to find fast changes of scenery if you travel through the state. On the Olympic peninsula you'll find rain forests, snow-capped peaks and miles of beach; in the northwest area, the San Juan Islands and snow-capped Mt. Baker. In the Puget Sound area, big cities (Seattle, Tacoma, Everett). In the southwest, miles of sandy beaches. In the central part of the state, you find many forest-rimmed lakes, streams and Grand Coulee Dam. In the east, the Snake River Gorge, Palouse Falls, Blue Mountains, Mt. Spokane and Sherman Pass. And in the north, the saw-toothed Cascade Mountains.

This varied scenery has attracted a proud, independent people who cherish variety and a stimulating environment. Of the state's 3.8 million people 14.7 percent are over age 60 and 10.6 percent are over 65. Counties with more than 20 percent over age 60 include: Jefferson, Pacific, San Juan, Chelan, Lincoln and Columbia.

Weather to Match the Mountains

Washington has 2 distinct climatic zones: the western portion, which is characterized by mild summers (average temperature 68°F.) and mild but moist and cloudy winters, and the eastern half, which has sunny weather most of the year but is 10 degrees hotter in summer and 10 degrees colder in winter. In the eastern part, Spokane averages 29°F. in winter, 46°F. in spring, 66°F. in summer and 48°F. in fall. In the western part, Seattle averages 43°F. in winter, 51°F. in spring, 65°F. in summer and 51°F. in fall. The western portion, where two-thirds of the population is centered, has very little freezing weather in the winter and only small amounts of snowfall at lower elevations. The average rainfall is 45 inches, 85 percent of which falls in the winter months. Eastern Washington can have several weeks of freezing weather in the winter and generally a fair amount of snow. However, for most of the year, days are clear and sunny.

More Than Adequate Medical Facilities

Washington has 178 doctors per 100,000 population (vs. the national average of 174), which is more than adequate for the population. A semi-private hospital room averages $154 daily, vs. the national average of $163. The state has 125 hospitals with a total of 16,138 beds, 293 nursing homes with 26,663 beds and 77 personal-care homes with 3,681 beds.

Good Housing at Reasonable Prices

The Evergreen State has many retirement and vacation homes for sale for under $50,000. Even good building lots sell for under $10,000. Many larger homes are available for $75,000 with an acre or more of land. Rents are scarce in some areas, but when available, usually start at $350 a month for a 2-bedroom apartment. Most of the pmpular retirement or resort areas have mobile-home parks with rents averaging $75 a month.

No Income Tax; High Sales Tax

Just the reverse of Oregon, Washington has no income tax but a relatively high sales tax. However, the total tax burden is low, ranking thirty-fourth at the lowest income bracket to forty-fourth at the highest.

Property Taxes —taxes are assessed locally at 100 percent of true value, and the tax is limited to 1 percent of full value (with additional levies subject to voter approval). Household goods and furnishings and all intangible property are exempt, and an additional $300 household exemption essentially exempts most other tangible personal property of individuals not engaged in business. Homeowners age 62 and over are eligible for other exemptions and deferrals, based on income.

Sales Tax—the rate is 4.5 percent, but most cities and counties add an additional 0.5 percent to bring the total to 5 percent. In addition, King County (Seattle) adds 0.3 percent to support mass transit. Food and most prescription medicines and medical devices are exempt.

In spite of the relatively low taxes, the cost of living (in the Seattle area) is 6 percent above the national average ($10,602 for a couple in Seattle vs. the national average of $10,022). However, this is lower than the rate in San Francisco and other major western cities.

Seattle Is the Cultural Center

Most of the cultural facilities in the state (and in the entire northwest) center in Seattle. The city has a symphony orchestra, opera association, art museum and 10 other museums and 6 professional theater companies. The $50-million Seattle Center, site of the 1962 World's Fair, has many artistic complexes. Yet the rest of the state has much to offer: flowers bloom early and many festivals center around the blooming of daffodils, apple blossoms, rhododendrons and lilacs. Washington also has 3 national parks, including the fourth oldest in the country, Mount Rainier National Park. The state also has 70 state parks, numerous campgrounds, guest ranches and resorts. Most major towns have either a museum or gallery, and Spokane has a symphony orchestra and civic theater, which presents major productions. Every town of any size has facilities for both summer and winter sports, for, as in Oregon, outdoor recreation is extremely popular.

A Leader in Services for the Elderly

Washington has an outstanding program for seniors, including hot-meal program and meals on wheels, transportation services (dial-a-ride) and legal services, health care at a day-care center or at home and a "health screening" that counsels preventive medicine, help in chopping wood, washing windows and other household chores (including shopping for groceries), up to $800 worth of home-repair work a year for low income seniors and caseworkers who represent older people with bureaucracies like Social Security. The Bureau of Aging contracts with 12 area agencies on aging to provide services on a local level. And a private lobbying group, the Senior Citizens Lobby, applies pressure on the state level to get programs passed through the legislature. One such program is designed to help keep seniors out of nursing homes and in their homes as long as possible. And a survey taken by the state shows that the senior services are reaching the people who need it the most—the poor, the infirm and the very old. Anyone over age 60 is eligible for these services.

For further information, write:

Bureau on Aging
Mail Stop OB43G
Olympia, WA 98504

MAJOR RETIREMENT AREAS

Seattle (pop. 500,000) has grown from a ragamuffin to a sophisticated lady. Now she combines the beauty and mystery of Hong Kong, the breathtaking views on ski-slope hills of San Francisco, the folksiness of Chicago and that bit of Western raffishness of Denver.

But Seattle has a claim to fame in its own right. Recently, *Town and Country* magazine called Seattle "the all-American city everyone dreams about . . . a squeaky-clean, spacious place energized by its physical surrounds and citizens' pride." *Family Circle* rhapsodized about the city's "charisma," "scores of freshwater lakes," and "most verdant greenery in the country." And *New West* magazine voted it the "best big city," rating it excellent in education and civic concern, good on affluence, economic and racial balance and lack of poverty. Its lowest rating went for housing, although values here are still better than in many similar places.

Climate and Environment. Nestled between Puget Sound (salt) and Lake Washington (fresh), Seattle sprawls across 7 hills and countless ridges. These are dwarfed by the Olympic Mountains to the west and the Cascades to the east. Seattle is warmed by the Japan Current, shielded by the Olympics from the excessive winter rains and protected by the Cascades from midwinter blasts. Winter averages 43°F., summer 68°F., with an average annual humidity of 72.5 percent. Average annual rainfall is 50 inches, most of it falling from October to April. Some snow falls during winter, most of it at higher elevations. There are 151 sunny days a year; when the sun shines it's like a just-engaged girl looking at her ring.

Medical Facilities. Seattle has 14 hospitals with a total of 3,623 beds, 12 clinics, and enough doctors (more than 2,000) to staff these and take care of the general population. It also has a Tel-Med service—175 3-to-5-minute tape recordings (in layman's language) on health topics.

Housing Availability and Cost. When Boeing, the aviation company, is booming, housing tends to be scarce and expensive. But when there's a slump in aerospace production, you can pick up good housing at reduced prices. Generally, figure on paying at least $60,000 for a small retirement home, $400 a month for rent, $50,000 for a townhouse or condominium. Some of the choicest residential neighborhoods are situated along Puget Sound south of Discovery Park, and across the Lake Washington floating bridges in Bellevue and Mercer Island. Some people live on houseboats on Lake Union and Portage Bay. And there are some special retirement facilities: *Hilltop House Retirement Home*, where rents are one-quarter of income for low-income seniors; *Horizon House*, where initial fees start at $10,000, with $300 a month for 3 meals; and several mobile-home parks with rents under $100 a month.

Cost of Living. It costs a retired couple at least $10,602 annually to live here (vs. U.S. average of $10,022). State and local taxes are 8.12 percent ($609) on a $7,500 income, 5.31 percent ($797) on $15,000 and 3.98 percent ($996) on $25,000. If you want to entertain and be entertained, it would cost $20,000 a year to live comfortably here.

Leisure-Time Activities. The 1962 World's Fair left Seattle with the Seattle Center, a complex that includes an opera house, playhouse, arena coliseum, the Pacific Science Center and the futuristically designed Space Needle. The Seattle Repertory is a top-notch professional group, the Seattle Symphony is world-renowned, the Seattle Opera outstanding. Seattle is big league in sports, too. The Kingdome, Seattle's seat of professional sports, hosts the SuperSonics and other winning teams. Add the Waterfront Park, Pike Place Market (a historic site like Boston's Quincy Market), Pioneer Square (where the city was founded), the Oriental international district and you have a kaleidoscope of activities and events that could keep your mind and body spinning all year-round. Downtown buses are free, and the World's Fair monorail links Seattle Center with downtown every 15 minutes.

Special Services for Seniors. The Seattle area offers an impressive array of services at reduced rates. Included are 10¢ bus rides ($2 a month) to anywhere in the county, pet license and tax discounts, free appliance parts, restaurant discounts and discounts at some pharmacies, food coops, tours and theaters, free tuition at Seattle Pacific University, several hot-meal sites, meals on wheels, transportation program, outreach program, day-care centers, volunteer opportunities through foster grandparent programs and Retired Senior Volunteer Program (RSVP), Elder Citizens Coalition (a political group of low-income seniors), senior services and centers, senior craftsmen program, a senior information center, senior services information and assistance program.

For further information, write:

> Seattle/King County Convention and Visitors Bureau
> 1815 Seventh Avenue
> Box GT
> Seattle, WA 98101

Sequim (pop. 3,000) and the *Dungeness Valley*, although only 70 miles northwest of Seattle, lie in the "dry shadow" of the Olympic Mountains, so rainfall averages only 16 inches a year. Temperatures average a maximum of 44.8°F. and a minimum of 31°F. in January and a maximum of 71.9°F. and a minimum of 49°F. in July. A day above 80°F. is rare, and blankets are needed every night, including July and August. Electrical storms are rare; tornadoes and hurricanes unknown. Snow, usually light, seldom lasts long. The town has 6 doctors, 4 dentists, 3 chiropractic clinics and 3 rest homes. Homes are mainly frame, selling from $50,000 to $100,-000. Some rentals are available from $300 a month. Condominiums are being built near the 2 golf courses and a condominium retirement development of nearly 100 units occupies the hillside on the south side of town. Other developments are planned, and new homes dot the backroads, byways and beachfronts. Taxes are only 1 percent of market value. Sequim has a movie theater, bowling alley, bridge and other clubs, fraternal organizations and a leisure-hour club for seniors. Excellent fishing (saltwater) is available all year-round, no license required. There is good pheasant and duck hunting in the area, and deer, elk and bear less than 1 hour away. Gardening is a popular activity—many seniors raise (in addition to flowers) apples, pears, cherries, strawberries, peaches, apricots, gooseberries, blueberries, tomatoes, peas, beans, rhubarb, cabbage, lettuce, carrots, turnips, radishes, celery, squash, brussel sprouts and asparagus. Adult-education classes at the high school and at Peninsula College in Port Angeles (see below) offer classes for seniors.

For further information, write:

> Sequim-Dungeness Valley Chamber of Commerce
> P.O. Box 907
> Sequim, WA 98382

Port Angeles (pop. 17,500), sitting atop the Olympic peninsula, has the Olympic Mountains at its back and Juan de Fuca Strait at its shoreline. Just 17 miles across the strait is Victoria, British Columbia. Port Angeles is the headquarters for Olympic National Park and county seat of Clallam County (pop. 46,600). Climate is typically marine, with fresh breezes.

Annual rainfall is 22.83 inches; snowfall 8.5 inches. Cool summer days average 65°F. to 75°F., occasionally going up to 85°F. Winter afternoons are in the 40°F. to 50°F. range, with nights in the 30's. Medical facilities are excellent, with an 86-bed hospital, 2 nursing care centers, 30 physicians and 17 dentists. Housing is reasonable, with small retirement homes selling for $50,000 and renting from $350 a month. Some apartment houses exist for seniors with low incomes. Real and personal property is assessed at 100 percent of fair market value; taxes are $163 per $10,000 value ($815 on a $50,000 home). Cultural facilities include an excellent library system with 140,129 books, Port Angeles Symphony, community concert association, more than 100 service and fraternal clubs and special programs for the elderly.

For further information, write:

Chamber of Commerce
1217 East First Street
Port Angeles, WA 98362

Port Townsend (pop. 5,700), located just east of Sequim, has been called "the dream that failed." It was once considered the most important town in Washington state, and there was talk of its competing with San Francisco as the most beautiful town in the West. Huge Victorian mansions were erected on lots that sold for as much as $500 a front foot. The only thing it needed to become the undisputed shipping capital of the Northwest was a railroad—which never came. And the city languished until the late 1950s and 1960s, when the town and its ancient mansions were discovered by restoration buffs and retirees. Many of these homes have been restored and are now selling for $100,000. But good 2- to 3-bedroom homes on ample lots sell from $50,000, with taxes 1 percent of market value. The general hospital has 42 beds and the Kah-Tai Care Center has 94 beds and a full nursing staff. Port Townsend has 7 physicians, 5 dentists and 2 chiropractors. Boating and sailing are popular here, and there's skiing nearby in the winter. Port Townsend has 2 9-hole golf courses, and there are swimming areas and walking trails throughout. The Centrum Foundation at Fort Worden State Park schedules cultural events year-round, the recreation department has senior events going most of the time and adult education and crafts are offered through the local school system.

For further information, write:

Chamber of Commerce
2437 Sims Way
Port Townsend, WA 98368

San Juan Islands. There are 172 islands nestled between the northwest corner of Washington state and Vancouver Island, British Columbia. The largest islands are *Orcas* and *San Juan* (each about 55 square miles) characterized by secluded coves, giant trees, freshwater lakes, modest motels and plush resorts. These islands enjoy the relatively rainfree climate of Sequim, Port Angeles and Port Townsend; only about 29 inches fall here annually. The year-round climate is mild, with no heat waves and little snow, frost or fog. *Friday Harbor* on San Juan has a hospital and dentist's office, and a flying doctor serves the islands. Waterfront homes are expensive, selling from $100,000, but you can buy a vacation or resort cabin or a small retirement home from $50,000. Taxes run 1 percent of market value. Orcas has the largest retiree population, with most older people living in small communities like *Deer Harbor, Olga* and *Eastsound.* The retirees have several clubs, and they have formed hobby groups and craft classes. Adult-education courses are available on San Juan and the island has major shopping facilities (prices tend to be 10 percent higher than on the mainland). These islands are best suited to those who enjoy outdoor activities, nature studies and solitary activities like arts, crafts, writing, painting and photography. Although there is some organized entertainment on the islands (including well-attended Saturday night dances), most of the inhabitants are proud individualists who prefer solitude. Several ferries leave *Anacortes* each day for the major islands of the group, and you can take your car (the islands have scenic drives). An island tour takes about 5 hours.

For further information, write:

Chamber of Commerce
Orcas Island, Eastsound, WA 98245
San Juan Island, Friday Harbor, WA 98250

Olympia (pop. 30,000), Washington's capital city, is surrounded by natural beauty—Mt. Rainier and the Olympic Mountains behind it, Puget Sound at its doorstep. It's a parklike community with fountains, sunken gardens and acres of lawn surrounding the capitol building. The rest of the city is manicured and green, with many fruit trees, shrubs and flowers in blossom most of the year. The temperature in January averages 38.1°F. and 63.9°F. in July. Precipitation is around 47 inches a year, 75 percent of which falls in the winter months. There are 228 physicians in the area and 300 hospital beds. Recreation areas flourish with 4 golf courses, ski areas and beaches within reach. Olympia was chosen in 1963 as the site for Panorama City, a 160-acre life-care retirement community of over

1,100 people with single or multifamily homes, a 5-story high rise, and garden and studio apartments with prices running from about $25,000. Fees average $450 a month and include all utilities, interior and exterior maintenance, lawn care, full hospital and medical coverage, security patrols, appliances, cable and closed-circuit television, basic telephone charge, carpeting, transportation and recreational and hobby-shop facilities to fit almost anyone's needs. Optional and special services include food service, restaurant, housekeeping services and a fully staffed 106-bed convalescent and rehabilitation center on campus. For further information on Panorama City, write 150 Circle Drive, Lacey, WA 98503.

For further information, write:

Chamber of Commerce
1000 Plum Street Box 1427
Olympia, WA 98507

Ryderwood (pop. 500), a former logging town in the southwestern part of the state, was purchased by a realty company in the 1950s and turned into senior estates. Homes were offered to retired couples on a 12-year deferred-payment basis, with total purchase price below $10,-000. Now resales are available for under $50,000, and some new houses and townhouses have been built for over $50,000. Still, housing is cheap and attractive here, and the town is centered around senior activities. Included is a nondenominational church, social club, men's and women's clubs, a library and a park. Hunting, fishing and gardening are excellent (rainfall totals 40 inches a year). Summers are cool and there is little snow in winter. The town is located at 300 feet altitude in a flat valley of 225 acres surrounded by mountains and streams and with its own community lake.

For further information, write:

Chamber of Commerce
Ryderwood, WA 98581

SUMMARY

Washington offers a varied and stimulating retirement in both urban and rural settings. But because of the fast-changing scenery and weather patterns, you must pick your place carefully unless you like perpetual rain and extremes of heat and cold. Most retirement centers are in the western portion of the state, where the weather is mildest and the scenery most spectacular. And with Washington's outstanding senior programs and services, retirement could be a pleasure. Here are my ratings of major retirement areas:

Excellent — Seattle area, Sequim
Good   — Port Angeles, Port Townsend, San Juan Islands, Olympia, Ryderwood

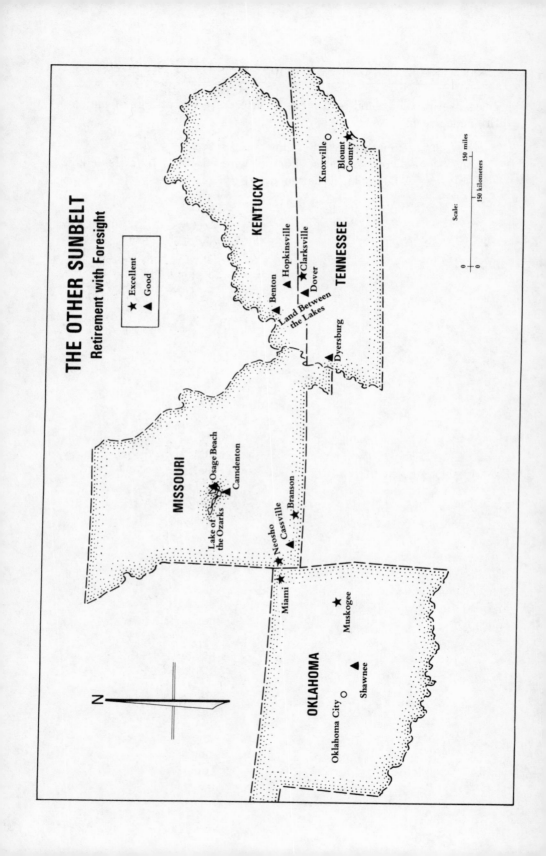

VIII.

THE BORDER STATES—

RETIREMENT WITH FORESIGHT

The states on the border between North and South—Kentucky, Tennessee, Missouri and Oklahoma—could be the retirement areas of the future. Far from being backwaters of the traditional Sunbelt states (North Carolina, South Carolina, Georgia, Florida, Alabama, Louisiana, Arkansas, Texas, New Mexico, Arizona, southern California and Hawaii) covered in detail in my preceding book, *Sunbelt Retirement,* these states have a lot to offer now and more to come in the future.

Generally, these states don't require the air conditioning of the Sunbelt nor the central heating of the Snowbelt. In an increasingly energy-conscious world, these states appeal for their energy efficiency. Also, they are just that much closer to the family up north and the resorts down south, so retirees can change scenery and weather in a matter of hours rather than days.

These states offer a wide range of economic, social and environmental factors to appeal to all personalities and pocketbooks.

1. KENTUCKY—FOR A NEW RETIREMENT LIFE

"My Old Kentucky Home" might be a sentimental ballad for some, but to others it's not only a possibility, but a probability—especially for retirees in western sections of Kentucky (and Tennessee) who call that area "Hubland, U.S.A." This is the Land Between the Lakes, a 170,000-

acre public demonstration area being developed by the Tennessee Valley Authority (TVA) in the Kentucky-Barkley lakes region. More than $35 million is being spent to preserve the natural features of this beautiful woodland while constructing new facilities for outdoor recreation. And with 15 cities, 35 towns and 25 lake developments in the area, many retirees are flocking here. This is especially drawing military retirees who can use the services and facilities at Fort Campbell (Hopkinsville), where an Armed Forces Retirement Center has been formed. Within the Ken-Bar region (as the Land Between the Lakes is called) retirees are being offered 170,000 acres of prime retirement land: 4,000 miles of shoreline along with countless lakes, rivers, springs, creeks and 25 golf courses.

Kentucky has 4 distinct sections—the historic northern arch, the bluegrass, the eastern mountains and western lakes—each differing in geography, economics and culture. The northern part is dominated by fine homes, good-looking horses and lush grasslands made blue by the limestone in the soil. The eastern highlands have rugged mountains, deep forests, lakes and natural rock formations like the Sky Bridge. Central Kentucky is bordered by the bluegrass region to the north and the Pennyrile plateau to the south and separated by a chain of low hills, the Knobbs. And the low, flat plain of western Kentucky is distinguished by that 40-mile long peninsula, the Land Between the Lakes.

Some 15.2 percent of Kentucky's 3.5 million population is over age 60, 11.0 percent over 65. Counties with more than 20 percent over age 60 include Ballard, Carlisle, Fulton, Graves, Hickman, Caldwell, Crittenden, Lyon, Todd, Trigg, Webster, Allen, Butler, Logan, Metcalfe, Robertson, Adair, Green and Harrison.

Moderate, Mellow Climate

The climate is generally moderate, with generous amounts of rainfall. Winters are short and mild and summers are moderate. Overall temperature averages 54°F. in the northeast and 58°F. in the southwest. Winter averages 37°F., spring 55°F., summer 75°F., fall 57°F.

Low Cost, Quality Medical Care

While a semiprivate hospital room in Kentucky averages only $106 a day (vs. the national average of $163 daily), there are only 128 physicians per 100,000 population, less than the recommended minimum of 133 per 100,000. There are 121 hospitals with 18,815 beds, 182 nursing homes with 13,981 beds and 139 personal-care homes with 6,969 beds.

Low-Cost Land and Housing

You can buy good recreation land for less than $1,000 an acre, and vacation homes go for under $50,000—some under $40,000. Building lots are available for as low as $500. Mobile homes sell from $15,000 and park rentals start at $50 a month.

Moderate Cost of Living

Kentucky ranks twenty-second in tax burden at the lowest tax bracket and twenty-ninth at highest levels.

Income Tax—rates on taxable income range from 2 percent on the first $3,000 to 6 percent on the next $8,000. Each person gets a $20 exemption, and those over age 65 get an additional $40 exemption.

Property Taxes—all property in Kentucky is assessed at 100 percent of fair market value. Land and buildings are taxed by the state and may also be taxed by local jurisdictions. The state rate is 31.5¢ per $100 of assessed valuation; taxes on a $50,000 home in Lexington run $545 annually. Persons over age 65 get tax concessions based on income.

Sales Tax—the rate is 5 percent with prescription medicine and grocery food exempt.

Parks Offer Senior Citizen Specials

Recreation is centered outdoors, and the Kentucky Department of Parks offers a series of "senior citizen specials" featuring games and activities for persons 62 and over at parks from late February through May. Participants can choose from activities such as arts and crafts, parties, games, a banquet and nature programs. Kentucky has two national parks, Cumberland Gap and Mammoth Cave, and its state parks are among the finest in the nation. Cultural activities are centered around university towns, and historical sites are scattered throughout the state, including many Civil War battlefields.

Services for Seniors

The Center for Aging and Community Development funds and helps set up local programs in major areas: nutrition, health care, financial assistance, housing, legal matters, leisure-time activities. Most direction and programs are at the local level and vary widely.

For further information, write:

Center for Aging and Community Development
403 Wapping Street
Frankfort, KY 40601

MAJOR RETIREMENT AREAS

Hopkinsville (pop. 30,000), in the Ken-Bar region, is the town nearest to Fort Campbell, 16 miles south. Fort Campbell is one of the nation's largest military installations. Many military retirees like to live in Hopkinsville because of its nearness to the fort's facilities (PX, hospitals, clubs), yet here they can lead an independent civilian life. The town itself lies in flat tobacco country and it is also a light manufacturing center.

Climate and Environment. The average annual temperature is 59.4°F., with a winter average of 38°F. and a summer average of 76°F. Normal average rainfall is 46 inches with mean annual snowfall of 10.90 inches. Relative humidity averages 79 percent at midnight, 84 percent at 6 A.M., 58 percent at noon, 62 percent at 6 P.M.

Medical Facilities. Hopkinsville has 1 general hospital with 245 beds and a mental hospital with 520 beds. There are 3 nursing homes with 262 beds, 4 personal-care homes with 321 beds, 7 clinics, 61 doctors, 20 dentists and 29 specialists, more than enough for the population.

Housing Availability and Cost. Housing is plentiful, with small 2- to 3-bedroom retirement homes selling for $40,000 and apartments renting from $350 a month. There are also 350 subsidized retirement units and 400 more luxurious ones with rents from $250 a month. The Christian Health Center has a high-rise apartment complex with units for the elderly. Building lots range from $10,000 to $25,000 and building costs per square foot are just over $30.

Cost of Living. Combined state and local taxes inside the city run $1.049 per $100 value (assessed at full market value). Thus, taxes on a $40,000 home run $419.60 a year. Outside the city the rate is 0.596, which means $238.40 on a $40,000 home.

Leisure-Time Activities. The town has a newspaper, a library with 107,419 volumes, 4 bookstores, 3 art galleries, 1 museum, 1 little theater, over 20 independent clubs plus an Elks Club and a private country club, 8 parks, 3 swimming pools, 2 golf courses, 18 tennis courts, biking, hiking and horseback riding in the area. A full range of adult-education courses is available at Hopkinsville Community College, as are a community concert series and performances by the Pennyrile Players. The Pennyrile Festival of Arts is celebrated during the second week of October and offers juried art exhibits, programs in drama and music and a garden tour. Twice yearly, in April and October, a professor at Hopkinsville Community College presents a "Highlights in Local History" program at the Pennyrile Area Historical Museum. Pennyrile Forest State Resort Park is located in northern Christian County about 20 miles north of Hopkinsville. Facilities include a 24-room lodge, 180-seat dining room, 1- and 2-bedroom cottages and efficiency cottages and complete recreational facilities. Hopkinsville is located just 30 miles east of the vast Land Between the Lakes.

Special Services for Seniors. Besides numerous senior clubs, Hopkinsville has an office on aging, a hot-meal program, homemakers and visiting nurse services, special health clinics, transportation services, a hot line, legal aid and a rehabilitation program.

For further information, write:

> Hopkinsville–Christian County Chamber of Commerce
> P.O. Box 565
> Hopkinsville, KY 42240

Land Between the Lakes, a 170,000-acre project being developed by the Tennessee Valley Authority, is in the Kentucky-Barkley lake region. It is a haven for hunters, fishermen, campers, hikers, boaters, bird-watchers and horseback riders. The 3 large family compounds bordering Kentucky Lake provide more than 800 well-defined campgrounds, 27 other lakes offer more limited camping and other recreational facilities are available. In addition to the lure of the region to sportsmen, retirees have a wide choice of employment opportunities in 5 cities—St. Louis, Evansville, Louisville, Nashville and Memphis—all of which are linked to the Ken-Bar region by interstate highways and inland waterways. Also, in the Land Between the Lakes are 10 colleges and universities, 9 state parks and 2 national parks, while 8 state and federal forests cover thousands of acres between the TVA dams. There are many established small towns and villages around the area, including Hopkinsville (above), that are suitable for retirement.

Many nearby retirement developments are underway offering good housing from $40,000, with taxes 1 percent of market value. With all the fishing and hunting in the area, many retirees literally "live off the fat of the land."

For further information, write:

> Land Between the Lakes, TVA
> P.O. Box KWW
> Golden Pond, KY 42231

Ken-Bar Lakes Enterprises
P.O. Box 126
Gilbertsville, KY 42044

Marshall County (pop. 25,000) lies just west of the Land Between the Lakes and consists of the towns of *Benton* (pop. 4,200), *Calvert City* (2,500), *Hardin* (600) and smaller communities in a land area of 303 square miles. The annual mean temperature is 59.5°F., annual rainfall 47.2 inches, with generally mild winters and light snowfall. The Marshall County Hospital in Benton has general hospital facilities, including a long-term care unit. There are 2 large hospitals in Paducah, 25 miles away. Good housing is available, with small retirement homes selling for under $40,000, building lots from $2,000, brick houses with full basements for under $50,000, several mobile homes for $20,000 and many places to rent from $300 a month. Taxes on a $40,000 home in Benton run $333.20 annually. There are 80 clubs in the area, ranging from civic to recreational clubs. The Marshall County Senior Citizens Club has a central office in Benton, with satellites in Calvert City and Hardin. A Zesta Club also meets in Benton. And, of course, Marshall County shares the recreational and educational facilities of the Land Between the Lakes.

For further information, write:

Marshall County Chamber of Commerce
Box 145, Route 7
Benton, KY 42025

SUMMARY

Kentucky appeals to those retirees, including military ones, who like the Land Between the Lakes area. Yet towns like Hopkinsville and Benton shouldn't be overlooked if you want to avoid too close an association with the resort area. Here are my ratings of the major areas:

Good — Hopkinsville, Land Between the Lakes area, Benton (Marshall County)

2. TENNESSEE—FOR A CHANGE OF RETIREMENT PACE

Some folks think that the Tennessee Valley Authority made the Volunteer State what it is today. While some natives might argue this, it is true that when the TVA tamed the Tennessee River it not only brought cheap energy to modernize rural areas, but it also created a state that is now largely urban and industrialized.

More than 40,000 square miles drain into the Tennessee River, and this water is controlled by 33 major dams that have created a string of lakes with a total surface of 625,000 acres and a shoreline of 11,000 miles.

The TVA not only made the Land Between the Lakes of northwestern Tennessee, it created the "Great Lakes of the South." The lakes in eastern Tennessee are particularly beautiful because of the contrasting mountain scenery. The dams have also made the Tennessee River navigable from north of Knoxville to the river's confluence with the Ohio River. And TVA's conservation, reforestation and other regional-improvement practices attract not only industrialists looking for new sites but tourists looking for new recreational areas.

Before you get the impression that Tennessee was created by the TVA, note that the state has 3 distinct areas. Western Tennessee, bordered by the Mississippi River, stretches its rich plains to central Tennessee, where the highland rim, central basin and farmlands predominate. In eastern Tennessee are the Great Smoky Mountains, where 16 peaks rise more than 6,000 feet, towering over lakes, valleys and the Cherokee National Forest. Each region has bred its own people with their own accents. Eastern Tennessee is home to the mountaineer who speaks with a twang, whose ancestors fought for the union in the Civil War and who votes Republican. Western Tennessee speaks with a magnolia flavor, fought for the Confederate States and votes Democratic. The people in central Tennessee are somewhere in between the mountains and the cotton fields, in both speech and outlook.

So you can have a change of scenery, accents, people and pace if you retire in Tennessee. Some 15.1 percent of the Volunteer State's 4.5 million residents are over age 60 and 10.7 percent over 65. Interestingly enough, the older residents are pretty evenly scattered throughout the state, and the only counties with more than 20 percent of the population over age 60 are Jackson, Giles, Perry, Benton, Carroll, Crockett, Gibson, Henry, Decatur and Hardeman.

Change-of-Pace Climate

The climate is described as "humid continental to the north; humid subtropical to the south." This translates into a statewide average of 52°F. in winter, 60°F. in spring, 85°F. in summer and 60°F. in fall. In Nashville, in the center of the state, winters average 47.4°F. and summers 71.8°F. There are 198 sunny days with an average annual humidity of 71.8 percent. Annual average rainfall is 54.41 inches, snowfall 2.5 inches.

Low-Cost, Moderately Good Medical Care

The average daily rate for a semiprivate hospital room is $108, vs. the national average of $163. The state has 147 doctors per 100,000 population, which is above the minimum of 133 but below the national average of 174. Tennessee has 160 hospitals with a total of 31,008 beds, 253 nursing homes with 18,387 beds, 37 personal-care homes with 1,705 beds. The best medical care is available in and around Nashville, Memphis, Johnson City, Knoxville and Chattanooga.

Good Housing at Low Cost

Good housing is plentiful at low cost. Small retirement homes sell for $40,000 and rent from $300 a month. Good recreational and farmland sells for under $1,000 an acre. And some mobile homes are available for under $20,000, with park rentals $60 a month. Some retirement housing is set aside for low-income seniors. Retirement villages are located in *Johnson City, Cosby, Crossville, Crab Orchard* and *Pleasant Hill.*

Low Cost of Living

The cost of living in Tennessee—especially in rural areas—is 10 percent below the national average. And Tennessee ranks forty-ninth in tax burden at both lower and upper tax brackets.

Income Tax —no tax on earned income; 6 percent tax on dividends and interest, but only 4 percent on dividends from corporations which have 75 percent or more of their corporate property in Tennessee. Persons 65 or older whose income is less than $6,000 ($10,000 if filing jointly) are exempt.

Property Taxes —residential property is assessed at 25 percent of value. Tangible personal property is assessed at 5 percent of value. A refund on all or part of property taxes paid on the first $6,000 of market value of residences is given to taxpayers 65 or older if their annual income does not exceed $4,800. Generally, taxes run under 1 percent of market value; the annual tax on a $50,000 home in Nashville is $485.

Sales Tax —rate is 4.5 percent but some cities and counties impose an additional tax up to 2.25 percent. The maximum local levy is $7.50 on the sale of any single item. Prescription drugs are exempt, and energy fuels sold for residential use are taxed at 1.5 percent.

Good Outdoor, Indoor Recreation

Nashville is the "Athens of the South" and home of country music. The mountains in eastern Tennessee (Great Smoky Mountain National Park) and the Land Between the Lakes area in western Tennessee offer various outdoor activities year-round. The 26 state parks are among the nation's finest, and many overlook lakes and have sandy beaches. Throughout the state there are colleges and universities offering classes for seniors, and many larger cities (Nashville, Knoxville, Chattanooga, Memphis) have symphony orchestras, museums, art galleries and other cultural facilities and events. Because of its strategic geographic location, Tennessee was a major Civil War battlefield, with many historic sites located throughout the state.

Special Services for Seniors

Numerous cities and towns support local senior centers, many of which are multipurpose. And a growing number of communities have demonstrated their interest in seniors' needs by providing needed services. The Department of Employment Security offers job counseling to persons over age 65, and job counseling services are also provided in larger cities and towns. There are many openings for volunteers in medical facilities, children's institutions, senior citizens' centers and the University of Tennessee extension service.

For further information, write:

> Tennessee Commission on Aging
> 535 Church Street
> 703 Tennessee Building
> Nashville, TN 37219

MAJOR RETIREMENT AREAS

Clarksville (pop. 60,000), 45 miles southeast of the Land Between the Lakes and 8 miles south of Fort Campbell, Kentucky, has been billed as the "ideal military retirement town." Rolling countryside laced with creeks, rivers and lakes surrounds the town, which has been a storehouse of traditional southern culture for two centuries. It is the Land Between the Lakes southern gateway and one of the most historic ports on the Cumberland River.

Climate and Environment. Temperatures are moderate, ranging from 30° F. to 49°F. in January, 48°F. to 72°F. in April, 68°F. to 92°F. in July and 48°F. to 74°F. in October. The humidity is moderate and in winter is higher than in summer. The sun shines 63 percent of the possible time. Rainfall averages 48 inches annually, with January or March the wettest months and October the driest. Snowfall averages 10.7 inches annually.

Medical Facilities. Clarksville has 1 major hospital with 194 beds, with a 40-bed addition under way. A new 241-bed hospital will also be available to military dependents at nearby Fort Campbell. There are 4 nursing homes in the area with a 340-bed capacity; 60 physicians; 30 dentists; 8 optometrists.

Housing Availability and Cost. Residents can choose rental or purchase of single family homes ($40,000 and up), apartment complexes, condominiums or subdivisions. Rentals (2-bedroom houses and apartments) range from $250 to $350 monthly. Building lots range from $3,000 to $20,000 and building costs approximate $35 a square foot. Mobile homes are available from $10,000 and there's plenty of rental space available.

Cost of Living. The tax rate in the city is $1.60 per $100 assessment (25 percent) and $3.55 per $100 in the county. Some stores offer senior discounts. Located in the heart of the Tennessee Valley Authority, retirees can live here for less than the national average.

Leisure-Time Activities. There is 1 daily and 1 weekly newspaper, a major library, bookstores, a university museum and art gallery, a community concert association, cable television, 4 radio stations, over 80 civic clubs and organizations, square-dance clubs, antique car clubs, a community chorale, area theater performances, continuing education classes, 11 parks and playgrounds, 6 municipal swimming pools, 2 golf courses, numerous tennis courts, biking, hiking, horseback riding and boating.

Special Services for Seniors. Clarksville has the Catherine Edmondson Senior Citizens Center; many churches have seniors clubs. There is a hot meal service for seniors and other programs. Clarksville has a homemaker service, visiting nurses, meals on wheels, a transportation program, an information and referral service and a legal aid service.

For further information, write:

> Clarksville Area Chamber of Commerce
> P.O. Box 883
> Clarksville, TN 37040

Dover (pop. 1,000) is the county seat of *Stewart County* (pop. 8,000). It is located in the northwestern part of central Tennesee, 20 miles west of Clarksville and only 5 miles east of the Land Between the Lakes area. Mean annual temperature is 59.1°F., with a mean maximum of 71.2°F. and a mean minimum of 47°F. Mean annual precipitation is 48.24 inches, and snowfall 5.6 inches. A medical clinic staffed with 1 doctor is in Dover and 5 medical doctors and 1 dentist practice in Stewart County. The nearest hospitals are in Clarksville and Paris (25 miles west). What housing is available runs $40,000 for a single-family small home, and some rentals are available from $300 a month. Dover's main attraction is that it is the nearest town to the Land Between the Lakes area with all its vast recreation facilities. It is also near Fort Donelson National Military Park, which was the scene of one of the decisive early battles of the Civil War (a victory for the Union forces).

For further information, write:

Stewart County Chamber of Commerce
Dover, TN 37058

Dyersburg (pop. 17,000) is the seat of *Dyer County* (35,000). It is located in the extreme western part of the state, 18 miles east of the Mississippi River and 78 miles northeast of Memphis. Mean winter temperature is 41.5°F., mean summer 81.8°F., mean precipitation 49.7 inches, mean annual snowfall 4.8 inches. The town has Parkview Hospital with 160 beds (expansion will increase this to 225 beds) and 2 nursing homes with 163 beds. There are 33 doctors and 14 dentists in the area. Good housing is available in several new subdivisions which are expanding on the northern edge of the city. Here, you can buy a new 3-bedroom home from $33,000 to $75,000. Several apartment complexes are available with rents of $150 to $300 a month. And some rental housing is available on a limited basis. Property in Dyersburg is assessed at 25 percent of value with a rate of $2.50 per $100; in the county, it is assessed at 25 percent at a rate of $2.80 per $100. This makes the effective rate 63¢ per $100 of full market value in the city and 70¢ per $100 in the county. For cultural attractions, the city has a community concert association, little theater, art council, McDowell Music Club and a major library. Many clubs operate through the 49 churches (48 Protestant, 1 Catholic) and there are many civic, service and fraternal organizations.

For further information, write:

Greater Dyersburg/Dyer County Chamber of Commerce
P.O. Box 443
Dyersburg, TN 38024

Blount County (pop. 72,000) in eastern Tennessee is good retirement country, especially around the towns of *Maryville* (pop. 17,000) and *Alcoa* (8,500). These towns nestle at the foot of the Great Smoky Mountains, adjoining metropolitan Knoxville with its cultural and educational offerings. The temperature averages 40.6°F. in January, 62.9°F. in April, 78.2°F. in July, 57.4°F. in October. The humidity in winter ranges from 58 percent to 81 percent, in summer 61 percent to 92 percent. Annual average rainfall is 47.69 inches, with July the driest month and April the wettest. Snowfall averages 13 inches annually.

Medical Facilities. There is 1 major hospital in the area with 334 beds, 4 nursing homes with 576 beds, 2 clinics, 78 doctors and 40 dentists, more than enough for the population.

Housing Availability and Cost. Housing is plentiful, with single-family homes ranging from $30,000 to $50,000, condominiums from $65,-000, mobile homes from $15,000 to $27,000, building lots from $6,000 to over $10,000, some rentals from $250 a month and 2 retirement residences: *Asbury Acres* with 96 units and 11 cottages and *Maryville Towers*, 118 units, both located in Maryville.

Cost of Living. Taxes are generally low, with the county tax on a $40,000 home running $310 annually. Other costs are moderate—among the lowest of all Southern cities of comparable size.

Leisure-Time Activities. The area has 1 daily and 1 weekly newspaper, a new main library with 35,000 books, 4 bookstores, 4 art galleries, 1 museum, a little theater group, good radio and television reception, many clubs appealing to most interests, adult-education classes at Maryville College, 10 parks, 3 swimming pools, 5 golf courses, 18 tennis courts and the Great Smoky Mountains Park only 19 miles away.

Special Services for Seniors. There is a senior citizen center with a full-time director at Everett Park. The center offers a hot-meal program, homemakers service, transportation program, special health clinics, income-maintenance program, legal aid, mobile units for the elderly and rehabilitation programs.

For further information, write:

> Blount County Chamber of Commerce
> P.O. Box 635
> Maryville, TN 37801

Maryville and Blount County are 30 miles from Gatlinburg, Tennessee and Highlands, North Carolina, which is the center of the Highlands, at the southern end of the Blue Ridge Mountains. This area includes some of the most scenic parts of North Carolina, South Carolina, Georgia and Tennessee. Novelist James Dickey set his best-seller *Deliverance* here, and the movie version was filmed on the nearby Chattanooga River. It is an area of deep blue lakes, dense woods, wildflowers and sleepy, small towns tucked back into mist-shrouded mountains. According to one study,

75 percent of the land is owned by people who plan to use it as a vacation or retirement retreat.

SUMMARY

Tennessee offers a change-of-pace retirement in scenery, people and places. The western part features the Land Between the Lakes area and the charm of the South; the eastern part the Great Smoky and Blue Ridge mountains and mountain people and attitudes. Here are my ratings of favorite retirement areas:

Excellent — Clarksville, Blount County
Good   — Dover, Dyersburg, Dyer County

3. MISSOURI—LAKE (AND LAND) OF OZARK RETIREMENT

Well might Missouri say "show me" to neighboring Kentucky and Tennessee. While those states boast of the Land Between the Lakes, Missouri claims both the Lake and Land of the Ozarks, one of the largest man-made lakes and one of the largest retirement areas in the United States.

This area lies, generally, in the southern part of the state and features dome-shaped hills, fertile valleys, deep caves, limestone bluffs, green forests, swift-flowing streams, great rivers and majestic lakes. This Lake and Land of the Ozarks attracts 20,000 retirees annually from neighboring states and from Texas. They come because they seek a quiet, rural setting, old-fashioned virtues and a lower cost of living.

The self-sufficient make it. The city folk who like to play at country living find the isolation, lack of organized activities and scarcity of ammenities confining—and leave. Some go home, but others stay around long enough to discover the other Missouri—the northeast Mark Twain country with its riverboat scenery, the central and southwestern prairies and the southeastern alluvial plain with its large springs and deep caves.

They also find up-to-date cities like Kansas City, which claims it has more per capita construction than any other city; and St. Louis, which has crowned its blues with the Gateway Arch—the nation's tallest monument.

Some 17.4 percent of the state's 5 million people are over age 60, and 12.9 percent over 65. These older folks are pretty well scattered throughout the state, but the Lake and the Land of the Ozarks claim the most retirees. Here is what they find in the Show Me State.

A Two-Zone Climate

The northern part of the state lies in the moist Great Lakes storm belt while the southern and western portions lie at the edge of the semiarid Great Plains. Statewide winters average 30°F., spring 56°F., summer 78°F.; fall 57°F. In Kansas City (in the northern part), winters average 38.7°F., summers 70.6°F., with 194 days of sunshine, average annual humidity 66.8 percent and annual rainfall 27.75 inches.

Low-Cost, High-Quality Medical Care

Missouri has 155 doctors per 100,000 residents, below the national average of 174 but comfortably above the minimum of 133. An average semiprivate hospital room costs $126 daily, vs. the national average of $163. There are 167 hospitals with a total of 35,437 beds, 459 nursing homes with 38,239 beds, 107 personal-care homes with 5,324 beds. Dental discounts are available to low-income seniors.

Unusually Good Supply of Housing

Missouri has a good supply of housing, ranging in price from under $10,000 to over $250,000. You can buy 12-acre retirement "farms" for as little as $31,500. And you can find a good supply of retirement retreats, small homes, vacation cottages, second homes and older homes for $40,-000 to $50,000. Rentals are available in the larger cities—Kansas City, St. Louis, Springfield, Joplin—from $350 a month. And Kansas City is the headquarters for the United Farm Agency, which specializes in small farms, ranches, retirement retreats and other specialized housing. For a copy of their latest catalog (published quarterly), you can call toll-free 1(800) 821-2599. Missouri residents call 1(800) 892-5785. You can write their national headquarters, 612 West 47th Street, Kansas City, MO 64112. Not surprisingly, the largest section of their national catalog features the state of Missouri.

Lower Cost of Living

Missouri's cost of living is below the national average. Using the average annual retirement budget of $10,022 for a couple, you could retire in Kansas City on $9,868 and in St. Louis on $9,836 annually. In tax burden, Missouri ranks twenty-ninth at the lowest level and thirty-eighth at the highest brackets. Property tax on a $50,000 home in Kansas City averages $590; for the same house in St. Louis the average tax is $820.

Income Tax —the rates on taxable income range from 1.5 percent on the first $1,000 to $315 plus 6 percent of excess over $9,000. Personal exemptions range from $1,200 (single) to $3,400 (married filing jointly).

Property Taxes —these range from 1 percent to 2 percent of market value. Persons 65 and older who own their homes or rent and who have household incomes of less than $8,500 (single), $9,000 (married) and who have resided in Missouri for the entire year may be entitled to a credit on property taxes or rent paid up to $500.

Sales Tax —the state rate is 3.125 percent but communities usually impose an additional 0.5 percent to 1 percent. Some add an additional 0.5 percent for mass transportation.

Big City Culture but Rural Isolation

Cultural activities are centered in the largest cities. St. Louis boasts the St. Louis Art Museum, the National Museum of Transport, the Steinberg Art Gallery, the Missouri Historical Society, the Jefferson National Expansion Memorial, the Missouri Botanical Garden and Powell Symphony Hall. Kansas City features the Atkins Museum and William Rockhill Nelson Gallery, the Lyric Theater, Kansas City Philharmonic, Starlight Theater, and the 85-acre Crown Center, a major shopping, residential and business complex. The riverfront, too, has been newly renovated and now features many good restaurants, shops and small businesses. In the smaller retirement towns (with the possible exception of Neosho and some others—see below), there are few organized activities and retirees must provide their own entertainment or become absorbed in projects which can range from a small farm or business to much-needed social or community service work. The self-sufficient retiree will find plenty to keep him busy; if you depend upon organized events and clubs, you'd better stick to the bigger cities.

Progressive State, Area Agencies on Aging

At all government levels, agencies on aging are unusually active. Nutrition sites have been established in each county, and the agencies have provided other programs, including multicounty rural homemaker services, transportation, information and referral, health care, legal services and many others. Other agency programs include a senior citizens lounge at the state fair and assisting tornado and heat-stroke victims (during the 1980 heat wave, Missouri was unusually hard hit because areas used to summer temperatures in the 80s and 90s had to cope with temperatures soaring over 100°F.). Missouri seniors also hold legislative rallies to pass needed legislation, and elect a "silver-haired legislature" that gathers each year to consider legislation and to push for passage of needed bills. This legislature has been effective in getting scores of bills passed which make life better for seniors. And in Kansas City, a growing army of older persons are being spared heart-breaking moves thanks to the Shepherd's Center, a remarkably successful program of 25 churches and synagogues. The center offers 18 services such as delivery of hot meals to people who are homebound, assistance with shopping, companion-aides, home repairs done at minimal cost, help with safety and security, education courses, group therapy, health maintenance, assistance with employment and hobbies and crafts. The center also trains people to set up centers elsewhere.

For further information, write:

Division on Aging
Department of Social Services
Broadway State Office Building
P.O. Box 1337
Jefferson City, MO 65102

MAJOR RETIREMENT AREAS

Neosho (pop. 11,000), located in southwest Missouri—175 miles south of Kansas City, 120 miles east of Tulsa, Oklahoma and 80 miles west of Springfield—has been called the Flowerbox City (for the many floral displays in civic areas) and the City of Springs (for the 9 springs located within city limits). In fact, its name derives from the Native American *Ne-ozho* or *Ne-u-zhu*, which means clear or abundant water. It is a hilly, woodsy area with an average temperature of 58.1°F. and an average annual rainfall of 42.9 inches and 12.1 inches of snow. January is the coldest (and driest) month with an average temperature of 36.8°F. and snowfall of 2 inches. July is the hottest month with an average of 79.2° F. May is the wettest month with 5.75 inches of rain.

Medical Facilities. The town has 1 general hospital, Sale Memorial, with 63 beds. It also has 2 osteopathic clinics, 2 convalescent homes (Neosho Senior Center for long-term care, with 94 beds and a staff of 83; Powell Boarding Home for ambulatory elderly with 4 on the staff). There are 15 doctors in general practice, 2 surgeons, 6 dentists and 5 chiropractors in the town—about adequate for the population.

Housing Availability and Cost. Housing ranges in price from $6,000 to $250,000, with the average small retirement home selling for $50,000. Neosho offers a wide variety of housing, including stately old homes, several apartment buildings and complexes and a multistory apartment house, *The Oaks,* for senior citizens with moderate income. Land sells for $1,500 to $4,000 an acre.

Cost of Living. Costs are moderate, with city taxes at 47¢ per $100 full valuation, county taxes of $1.80 per $100 full valuation. This makes the effective tax on a $50,000 home $1,135—higher than in some areas, but worth it for the services and recreation it buys.

Leisure-Time Activities. Neosho offers good indoor and outdoor recreation. It boasts a community recreation center with a full-time director; a beautiful golf course with grass greens and surfaced cartways, 4 public tennis courts, an Olympic public swimming pool, access to lakes and rivers which offer good fishing (bass, bluegill, catfish, crappie) and good hunting areas (deer, rabbit, squirrel, turkey, quail, dove). Trail hiking, horseback riding and rock hounding are also available in the area, as well as camping and picnicking. Indoor activities include a historical museum, 1 city and 1 county library with 70,000 volumes, 2 movie theaters, and 1 amateur little theater group, the Big Spring Community Theater Group. Adult-education courses are available at Crowder College, a 2-year junior college. Annual events include the Dogwood Tour in April, Fall Festival (arts and crafts) in October and Christmas Parade in December.

Special Services for Seniors. Neosho has a senior citizens club and a chapter of the National Association of Retired Federal Employees. Seniors also belong to many of the more than 40 other clubs, including American Legion, Knights of Columbus, Kiwanis, Rotary, Masons, American Association of University Women, American Business Women, Soroptimist and Fortnightly Club.

For further information, write:

Neosho Area Chamber of Commerce
308 West Spring Street
Neosho, MO 64850

Branson (pop. 3,000). This resort town lies 38 miles directly south of Springfield. It is in the heart of the Ozark retirement area (about one-third of the residents are retirees) in a region which provided the setting for Harold Bell Wright's novel *The Shepherd of the Hills.* For a small town it has an excellent hospital, and there's a wide variety of housing, including apartments, condominiums, single-family housing, mobile homes and small farms. The town offers varied recreational activities in the adult community center, including arts and crafts, pot-luck suppers, special lectures and activities. Outdoor recreation includes golf, tennis, gardening, hunting and fishing. On Lake Taneycomo, near Bulls Shoals and

Table Rock lakes, you'll find excellent trout fishing, as well as bass fishing in nearby lakes. The town boasts many retiree clubs and clubs with a good portion of retiree members.

For further information, write:

Chamber of Commerce
Branson, MO 65616

Cassville (pop. 2,000), midway between Branson and Neosho, is an Ozark retirement town boasting some unusual scenery: 7 miles south lies Roaring River State Park, a 3,459-acre camping, picnicking, hiking, trout fishing and swimming area; Mark Twain National Forest, offering flat trips and fishing, hunting, camping, picnicking and horseback riding; Crystal Caverns, containing many rare formations including black stalactites, aragonite crystal and calcite ice; Ozark Wonder Cave, 7 rooms with multicolored onyx, stalactites, and stalagmites. The town itself offers adequate medical facilities (with access to larger nearby hospitals), a fair supply of housing and leisure-time activities including retiree clubs and clubs that retirees belong to.

For further information, write:

Cassville Chamber of Commerce
Cassville, MO 65625

Camdenton (pop. 1,800) is a resort town 10 miles south of Lake of the Ozarks, formed by the impounding of the Osage River. One of the largest man-made lakes in America, the lake features almost 1,400 miles of dragon-shaped shoreline accented by sparkling blue water, white limestone bluffs and lush green forests. The Lake of the Ozarks features excellent fishing, boating and swimming. And although it is a popular recreation area, it provides a quiet solitude from the modern bustle. *Osage Beach* (pop. 1,100) is the resort town right on the Lake of the Ozarks and offers retirement possibilities. Seasonal events include the Ozark Opry and Jamboree (country music). Attractions in the area include Bridal Cave (scene of more than 720 weddings), Kelsey's Antique Cars (cars from 1899), Camden County Historical Museum (antique tools, pioneer furnishings, crafts) and Lake of the Ozarks State Park (the largest state park in the state).

For further information, write:

Lake of the Ozarks Association
P.O. Box 98
Lake Ozark, MO 65049

Other good retirement towns include (with zip code): *Aurora* (pop. 5,500; 65605), *Ava* (pop. 2,500; 65608), *Forsyth* (pop. 1,000; 65653), *Excelsior Springs* (pop. 9,500; 64024), *Gainesville* (pop. 1,000; 65655), *Joplin* (pop. 40,000; 64801) and *Springfield* (pop. 130,000; 65801).

SUMMARY

Missouri offers away-from-it-all retirement at below-average price. However, the best retirement areas lie in the Land of the Ozarks or near the Lake of the Ozarks, in small towns which lack organized activities and big-city amenities. If you're a self-sufficient retiree with a project or involvement in community or service work, you'll do well. But if you need a fun-and-games atmosphere, look elsewhere. Here are my ratings of major retirement areas:

Excellent — Neosho, Branson
Good   — Cassville, Camdenton, Osage Beach

4. OKLAHOMA—THE UNKNOWN RETIREMENT EMPIRE

Oklahoma is more than just OK—it's on its way to becoming a new retirement mecca as more people discover it as a great place to visit and a better place to live.

Most of the interest centers in the eastern part of the state, which is far different from the dust bowl which lies further west. This eastern area normally gets 45 to 50 inches of rain and has more than 70,000 lakes and ponds—including massive Eufaula Lake with its 2,600 miles of shoreline. The federal government built many lakes to provide water for the McClellan-Kerr-Arkansas River Waterway, a barge system that connects Tulsa with the Mississippi River. The lakes spawned many state-owned lodges, the grandest of which is Shangri-La on the Grand Lake of the Cherokees northeast of Tulsa. The resort boasts an airport which can accommodate large corporate jets, and the area offers golf, tennis, swimming and boating.

But much of the development is new, and the lack of building in the past has left the area with abundant clear water, clean air and a population density that is a tenth that of the Northeast. It has also left this part of the state with the country's highest concentration of nonreservation Native Americans—40,000, representing every tribe (the state was originally settled by the so-called 5 civilized tribes—Cherokee, Chickasaw, Creek, Choctaw and Seminole). In "turnabout is fair play," the Native Americans have absorbed the grain farmers from the Midwest, mountain-

eers from Appalachia, cotton growers from the South and oil drillers from
Pennsylvania, who also occupy the land. In few places do Native Americans and whites blend as well as they do here, where Native American
ancestry is a source of pride. The most famous "Cherokee kid," from
Claremore, gained fame as Will Rogers.

While most retirement communities lie in this eastern section, you
shouldn't overlook other parts of the state. The southeast consists of
forested mountains, green valleys, rushing streams, rolling plains, and
the Red River bottom. The central part features granite mountains that
post sentinel over prairies, lakes and rolling plains. The northwest flatland
is covered with gleaming white salt, and the Panhandle, the extreme
appendage of this area, contains rich wheat, ranches and cattle.

Some 16.8 percent of the Sooner State's almost 3 million population
is age 60 and over, and 12.3 percent is over 65. Counties with more than
25 percent of the population over age 60 include Craig, Delaware, McIntosh, Marshall, Hughes, Alfalfa, Grant, Jefferson, Beckham, Greer, Har-
mon, Kiowa, Dewey, Ellis and Woods.

Temperate But Variable Climate

As the elevation rises steadily from the southeast to the northwest,
the temperature depends upon which part of the state you're in. Here is
how temperature varies in various seasons in various parts of the state:

Section	Spring	Summer	Fall	Winter
Central/NE/SW	62°F.	82°F.	63°F.	38°F.
Northwest	57°F.	80°F.	60°F.	35°F.
Southeast	63°F.	82°F.	64°F.	42°F.

In Oklahoma City, in the center of the state, you can get even more
variation, with winters averaging 45.2°F., summers 74°F. with 226 sunny
days and an average annual humidity of 65.5 percent. Precipitation averages 27.63 inches annually and snowfall 12.8 inches annually.

Low-Cost, Quality Health Care

While the cost of a semiprivate hospital room is only $121 daily (vs.
a national average of $163), Oklahoma has only 128 doctors per 100,000
residents, far below the national average of 174 and below the acceptable
minimum of 133. The Sooner State has 156 hospitals with a total of 17,100

beds, 373 nursing homes with 29,481 beds and 21 personal-care homes with 1,103 beds.

Low-Cost Land and Housing

Both land and housing seem unusually good buys. A 5-acre "retirement ranch" sells for $35,000, a 60-acre self-sufficient farm for $50,000, single family "rural havens" for $25,000 and land for $500 an acre. However, for most desirable housing in major retirement areas, figure at least $30,000 for single-family homes and rents from $300 a month for 2-bedroom apartments.

Low Cost of Living

The cost of living and taxes are below the national average. The property taxes average 1 percent for housing, with the taxes on a $50,000 home in Oklahoma City averaging $545 annually. The tax burden is among the lowest, ranking forty-seventh at lowest brackets and thirty-third at highest. Many communities give senior discounts ranging from 10 percent to 20 percent on drugs, groceries, sports events and even eyeglasses. Food coops offer 33 percent savings on fresh fruit, vegetables, and staples; baked goods are available at 10 percent discount; and state lodges and parks give a 10 percent discount to seniors and a 50 percent discount on recreational use. In Oklahoma City, an older person pays only $5 for a coupon book worth $10 in transportation fares, including cabs. In Tulsa, low-cost dentures are available for $250. The Oklahoma State Fair has a Senior Citizens Day when seniors get in free. And some banks offer free checking accounts to seniors.

Here is a further breakdown of taxes:

Income Tax —rates on taxable income, for couples filing jointly, range from 0.5 percent on the first $2,000 to 6 percent on over $15,000. Individuals filing separately halve the income brackets (on first $1,000, 0.5 percent).

Property Taxes —rates are set locally, with a maximum assessment of 35 percent of full value. There's a general homestead exemption of $1,000 with an additional $1,000 for those whose household income does not exceed $4,000. Persons age 65 and over whose income does not exceed $6,000 may claim relief for property taxes in excess of 1 percent of income to a maximum of $200.

Sales Tax —the state rate is 2 percent, but most cities levy an additional 1 to 2 percent. Exempt are motor vehicles and homes, travel trailers, gasoline, cigarettes, 3.2 beer, water service.

Little Indoor, Big Outdoor Culture, Recreation

Most of the museums, galleries, art and music are in the larger cities, Oklahoma City and Tulsa. Tulsa has Oklahoma's only opera company, along with a civic theater, ballet company, symphony and a new $19-million performing-arts center. Oklahoma City has the strikingly modern Oklahoma Theater Center, which offers live theater from fall through spring. It also has an underground shopping mall that connects most major downtown buildings and which offers a complete range of shops and businesses—so much so that it is possible for anyone who works or lives downtown to avoid the summertime altogether. One luxury Oklahoma is short on: bars. Oklahoma is probably the driest state, with liquor available only at package stores. Some restaurants sell 3.2 beer, and they allow you to bring your own bottle for dinner. It is possible to purchase a drink at a private club whose rules for membership are sometimes lax, but if convenient watering holes are part of your life-style, you'll have to find a wetter state.

Many Services for Seniors

The Oklahoma Special Unit on Aging provides and sponsors many services, including multipurpose centers, congregate nutrition programs, information and referral, outreach and escort, transportation systems, legal counseling, homemakers services, home health care, volunteer opportunities, advocacy assistance, home-repair projects, training programs and special activities. Services are also available through the area agencies on aging which blanket the state.

For further information, write:

> Special Unit on Aging
> Department of Institutions,
> Social and Rehabilitative Service
> P.O. Box 25352
> Oklahoma City, OK 73125

Oklahoma City is also headquarters for the National Association of Mature People, which offers insurance, travel, discount and other special programs for older people.

For further information, write:

> NAMP
> 2000 Classen Center
> Oklahoma City, OK 73126

MAJOR RETIREMENT AREAS

Muskogee (pop. 43,000), about 40 miles southeast of Tulsa, is a diversified industrial center near the confluence of the Verdigris, Grand and Arkansas rivers. It is also an important agricultural center and is headquarters for the United States Union Agency for the Five Civilized Tribes. About 16.6 percent of the residents are retired.

Climate and Environment. The town is surrounded by low, gently sloping hills, blending into a rich, flat-to-rolling farming section. The climate is subtropical. Winters are comparatively mild, with only an occasional outbreak of cold air. January averages 38°F., with only 5 days a year when the temperature fails to rise above freezing. April averages 50°F. But summers are usually hot, with July averaging 11 days when the temperature goes over 100°F. However, a relatively low humidity (55 percent) and a good southerly breeze usually ease the discomfort of the high afternoon temperatures and provide for a pleasant night. October days are mild and mellow, averaging 73°F. Rainfall averages 42 inches a year, with January the driest month and April the wettest. The area is relatively free from noise or air pollution.

Medical Facilities. Muskogee General Hospital has 300 beds and is fully accredited. A $24-million expansion program has recently been completed. A Veterans Administration hospital has 247 beds and a staff of 26 doctors and 4 residents. A total of 91 doctors are on the staff at Muskogee General and provide both general practice and major specialties. The city has 24 dentists, 9 optometrists, 3 osteopaths, 7 chiropractors, 2 podiatrists and 10 nursing homes with a total of more than 600 beds. All told, medical facilities are adequate for the population.

Housing Availability and Cost. Housing is generally plentiful with single-family, 2-bedroom homes selling from $30,000. The town also has the 200-unit, 11-story Honor Heights Towers, which provides housing for low-income elderly (at a quarter of their income) and more units are under construction. Building lots sell from $1,500 and apartments are generally plentiful from $300 a month. Some vacation homes are available from $25,000 around the lakes.

Cost of Living. Costs are generally lower than average, with some senior discounts (mainly on drugs) available. Seasonal produce and local meats reduce costs, and energy costs are lower than usual. Retail sales tax is only 4 percent. Some employment is available through the state and local employment offices and through the Kiwanis Senior Citizens center. Maximum combined taxes run $88 per $1,000 valuation, with the assessment ratio running under 15 percent of true value (the ratio can't exceed 35 percent).

Leisure-Time Activities. Muskogee has its own local paper, a library with 90,000 volumes, 9 bookstores, 3 art galleries, 1 museum, a little theater, good radio and television reception (cable) and some 100 clubs, ranging from Alcoholics Anonymous to YWCA. Included are branches of the American Association of Retired Persons, Muskogee County Retired Teachers and many clubs (service, arts and crafts) to which retirees belong. Adult-education classes are available at Connors College. There are 32 parks, 3 swimming pools, 2 golf courses and 13 tennis courts in the area, and biking, hiking and horseback riding are also available. Muskogee has an exceptionally large number of accomplished artists in the area, and a number of showings are scheduled each year. A most interesting collection of Native American art is on exhibit year-round at the Five Civilized Tribes Museum in Honor Heights Park.

Special Services for Seniors. Muskogee has a local office on aging and the Kiwanis Senior Citizens Center. It offers a hot-meal program for seniors, homemaker services, visiting nurses, meals on wheels, transportation program, a hot line service and other emergency services for seniors.

For further information, write:

> Muskogee Chamber of Commerce
> P.O. Box 797
> Muskogee, OK 77401

Miami (pop. 15,000), located in the extreme northeastern corner of the state, 80 miles from Tulsa, at the headwaters of Grand Lake, boasts many recreational facilities. The temperature averages 60°F. annually, with average rainfall of 42 inches and snowfall of 9 inches. The town has 2 hospitals with 145 beds, 3 nursing homes, 3 clinics, emergency service, 26 medical doctors, 15 dentists and 5 specialists, adequate for the population. Housing is plentiful, with small retirement homes selling for $30,000 and condominiums, coops, townhouses and mobile home/modular units available. Miami Towers offers special units for seniors and other apartments rent from about $250 a month. Building lots sell from $5,000, with building costs ranging from $26 to $40 a square foot. Other costs are about average or below, with some exemptions and discounts for seniors. Miami has 1 newspaper, 2 public libraries (1 college) with over 80,000 volumes, 2 bookstores, 1 art gallery, a museum, little theater, good radio and television reception, 45 clubs, arts and crafts courses, a park, 2 swimming pools, a golf course and 19 tennis courts. The town has 2 senior centers, 2 senior clubs, a hot-meal program for seniors, minibuses for transportation and special counseling programs for seniors.

For further information, write:

Miami Chamber of Commerce
P.O. Box 760
Miami, OK 74354

Shawnee (pop. 35,000), located 35 miles east of Oklahoma City, is a diversified industrial and agricultural center. January temperatures average 39.7°F. and July 82.4°F. Rainfall averages 36.12 inches annually with about 6 inches of snowfall. Shawnee has 2 hospitals with 214 beds, 9 nursing homes with 688 beds, 3 clinics, emergency service, 46 medical doctors and 13 dentists, about adequate for the population. Housing is generally scarce, although there is a senior citizens retirement center. Some senior discounts are available, mainly in drugs, and some local food bargains help offset costs. The town has 1 daily and 1 weekly newspaper, a bookstore, art gallery, museum, little theater, good television and radio reception, 80 clubs and adult-education classes. Swimming, golf, tennis and other outdoor activities are available. Shawnee also has a senior center, 2 chapters of the American Association of Retired Persons, counseling services for seniors, homemakers service, visiting nurses, transportation program, hot-meal program, emergency service, rehabilitation programs, large-print books in the library and a mayor's council on aging.

For further information, write:

Shawnee Chamber of Commerce
P.O. Box 1613
Shawnee, OK 74801

Other towns worth investigation are (with zip code) *Ardmore* (pop. 26,000; 73401) and *McAlester* (pop. 17,000; 74501).

SUMMARY

Oklahoma offers low-cost retirement living in an as yet relatively undeveloped section of the country—the *eastern* part of the state. You can buy small retirement homes for as little as *$30,000*, and enjoy a temperate climate in a fertile, lake-studded land. Here are *my* ratings of major retirement areas:

Excellent — Muskogee, Miami
Good — Shawnee

EPILOGUE—

FINDING YOUR RETIREMENT

EDEN

I've tried to include every possible Retirement Eden within the scope of this book. I contacted all state units on aging and followed up every recommendation from these and other sources. If I've omitted some places it's because I've found that the welcome mat is no longer out there or the places no longer qualify as Retirement Edens.

However, the places I have included do offer some advantages to satisfy your basic needs and wants. To help pinpoint the best places for you, in Table VIII I've rated the states as to how they compare in the 6 yardsticks that make up Retirement Edens.

Here are the states that rank excellent or good in each category:

Climate and Environment

Rhode Island
Connecticut
Maryland
Virginia
Northern California

Western Nevada
Oregon
Kentucky
Tennessee
Missouri

TABLE VIII. HOW THE VARIOUS STATES COMPARE AS RETIREMENT EDENS
(1=Excellent; 2=Good; 3=Fair; 4=Poor)

State	Climate and Environment	Medical Facilities	Housing Availability and Cost	Cost of Living	Leisure-Time Activities	Special Services for Seniors
Massachusetts	3	1	2	4	1	3
Vermont	3	2	2	4	2	2
New Hampshire	3	3	2	2	2	2
Maine	3	2	2	3	3	2
Rhode Island	2	2	3	3	2	2
Connecticut	2	2	3	3	2	2
New York	3	2	3	4	1	2
New Jersey	3	2	2	4	2	2
Pennsylvania	3	2	2	3	2	2
Maryland	2	2	2	3	3	3
Virginia	2	2	2	2	2	2
Ohio	3	3	2	2	2	1
Indiana	3	4	2	2	3	2
Wisconsin	3	3	2	4	2	2
Minnesota	3	2	2	3	2	1
Colorado	3	2	2	2	2	2
Utah	3	2	2	2	2	3
North Dakota	4	4	2	2	3	2
Idaho	4	4	2	2	3	3
Northern California–Western Nevada	1	1	4	4	1	1
Oregon	2	2	3	3	2	2
Washington	3	2	2	3	2	1
Kentucky	2	4	2	3	2	3

TABLE VIII. HOW THE VARIOUS STATES COMPARE AS RETIREMENT EDENS
(1 = Excellent; 2 = Good; 3 = Fair; 4 = Poor)

State	Climate and Environment	Medical Facilities	Housing Availability and Cost	Cost of Living	Leisure-Time Activities	Special Services for Seniors
Tennessee	2	3	2	2	2	2
Missouri	2	3	2	2	3	1
Oklahoma	3	4	1	1	3	2

Medical Facilities

Massachusetts
Vermont
Maine
Rhode Island
Connecticut
New York
New Jersey
Pennsylvania
Maryland

Virginia
Minnesota
Colorado
Utah
Northern California
Western Nevada
Oregon
Washington

Housing Availability and Cost

Massachusetts
Vermont
Maine
New Hampshire
New Jersey
Pennsylvania
Maryland
Virginia
Ohio
Indiana
Wisconsin

Minnesota
Colorado
Utah
North Dakota
Idaho
Washington
Kentucky
Tennessee
Missouri
Oklahoma

Cost of Living

New Hampshire
Virginia
Ohio
Indiana
Colorado
Utah

North Dakota
Idaho
Tennessee
Missouri
Oklahoma

Leisure-Time Activities

Massachusetts
Vermont

Wisconsin
Minnesota

New Hampshire   Colorado
Rhode Island   Utah
Connecticut   Northern California
New York   Western Nevada
New Jersey   Oregon
Pennsylvania   Washington
Virginia   Kentucky
Ohio   Tennessee

Special Services for Seniors

Vermont   Wisconsin
New Hampshire   Minnesota
Maine   Colorado
Rhode Island   North Dakota
Connecticut   Northern California
New York   Western Nevada
New Jersey   Oregon
Pennsylvania   Washington
Virginia   Tennessee
Ohio   Missouri
Indiana   Oklahoma

But before basing decisions on these ratings alone, there are some personal and practical facts to consider under each category. I used the checklist on pp. 289–290 in seeking information for this book; you can adapt it for your own search.

Here are other points you might want to consider:

1. Climate and Environment. If you are used to a 4-season climate, you might find the perpetual fall of the San Francisco Bay area monotonous. However, it is possible to find a moderate 4-season climate in states like Virginia and Missouri and in the foothills of the Sierras in Northern California. Also, realize that daily and seasonal extremes are possible in the best places. It is not uncommon for the temperature to drop 30 degrees or more daily in the mountains of Colorado, and it is not unusual for a place with a mild winter temperature (like the Oregon coast or Seattle) to have almost perpetual rain during that season. You can find out these daily and seasonal patterns by writing to the chambers of commerce, by visiting (and staying) off-season as well as on-season and by getting a free list of communities on which climate data has been prepared

FACT SHEET FOR RETIREMENT EDENS

GENERAL: Name of Town_____Population_____Location
(nearest reference point)_____Elevation_____Percent
retired_____Other (specify)_____

1. CLIMATE AND ENVIROMENT: Temperature range or average: January_____
_____April_____July_____October_____.
Humidity range: winter_____summer_____. No. of sun-
shine days_____Rain (inches)_____Driest month_____
_____Wettest month_____Snowfall (inches)_____
Noise or population (specify)_____

2. HEALTH FACILITIES: No. of Hospitals_____beds_____.
Nursing homes_____beds_____Personal-care Homes___
_____beds_____.Clinics_____Emergency service
_____No. of medical doctors_____Dentists_____
___Specialists_____Special medical facilities (specify)_____
___. Is area noted for special health facilities or attributes (air, water, climate–
specify)_____

3. HOUSING AVAILABILITY AND COST: General housing availability (plentiful,
scarce–specify)_____. Special retirement housing units (specify)_____
_____. Price range of 2-bedroom units of: single-family houses_____
_____condominums and coops_____townhouses_____mo-
bile homes/modular units_____Building lots (cost range)_____
_____Building costs (total per sq. ft)_____. RENTALS (1-or 2-bedroom)
of houses_____apartments_____nonprofit retirement
housing_____foster homes_____vacation homes_____
_____Off on season differentials_____

4. COST OF LIVING: Personal income or property tax (specify)_____
Residential tax rate (specify)_____Effective property tax on $40,000
home_____. Special tax concessions for seniors_____. Retail sales tax_____Sales tax exemptions_____Senior discounts (specify)_____Food cost (high-low)_____Local
food bargains (specify)_____Energy costs (high-low)_____
___General living costs compared to similar communities_____What

jobs available for seniors_____Other ways to increase income (business, sales—specify)_____What job counseling available for older people_____Nonprofit agencies for elderly (specify)_____ Other ways to reduce living costs (specify)_____

5. LEISURE-TIME ACTIVITIES: Local newspapers_____Libraries_____ _____(no. volumes)_____Bookstores_____Art galleries_____Museums_____ Little theater_____ __FM radio_____Public TV or cable_____General TV (reception quality and no. stations)_____General radio (reception quality and no. stations)_____No. Clubs_____gardening_____ _____book_____crafts (specify)_____hobby (specify) _____chess_____bridge_____other (specify) _____Adult-education classes (specify)_____Parks_____ _____Swimming pools_____Golf courses_____Tennis courts_____Biking, hiking, horseback trails (specify)_____ _____ Other (specify)_____

6. SPECIAL SERVICES FOR SENIORS: Senior centers_____Senior clubs (specify)_____Office on aging_____Counseling services for seniors (specify)_____Hot meal program for seniors_____ _____Homemakers services_____Visiting nurses_____ Meals on wheels_____Transportation program_____ Special health clinics_____Income maintenance program_____ _____Hotline service or emergency service for seniors (specify)_____ Legal aid_____Mobile units for elderly_____Rehabilitation programs_____Other special senior programs (specify)_____ _____

by writing to the National Climatic Center, Federal Building, Asheville, NC 28801. You can obtain a report about the weather in any given month for 20¢, or an annual report for the same price. You can also subscribe to the reports on a given community; for $2.55 you will get the 12 monthly reports and the annual report (an order must be for at least $2).

   2. Medical Facilities. Just because states like Massachusetts or Minnesota have good health facilities doesn't mean that there's a doctor or a hospital that will take care of you. If health care is important, make sure you arrange for a new doctor before you move. Your present doctor may be able to make such an arrangement or you can get referrals from the local county medical association or hospital. Also, make sure your doctor feels that a move will benefit your health, and that you aren't trading one problem for another. I know a woman who moved from Michigan to southern Arizona for her arthritis. Her doctor thought the hot, dry climate would be good for this disease, and it was. But the woman also has asthma, and the dust made it worse. So she had to escape to Prescott, Arizona (in the central mountains) to get relief for her asthma, although her arthritis started acting up again. You probably won't know if a place will treat you kindly unless you've lived there a full year (and until your body has adjusted to the new climate and perhaps altitude). Also, drinking water has become a problem in some areas and you should check this out. You can get a detailed set of guidelines for sizing up a local public water supply by sending for a free copy of "Manual for Evaluating Public Drinking Water Supplies," Water Supply Division, Environmental Protection Agency, Washington, D.C. 20460.

3. Housing Availability and Cost. Try it before you buy it. You're better off renting or leasing your present home and renting or leasing a home (the kind you'd like) in your new place. Then, after 6 months or so, if you decide that you want to move permanently, you can sell your former home and buy the new place. An alternative is to swap homes. You can do so through the following agencies. They generally charge $20 for an entry, let you make your own arrangements and request that you submit your listing 6 months before you want to make a swap. Write for details from:

Vacation Exchange Club
350 Broadway
New York, NY 10013

Holiday Exchanges

Adventures in Living
Box 278

P.O. Box 878
Belen, NM 87002

Inquiline, Inc.
35 Adams St.
Bedford Hills, NY

Winnetka, IL 60093

If you do buy new housing in a new place, don't trade down too far. As one retiree who moved into a smaller home said, "It's like Monopoly, when they send you back to 'Go' and you find yourself in a little house like the one you had as a bride." One real estate agent told me, "People with an $85,000 house to sell usually hope to find one for $40,000, but when they see what they can get for the money, they usually have to raise the price. A move from an $85,000 to a $60,000 house is about right." Also, consider the stress involved in getting used to a different type of home and new surroundings. This could be especially hard on city folks who opt for country living. If you're in that category, you might send for the U.S. Department of Agriculture's book *Living on a Few Acres,* which has a chapter, "Consider the Tradeoffs Before Leaving the City." You can get the book for $7 from Superintendent of Documents, U.S. Government Printing Office, Washington, D.C. 20402.

Another way to check out housing availability and cost (and if the place is suitable for you) is to write the chambers of commerce listed under each town in this book, and specify what you need or want. Chambers of commerce usually act as screening committees for realtors in the area, and will send you a list of such agents and what is available at what price. The chambers also act as screening committees for the town as a whole, and their response (or lack of it) will give you an idea if the welcome mat is out or not.

4. Cost of Living. It is not *where* you live that determines your cost of living, it is *how* you live. If you want the same things you have now, and the same services and conveniences, chances are it will cost you the same (in one form or another) as it does now. The only way to take advantage of a low-cost area is to settle in like a native and put up with any inconveniences or lack of services you find there. Also remember that just because a state like New Hampshire doesn't have a sales or income tax doesn't mean that they won't have these taxes forever. And low taxes usually mean a low level of services. In the case of New Hampshire that means poor garbage disposal and poor schools. Prices in rural areas can be high where freight costs and lack of competition give local merchants free rein. In addition, if you have to pay for gallons of gasoline or scarce public transportation to get anywhere, and if your insurance rates are higher because fire or police protection is lower, then you're probably not better off there than in a higher-taxed area. Also, you must establish residency and usually live in a place for a year before you are eligible for any special senior citizen or homestead tax exemptions.

5. Recreation and Culture. Chances are you'll want the same or even better recreational and cultural facilities than you have now. If libraries or bowling alleys are important to you, make sure you have access to them in your new community. Also, check radio and television reception. This is especially important in remote regions (although many rural areas are ahead of cities in having cable television). Fortunately, many of the communities with high percentages of retirees have more civic, service and social clubs and organizations than other towns. Your best way to go from being a stranger to becoming a neighbor is to join a club, house of worship, volunteer group or civic enterprise of your choosing. Better still: transfer membership in a national organization (Rotary, Lions, Kiwanis, Boy and Girl Scouts, Cancer Society, League of Women Voters, etc.) to the local chapter in your new community. In this way you'll have an instant group of new friends. To keep abreast of social activities as well as climate, medical facilities, housing costs and general business developments, I strongly urge you to subscribe to the local weekly or Sunday newspaper. It will keep you up-to-date while you're contemplating a move.

6. Special Services for Seniors. Probably the most important services are transportation and hot-meal program. Transportation is often poor or lacking in rural areas, yet you'll need it to go shopping, see the doctor and transact other business and social activities. The new community should have a "dial-a-ride" or minibus program for seniors, and some sort of emergency ambulance service. And don't overlook the daily hot-meal program, where seniors gather for a nutritious meal and pay what they want or can afford (the usual contribution is under $1). You not only get a good, well-balanced meal, you meet other seniors and engage in social activities (meals are usually held in a senior center or other recreational facility). I've found that these meal programs are popular with the rich as well as the poor, who gather as much for the social activity as for the meal.

You may have other needs and wants, and you'll want to make sure that the new move will lower your cost of living and improve your lifestyle. Chances are, if you pick a new place because you like it and it likes you, you'll find yourself among more people with similar interests and backgrounds than you do now. And you'll be happier, healthier and wealthier in your Retirement Eden.

BIBLIOGRAPHY

CARLISLE, NORMAN and MADELYN. *Where to Live for Your Health.* New York: Harcourt Brace Jovanovich, 1980.

COOLEY, LELAND F. and LEE M. *How to Avoid the Retirement Trap.* New York: Nash, 1972

DICKINSON, PETER A. *Sunbelt Retirement.* New York: Elsevier-Dutton, 1980.

———. *The Complete Retirement Planning Book.* New York: Elsevier-Dutton, 1976.

FORD, NORMAN D. *Where to Retire on a Small Income.* New York: Harian Publications, 1979.

FRANKE, DAVID. *America's 50 Safest Cities.* New Rochelle, New York: Arlington House, 1974.

FRANKE, DAVID and HOLLY. *Safe Places.* New Rochelle, New York: Arlington House, 1973

MORRISON, MORIE. *Retirement in the West.* San Francisco: Chronicle Books, 1976.

INDEX